DATE DUE			
MAR 2 5 97			

Also by Barry Rubin

The Arab States & the Palestine Conflict

The Great Powers in the Middle East:
Nineteen Forty-one to Nineteen Forty-seven;
The Road to the Cold War

Paved with Good Intentions:
The American Experience & Iran

Secrets of State:
The State Department & the Struggle over
U.S. Foreign Policy

Modern Dictators

Third World Coup Makers, Strongmen, and Populist Tyrants

BARRY RUBIN

McGraw-Hill Book Company

New York St. Louis San Francisco Auckland Bogotá Hamburg
Johannesburg London Madrid Mexico Milan Montreal New Delhi
Panama Paris São Paulo Singapore Sydney Tokyo Toronto

1 2 3 4 5 6 7 8 9 DOC DOC 8 7

ISBN 0-07-054161-2

LIBRARY OF CONGRESS CATALOGING-IN-PUBLICATION DATA

Rubin, Barry M.
  Modern dictators.
  Bibliography: p.
  1. Dictators.   2. Comparative government.
I. Title.
JC495.R83   1987   321.9   86-18543
ISBN 0-07-054161-2

BOOK DESIGN BY KATHRYN PARISE

There is nothing more difficult to carry out, nor more dangerous to handle, than to initiate a new order of things . . . partly from the incredulity of mankind, who do not truly believe in anything new until they have had actual experience of it.

—Niccolò Machiavelli,
The Prince

Why, man, he doth bestride the narrow world
Like a Colossus; and we petty men
Walk under his huge legs, and peep about. . . .
Men at some time are masters of their fates:
The fault, dear Brutus, is not in our stars,
But in ourselves, that we are underlings.

—William Shakespeare,
Julius Caesar

Politics are just as much a part of life as gambling or poetry; and it is extremely instructive to see how impotent the political opinions which men think, are to produce action, and how potent the political prejudices which men feel, are to produce it.

—George Bernard Shaw,
letter of December 2, 1894

Historians have on the whole been less shocked by foolishness, cruelty, lack of compassion, missed opportunities, and various tragedies than sociologists and students of political science, simply because historians have been preoccupied with what actually happened rather than with what should have happened.

—Walter Laqueur,
A World of Secrets

Preface

The evolution of dictatorship is as much a part of history as the development of democracy. In our era persuasion has become as powerful a force as repression in creating and maintaining such regimes. Debates over the nature of these systems are at the center of the contemporary U.S. and European foreign policy debates. The flourishing of dictatorship has challenged views of history flavored with optimism and based on a deterministic view that material development brings political progress. At the same time a vision of the world too narrowly focused on the conflict between communism and capitalism must be refocused to understand the emergence of a Third World. In fact, it is impossible to defend the West without such an understanding. Our current discussion of dictatorship, much influenced by earlier analyses of "totalitarianism" based on Hitler's Germany and Stalin's Russia at their peak of control and repression, needs to be updated. This model applies only imperfectly to contemporary dictatorships, particularly those in the Third World.

I have long been interested in the nexus among belief systems, pragmatism, and the process of making politics and foreign policy. It has seemed to me that different national histories and political cultures produce their own internally logical systems that may seem the exact opposite of reality to other people but that may function well for those who know how to use them. To put it briefly, one person's political pragmatism is another person's political suicide. The lower level of analysis is amoral and detached. At a higher level, however, one must judge the cost and worth of these choices. In discussing such topics as repression and corruption, I am trying to understand what works and what does not from the point of view of governments. I also want to discover to what extent dictatorships are inevitable in certain countries at this time.

In a book on the United States and Iran, *Paved with Good Intentions*, I followed the transformation of a country from a traditional to a modern dictatorship, along with U.S. efforts to understand and deal with this crisis. In another work, *The Arab States and the Palestine Conflict*, I studied how the Arab-Israeli issue became a focus for Arab states' politics and actions, bringing out the close connection between internal political struggles and foreign policy. The situation showed how a strategy that worked well for holding or seizing power within a country could be disastrous from the point of view of achieving goals on the international level. In a book on U.S. foreign policy, *Secrets of State*, I looked at the American policy-making system, noting how personality and bureaucratic considerations within the government intersected with the events and problems of the outside world. Central, too, in this process was the peculiar U.S. way of looking at the world, defining America's role in it, and making national decisions.

This book turns to the dictators themselves who run so many of the countries in the Middle East, Latin America, Africa, and Asia. It attempts to explain how dictatorship became the dominant form of government, how it takes power and survives or changes, and how it poses challenges for the democratic states of the world. My object is to write, on the one hand, for policymakers and those involved in contemporary affairs and, on the other, for the general public interested in comprehending an increasingly enigmatic world that affects, even threatens their lives.

To be useful, writing must communicate ideas derived from a close study of people, structures, and events in the real world. Complexity and disorderliness, inevitable in human society, undercut attempts at generalization. The purpose of this book is to make useful cross-national observations which help to clarify the mass of detail and the swirl of events. I do not claim the analysis herein is perfect or all-encompassing. The point is not to find some esoteric exceptions but to use whatever guidelines for comprehension can be derived here.

A number of friends and colleagues have been most helpful in this study. Travel abroad has also broadened my perceptions of how foreign systems work. I would like to thank Gérard Chaliand, Patrick Clawson, Michael Clough, Stephen David, Douglas Friedman, Richard Feinberg, Herbert Howe, Lillian Harris, Walter Laqueur, Robert A. Manning, Jennifer Noyon, Marina Ottoway, and Nina Serafino for their help and encouragement. Of course, the contents are my responsibility alone. I would also like to thank Dan Weaver of McGraw-Hill for his faith and cooperation.

Barry Rubin
Washington, D.C. 1985–1986

Contents

Introduction: Crises and Paradoxes

The world suddenly became a lot more difficult for Americans to understand in the 1970s and 1980s. Dozens of Third World countries underwent a seemingly endless series of coups and revolutions. The problems and demands of nations in Asia, Africa, Latin America, and the Middle East increasingly became the focus of international issues and crises. Third World dictators, whose personalities and motives were mysterious to Westerners, dominated the headlines.

Cambodia's new Communist rulers massacred millions of their own countrymen. Ugandan dictator Idi Amin played the tyrant at home and the clown abroad. Iran's Ayatollah Khomeini held U.S. diplomats as hostages and defied America to do something about it. Libyan leader Muammar al-Qaddafi threatened to cut off President Reagan's nose.

Americans, accustomed to thinking of dictators as necessarily unpopular, find unfathomable why tyrants seem to be dominating the Third World and are often able to inspire fanatical loyalty among their people. They find the increasing number of political strong men sponsoring anti-Americanism, terrorism, and aggression against neighbors to be incomprehensible.

Seemingly popular, democratic revolutions against dictatorships in Iran, Nicaragua, and elsewhere created new kinds of repression and dictatorship. Some Third World countries seemed incapable of achieving stability; in others, rulers clung to power despite frequent defeats, failures, and broken promises. And many of these leaders were so colorful, their policies so apparently strange and contradictory that insanity seemed the only logical explanation for their behavior.

The Third World dictators' rhetoric was difficult to decipher. They called their aggressive wars "liberation." Their brand of freedom resembled servitude, their state-run media were mouthpieces, and their systems of "true" democracy seemed to be despotism. And yet the more the West backed their domestic rivals, the more such "moderates" were discredited as puppets and traitors. The populist dictators often aligned themselves with the Soviets, and their triumphs over pro-Western (and often equally unsavory) regimes were a measure of declining U.S. influence and failed U.S. policies over the last thirty years.

In the nineteenth century democracy was regarded as the grand prize of civilization, a system reserved for the most advanced in wisdom, the most superior in race. This justification was used to explain limits on the right to vote and to participate in politics. The masses of people, those whose lack of property or education, race, or gender caused their exclusion from these political rights, clamored and struggled to gain equality.

Similarly, a key rationale of European empires was that their colonial subjects were incapable of governing themselves. Movements in the colonies sought independence but generally accepted the mother country's definitions of economic development and of a just political order. They proclaimed their right to self-determination and self-government, decrying the denial of democratic rule and the continuing poverty of their peasant masses. Resenting the label of inferiority, they insisted on their devotion to and capability for democracy.

"Democracy," said Winston Churchill, "is the worst form of government, except for all the other forms that have been tried from time to time." That idea seemed self-evident in those terrible days of the 1930s and 1940s when a Soviet dictatorship sent millions of its own people to concentration camps and the Nazi regime threw millions into death camps, used prisoners as slave labor, and set off a war that killed 50 million people.

Today there are many dissenters to Churchill's view among the ruling classes and intellectuals in dozens of Third World countries. When the twentieth century began, absolute monarchies and despotisms were seen as predemocratic systems, doomed to extinction by an inevitable progress. The following decades, however, have spawned new kinds of dictatorships that self-confidently proclaim themselves a superior new wave of history, arguing they are more democratic than states stressing personal freedom, the right to dissent and debate freely, fair elections, and the due process of law. Their claims receive formal approval at the United Nations and international conferences. Consequently, the most successful representative democracies now exist side by side with the most powerful dictatorships ever known.

The expression "Third World" refers to the less developed countries of Africa, Asia, Latin America, and the Middle East. From 1945 on dozens of new countries in these areas achieved independence from European colonialism. Their new leaders were full of plans for rapid development and progress. Foreign well-wishers even proclaimed that the West would find much to learn from Third World political, economic, and spiritual innovations. But the second half of the twentieth century became an era of tragedy rather than of glory for the Third World.

For many of these countries, political stability and economic progress were elusive. Continued foreign intervention and manipulation mocked their rhetoric of proud independence. Third World efforts to unite in making demands against industrial states (the "North-South" dialogue) or to create their own nonaligned bloc collapsed in bickering or remained impotent in practice.

Few Third World states—mainly Middle East oil exporters and small Asian export-oriented economies—made major progress in economic development. And where it occurred, development often brought social change and an intellectual ferment more conducive to political upheaval than the relative stagnation of earlier decades. National leaders, ideological blueprints, and international movements (Pan-Arab, Pan-African, Islamic, and nonaligned) failed to deliver on their promises. Only swelling national pride, ideological enthusiasms, and a drive to preserve cultural authenticity provided psychological sustenance to make up for the lack of material gains.

Dictatorial types of government proved far more adaptable to these conditions than did fragile democracy. By the 1980s much of the Third World was ruled by politicians or military officers boosted into power by force of arms or by force of personality. Unchecked by laws and unwilling to allow opposition, these leaders set their nations' courses with a relatively free hand.

The dictators found it hard enough to gain absolute control at home. Obtaining international power and economic wealth was even more difficult. Leaders used fiery rhetoric as a substitute for their lack of international influence and tried to gain political leverage with new tactics, including the export of ideology and subversion, state-supported terrorism, alliance with the Soviet bloc, and regional alignments. But if leaders demagogically stirred up their own people to cement loyalties, this rising nationalism also made for frictions between countries and interfered with slogans of Third World cooperation. Since the leaders' goals and interests were often at odds with those of other states, the Third World became a hotbed of conflict rather than the model of mutual support so ardently portrayed by its publicists.

Hopes for the Third World fell far from the wave of euphoria that accompanied decolonization and independence in the 1950s and 1960s. The trendsetters were giants who acted, and sometimes saw themselves, as political demigods. Sukarno in Indonesia and Gamal Abdel Nasser in Egypt, Kwame Nkrumah in Ghana and Julius Nyerere in Tanzania, Sékou Touré in Guinea and Jawaharlal Nehru in India. Some of them were charter members of the nonaligned movement, founded at Bandung, Indonesia, in 1955 as well as of a new style of government.

The U.S.-Soviet conflict, dividing the world into East and West, Communist and capitalist, totalitarian and democratic, was complicated by the rise of an independent Third World. Since Europe was stable, the Third World became the focus of great power struggle and provided the audience for whose applause the two great powers vied. The deadlocked U.S.-USSR competition allowed Third World leaders a greater latitude in shaping international events; Washington and Moscow, in turn, influenced, manipulated, and intervened in—but rarely controlled—Third World developments.

Regional problems set off crises in their own right as well as became sites for new Cold War battles. For example, the three bloodiest conflicts since World War II—the Korean, Vietnam, and Iran-Iraq wars—involved Third World dictators in Pyongyang and Seoul, Hanoi and Saigon, Tehran and Baghdad. The United States and USSR reacted to rather than regulated these crises.

In the 1970s and 1980s Third World turmoil increased at a steady pace. Ethiopia had a revolution and fought a border war with Somalia; Nicaraguan dictator Anastasio Somoza fell to Sandinista guerrillas, who dragged the country toward their variety of Marxism. Most of Latin America, despite spells of democracy, still seemed vulnerable to the return of military dictators. Iran's revolution replaced the Shah's traditional dictatorship with a dramatically different Islamic radical one under Ayatollah Khomeini. Syria's President Hafez al-Assad imposed his power on Lebanon; Libya's Muammar al-Qaddafi became the impresario of international terrorism and tried to foment unrest in Africa and the Middle East. In Asia modernizing dictators oversaw dramatic economic development in South Korea, Taiwan, and Singapore.

This was a world far different from what Americans had grown to expect in the two decades after 1945. During those years U.S. presidents, confident and arrogant enough to see neutrality as treason to the Free World, were able to support or engineer the overthrow of troublesome nationalist Third

World regimes and replace them with pro-Western military governments. This program was followed in Iran and Guatemala and, more indirectly, in Indonesia, Zaire, Ghana, Argentina, Brazil, and elsewhere.

By the late 1960s, however, the patterns of international politics were changing as new power centers developed around the world. While the United States remained the single strongest country, the Soviets had developed global military and aid capacities, and Western Europe and Japan became major economic powers. Third World governments learned more sophisticated political techniques and means of control while finding foreign support in Moscow or elsewhere. The collisions Britain and France faced with Third World nationalism had earlier convinced them to give up their empires. Now the United States discovered that historic imperial techniques no longer worked.

The Vietnam War was a foreign policy disaster that warned Americans of a need to reevaluate their role in the world and to readjust to changing realities. U.S. intervention turned into a bloody, futile enterprise and a dangerously divisive issue at home. The United States was forced into an agonizing reappraisal: Was the root of the conflict expansive communism or powerful Third World nationalism? Did the U.S.-backed South Vietnamese government fall because it was not democratic enough, as liberals tended to argue, and therefore forfeited popular support and—through its dependence on the Americans—national legitimacy? Or did North Vietnam win, as conservatives suggested, because Americans lacked will and unity? Essentially, however, Hanoi had found a more effective kind of populist, nationalist, and efficiently repressive dictatorship than had Saigon. Communist North Vietnam's system was only partly Communist in origin and as far beyond South Vietnam's traditional dictatorship as an automobile over an oxcart.

After the Vietnam debacle Americans also debated other fundamental foreign policy questions: What was the most effective way to combat apparent advances in Soviet influence throughout the Third World? How had anti-Americanism spread so widely, and what had the United States done to foster it? Were Third World radical nationalist or Marxist regimes necessarily antithetical to U.S. interests? Why did America's allies collapse so frequently, so much more often than their more leftist rivals? Did U.S. pressure for reforms in conservative dictatorships help stabilize those countries or make them prey for anti-American revolutions?

President Jimmy Carter tried to answer these problems from a liberal perspective. Believing that Moscow did not control all developments in the Third World, Carter's administration argued that the Soviets were not ten feet tall and that Americans should not have an exaggerated fear of communism. The United States, it argued, could effectively compete with the Soviets for influence even in states with radical regimes. American concessions would help improve relations with the Third World and dispel anti-American feelings.

While suggesting moderation and compromise with African, Arab, and Latin American regimes, the Carter administration also proposed a set of policies for dealing with allied dictatorships like Guatemala, Nicaragua, Iran, and the Philippines. The Carter administration believed that these countries could avoid a revolution, coup, or guerrilla insurgency by showing greater respect for their citizens' human rights and for democratic principles. By accepting or even encouraging inevitable change, these policymakers thought, Washington could moderate the direction and soften the impact of events.

Carter's approach during his 1977–1981 term had impressive successes: treaties returning the Panama Canal to Panamanian sovereignty, arranging Zimbabwe's independence under a black majority government, mediating the Israel-Egypt peace at Camp David, improving the U.S. image in Africa, and promoting a return to civilian governments in Latin America.

Yet Carter's foreign policy was judged a major failure. Events in the second half of his term seemed to encourage a more conservative assessment of the proper U.S. policy toward Third World problems and crises. The Soviet invasion of Afghanistan in December 1979 confirmed a pessimistic view of

Moscow's chronically expansive imperialism. The use of Cuban troops in Angola and Ethiopia, to ensure the survival of Soviet clients, was taken to indicate that Moscow was a direct threat in the Third World and a major cause of instability there. A soft U.S. policy, refusing to use force to help allies and punish foes, would only give the Soviets a further edge.

A parallel experience came out of 1978–1979 revolutions in Iran and in Nicaragua that replaced pro-U.S. dictatorships with anti-American radical regimes. Ronald Reagan and other conservatives subsequently argued that Carter's policies had undermined the old rulers and allowed them to be replaced with governments detrimental both to U.S. interests and to their own citizens. Many Americans interpreted the Iranian hostage crisis as proof that a conciliatory policy allowed extremists to believe they could insult the United States at will.

In short, Carter's friendliness and flexibility toward the Third World resulted in steep political costs at home and relatively few benefits abroad. When Reagan claimed that only a tougher America could win respect, that the Soviets were the source of Third World problems, and that radical nationalist dictators must be faced down, the American people were ready to listen. Iran's holding of fifty-two U.S. Embassy officials for almost fifteen months, a crisis continuing throughout the 1980 election campaign, seemed living evidence of a hostility that no moderation could dissipate. The Vietnam syndrome had been replaced by the Iran syndrome as Reagan won huge election victories in 1980 and 1984.

The American political tradition has a surprisingly contradictory attitude toward dictatorship. On the one hand, the framers of the U.S. Constitution assumed that governments were naturally prone to becoming dictatorships. Therefore, they divided power among institutions (executive, legislative, judicial) and jurisdictions (federal, state, and local) in a system of checks and balances to prevent an excessive concentration of power.

On the other hand, the long, relatively untroubled continuity of democracy that followed allowed later Americans to consider dictatorship a deviant form of government which is bound to be unpopular and can survive only through repression. In view of the pragmatism of American politics, the power of ideology, desperation, and demagoguery that lie at the foundation of dictatorship's appeal is hard to comprehend. The United States' national success and stability make alien the Third World's trauma of underdevelopment and humiliating national weakness, including subservience to foreigners.

Nor does the European idea of realpolitik—that a great power should seek its allies on the basis of national interest and without regard to their internal systems—appeal to Americans. They have always been more willing to become involved in international affairs when some high principle is at stake. World War I was fought to "make the world safe for democracy." World War II and the Cold War were accepted as struggles for freedom against totalitarianism. The Vietnam War was so controversial because policymakers ultimately could not convince the public that such principles were at stake or were worth the price being paid in lives and treasure.

These principles hold true across the American political spectrum. Liberals argue that radical Third World regimes often show greater economic progress and correct old injustices. They believe that anti-American behavior is a reaction against past and present U.S. actions and add that the United States has a moral responsibility for the depredations of dictators who are its allies. Such miscreant regimes invite Communist revolution.

Conservatives justify support for "milder" rightist dictatorships as preferable to Communist ones since the former are deemed less thoroughly repressive, less dangerous for U.S. interests, and more likely to change in a democratic direction.

Rightist dictatorships, conservatives conclude, are more acceptable both morally and in terms of U.S. interests than are leftist dictatorships. Liberals believe the opposite. Still, in practice U.S. policymakers have been inclined to support the status quo in accord with President Franklin Roosevelt's dictum about the then-ruling member of the Somoza family: "He may be an SOB, but he's our SOB."

American predilections to expect the decline of dictatorships were reinforced by a misleading scholarly and popular analysis of Third World trends in the 1950s and 1960s. As interest rose about the new or soon-to-be independent countries, academics predicted that the Third World would follow the West's historical pattern. An agrarian-oriented "traditional society," in which people's loyalty lay with religion, tribe, and extended family, would be replaced by an urban, change-oriented "modern" society characterized by individualism, industry, and allegiance to nation-states. This evolution would follow technologically determinist lines: Certain forms of communication (the telephone and television), production (the factory and machinery), and thinking (the scientific method, modern sociology, and psychology) would forcefully shape the institutions of any society that used them.

The erroneous predictions of Western European and American observers were held by most of their counterparts in the Soviet bloc. Soviet Communists also expected developing societies to become more and more like them, inevitably following a road leading first to capitalism and then, through either Communist-led revolution (as in China or Vietnam) or a revolutionary dictatorship following the "noncapitalist road," toward what Moscow considered socialism.

Events taught something quite different from what everyone in the West, the Soviet bloc, and the Third World expected. A new kind of political regime arose in the Third World: the modern dictatorship that combined populism, nationalism, mobilization, and repression.

CHAPTER ONE

Populist Tyrants

"The Third World," wrote Frantz Fanon, a Martinique-born psychologist who participated in Algeria's independence struggle, "ought not to be content to define itself in the terms of values which have preceded it. On the contrary, the under-developed countries ought to do their utmost to find their own particular . . . methods and a style which shall be peculiar to them." Much of the Third World followed this advice. Rather than accept a Western democratic or Soviet Communist form of political organization, it developed a new type of system— "modern dictatorship"—that displaced the colonial rule, halfhearted democracies, and "traditional dictators" who ran Third World countries.

Before the rise of modern dictators through coup or revolution, many Third World rulers led systems that can be called traditional dictatorships. They were conservers and manipulators of the existing order, more concerned with redividing wealth to their advantage than in making social or political change, even when they favored economic development. As the proprietor of government, the traditional dictator preferred political passivity from the masses, fearing that anything else would produce demands for changes in the system. Those who actively opposed the ruler were suppressed; the rest were intimidated when necessary and otherwise ignored.

Traditional dictators like the Shah of Iran, Anastasio Somoza of Nicaragua, Haile Selassie of Ethiopia, or Ferdinand Marcos of the Philippines ruled through direct personal control of the national finances and military forces. Decisions were centralized in their own hands, lieutenants served at their pleasure, and cooperation among top officials was discouraged lest it produce political conspiracy. The traditional dictator sought to become not a popular celebrity but a regal one, preferring to be feared and rich. He offered his subjects many punishments and few incentives.

For traditional dictators, change was inherently threatening. Machiavelli wrote, "There is nothing more difficult to carry out, nor more dangerous to handle, than to initiate a new order of things. For the reformer has enemies in all those who profit by the old order and only lukewarm defenders in all those who would profit by the new order." This warning contains an important clue to any would-be modern dictator. He must organize and mobilize the beneficiaries of change in order to overcome those whose power and privileges he has seized.

Communists have seen the solution to this problem as organizing for class warfare; Fascists have stressed the conflict between nations and ethnic groups. In each case, however, the object has been to convince one section of the population that its interests lie in supporting the government against other groups. Consequently, both systems developed the most sophisticated and comprehensive ways of winning support—ideology, political party, mass rallies, control of the media and schools—and of repressing opponents or targeted victims.

This apparent paradox is the foundation of modern dictatorships. A dictatorship can be defined as a system of government ruled by a relatively small number of self-appointed people who hold absolute power over any organized institutions or system of laws. A modern dictatorship is a dictatorship that succeeds in overcoming the gap between rulers and ruled by convincing a large portion of the people—through persuasion, benefits, and organic links—that they should support it.

The Third World modern dictator melded the inventions

of Marxism and fascism with his own national history and conditions to gain a new kind of legitimacy as a populist (the people's tribune), nationalist (the country's defender against imperialism), revolutionary (destroyer of the old order), and socialist (mobilizer and manager of the nation's economy).

The incredible popularity of such different modern dictators as Nasser and Castro, Khomeini and Julius Nyerere of Tanzania, shows the power that can be unleashed by a leader who cares or even pretends to care for the masses who have been so ignored in the past. And the enthusiastic response of the masses—those whom Argentine dictator Juan Perón called *descamisados* ("the shirtless ones") and Iranian dictator Ayatollah Ruhollah Khomeini labeled the *mostazafan* ("the downtrodden")—was perfectly logical.

It is of the greatest importance to understand that the modern dictator does not operate purely on the basis of illusion. Most Third World countries face a tremendous uphill struggle against poverty, lack of economic infrastructure, and much stronger foreign powers. They are desperately trying to compress two centuries of Western economic and political evolution into two decades.

As alternative models of development are tried and seen to fail, confidence is lost and hopes are shattered. Knowing that many Westerners believe them incapable of steady government or successful progress, Third World elites, intellectuals, and army officers try to figure out why previous efforts failed. Experience with war, famine, anarchy, and drift make them eager for a new regime that can bring stability, unity, and pride. Even if a populist dictator's gifts are largely rhetorical, these words at least provide an oasis in a generally dismal present.

Consequently, when a Perón, Khomeini, Nasser, Nyerere, or Castro takes power in the aftermath of a coup, revolution, or independence, a large proportion of the population will rally to his call. It will view its leader as having brought national salvation and self-respect, improvement in living standards, opportunity for education, and personal advancement. At the same time he preserves the culture's "authenticity" and dispenses a sense of community and purpose alongside a greater degree of social justice. He speaks the rough language of the people in terms comprehensible to them, explaining what is wrong with the world as it is. He ridicules the pompous notables or superior foreigners and explains how the much victimized common people will finally emerge victorious.

In a revolution's early days, at least, the leader does exactly what he promises. The old system collapses with surprising swiftness and completeness. Colonialism, expected to last for decades, ended almost overnight in the late 1950s and early 1960s; traditional dictatorships, thought to be invulnerable, crumble. The oligarchy's seemingly unchallengeable power evaporates. The last, at least in the regime's rhetoric, have become first. Fidel Castro nationalizes the sugar mills; Perón raises workers' wages, Nasser takes over and runs the Suez Canal, Qaddafi seizes Libya's oil; Iran holds Americans hostage without effective reprisal. The oligarchy at home or the superpower is shown to be a paper tiger, drowned like Pharaoh's army by the sea. No wonder the dominant mood is apocalyptic.

And who is the architect of this apparent miracle? The leader who reaches out to the people, who wants and needs their support, whose reforms give them the possibility of having land, going to school, and rising to positions of respect. He teaches that their customs and culture are superior, not inferior, to those of the proud—but inwardly materialistic, decadent, or imperialistic—West. The more the leader turns the old hierarchy upside down, the more those who were once on the bottom approve. Thus can one simultaneously be both popular and a dictator.

If former officials, policemen, or the wealthy are imprisoned or executed in the regime's first days, this will not disturb the mass of people who previously suffered under their rule. If others flee into exile, this only consolidates the modern dictatorship, removing its opponents and the fainthearted.

The new regime turns criticism by Western states or international organizations to its own advantage. Foreigners have no right to condemn the new system as tyrannical and undemocratic, the modern dictatorship argues, for they did nothing when the people were being tortured and exploited before. At best, they did not overthrow the old regime; at worst, they gave it political, economic, and military assistance. Not having complained about the murder of peasants, they now cry out at the executions of the former elite. It is easy to believe that these criticisms of the revolution are not only hypocritical but conspiratorial. The fear of returning to the old order inspires even more support for the new regime.

Of course, cynicism grows with time. Some rise high enough to suffer in new repressions, for in modern dictatorships the "torturable class" is not the poorest but the new elite, officers or intellectuals who might challenge the dictator. Others find promises are unfulfilled. Yet the revolution also gives opportunities to many energetic, talented, or opportunistic members of the lower classes. The official, soldier, manager, party member, youth activist, trade unionist, peasant given land, and members of the leaders' tribal, regional, or religious group feel their gains or very survival are dependent on the regime.

If a dictatorship is going to survive very long, however, in the face of growing internal dissent and the inevitable inability to fulfill all its promises, it must stress this organizing principle. While democratic regimes rest on support of at least 51 percent of the people, modern dictatorships need a base of at least 20 or 30 percent active support and participation in its party, mass, and security organizations. Many leaders learned these lessons, and in Africa and the Middle East dictators' length of tenure had increased noticeably by the 1980s over the 1960s.

While dictatorships are above the law, no regime can repeal the laws of political survival. Democratic leaders, who also want to stay in power to preserve their positions and privileges, must accept the inevitability of peacefully stepping down. Leaving office, however, rarely brings them the risk of death, imprisonment, or exile, while for dictators and their main collaborators, these are the very penalties of defeat. For dictators, political survival may be the only way to physical survival.

Ironically, the new-style dictatorship's determination to

15

survive means it cannot ignore domestic public opinion. Abroad the ruler may even appear insane, but whether he is crazy can be better judged by whether his behavior damages his standing at home. A leader like Idi Amin, who undermined his own position by endless murders, or like Central African Republic President Jean Bédel Bokassa, who crowned himself emperor amid costly pomp, has obviously lost touch with reality. Yet insulting foreign powers or making incredible boasts may be smart politics by enhancing domestic popular support. In this context the actions of Qaddafi and Khomeini reflect the views of many of their countrymen and are politically shrewd.

Most dangerous are economic austerity measures that lower living standards; it may be politically safer to go into hopeless debt than to court unpopularity through painful austerity measures. Similarly, sharing views like xenophobia, socialist egalitarianism, Islamic fundamentalism, and ethnic hatred may be far less dangerous than challenging them or appearing too Westernized. Such situations may be called the law of logical political irrationality; leaders (even dictators) often make decisions designed to enhance their popularity even when these choices exacerbate, rather than solve, problems.

As a charismatic leader whose speeches, public personality, physical appearance, and promises must appeal to at least a large section of his people, the modern dictator is already quite different from the traditional dictator, who was indifferent to his public image except purely for the sake of his own ego. The modern dictator places himself at the apex of a four-layer pyramid: active supporters whose group loyalty or belief in the ruling ideology is coupled with their enjoyment of power and privilege, patriotic nationalists who believe the new regime is moving the country forward, beneficiaries from material gains like land reform, and those who give loyal lip service from fear of punishment.

One of the modern dictator's main attributes is his ability to communicate directly with the masses. What need is there for any independent parties, newspapers, and legislature or for contested elections when the identification of people with a leader bypasses all these devices? A mainstay of modern

16

dictatorship is the idea that this direct link between masses and dictator is a system superior to parliamentary democracy. In Nazi Germany it was called the Fuhrer principle; the Italian Fascist creed stated, "Mussolini is always right." In the Soviet Union it became Stalin's "cult of personality"; Mao Zedong's *Little Red Book* called it the "mass line"; North Korea's Kim Il Sung named it *juche*. Equally, it has been Peronism, Nasserism, the Islam of "Imam" Khomeini, Qaddafi's "third way," and many other ideologies built around the leader's thoughts and personality.

"I am your dreams," said Kemal Atatürk, the founder of the Turkish Republic in the 1920s. While Atatürk, who favored evolution toward Western-style democracy, quickly added that he was not superhuman, the modern dictator does want to portray himself as the embodiment of the people's collective aspirations and personal hopes. He wants them to identify with him, to be in awe of his brilliance and decisiveness, and to trust him as the guardian of their interests. This relationship between leader and ruled is the new version of the medieval divine right of kings based on the relationship between the monarch and God.

The fundamental ideal of modern dictators is the nation as army, the people as troops to be disciplined and highly organized. Dissent is an unnecessary luxury. These authoritarian ideas have been justified by ideological systems developed by revolutionary or mercenary intellectuals. They decry democratic institutions as decadent and inefficient for development and as illusions proffered by imperialism and capitalism. All dictators are unwilling to accept and many are psychologically incapable of understanding the role of a free press, multiparty system, parliament, free-enterprise economy, academic freedom, and independent trade unions.

Just as the modern dictator seeks popularity and a political base of support, so he must also discredit and repress his opponents. The dictator achieves the former end by branding dissidents as "counterrevolutionaries," "feudalists," "antipatriotic elements," and "servants of foreign powers." The modern dictator makes himself legitimate by making the old order illegitimate; he makes himself strong by rooting out the former social system and loyalties. In countries where the pace of change is pressed by modernization, national survival, and human need, the modern dictator is taking the most expedient course.

To permit dissent is to risk opposition; to allow opposition is to risk the regime's survival. If the emperor has no clothes—when the regime's problems or hypocrisies become too obvious—there is all the more reason to stop anyone from saying so. In this context, intolerance is a virtue and sentimental weakness is a potentially fatal political vice.

Repression is the other side of the search for support. There are, however, many different kinds of repression. The modern dictator seeks to make his suppression acceptable to nonopponents by discrediting any of those who challenge his authority. On this point he may be more demanding but also more successful than the traditional dictator. He instinctively understands Machiavelli's injunction "Men must be caressed or annihilated; they will revenge themselves for small injuries, but cannot do so for great ones; the injury therefore that we do to a man must be such that we need not fear his vengeance."

In traditional dictatorships, resisters can comfort themselves with the knowledge that they will be heroes to the silent, cowed masses. International or regional organizations will sing their praises; they may emerge after long prison terms to take their places as leaders of a new society. But modern dictatorships leave no space for ideas other than their own. Fanon justifies this approach by the needs of the struggle: "Truth is the property of the national cause. . . . Truth is that which hurries on the break-up of the colonialist regime; it is that which promotes the emergence of the nation; it is all that which protects the natives, and ruins the foreigners."

This is in no way to deny that traditional dictatorships engage in horrible injustices and tortures. Their ferocity is not necessarily less intensive; it may often be less systematic. Antidemocratic opponents of the regime who emerge from prison or exile to take power will be even tougher. They are not going to allow others to follow their example and survive to make a

revolution against themselves. Milovan Djilas, dissident and
ex-Communist leader, wrote that when the Yugoslav Communists came to power, they knew exactly how to strengthen
the prisons where they once resided in order to isolate and
demoralize those to be incarcerated there.

So modern dictators go farther than the cynical but sometimes more flexible traditional dictator by robbing their opponents of any justification. No decent person could rebel
against the patriotic people's government. Critics or dissidents
must be counterrevolutionaries, traitors, sellouts to foreign
powers, and so on—all the epithets which, for the traditional
dictator, are embodied in the label "Communists."

Even when inaccurate, this last accusation makes some
sense. After all, the traditional dictator had no problem with
private-enterprise capitalism. It did not interfere with his rule;
on the contrary, it was a rich source of profit and kickbacks.
His friends were given monopolies or franchises to ensure
their loyalty and livelihoods. The dictator personally accumulated land and businesses, as did Nicaraguan dictator Anastasio Somoza, the Shah, and Philippine President Ferdinand
Marcos. The resulting corruption wasted national resources,
alienated and squeezed out the local businessmen, and skimmed
off foreign aid and loans.

But the modern dictator and his allies cannot abide any
strong institutions outside their own control. The means of
production are nationalized for both political and economic
reasons. State control directly profits those in power, can be
manipulated for political patronage, and may be operated at
a loss to gain the support of consumers and workers. On the
economic level, state enterprises are the only way underdeveloped states have of carrying out large or innovative economic projects with their own resources or dealing equally
with multinational corporations.

A host of new institutions are created to supplement the
government itself. These groups, called "transmission belts"
in Communist terminology, are designed to carry information
up the line to the leadership and orders down the line to the
membership. Although controlled from the top, the party,

unions, the media, and women's, peasants', labor, student, and youth groups give the system some self-correcting capacity and the rank and file some means of making their problems heard. Ultimately, of course, these groups are more concerned with propaganda than with representativeness, implementing orders rather than raising objections, and uprooting dissenters rather than eliminating corrupt or incompetent officials.

These groups also provide a way to distribute benefits and bribes. By rewarding tens of thousands of officials and activists, the regime broadens its base of support far beyond the few top leaders and their families. These groups can defend the government and uncover opponents while spreading its influence and ideology throughout neighborhoods, workplaces, and the provinces. In contrast with the almost isolationist elitism of the traditional dictatorship, the modern dictatorship spreads its tentacles far and wide. The ideal is to give the regime total control over political, economic, social, and intellectual life. Nevertheless, these are hardly "totalitarian" regimes because their efforts fall so short. They lack the resources and infrastructures. If totalitarianism is the highest stage of dictatorship, in this respect, too, the Third World is underdeveloped.

At the same time, however, modern dictatorships do not stem from underdevelopment but rather are products of the modernization process itself. As the Third World adopted statehood, telecommunications, modern dress, assembly lines, United Nations membership, professional armies, and twentieth-century business methods, it reshaped and reinterpreted these things to fit the existing culture. Western expectations underrated this process. What had once appeared to be the only way of coping with modern technology turned out merely to be only the way nineteenth-century American, British, or French society had handled the problem. A Chinese, Nigerian, or Iranian solution might be quite different because of different social and cultural starting points.

The industrial and political revolutions of the eighteenth and nineteenth centuries in America and Western Europe brought severe social and psychological shocks to those societies. But modern technology's effect on the Third World was

20

even more dramatic because it came all at once, in contrast with the West's gradual evolution. Further, change in the West came through internal development, not as an import from abroad.

In the West, the destabilizing strain of eighteenth- and nineteenth-century industrial and political revolutions and of scientific and technological change—the birth of great industrial cities, the transformation of peasants into workers, the formation of new states, the need for mass education, the destructive power of standing armies, and so on—had forced a series of changes over a century or more. And even then these pressures gave rise to incredible social and psychological dislocation, the French and Russian revolutions, fascism and wars. It was not an easy transformation.

But these same upheavals arrived in the Third World all at once, as complete packages that had to be blended with what already existed. Further, change in the West came through internal development, not as an import from abroad. The West entered the Third World as an imperialist conqueror seeking to impose new economic and cultural patterns. Ideas and institutions Westerners took for granted appeared to the Third World not as natural companions of modernity but as an invasion of alien mores, in conjunction with foreign rule, that could be changed or even rejected. The traditional culture was unable to preserve itself intact but was the starting point in a process of reinterpreting Western concepts of democracy, nationalism, justice, and society even while accepting the Western science, technology, machinery, weapons, and knowledge that were spreading throughout the world.

The point here is that change was neither as total nor as Westernizing as had been predicted. Instead, the result was a hybrid of traditional society and imported ideas and material goods to produce something quite new. Traditional political structures were "modernized" into new forms of authoritarian rule; "modern" concepts learned at Western universities were used in hitherto unexpected ways.

Traditional world views or institutions were never displaced by an internal modernization process—as feudalism was destroyed in Western Europe—but were broken by external colonialism. Consequently, these ideas and structures were not invalidated in much of Asia, Africa, and the Middle East. Since the "old" behavior and thinking could not stave off this challenge and the "modern" Western ideas could not triumph completely, the result was a hybrid which contained a strong streak of traditional thinking. The old culture and structures of authority became part of a national patrimony to be upheld against foreign penetration by leaders preaching unity and nationalism; the old communal egalitarian practices were taken to validate the kind of socialism and populism also embodied in modern dictatorship.

Four examples of how the Third World integrated Western innovations with local traditions illustrate the point:

Religion, politically weakened in the West, seized on modern nationalism and promotional techniques to embody a sense of nationhood and community in Third World countries.

The army, professionalized and highly trained in the West to deal with expensive, advanced weapons, became depoliticized. In the Third World, similar training and a claim on so much of the national budget made soldiers more concerned with political and financial matters, convincing them they could better run the country.

Ideology, developed in the West as a conscious and consistent body of political thinking, was used by Third World rulers to organize and mobilize broad support while justifying their repression and monopoly on power.

Electoral democracy, the centerpiece of Western government, fostered political pluralism and independent organization by the citizenry to pursue their goals and protect their interests. The abuse of this system

in the Third World discredited it. Modern dictatorships substituted a "higher" stage of participatory democracy that stifled dissent and became a chain of
command promoting the citizens' obedience to the
rulers.

Western social science thought religion to be the product of
a prescientific world view and expected it to decline as societies
developed. On the contrary, the influx of Western ideas forced
religious institutions to adapt and fight back while the upheaval caused by the modernization process triggered a renewed search for political and cultural identity that often
strengthened the political importance of religious identity. Nowhere was this more true than in the Islamic world. As one
Arab official put it, "We accepted the manifestations of a modern civilization but refused its rulings. . . . People became confused and they ran away to find comfort in Islam." Islam did
not merely react to such perceived threats as secularism or
women's equality, it actively used the new technologies—television and radio broadcasts, printing plants and tape cas-
settes, faster transportation—on its own behalf.

Iran is the most obvious example—and is the only place
where an Islamic fundamentalist movement took power—but
the same techniques were used from Morocco to Indonesia by
other groups. In most of these countries the power of the
urban clerical hierarchy had declined over the centuries as
local beliefs and compromises with custom eroded religious
orthodoxy. The new technology allowed the big-city mullahs
to rebuild communications with the countryside, increase the
number of their students, and distribute sermons and religious
literature more widely than they had ever been able to do
before. This reinvigoration of the clergy was an important
factor in the Islamic revival.

Urban migration, the search for national identity, and the
growth of mass education also encouraged an upsurge in the
importance of religion. In Egypt, Iran, Tunisia, and other
countries people moving from villages to cities sought to trans-
plant familiar sources of authority and belief to cope with their

bewildering new environment. Saudi Arabia used closed-circuit television to maintain the classroom separation between the sexes; in Malaysia ethnic Malays promoted Islam as a unifying factor in winning political control over the Chinese minority.

Students often supplemented their Westernized technical training with fundamentalist politics without sensing any contradiction between the two. The founders of Egypt's two main Islamic radical groups held, respectively, a doctorate in science and a bachelor's degree in agriculture. Unlike earlier fundamentalists, who rejected Western technology, the new generation saw these imports in pragmatic terms: as value-free techniques that could be used for their own purposes.

Whatever form it takes, industrial society in Moslem countries will include a distinctively Islamic flavor. One of Egypt's leading sociologists, Ali E. Hillal Dessouki, explains: "The issue is not Islam versus anti-Islam but one of medieval versus modern Islamic thinking." Even the "medieval" fundamentalists are modern in their strategy, if not in their theology. In Latin America Catholic "liberation theology" has, with less success, sought to play a similar role in political mobilization.

The idea of the armed forces as a legitimate ruling group is another adaptation of Western institutions to Third World conditions. Certainly, the military often filled a highly political role in Europe, particularly in countries like Spain and Greece, the problems of which were similar to those of the Third World. Yet Western evolution was toward a professional military establishment under civilian control. Giving the soldiers advanced equipment and better training consolidated this role.

In the Third World, however, the construction of modern armies only enhanced the soldiers' political ambitions. The desire for up-to-date weapons and technology made them demand a larger share of the national budget. Training in broader national security problems encouraged them to see themselves as most able to rule the state and preserve its interests.

Certainly, when the army is willing or able to detach itself from the old order, it often has the best chance to lead a revolutionary transformation to a modern dictatorship. Niccolò Machiavelli wrote in *The Prince*, "All armed prophets have conquered and all unarmed ones failed," an idea updated by Mao Zedong as "Political power grows out of the barrel of a gun." Revolutionaries who distrust the military as innately conservative or undemocratic prescribe protracted armed struggle to construct an alternative army. In Latin America, where the officers are closely tied to the socioeconomic status quo, the destruction of the old military establishment is necessary for a thoroughgoing revolution, as happened in Nicaragua and Cuba. In places like Algeria, Angola, and Mozambique, where independence had to be won through war, guerrilla struggle was the basis for creating a national armed force the master of which held the key to power in the new state.

But the armed forces have advantages in addition to their monopoly on weaponry. Often they are the most durable national institution. United by discipline and often dominated by a tribal, regional or communal solidarity, the military is confident that it can best deal with the modern world, cleaning up the mess made by corrupt and divisive politicians. Civilian leaders often lay the groundwork for coups when they politicize the army by calling on it to put down rioters or dissidents.

In many countries the army was not considered an honorable career for sons of wealthy families and became a means of upward mobility for boys from lower-middle-class or poor backgrounds, outcast ethnic groups, or backward regions. Any young man becoming an officer in Africa, the Middle East, or Latin America must be well aware of his profession's political possibilities. In many parts of the world officers might be embittered outsiders quite willing to overthrow the political and economic order rather than members of the establishment. The great exception is Latin America, where officers usually follow their long tradition of allying themselves with the ruling class. They are motivated by a well-entrenched, conservative Catholic and anti-Communist ideology; social and personal contacts integrate them into the oligarchy.

Once in power, military rulers know they have to control the rest of the army, particularly if they shed their own uniforms, so as not to be displaced by men like themselves. A clever system of controlling admission to the officer corps, political indoctrination, multiple intelligence agencies to watch the soldiers and each other, as well as manipulation of assignments, transfers, and promotions is developed. To weld together the faction, some organizing principle—a combination of ethnic identity, regionalism, ideology, party structure, mutual loyalty, and other factors—has to be found. Gradually the soldier-politicians have learned how to keep themselves in power.

Western ideologies are also adapted and changed for Third World purposes. Marxist and social democratic thinking has been given a strong dose of Arab nationalism in the Middle East and a large degree of nationalistic and even tribalist content in Africa. In Western Europe radical political movements sought to redistribute existing wealth and to overturn perceived class rule. By way of contrast, Third World revolutionaries emphasized the promotion of national sovereignty and identity through unity and the creation of wealth through development.

The whole idea of politics had a different connotation in the Third World compared to the industrialized West. In the United States and Western Europe most political thinking questioned the authority of the state over the people as a way of challenging the rule of a small minority. The trend was to encourage the organization of independent organizations— trade unions and trade associations, ethnic groups and occupational lobbies, multiple parties and competing newspapers— to break up any monopoly of political and economic power.

In the Third World, these institutions rarely accumulated such power and independence until quite recently; government was deemed to be the property of the elite—or even of foreign colonialists—rather than the business of the masses. Any independent involvement in such affairs was dangerous, as the fate of thousands of imprisoned or murdered workers, peasants, and their organizers showed.

Traditional dictatorships continued this pattern. In them, workers found little sympathy or redress of grievances from the government. Local businessmen or foreign employers usually lacked any sense of social conscience; trade unions were ineffective or nonexistent. The constant supply of unskilled labor available from the countryside vastly exceeded the limited number of jobs available and kept down wages and the job security of urban workers.

In the countryside peasants working for bare subsistence in isolated villages knew the landlord as their political authority. Their own country's name was a distant abstraction that inspired little loyalty or enthusiasm. From long experience they viewed the government with suspicion—as an oppressive collector of taxes, impresser of young men for the army, and reliable ally of the local oligarchy.

The idea that the government was supposed to serve the needs and be responsive to the wishes of the people, then, was as alien to the twentieth-century Third World as it had been to eighteenth-century Europe under the reign of kings. But the situation in Western Europe and America eventually produced democracy while the political attitudes and experiences of the Third World were conducive to the appeal of modern dictatorship.

The Third World's political course was shaped by several factors: the example of European totalitarian thinking and practice, the weakness of an independent middle class or of institutions demanding limited government, the lack of national political traditions, the pressure of time and underdevelopment, the exigencies of the struggle against colonialism or traditional dictatorship, and the real or perceived threat from foreign powers.

One of the foremost causes for the appeal of modern dictatorship was the apparent failure of Western-style democracy. In fact, Third World people's contacts with parliamentary, pluralist, electoral systems were often negative. In Middle Eastern countries like Egypt, Syria, Iraq, and Sudan, in Asian nations like South Korea or Pakistan, and in many states in Africa, political parties tended to be controlled by big landowners, urban magnates, and wealthy merchants who were concerned with the masses only when they needed their votes.

The politicians' factional disputes, personal frictions, quarrels over the spoils, and finely worded platforms meant nothing to the poor majority.

Given the nature of these systems, relatively few people had an active interest in open elections or free debate; fewer had commercial interests jeopardized by state control of the economy. Freedom of speech meant little to those denied it under the old regime. When newspapers were only organs of the oligarchy, when the main function of the courts and police was to trample on rights, people could not have much expectation of press freedom or impartial justice.

Democracy as known in the West was discredited as not only an import but a failed one at that. Every time a traditional dictator boasted of his anticommunism, called his regime part of the Free World, praised the United States, or extolled the benefits of capitalism, he was encouraging the opposite point of view on those opposed to his regime. When Third World parliamentary systems were manipulated by outsiders, paralyzed by corruption, swept by internal conflicts, incapable of challenging the power of foreigners or the tragedies of economic development, they were judged to be incapable of meeting the needs of the nation or the masses.

When democracy appeared too fragile and slow a process to meet Third World needs, the modern dictator had a seemingly more dynamic system to propose. The ceremonies and guarantees of "free" elections, speech, press, etc. were less missed for never having been enjoyed. Political checks and balances on the power of the leader and his party would just waste time, energy, and strength. In an emergency situation, argues the modern dictator, such ideas as due process and legality are, at best, luxuries and, at worst, tools of internal exploiters and foreign imperialists.

The unity required by the independence struggle, a revolutionary movement, or even a coup did not convince leaders of the value of political debate and dissent. It was difficult for them to conceive of opponents as anything other than traitors or as architects of a new revolution. For those believing themselves to be victims of colonialism or imperialism, Western talk of human rights or democracy often seemed like a fraud.

This bitter antagonism was most articulately expressed by Frantz Fanon: "All that the native has seen in his country is that (the authorities) can freely arrest him, beat him, starve him." So great is the resulting skepticism that "when the native hears a speech about western culture he pulls out his knife" because these so-called values have only made him the victim of repression and aggression.

Machiavelli sought to inspire the unification of his Italian homeland and instead became a guide for feudal autocrats. Marx wanted to be the liberator of humankind and instead became the founder of the most effective form of cruel dictatorship. Similarly, Fanon wanted to bring real freedom to the suffering Third World and instead laid down the guidelines for modern dictatorship there. In Fanon's writings one finds the arguments that were later used as apologies and justifications by the new rulers.

"The customs, traditions, and myths of the colonized people," wrote Fanon, were taken by Europe as "the very sign of the poverty of spirit and of their constitutional depravity." And the very fact that the West had condemned them made them all the more worth defending. Yet the Third World politician was caught in difficult contradictions. He wanted stability and unity at the same time as he sought revolution and change. He wanted to root out and defeat the West at the same time as he desired its rewards and products. But once dictatorship had broken the fragile chain of pluralism, it was much harder to restore the norms of democratic life, much easier to disrupt it again.

Thus, the Latin American militaries acted in the name of preserving traditional values against the subversive influx of Western liberalism and modernism. Coups were justified as resolving the inability of civilians to cope with the country's problems and the promises of radical populists that went beyond what the nation could afford.

In Africa the leaders of the independence movements,

who thereafter became the countries' first presidents—and usually presidents for life—promised an African socialism and policy that continued the idea of a united people battling foreign influence. Sometimes disillusion with quarreling parties and internal strife convinced officers to take over, proclaiming they would institute a truly authentic indigenous system to replace the politicians with their luxurious life-styles and European suits. Where Europeans refused to grant independence, radicals called for an armed struggle that would not only triumph in the end but also create the embryo of a new society based on mutual cooperation and "scientific socialism."

In the Middle East the rejection of parliamentary systems was almost always irreversible. In Egypt, for example, the Wafd party repeatedly won elections throughout the 1920s, 1930s, and 1940s on the basis of its liberal nationalist platform and wide organization among the peasantry. The king and corrupt landlord parties kept it out of office through electoral fraud and suspension of the constitution. The Wafd itself became tarnished with corruption and linked to British manipulation. Egyptians turned to more radical and violent groups, including Communists and Islamic radicals, until Colonel Gamal Abdel Nasser seized power in 1952. He cut the knot that had deadlocked thirty years of efforts to fulfill national and popular aspirations, instituting land reform, expelling British influence, and making Egypt leader of the Arab world. Obviously Nasser's alternative seemed more attractive than what had gone before. In the 1950s and 1960s one Arab state after another was taken over by similar modern dictatorships, which often consciously imitated Nasser's regime.

A successful mixture of repression, popular appeal and thoroughgoing organization has often allowed modern dictatorships to replace traditional dictatorships and to remain in power for some time. This process, writes political theorist Michael Walzer, may be seen "as the absolute reversal of radical politics; popular movements are demobilized . . . revolutionary hope is turned into an ideology of domination; social control is intensified to the point where commitment and self-discipline lose all meaning."

Such a description is not altogether accurate. While Third World modern dictatorships are institutionally weaker than the Soviet government, they have a better chance of maintaining a real measure of support and legitimacy at home. Few Russians believe in communism; the Eastern European satellite regimes are imposed by Moscow. But many Third World citizens are still relatively positive about their government and ideologies. Nationalism is a potent force. The younger nations still hope for utopia, gain enthusiasm from recent revolutionary reforms, and believe that only the mobilization of their people and resources can preserve independence and bring desperately needed development.

Further, Third World modern dictatorships can increase their popularity by retaining many aspects of their nations' past political styles. They are more tolerable for their citizens when they fit existing cultural norms and demonstrate a much larger degree of flexibility than one might expect from such labels as "totalitarian" or "authoritarian."

When one deals with the Third World, the impressive edifice of institutions, statistics, laws, and ideologies—often modified in the rulers' pragmatic drive to keep power—should never be taken at face value. Nepotism continues to benefit relatives and those from the same tribes, regions, or ethnic groups as the rulers. Bribery is a common shortcut to getting things done. Personal relations are still more important than bureaucratic rules, which are not taken seriously, especially outside the capital, and there are dozens of ways around regulations. Organization is never as rigid or impressive in practice as it is on paper. More than one supposedly all-powerful leader has commented, like Khomeini, "No matter what I say, people interpret it as it suits them." These realities, at first appearing as shortcomings or weaknesses, make people's lives easier and the political system more acceptable.

Modern dictatorships' tremendous problems of continuity also undermine their rigidity. If so much depends on one man, the ideology and even the regime often cannot survive his death. The demise of three Soviet leaders in three years showed Moscow's sclerotic leadership but also demonstrated the regime's strength. Many Third World states have not yet survived such transitions, though Egypt, Kenya, and others have shown it can be done.

Nevertheless, although a given modern dictator may be replaced or overthrown, his successor will generally impose a similar regime, using the same techniques. The old, traditional power structure of kings, chiefs, and landed notables is not likely to be restored. Democratic interludes only collapse in the face of some new challenge from the military or a charismatic civilian leader.

Essentially, then, modern populist dictatorship is a technique which transcends the coloration of its practitioner's specific ideology. Khomeini's Islamic fundamentalist Iran has, as we will see, a great deal in common with Castro's Communist Cuba. And more of the difference is due to cultural factors than to ideological ones. While liberals take too seriously the egalitarian and progressive words of the one-party regimes, conservatives take too seriously their left-sounding rhetoric and alignments with the Soviet Union.

In fact, technique has replaced ideology as the foundation of Third World regimes, or to put it another way, ideology has become a manual for the technique of gaining and maintaining power. The twentieth century is not only the age of progress in transport and communication, chemistry and medicine but also the age of "progress" in the art of dictatorship. One can no more survive with nineteenth-century methods of dictatorship than with outdated industrial or agricultural techniques.

On the other hand, Third World politicians and intellectuals who have been the victims of such regimes' destructive and foolish policies resent what they see as a Western assumption that their societies are incapable of maintaining democratic systems. Yet they are the last people who should underestimate the new tools that dictators possess which permit and reinforce their hold on power.

There are ways in which the innovations of modern dictatorships are steps forward over the old regimes. By activating at least some workers and peasants and teaching them that at least in theory they have political interests and that government exists to serve them, the regimes of Nasser, Perón, Castro, Khomeini, and others may prepare the ground for development and progress. There are also material benefits in the form of land reform, better health facilities, more education, opportunities for personal advancement, and even higher living standards in many modern dictatorships compared to their predecessors.

Yet better organization also implies tighter controls, less personal freedom, and more widespread repression. By undermining dissent or independent organization, by being so effective in rooting out alternative institutions, the modern dictatorship makes itself harder to replace and hence tends to freeze society in its own image. Even Machiavelli recognized that "it cannot be called virtue to kill one's fellow-citizens, betray one's friends, be without faith, without pity . . . ; by these methods one may indeed gain power, but not glory."

Since modern dictatorships tend to be stronger than traditional ones, the latter are at a major disadvantage in any internal or international conflict. Washington has often ended up on the losing side by supporting traditional dictatorships. It has also repeatedly tried, with far less success recently than in the 1950s, to overthrow populist dictatorships which it saw as communistic or as inherently pro-Moscow.

Finally, Third World modern dictatorships are subject to complex pulls in the global competition between the United States and the USSR. They have rejected the Western democratic and private-enterprise model and have adapted many ideas from the Soviet Union. Even those who would have been horrified at being thought Communists found in Moscow's system of state control—single-party rule, mass organizations directed from the top, government ownership of the economy, strong repressive apparatus, all-encompassing propaganda, style of rhetoric, and so on—much that was applicable for their own dictatorships.

Further, the Soviets had apparently industrialized quickly and by means of their own willpower rather than, as seemed the case with the United States and Western Europe, through slower historical processes. In short, the Soviets had faced problems closer to those confronting the Third World: building a modern state overnight, assembling a self-perpetuating ruling group, destroying the old order, subordinating the army, creating national loyalties where none hitherto existed, and defending itself against a hostile outside world.

Some factors do compel the modern dictatorship toward the Soviets: common opposition to democracy as decadent, lip service to socioeconomic revolution, and blaming problems on "Western imperialists." As the world's first successful modern dictatorship the Soviets have a special appeal. Moscow's foreign policies also forge important links. Many countries rely on Soviet bloc arms and advisers for their secret police and military forces. The USSR takes a strong stand on Arab-Israeli and southern Africa issues that create political support and debts from Third World regimes.

These common characteristics give Moscow some real, but hardly irreversible, advantages. But Third World dictatorships always put their own interests first. They are more nationalistic than Communist and are more interested in maintaining power than either form of ideology. Even regimes in Ethiopia, Angola, Mozambique, or South Yemen that use Marxist-Leninist jargon and model their parties explicitly on Soviet experience still behave in tune with their internal political needs and cultures.

While Moscow was often a useful source of support and inspiration, few leaders were willing or able to imitate too closely its structure. From the Third World's standpoint the USSR was part of the industrialized "North." Conditions there were in many ways quite different from those faced by Third World regimes. The Soviet economy did not work so well, and its technology was inferior to that of the West. Soviet aid often turned out to be limited—except for selling arms in exchange for hard currency—and had a political price tag attached. Some modern dictatorships have learned these lessons; others are impelled by national interest, ideological enthusiasm, or lack of an alternative toward dependence on Moscow.

It seems cruel to blame the often victimized Third World

for its difficulties, considering colonialism's past and the great powers' misdeeds. Yet after a quarter century or more of independence the Third World's problems are also a result of its own leaders' misrule, exploitation, and corruption. Ignoring or even covering over this fact benefits no one.

An Algerian journalist once solicited from me a range of negative comments on the current state of U.S. politics and policies. "And what," I asked, "is happening in Algeria?" He was shocked. "But that's my country!" In other words, Americans should be willing to criticize their country's shortcomings, but the same behavior could not be expected from Third World citizens. Repression, insecurity, and a cultural preference for consensus make many Third World people feel such self-criticism is unnecessary and undesirable. If the United States is not immune from criticism—and in fact benefits from realistic assessments of its strengths and weaknesses—the same rule applies to other countries.

The transformation from colony or traditional dictatorship to modern dictatorship is a turning point in a nation's history. The basis of that process has been an undermining of the old society by internal change—better transport, education, communication; economic growth and urban migration; rising nationalism; new revolutionary techniques—and by foreign ideas and models that attract the cosmopolitan intellectual and military elites.

CHAPTER TWO

The Lessons of European Totalitarianism

Precisely at 1:00 P.M. on August 22, 1939, two huge German Focke-Wulf Condor planes landed at Moscow airport. Berlin's Foreign Minister Joachim von Ribbentrop came down the stairs to be greeted by five Nazi flags outside the terminal and a Soviet military band's rendition of the Nazi anthem. Members of the German Embassy staff clicked their heels and gave the Hitler salute; the Soviet welcoming delegation preferred a simple handshake with Ribbentrop. That afternoon Ribbentrop and Soviet Foreign Minister Vyacheslav Molotov initialed a nonaggression pact. Molotov commented shortly thereafter, "Fascism is a matter of taste."

Secretly the two governments planned for the division of Europe and the Middle East between themselves. No wonder that Ribbentrop could barely suppress a triumphant smile when he climbed back aboard his plane. As a first step in joint aggression Germany invaded western Poland barely a week later; the Soviets took over eastern Poland. Would Hitler have dared start World War II without Stalin's neutrality and cooperation?

The moment marked the apex of a new kind of dictatorship that conquered country after country, creating a nightmare of murder and repression while graphically demonstrating techniques for rule that were as politically effective as they were horrible.

News of this unexpected alliance shocked the world. After all, Soviet communism and German fascism were considered, by each other and by most observers, polar opposites. Their cooperation did not demonstrate that they were identical, but it did show that there were some very important common threads in these new forms of dictatorship. In some respects their organizational and psychological techniques were more important than the differences in their proclaimed goals.

Although dictatorship is a very old form of government, these new regimes, with their regimented parties, mass rallies, concentration camps, and passionate promotion of hatred, represented something quite different from the forms of government of most states since the first civilizations were established by the empires of kings and generals.

Historically rulers gained legitimacy from conquest, inheritance, and religious authority. Egypt's pharaohs, South America's Inca and Aztec rulers, Persia's shahs, China's emperors, and many others followed this pattern. Absolute monarchy, as the only type of government, did not have to defend its propriety. Since it had no democratic pretensions or literate citizenry, there was no effort to appeal to the masses; their loyalty could be taken for granted.

Ancient Greece and Ancient Rome added a new twist by granting some nonaristocrats political rights as "citizens," an invention giving those states a broader popular base than any previous regimes. Even this limited degree of democracy proved impermanent. Rome became an empire, and after its collapse, feudal systems arose based on a compact for protection and military service between serfs and nobles, nobles and kings.

As power was concentrated in the monarch's hands, the nobility and church were subjugated, but aristocrats and cities (or, more correctly, their merchant classes) gradually gained rights in addition to their obligations. Again, legitimacy and stability were ensured by a social contract; kings did not have to convince their subjects to vote or fight for them.

Dispersion of power gradually made room for more open political debate and the emergence of parliaments representing the landed gentry and growing middle class. Throughout the eighteenth and nineteenth centuries political and electoral rights were granted to larger groups that challenged the legitimacy of absolute monarchy and demanded a greater voice and role in government.

Advocates of democracy questioned the rule of a small closed elite as nationalism emerged to challenge the definition of existing states. The English, American, French, and Dutch revolutions developed the remarkable idea that government should depend on the consent of the governed and that monarchy was not necessary for a stable political order. They limited authority by constitutions, guarantees for citizens' rights, and balancing of the executive's powers against those of an elected legislature. The pluralism and flexibility of democratic societies encouraged progress. Capitalism sought to reduce political authority in favor of a productive private economic sector; intellectuals argued for social and economic reforms.

This greatly simplified history applies to a relatively small number of countries. Empires centered in the Middle East, Russia, and China provided a different model of powerful centralization, uneroded religious legitimacy, and philosophical traditions stressing the primacy of state over citizen. For whatever reasons, parliamentary democracy developed independently only in Western Europe and North America. Since European imperialism smashed the existing systems in the rest of the world, it is impossible to know how they would have developed if left undisturbed, nor is it easy to separate the legacy of colonialism from that of the previous, indigenous tradition.

Even Europe only partly followed a pattern of democratic development, becoming the testing ground for new forms of dictatorship just when the form seemed headed for extinction. The Communist regime of the USSR and the fascist regimes of Germany and Italy proclaimed themselves superior to decadent parliamentary systems. Their ideologies fueled a wave of imperialist aggression and served as the rulers' tools for regimenting society.

There has been a bitter, politicized debate over whether communism and fascism are siblings or even twins. The tragedies of World War II make pressing the point seem repugnant, but it is not necessary to enter that debate to see that the systems have much in common. To Third World observers seeking hints for their own politics, the similarities were usually more important than the differences.

Communism and fascism both used and perverted some of the late nineteenth and early twentieth centuries' most advanced ideas. Extolling management, organization, science, and economic development, they celebrated the power of humankind over nature, society, and other people. Using military discipline and mass production as models for ordering the masses, they glorified repression against critics or opponents and demanded the populace's enthusiastic support. They built a single hierarchical party in authority over government and a comprehensive ideology to direct all aspects of culture and education.

The fascists explicitly extolled the cult of the leader as infallible demigod; the Communists condemned it in words but deified Stalin in practice. The Fascists were fanatic nationalists; Stalin spoke of internationalism but pursued Soviet interests over the bodies of foreign Communists and neighboring countries. To eliminate real or imagined opponents, a system of concentration camps, surveillance, secret police, informers, and torture was established on a scale hitherto unknown in history.

While the resulting regimes were horrendous dictatorships with torturers, death camps, and megalomaniacal rulers who wasted their people's lives and their nation's resources, these systems clearly had effective ways to obtain and keep power. Both Hitler and Stalin were popular at home except among political or ethnic minorities that soon became their prisoners or victims. Through organization and central planning the two leaders accelerated economic development and built strong armies. Russia and Germany, the countries most devastated and humiliated by World War I, emerged in the 1930s as proud and powerful world powers.

Charismatic leaders, made to seem just and attractive by the concentrated power of modern public relations techniques (as political propaganda), proved able to win mass adulation. Parliamentary democracy was portrayed from both left and right as decadent, anarchic and outdated. Foreigners were enemies; rivals were demons; the old ruling classes were finished. The people could be stirred to revolutionary action, then manipulated into officially approved activity and acquiescence. The army must be politicized. At the same time it must come under the party's control to guarantee its loyalty.

These new, totalitarian modern dictatorships were not extensions of the past patterns of monarchy and empire. Those historic regimes were constrained by tradition but also did not need to make populist appeals or encourage mass mobilization. Instead, the modern dictatorship was a counterdemocracy, providing an alternative way to deal with the mass politics of the twentieth century.

Third World politicians and militants—reading propaganda, visiting Berlin or Moscow, or picking up Marxism during studies at French or British universities—were impressed by the apparent ability of communism and fascism to revitalize previously declining nations while Western democracies were helpless in the face of the Depression of the 1930s. German and Soviet political unity, military might, economic strength, ideological identity, and nationalistic revival were appealing for people seeking these same things. The facts that neither Germany after 1918 nor the USSR was a colonial power and that they condemned imperialism and were enemies of the British and French empires made them more attractive to downtrodden peoples.

Latin American military officers were impressed by Mussolini's corporate society. Some independence fighters in India and elsewhere in Asia became sympathetic to a resurgent, militaristic Japan challenging the European colonial powers.

Arab nationalists thought Germany's unification and renaissance a model for emulation. Before World War II fascism seemed to inspire far more interest than Marxism in the Third World.

Few Arabs, Africans, Latin Americans, or Asians became Communists or Fascists. Such parties were usually fringe movements whose identification with foreign powers brought subsidies but also made them seem unpatriotic. In addition, explicit fascism was discredited by the Axis defeat in World War II, while Marxism was unacceptably atheistic, insufficiently nationalist, and often effectively repressed by colonial authorities or local regimes.

Future Third World leaders were seeking not a total philosophy of life—they already had their own cultures and histories—but a blueprint able to win them political power and to guide economic development. The idea that politics could be studied and practiced as a science was particularly appealing to intellectuals. The parallels between revolutionary strategy and the fundamentals of military organization and tactics fascinated young officers.

The ability of the Communists and fascists to grow from small, ridiculed fringe groups to become masters of their societies made their techniques seem undeniably successful. Third World thinkers in the nineteenth century had attributed the secrets of the West's success to constitutions, secularism, and technology. Now they found the dynamism of these new movements worthy of emulation.

Communism and fascism had a number of theoretical views and practical politics in common. Both condemned capitalism as inefficient, weak, divisive, and oppressive. They ridiculed electoral democracy as biased, ineffective, and slow. They pinned responsibility for national problems on scapegoats who could be made unpopular: foreigners, classes, or ethnic groups. For the remaining citizens, the two systems urged unity and demanded obedience.

They also shared a parallel system of incentives and punishments for winning loyalty and destroying opposition. The Fascists did not abolish private business corporations but felt it sufficient to secure political control over their operations. The Communists seized an economic monopoly to eliminate any alternative centers of authority and, for this reason, gave control of these enterprises to the state rather than to the workers.

Both systems, then, were sophisticated efforts to combine the centralized authority and repressive power of dictatorship with the mass support and popular cooperation enjoyed by democracy.

Karl Marx, of course, thought of himself as a new Prometheus rather than as a new Machiavelli. Although he gave relatively little thought to the nature of a socialist government, he was naïvely sure it could easily solve the economic and political problems it would face in suppressing the bourgeoisie and allowing the proletariat to enjoy true control of society and individual freedom. With almost deterministic confidence, he believed that such a state, possessing economic, political, and military power, would produce a utopia. Marx said that in capitalism the proletariat was victimized by "false consciousness," a failure to understand its "true" interests, but he did not see how regimes calling themselves Marxist would extend such manipulation to heights previously undreamed.

But the very idea of a "scientific" theory of rule and revolution was intolerant of any alternative views. The idea that all political thought and practice was class-based laid the basis for destroying pluralism as a bourgeois ploy. If opposition to Marxism was false consciousness, then those with a true understanding were justified in imposing their views on everyone else.

The Leninist view was a natural outcome of this philosophy. In the words of Fidel Castro, "Whoever stops to wait for ideas to triumph among the majority of the masses before initiating revolutionary action will never be a revolutionary. . . . Humanity will, of course, change. . . . But this is not a revolutionary attitude." Electoral democracy, then, had three major problems: It was a tool of the bourgeoisie, prevented revolutionary change, and intensified an erroneous view of the world held even by the working class. Violent revolution followed by an enlightened dictatorship was the necessary alternative.

Marx thought this new system would involve true mass participation—a democracy for the majority and suppression of the old ruling class—rather than a dictatorship of a single leader and the top party officials. When Marx did consider the problem of charismatic dictatorship, he saw it as a flimsy, unworkable system. Marx compared Louis Napoleon, the populist dictator of France from 1852 to 1870, to his uncle Napoleon Bonaparte and concluded that while the latter's rule had been a tragedy, Louis's regime was only a "farce."

Marx failed to grasp how men like Louis, or even Napoleon Bonaparte for that matter, could seize the reins of power, subordinate the state to their egos, and use the masses' real desires and loyalty for their own ends. He could not fit his view of class rule and class struggle into these real situations except by viewing such dictatorships as merely a front for capitalists rather than as a new type of political system. Marxists committed the same error in the 1930s, when they could envision fascism only as a dictatorship of the capitalists. They had a similar difficulty in understanding Stalinism since such a terroristic dictatorship, by definition, could not happen under a Marxist "workers'" regime.

By defining the raw material of history as the economic productive forces, Marx left out the raw power of human psychology, nationalism, and xenophobia, the life experiences of individuals and the historical experience of societies, and a host of other factors. Like a scientist combining benign chemicals to form a compound explosively different from what he expected, Marx thought his theory of action would bring a perfected society; instead, his ideas of class struggle, scientific socialism, the fraudulence of "bourgeois" democracy and rights, and the false consciousness of the masses all helped create a formula for comprehensive dictatorship.

Russian novelist Feodor Dostoevsky provided a view at odds with Marx in *The Brothers Karamazov*. The nineteenth-century Russian intelligentsia was painfully aware of czarist injustices: Peasants were brutalized and tied to the land; the autocracy was slow to industrialize and even slower to democratize. Most of the country's best thinkers realized that a violent revolution was inevitable; many of them believed it to be desirable.

Dostoevsky, a former revolutionary turned conservative, writes about a sixteenth-century Spanish Inquisitor whose philosophy is similar to that of later advocates for populist dictatorship. "People are more persuaded than ever that they have perfect freedom, yet they have brought their freedom to us and laid it humbly at our feet," he explains. In exchange, the rulers will give them material benefits, ideas to believe in, and leaders to worship.

"Humanity will proclaim . . . that there is no crime . . . there is only hunger," says the Inquisitor on the primacy of living standards over liberty. As for ideology, he adds that only those "who can appease their conscience can take over their freedom. . . . For who can rule men if not he who holds their conscience and their bread in his hands?"

Dostoevsky's characters argue, however, that the Inquisitor really believes that his way is necessary to help humanity. The author understood that the dictator who believes his own ideology is more dangerous than a cynical manipulator because he embraces crimes as a necessary foundation for progress. The pro-Stalin playwright Bertolt Brecht makes this point in *The Good Woman of Szechuan*: that it is "necessary to be cruel to be kind" to humanity. With confidence that the righteousness of his cause obviates the demands of conscience, the modern dictatorship can tell followers, in Dostoevsky's words, "Every sin will be expiated, if it is done with our permission."

Twentieth-century history mirrored the preoccupations of both Marx and Dostoevsky. Marx predicted and advocated the right and power of the economically and nationally deprived to make revolutions. Dostoevsky was right to warn that these movements might produce only new kinds of problems and oppressions.

Oppression and imperialism were the midwives of the twentieth century's revolts, as Marx predicted, and tragedy and horror were often the result, as Dostoevsky warned. National disaster in World War I, with its terrible loss of human life, incompetent leadership, economic hardship, and intellectual disillusionment, planted the seeds of totalitarian revolution in Russia and Germany. The war undermined the idea of progress, showed the hypocrisies of democracy, subverted the old order, and brought centuries-old monarchies crashing down.

While Marx had said little about the conduct of socialist regimes, Vladimir Ilyich Lenin, the Russian socialist who extended Marx's theory and led the first successful Marxist revolution, developed the strategy and tactics for seizing and holding power. For him, only the destruction of all competing ideologies, parties, factions, and leaders could guarantee a revolution's success. When czarist Russia collapsed, Lenin's brilliant, ruthless leadership brought the Bolsheviks to power in 1917. The Russian Revolution was indeed a turning point in world history, not as a new phase in human freedom but as a landmark in the development of modern dictatorship.

Lenin's single greatest contribution was his creation of a disciplined revolutionary party as a powerful weapon in taking and holding power. The party was like an army engaged in warfare: it needed authoritarian leadership and could not afford internal democracy. Besides, Lenin argued, democracy was only a mask for the rule of the bourgeoisie: " 'Freedom of criticism,' means freedom for an opportunist trend" and would debilitate the revolutionary struggle's necessary discipline and unity. "We are marching in a compact group along a precipitous and difficult path. . . . We are surrounded on all sides by enemies, and we have to advance almost constantly under their fire."

Even the working class was a barrier to revolution because it preferred to seek better wages and conditions through trade unions and reforms. "Class political consciousness can be brought to the workers only from without" by a Communist party led by professional revolutionaries. The party was the general staff of the revolution, its leader was commander in chief.

As he had predicted, Lenin exercised control over the party, and the party ruled over Russia. He had a keen sense of the proper timing and interim stages of action needed to achieve victory. Alliances with other groups or promises to the masses were only tactics, to be abandoned, if need be, at the opportune time.

In theory, Lenin was suspicious of charismatic leadership. "Demagogues are the worst enemies of the working class . . . because they arouse base instincts among the masses," he wrote. But he also appreciated this shortcut's value and never hesitated to use it. The ideal leader should be a "tribune of the people." Besides, for Lenin terms like "demagogue," "opportunist," or "traitor" had no intrinsic meaning but merely defined anyone who disagreed with his political line of the moment.

Just as Lenin saw no need for democracy within the party, so he felt no need for guaranteeing the rights or participation of citizens in his socialist state. Capitalist democracy was a sham: "The oppressed were allowed, once every few years, to decide which particular representatives of the oppressing class should be in parliament to represent and repress them!" The proletariat needed the state "not in the interests of freedom, but for the purpose of crushing its antagonists." When there was no one left to be suppressed, the state would wither away, but of course, there is always someone to be suppressed. Lenin's system eliminated not only the old rulers' "monopoly" on freedom but also the right to assemble, speak freely, control the trade unions, read uncensored news, decide where to live within the country or to travel abroad, vote, practice religion, etc. of the workers, peasants, professionals, and intellectuals who made up the total population of the Soviet state.

After Lenin's death in 1924 Stalin tightened his control over the party and state apparatus by placing his followers in key positions. Stalin's rival, Leon Trotsky, correctly predicted that the dictatorship of the proletariat would become the party's dictatorship, the party's dictatorship would be the central committee's dictatorship, and even that would be reduced to the rule of Central Committee Chairman Stalin. Yet Trotsky produced no alternative; as a Communist he could only defend the party's collective dictatorship.

In the late 1920s Stalin purged Trotsky and his supporters; throughout the 1930s he murdered even subservient political and military leaders whose stature might make them competitors. Close comrades of Lenin were tortured or psychologically browbeaten into confessing fabricated crimes as traitors, spies, and foreign agents. Millions of party members, peasants, and others were sent to slave labor camps or shot. Ferocious repression of dissent was a basic principle of men who, themselves having seized power, were aware that others might follow their example. In this context the political insanity of Stalin and Hitler was not their massive atrocities but a pathological, counterproductive fixation on killing people who posed no real threat to them.

Despite their brutality, these regimes were able to suppress truth at home and fill the void with propaganda. The system made the repression acceptable to many of their people and frightened the rest into silence. Germans who turned against Hitler did so mainly because he was losing the war; Stalin has been rehabilitated by his successors. The point is that modern dictatorship cannot be based on repression and fear alone, although it uses those tools with previously undreamed-of efficiency. To succeed, it must also give material benefits, pride in national strength, and a sense of legitimacy to a sizable proportion of the population. In short, it must give its people reasons for being loyal.

In Soviet communism the promise of a better life was coupled with a leadership cult, patriotism, party control over all parts of society, central direction of the media and economy, a paranoid fear of internal and external enemies, and an extremely effective secret police. Stalin wrote quite frankly about this mixture of indoctrination, intimidation, and organization. Everything must be "directed according to a single plan. . . . The seizure of power is only the beginning. . . . The whole point is to retain power."

All the property of the old ruling classes must be expropriated, and their individual members exiled, killed, or politically neutralized. Even this was not sufficient, wrote Stalin, because the old order's strength was deeply rooted in its "connections, habits of organization and management, knowledge of all the 'secrets' (customs, methods, means and possibilities) of management, superior education . . . technical personnel and (cultural) force of habit." Such a dangerous and well-entrenched foe could be overcome only by the state's total control over wealth, means of communication, education, and information.

Force is justified against the "bourgeoisie" and anyone who sides with it, meaning, by definition, anybody who criticizes the government or new rulers, deeds and decisions. By weakening a revolution already besieged by foreign plotters and by traditional patterns, they are "objectively" in the enemy camp. Stalin wrote, "The dictatorship of the proletariat cannot be . . . democracy for all" but is still better than capitalism, under which "there are no real 'liberties' for the exploited."

One must always remember that a Third World intellectual, politician, or military officer, reading this material or observing Soviet practice, need not believe in communism. Substitute Arab nationalism, African socialism, Islamic fundamentalism, or the personally tailored ideologies of different dictators, and the modern dictatorships' rules of power still hold good, just as Machiavelli's strictures served the prince-politicians of his day.

The Marxist literature instructs revolutionary forces to proceed covertly and by stages but always to be guided by a small disciplined minority capable of outmaneuvering and out-organizing enemies and allies until the day it can destroy them. The keys to success are determination and a consistent strategy able to "concentrate the main forces of the revolution at the enemy's most vulnerable spot at the decisive moment." Lenin explained: "Certainly, almost everyone now realizes that the Bolsheviks could not have maintained themselves in power for two and a half months . . . without the strictest, truly iron discipline in our Party."

Surprisingly, Stalin said his regime's work style should incorporate "American efficiency," which he called an "indomitable force which neither knows nor recognizes obstacles; which with its business-like perseverance brushes aside all obstacles." While rejecting Western democracy, modern dicta-

48

torships have always been eager to use its technological and scientific innovations. But dictators reject the view that technology is socially or politically deterministic, believing it can be adapted for their own purposes. Communists, Fascists, and Islamic fundamentalists, among others, have paid special attention to indoctrinating technicians whose expertise might seduce them away from the ruling ideology. The Chinese Cultural Revolution, for example, aimed to ensure they would be "Red as well as Expert." Ayatollah Khomeini purged universities on the same principle.

Similarly, fascism, the system most at odds with bolshevism, ironically adopted many of its methods. World War I was followed by a very severe economic depression and a great deal of labor (and antilabor) violence. The transformation of rural peasants into urban workers brought misery and psychological dislocation; the lower middle class and peasantry felt threatened by economic disaster and political instability. Upper and middle classes feared Marxist takeovers; workers wanted more power and higher living standards. Intellectuals sought dramatic solutions to society's problems and their own malaise.

In Italy ex-socialist Benito Mussolini took power with his militaristic Black Shirts and with a weak monarch's acquiescence in 1922. "A revolution is a serious matter," he said, "not a court conspiracy, nor a change of Cabinet, nor the rise of one party replacing another." While Mussolini's arrogance and disastrous foreign adventures made him seem clownish in retrospect, he was popular at home and respected abroad for most of his two decades in power. In that era's well-known phrase, he had "made the trains run on time." His bombast over building a new Roman empire and conquest of Ethiopia stoked Italian pride.

Mussolini boasted that his "corporate state" conciliated management and labor, but this was no more real than Soviet talk of proletarian rule. He demanded absolute personal control. There must be, said Mussolini in a 1933 speech, a "single political party, in order that political discipline may exist alongside of economic discipline and . . . unite everyone above con-

49

trasting interests." The basis for all this was "a totalitarian State
. . . which by absorbing the energy, interests and aspirations
of the people, may transform and uplift them."

Historian Walter Laqueur points out that to understand
such regimes, it is crucial to remember that "while not all
decisions are actually made in and by the center, *no* truly
important decision is made without the knowledge, let alone
against the wish, of the leader. It is equally important to realize
that while not all decisions are made by the supreme leader,
all *could* in principle have been made by him."

The personality of the leader is one pillar of the system;
ideology is another. Class unity would supplant class conflict
by promoting nationalism, love of and obedience to the leader,
and hatred of opponents who refused to accept the national
consensus. Mussolini and Hitler tried to deflect natural internal antagonisms outward against foreigners, Jews, liberals, socialists, and Communists. Similar regimes were established in
Spain and Portugal and as collaborators with Hitler in France,
Romania, Hungary, Norway, and parts of Yugoslavia and
Czechoslovakia.

Germany's seeming hypnosis by a fanatical, irrational
movement, despite the country's noble cultural and intellectual
tradition, has long fascinated and mystified the world. The
complex mix of causes included the humiliations and traumas
of defeat in World War I, the high reparations payments, and
international subordination, as well as rampant inflation and
unemployment in the Depression of the 1930s, the displacement and disruption of old classes and ways, traditional intolerance and a yearning for order, and the failure of the weak
Weimar Republic.

Democracy's shortcomings were a major factor in Hitler's
rise. The compromise endemic in parliamentary politics was
attacked by both right and left. Leftist intellectuals ridiculed
the republic while rightists blamed Germany's World War I
defeat on a leftist-liberal "stab in the back." The republic was
powerless against rising street violence and unemployment.

In *Mein Kampf*, written in prison after a failed 1923 coup
attempt, Hitler described parliaments as deadlocked or in the

control of selfish interests; majority rule was merely a "mob thrown together by more or less savory accidents." Democracy produced cowardly leaders afraid to displease constituents.

Those chosen to represent the people were ignorant, corrupt, conceited dilettantes. Electoral democracy can "only please the biggest liars and sneaks . . . because it is inevitably hateful to an honorable, straightforward man." In contrast with this "Jewish" institution was "truly Germanic democracy characterized by the free election of a leader (to) assume all responsibility." Such a system promoted heroism and dynamic action.

Instead of marching decisively forward, parliamentary states went in confused circles. Dramatic change was needed to solve problems, but democracy was a formula for continuity with the past. Reform was insufficient; revolution and a total transformation of society were necessary. Hitler's distaste for compromise and his belief that democracy was only a mask for domination and exploitation matched Lenin's critique of "bourgeois" systems.

"The Leader," wrote Hitler, knows the "broad masses . . . can be moved only by the power of speech (unleashing) volcanic eruptions of human passions . . . not the lemonade-like outpourings of literary aesthetes and drawing room heroes." He inflamed Germany with an image of a resurrected nation smashing its enemies and fulfilling its potential. His party's success depended on "the fanaticism, yes, the intolerance, with which its adherents uphold it as the sole correct movement, and push it past other formations of a similar sort."

Hitler wanted the Nazi state to become "a community of physically and psychically homogeneous creatures," where strength—undiluted by sympathy for enemies—was more important than character or education. Racial solidarity and, more important, extreme nationalism were an ideology aiming to compete with class solidarity. Employers, for example, should not show "pigheaded short-sightedness" in failing to recognize that economic development required concessions to the workers for the sake of national solidarity. While racism and anti-Semitism are the characteristics most remembered about Nazi Germany, they were secondary elements in Hitler's ability to gain and hold power. The German people supported the regime because of its nationalist appeal and viable claim of success.

It is easy to forget that Germany in the 1920s and 1930s was a country that felt itself crushed under foreign power, almost as if it had been turned into a colony. The victorious Allies in the First World War had forced onto it responsibility for the disastrous conflict. Germany was deprived of its military forces, lost control over some of its most valuable territory, and was saddled with a measure of economic servitude to pay reparations. Some foreign observers saw the Hitler regime in its first years as an understandable reaction of an oppressed and mistreated nation. Certainly his message of angry xenophobia and justification for Germany was a powerful and effective one.

Yet Hitler's success was also due to his mastery of the technique and structure of modern dictatorship. While Stalin's innovations preceded or paralleled his, Hitler was not bound by the rhetoric of Marxism-Leninism on the proletariat and democracy. He could openly express—in the most direct and ruthless manner—the inner secrets of this new political style: national chauvinism, militarization of society and fanatical insistence on unity, control of culture and the media, direction of the economy, organization of almost everyone into groups supporting the regime, pervasive ideology, linkage of career success with at least lip service to the government's goals, effective secret police, and destruction of the opposition. All this rested on the popular appeal of a leader who could persuade listeners and win millions of votes, alongside a program that combined nationalism and populism in a new formula—national socialism—appropriate to the needs and nature of his country.

By 1933 opposition to Hitler was divided as the other left and right parties fought among themselves. Communists attacked Socialists and claimed, "After Hitler, our turn." Some conservatives betrayed the republic to make a deal with the Nazis. Hitler's passionate speeches made converts, and his followers built a powerful party, private army, and propaganda machine. His ideology exalted those who felt themselves exploited, found scapegoats for their resentments, and stressed German superiority. No matter how much the content of his ideology differed from Lenin's, Hitler followed a Leninist strategy far more effectively than did the German Communists.

While Hitler's charismatic leadership allowed the Nazis to seize power, destroy all opposition, and conquer most of Europe between 1939 and 1942, the same personalism spelled the system's doom. Neither the party nor any other institution could counter Hitler's military errors, obsessions, and increasing isolation from reality. Military defeat destroyed the expansive fascism and militarism of Germany, Italy, and Japan; the Nazis' insane crimes discredited their ideology. Hitler committed suicide, Mussolini was hanged, and their puppets elsewhere suffered deserved fates. If they had not gone to war against more powerful opponents, there was no existing force or factor that seemed capable of destroying their regimes. Future dictators were offered an important lesson: It is far easier to gain total control of your own country than to attack neighbors, inviting foreign resistance that might overthrow you.

Stalin, of course, ended up on the anti-Nazi side only because Hitler invaded his hitherto loyal ally. The Soviet dictator continued to unleash more oppression on the USSR and its new Eastern European empire until his death in 1953. Successors trimmed the extreme aspects of his repression, though not the monopoly of power.

The direct influences of Communist or Fascist ideas on Third World political figures and the regimes they later led can be traced in some detail. Differences between the two ideologies made them appeal to different groups. There were Latin American officers like Juan Perón who admired the corporate state and Pan-Arab nationalists like Gamal Abdel Nasser who also hated the British and Jews and admired German unification (but who later allied himself with the Soviets); African students like Sékou Touré and Kwame Nkrumah learned Marxism in Paris or London, and Chinese, Vietnamese, and others started Communist parties under the guidance of Stalin's Third International.

While the theory and practice of European totalitarianism were of central importance in the history of dictatorship, this in no way implies that later Third World dictators are being equated with Hitler and Stalin. Equally, there is little to be gained from political theories that make the Hitler and Stalin systems archetypal "totalitarian" regimes. It is not very useful to take the two most totally repressive, relentlessly ideological governments in the century as the baseline for defining a political system, particularly since each required an industrialized state, a highly structured ideology, advanced technology, and a distinctively pathological edge.

Certainly, these are not very exact models for understanding Third World dictators far less capable of "successfully" inflicting power and ideas on their own societies. Third World modern dictatorships have been weaker and generally less ambitious, fanatical, and extreme than the European totalitarian systems at their peak.

Further, these European examples are only part of the modern dictators' heritage and only partly fit into the conditions they face. Local history and tradition are the third and most immediate source of inspiration for contemporary Third World dictators. The diversity of Third World cultures and histories means that despite similar techniques of rule, leaders' ideologies and styles vary enormously from continent to continent and from country to country. Yet Third World societies still have a great deal in common regarding their social, economic, and political structures.

For example, in contrast with the Marxist and Fascist emphasis on internal struggle, Third World regimes have put a greater stress on the country—itself an infant whose survival cannot be taken for granted—as a community of like-minded people. The village, tribe, and extended family clan are seen as models for the nation. As in the European dictatorships, the duty of group solidarity becomes linked with that of patriotism, but the object is the rapid and lasting achievement of such unity rather than its disruption by internal conflict.

It is easy to see why Third World leaders seeking indigenous ideologies claim capitalism and communism do divide the people into battling classes and groups. Democracy and free speech cause factional strife and criticism; Marxism exalts one class and incites it to hate and suppress the others. These systems are often seen as alien to national needs and traditions. Unity is highly prized both because it fits with the "homogeneous community" concept of past history and because it is a basic necessity if the nation and regime are going to survive. Thus, different dictatorships invent their own "third way," allegedly better than capitalism or communism, democracy or "proletarian dictatorship."

Such political and philosophical positions are complemented by similar foreign policy views. Each regime is faced with constant demands to take sides in the East-West conflict. Traditional dictatorships generally prefer strong links with the West. Modern dictatorships' structure and rhetoric make them more akin to the Soviet Union, but they generally want to minimize taking sides in the U.S.-Soviet rivalry, professing nonalignment to maximize aid and play off the big powers.

Just as a modern dictator prefers to be seen as an important figure independent of the two blocs, so he also wants to be considered father of his country, above faction and criticism. If the local community parallels the nation, the national leader is equivalent to the family head or clan chief. Like such a local notable, he does not welcome challenges from dissidents or journalists. African tribalism, Asian Confucianism, Middle Eastern Islam, and Latin American paternalism all preach respect for the leader.

The pragmatic value of this approach must be emphasized. Underdeveloped states are held together by weak bonds. Disunity can easily turn into anarchy. Competing parties often mirror and reinforce tribal, religious, and regional conflicts; civilian politicians and electoral systems have repeatedly brought deadlock, corruption, and insolvable conflict. The predominance of modern dictatorship is as understandable a response as it is a regrettable one.

Nevertheless, while differences inherent in the wide variety of countries and individual dictators are extremely important, European totalitarianism formed a foundation for the Third World modern dictatorships that came later. "Definitions are never absolutely perfect," Walter Laqueur has written. "The basic task is not to find ingenious formulas but to reach a deeper understanding of the essential character of certain political regimes, and the direction in which they are likely to develop."

CHAPTER THREE

The Rise of Third World Modern Dictators

All Third World regimes, parties, and politicians must answer an essential question: Why are we behind? Each conclusion suggests a different response. Originally, Third World thinkers attributed Europe's advancement to constitutionalism or technology. Those stressing Western democracy's importance favored political reform at home; those emphasizing Western products and techniques favored a more materialistic form of adaptation. A Japanese intellectual wrote, "Why are they . . . strong? Why are we . . . weak? We have one thing to learn from the barbarians: solid ships and heavy guns."

Japan's modernized militarism met with great success. Tokyo's defeat of Czarist Russia in 1905, the first major Third World victory over Western armies, made a tremendous impression throughout the colonial world. Only after a devastating defeat in World War II and U.S. occupation did Japan add political to technical imitation. Today observers explain Japan's economic success by stressing indigenous cultural factors—the Japanese style of teamwork, loyalty, decision by consensus, and so on—over borrowings from the West.

Technology cannot be merely grafted onto a backward society. Buying weapons, for example, does not guarantee the political unity, professional competence, maintenance skills, and discipline needed for a successful military elite. There are other necessary factors involved in narrowing the relative gap in wealth and power between the developed and underdeveloped states. Neotraditionalists—Islamic fundamentalists, Latin American conservatives, African socialists—blame relative backwardness on abandonment of historic values.

This posture poses, however, another contradiction between reality and theory, between ideology and practice. Officially the Third World wants Western living standards but not Western life-styles. At the same time the popularity of Western television programs, movies, music, clothes, and other artifacts makes political leaders nervous about the impact and cost of these goods. Of course, the rulers, who get stereos, Mercedeses, and other fine imports, are quick to point out the threat of Michael Jackson T-shirts. They feel even more threatened by the thought of importing freedom of speech, freedom of the press, political pluralism, or economic competition.

Blaming underdevelopment on the West is a central part of contemporary Third World ideology, especially but not exclusively in modern dictatorships. As colonialism once looted the Third World, they say, so neocolonialism now exploits it by unequal terms of trade, political intervention, and cultural imperialism. It is thus necessary to break with the West and its style of thought and government, through some form of Marxism, so-called scientific socialism, or nationalism. Isolation from foreign influence may be seen as a step forward; criticism from Western governments and media are to be expected as their complaints over having lost another victim.

In Latin America and Africa high hopes for a new era of elected civilian leadership have in the past been repeatedly disappointed; in the Arab world the possibility of genuine parliamentary-based systems is generally absent. The problem is not only the ambitions of would-be dictators but the political and military elite's profound rejection of structures deemed inevitably linked with underdevelopment and dependency.

Despite their common objectives, strategies, and ambitions, modern dictators fill a whole spectrum of types. The self-styled Communists have the most consistent tight and top-down political organization and nationalized economies, but even they include much variety: China, previously the most doctrinaire, now the most flexible; Cuba, a typical strong man regime with a Marxist overlay and heavy Soviet subsidies; Vietnam, where the Communists have forcibly preempted nationalism; North Korea and Romania, with egomaniacal leaders trying to found hereditary dynasties; and the regimes of Eastern Europe and Afghanistan, the "popular" bases of which consist of the Soviet army. The story is told that Poland's Communist dictator, Wojciech Jaruzelski, goes to Lenin's tomb in Moscow to ask for advice from the Soviet leader. "Comrade Lenin, the situation in Poland is terrible," he says. "The reactionaries are rising up and trying to restore capitalism. What should we do?" Lenin replies, "Arm the workers!"

While most Westerners think the USSR and Marxist ideology obvious failures, many African and Middle East leaders have a different attitude and find in them some useful analysis for understanding of and suggestions for dealing with their own condition. Equally there is a belief in socialism, however it is defined, as the way out of their dilemmas. When such regimes are said to be turning away from statism, this usually means they are more willing to deal with foreign multinational companies or to permit small-scale family farming or commercial enterprise among their citizens.

The national particularities and the common characteristics of modern dictatorship are demonstrated by three of the system's earliest practitioners, each of whom made a revolution that forever changed his country: Kemal Atatürk of Turkey, Juan Perón of Argentina, and Gamal Abdel Nasser of Egypt. All career military officers, they stood outside the old alignments of political factions and ideologies. The first two were particularly influenced by fighting (Atatürk in World War I; Nasser in the 1948

Arab-Israeli War) in wars lost partly as the result of the incompetence and corruption of their political leaders.

In some ways Atatürk was the first of the modern Third World dictators; in others this student of Voltaire and Rousseau was the last in a line of European democratic revolutionaries. When he came to power in 1922, many ideas that would be shredded in later decades were still intact; parliamentary democracy was a symbol of development, and Westernization seemed the route to modernization. "As the cultural level of a nation is raised," he predicted, "the fields of application of individual liberty too shall increase." The Communist and Fascist experiments that so fascinated Nasser and Perón had not yet shaped the political rhetoric and behavior of the age.

The Ottoman Empire, including the Balkans and much of the Arab world as well as modern Turkey, was for more than 600 years ruled by hereditary sultans. Personal and group identity was defined by language and religion rather than by loyalty to a nation-state. The rise of ethnic nationalism and the nibblings of European powers had reduced the once-powerful empire to being the backward "Sick Man of Europe."

Disgusted by the empire's decay, officers formed a secret group best known as the Young Turks. Their 1908 coup, the first Third World military takeover, was greeted with dancing in the streets of the capital, celebrating the new era. But the Young Turks' attempts at centralization and Turkification alienated the subject peoples and provoked new revolts and defeats, culminating in ruinous involvement in World War I. Four years later, by 1918, the empire lay destroyed, 20 percent of its people had perished from hunger or disease, and the nation was occupied by foreign armies.

A prostrate country was willing to accept radical change. Atatürk, who had proved himself the most competent and heroic of generals in the war, withdrew to the interior, raised an army, and formed a new government. From 1919 to 1922 he won a series of victories, expelling the occupying Greek Army and forcing diplomatic concessions from the European powers. At the end Turkey preserved its independence and home territory.

Describing Atatürk in the midst of his campaigns, in July 1921, U.S. Navy officer Robert Dunn reported, "His youthfulness struck you: the high cheek bones, somewhat hollow cheeks, small reddish and very trim mustache, steel blue eyes." His face was "not intellectual but subtle and mercuric. . . . You got a sense of concentration in the brain behind, with immense possibilities of inexorability, cruelty even, yet of complete realization of all points at issue and a broad outlook."

A grateful, desperate populace acceded him total authority. "If I wanted," he said shortly before his death in 1938, "I would have forthwith set up a military dictatorship. . . . But what I had in mind was to help set up a modern state for my nation." His experience with the horror of war made him eschew imperialism with the motto "Peace at home, peace abroad." It was better to let the empire go and avoid foreign adventures. National pride did not necessitate international hatreds.

He stood so far above his contemporaries that no serious rivals could emerge; his popularity minimized any need for repression. At the same time his strong powers of leadership made his countrymen see Atatürk in the superhuman image of the charismatic leader. There are two Atatürks, he said in one famous speech. "One is sitting before you, the (man) of flesh and blood, who will pass away. There is another whom I cannot call Me. It is not I that this . . . personifies, it is You— all you present here, who go into the farthestmost parts of the country to inculcate and defend a new ideal, a new mode of thought. I stand for these dreams of yours. My life's work is to make them come true."

Atatürk almost single-handedly preached and propagated the doctrine of development and modernization. He ordered the Turkish language simplified and converted to European script, eliminated the Muslim clergy's power, revised the legal code, and mandated unveiling and legal equality for women. The state founded and ran new industries and built a national network of educational institutes, the village hearths.

Symbolic measures were important as well. The Oriental fez, which Atatürk called "a sign of ignorance, of fanaticism, of hatred against progress and civilization," was replaced by the hat, "the customary headdress of the whole civilized world." In the same spirit he decreed that Turks take family names for the first time; parliament voted him the name Atatürk, "father of the Turks."

"We now belong to the West. We cannot attempt to attain and surpass the level of contemporary civilization merely by boasting about our old Civilization," explained Atatürk. Progress necessitated social change, science, knowledge, and cultural advancement. But to achieve this, the people had to be roused and united as they had been for the war of liberation. "Our people does not (consist) of castes or classes whose interests differ," Atatürk said. "Quite to the contrary, it is made of classes whose existence and efforts are mutually needed. . . . The farmer needs the artisan, the artisan needs the farmer and the farmer needs the merchants, and . . . all of these need not only each other, but the worker as well."

Even though the country was in ruins, he said in 1920, vigorous life would spring up only if the people abandoned their historic passivity and became willing to shape their own lives. Five years later he noted, "The real author of the political and social reforms realized by the Turkish nation in recent years is that nation itself. It's you! If the nation did not possess this capacity, no power would have sufficed."

His ideology's basic principles were symbols of these objectives: Republicanism meant the elimination of monarchy and the institution of representative rule. Statism embodied the government's leading role in promoting economic development. Reformism called for a willingness to change society. Nationalism brought a sense of identity as Turks put loyalty to the country above sectarian or factional interests. Secularism sought the separation of religion from politics, a difficult task in an overwhelmingly Muslim country. Populism taught that leaders must be responsive to the people's will.

Sometimes, but surprisingly rarely during his years as president between 1922 and 1938, Atatürk misused his power. More important, however, he laid the foundation for a different kind of system. "The nation must be vigilant towards its government," he had warned. "Sovereignty cannot be founded upon fear. And sovereignty which is supported by guns shall not last."

In short, Atatürk understood that democracy enhances national life and corrects the errors of a leader's egotism, miscalculation, or selfish interest that, if unchecked, could lead to disaster or oppression. "The press," he lectured in 1930, "helps prevent abuses and forces the government agencies to perform their duties correctly," although, he added, "it should also be remembered that it is easier to criticize than to create." But the catastrophe of the Young Turks, in their own way an embryo modern dictatorship, was a lasting lesson for him. "It is painful for a country and its people to be ravaged by the enemy," he warned. "But it is even more painful for the people to be exposed (to misfortune) by those who are of their very own race and whom they regard as great and keep at their head."

Despite periodic instability in later years, Turkey remained a nonaggressive and persistent democracy, the tradition was deeply implanted. The army saw itself as the repository of Atatürk's ideology, and Atatürk himself remains his country's incomparable hero and positive example. So popular does he remain that many Turks reject the idea that Atatürk was a dictator at all. They believe he was a national leader whose universal popular support meant his regime was democratic and whose inspired leadership was worthy of being followed without compulsion. Many—but probably a smaller proportion of—Egyptians, Chinese, Tanzanians, and Iranians would speak of their charismatic dictators in similar terms. In fact, this very type of identification is a prime characteristic of modern dictatorship.

Despite Atatürk's success, however, his example had little direct effect in the Middle East because his revolution's secularism and conscious Europeanizing policy made it unacceptable to other Muslim countries. Still, many of Atatürk's ideas on class, unity, patriotism, and populism would be independently reinvented by Third World leaders in later years. "Our government . . . has no resemblance to governments described in books," he said, defining it as "belonging to the people as a whole in contrast to an old regime that belonged to an individual or group of individuals." This was a precise statement on the modern dictatorship's self-image and view of its traditionalist predecessors.

There are parallels between the systems established by the Atatürk and Mexico's revolution during the 1920s. The Mexican Revolution, also intent on modernization, land reform, and secularism, found continuity through the appropriately named Party of the Institutionalized Revolution (PRI), whose political machine took over much of the economy and a wide range of peasant, worker, cultural, and other organizations. The two main threats to PRI dominance were defused: The army was depoliticized, and the president was limited to a single six-year term. Despite a large degree of democracy, no opposition party was allowed to defeat the PRI in a national election. Again, however, this system did not take root anywhere else in Latin America.

The idea of parliamentary democracy as an integral part of progress was overwhelmed by the examples of Germany and the USSR. Although few Third World leaders became Fascists or Communists, they were not persuaded that a dictator should educate his people toward democracy, a free press, individual rights, peaceful foreign policy, and pluralism. Aside from ideology, there were few men capable of seizing total power and then being willing to use it to make their continued rule unnecessary.

Perón and Nasser rose to power in the wake of World War II. Observation of other countries as well as their own experiences and political instincts taught them to use revolutionary techniques for setting in motion socioeconomic revolutions. Despite their countries' different traditions, the two men had a remarkable amount in common.

Both were military officers who, coming of political age in the 1930s, found their countries under incompetent leaders and patronizing foreign influence. Britain had tens of thousands of troops stationed in the Suez Canal area, and its diplomats were able to make and break Egyptian governments.

When the all-powerful British high commissioner was going home on leave in 1940, he teased Egypt's prime minister by saying, "Ali, don't let anything bad happen while I'm gone." "Oh, Sir Miles," replied the politician, "nothing bad ever happens when you're not here."

In Argentina British companies owned virtually all the railroads; foreigners owned and managed 45 percent of local industry. Neither country was a colony, but the intellectuals and politicians of each were obsessed by the lack of full national independence.

In addition to frustrated nationalism, the ruling establishment's isolation from the people and inability to cope with their needs provoked discontent. As a slim, handsome young man King Farouk was crowned king of Egypt in 1936 amid great hopes for his rule. A decade later Farouk was obese, corrupt, preoccupied with womanizing, and incapable of standing up to British pressure. The adoration had turned to ridicule. Yet the main alternative to the palace, the populist Wafd party, was also discredited by scandals, splits, and a willingness to accept British patronage.

Argentina, like most Latin American countries, was governed by alternating civilian and military regimes. Despite its productivity in grain and meat, Argentina did not live up to its economic potential. Landowners ran the country for their own benefit, showing little interest in industrialization. The European-oriented elite looked down on the poorly paid rural and urban workers and bitterly fought their unions. Since Argentina was one of the region's most urbanized, developed countries—as was Cuba at the time of Fidel Castro's revolution—the social and economic gap was all the more conducive to discontent.

While mainly shaped by their own cultural and national traditions, Perón and Nasser were also inspired by fascism, in large part because it corresponded to their nationalistic, anti-British interests. Perón was sent on a military mission to Italy in early 1939—his first visit to Europe—and stayed until the end of 1940. He was convinced that the Nazi and Fascist regimes were great successes, being particularly impressed by

65

charismatic leaders' manipulation of trade unions and their show business techniques in handling crowds. But Perón was too generous toward the workers, less violently repressive, too opportunistic, and never consistent enough to embrace this ideology, despite his pro-Axis sympathies during World War II.

Nasser cooperated closely with German spies during the war and would have been a likely collaborator if General Erwin Rommel's Afrika Korps had captured Cairo in 1942. Like Perón, however, Nasser was essentially a pragmatic nationalist looking for a workable philosophy of power and willing to move from "left" to "right" as the occasion required. Both dictators were determined to become architects of revolutions irreversibly changing their countries' course, not just military officers taking their turns in power.

Perón put it best: "I returned (from Europe) at a moment when the (political) battles, as usual, were being rigged. I asked myself, 'What would happen if someone began to fight for real and announced I'm going to play to win?' " Soon after he had come back, Perón joined a secret military society that successfully staged a coup in 1943, and he became top aide to the new junta's nominal leader.

His most brilliant move was to take the seemingly unimportant position as secretary of labor and public welfare. Perón energetically spoke in radical rhetoric to the unions—while reassuring employers in corporate-state terms—and supported demands for better pay and conditions. As biographer Joseph Page wrote, "For the first time a government was treating workers with respect instead of repression. They were beginning to feel like citizens who mattered, and they owed this psychic gratification to the colonel." Perón so successfully manipulated military assignments, courted civilian politicians and unions, and built popular support that he was elected president by a landslide within two years.

When the junta arrested the increasingly powerful Perón and abandoned his prolabor policies in October 1945, hundreds of thousands of workers poured into Buenos Aires to demonstrate. They walked for miles and waited for hours to acclaim their hero. Argentina had never seen anything like it. The police were overwhelmed, and the flustered junta practically had to beg Perón to rescue it. They freed him and called elections.

When the rich and their newspapers ridiculed Perón's supporters for their poverty and lack of manners, he proudly called his followers *descamisados* (the shirtless ones). When the Communist and Socialist parties lined up against him, Perón lambasted the "oligarchy-Communist alliance." After U.S. Ambassador Spruille Braden attacked him, Perón told the Argentines that they had to choose between "Braden or Perón." The effect was electric: Perón was elected president, and his supporters captured parliament with two-thirds of the vote.

Perón's popularity was not based on speeches alone. Wages of skilled industrial workers went up 27 percent and those of unskilled by 37 percent, during Perón's first five years in power. He raised fringe benefits, instituted social security, and appointed working-class men and women to high government positions. While supporters enjoyed material benefits, Peronists harassed opposition meetings, beat up critics, filled judgeships with supporters, and bought up newspapers. To ridicule the snobbish upper class, Perón set up a fish market on the steps of the elite's most exclusive club.

Perón was able to stigmatize the opposition as greedy and unpatriotic while convincing the common people he was on their side. He justified controlling the press to prevent it from being "weapons of economic disturbance and social divisiveness, [or] vehicles of foreign ideas or political ambitions." Perón's equally charismatic wife, Eva, made fiery speeches attacking the oligarchy and set up her own foundation to distribute money to the needy. Critics charged that Evita Perón's funds were lining the pockets of the Peróns, but these complaints did not deter the Peronists' fanatical devotion to the former movie star.

The dictator's real problem was that he did not dare touch the officer corps and failed to break the oligarchy's power.

Perón could not carry through a full revolution. As the economy went into decline, conservative officers rose and forced him to flee in 1955.

Three years earlier, with Perón still at the peak of his power, Egypt's Free Officers, a secret military group under Nasser's leadership, staged a bloodless coup against King Farouk. Nasser saw this event as the culmination of a century of gallant nationalist struggles. For the first time since the pharaohs Egypt had a truly indigenous ruler.

Nasser, like Perón, stood behind a higher-ranking figurehead before emerging as champion of the masses. First, however, Nasser consolidated the officer corps' support, decisively defeated the powerful Muslim Brotherhood and the Communists, and stole their constituencies. Perón's support came from workers and unions, but Egypt had little industry. Nasser courted the peasants and urban lower middle class. Land reform and rural development efforts pleased the former; nationalization of foreign assets favored the latter. Nationalistic foreign policy appeased all of them.

Instead of acting like desperate natives, humbly asking for justice, Egyptians wanted their country to stand tall, taking what was rightfully theirs, becoming a factor of consequence in the world, and claiming leadership of the Arabs. Nasser first secured British military withdrawal from the Suez Canal, bought Soviet bloc arms, and then seized the Canal. Militarily defeated by an Anglo-French-Israeli invasion in 1956, Nasser turned it into a diplomatic victory. Overnight he became the Arab world's hero. Nasserist movements, Radio Cairo's appeals, and Egyptian intelligence machinations stirred rebellion in Jordan, Lebanon, Syria, and Iraq in the 1950s and 1960s.

Nasser's Egypt was also an influential model for black Africa, then on the verge of independence. A writer visiting Cairo from Cameroon in 1960 thought an Egyptian military parade "not just a show to boast prestige, but the real 'march of liberation' by a whole people, which only yesterday was under foreign domination." A factory "owned and run by Africans" was no routine thing but "a revolutionary experience . . . and makes even a steel bar a symbol of emancipation." He concluded: "That this daring experiment has resulted in a dictatorship is in itself unimportant. What counts is that it has not resulted in anarchy." Such reactions show how possessing a strong military, a nationalized industry, and a stable government able to perform these miracles was the highest, even revered priority for the newly independent states.

Foreign policy had been relatively unimportant for Perón, whose country lay deep within the U.S. sphere of influence at a time when Washington was at the height of its international power. Nasser was more favorably situated in time and place. He became a founding member of the nonalignment movement and played off U.S. and Soviet power, tilting toward the latter. Perón's insults to Washington were popular at home; Nasser said tauntingly that if the Americans did not like his policy, they could go drink the Nile.

The fact that Nasser was dependent on U.S. food aid and Soviet weapons did not prevent him from being universally seen as a progressive, independent, anti-imperialist leader. The important thing was that no one thought the need for aid was determining his policies. On the contrary, Nasser's ability to obtain Washington's assistance while flouting its interests and to play both sides of the Cold War street seemed to demonstrate the value of nonalignment and Third World leverage in using superpower rivalry to its own advantage.

Equally paradoxical for Americans was the Third World's apparent willingness to ignore Moscow's imperial arrogance in establishing its own bases, providing substandard equipment, meddling in internal politics, and forcing Egypt deep into debt. Such practices eventually stirred Egyptian resentment and reaction. But in the 1950s and 1960s other peoples saw the "success" of Egypt's pro-Moscow brand of nonalignment as showing the Soviets as a reliable ally, generous in development efforts and helpful in removing the Western yoke.

Like Perón, Nasser was more successful at redistributing wealth than at creating it. Yet his land reform, establishment of cooperatives, improvement in health care and educational opportunities, and subsidies or price controls on many goods did improve the living standards of many Egyptians. When, as so often happened, his programs fell short of his promises, Nasser's ability to give the people a cause to believe in inspired a willingness to make sacrifices.

To demonstrate that Nasser did not solve Egypt's economic and social problems only makes more impressive the psychological factors that guaranteed his popularity. Rationing was accepted as promoting equality while subsidies helped the peasant and urban masses. The Aswan Dam fulfilled a national dream, though it did not live up to its predicted economic potential. State enterprises made Egyptians feel they had a stake in the ownership of the national wealth. Even if production was less efficient and goods were of lower quality, they were more widely distributed than before.

Western experts who went to Egypt repeatedly pointed out the weaknesses of that country's policies. Too much money was being spent on the army, the huge, stifling state bureaucracy, and subsidies on food so high that peasants fed their livestock on bread. The population was growing at a frightening rate.

This critique might be logical, Egyptians replied, but was politically unacceptable because changes would threaten the basis of the regime. Cutting the military budget might make angry officers lead a coup. Reducing the bureaucracy would throw out on the street the kind of young, educated men who would be the natural leaders of a revolution. Slicing subsidies, as Anwar al-Sadat discovered in 1977, could set off massive riots. In short, Egypt's policy might be economically irrational but made very good political sense, a paradox typical of modern dictatorships and a factor promoting mounting debts and disappointing economic growth rates in the Third World.

While solving few of Egypt's development problems, Nasser's policies led to outright catastrophes abroad. Cairo's military intervention during the 1960s in the Yemen civil war was a costly, unwinnable enterprise similar to the U.S. experience in Vietnam. Far worse, in attempting to show his militancy and Arab leadership, Nasser threatened Israel with extinction and went to the brink of war. In June 1967 Israel smashed the Egyptian Army in six days and captured the Sinai peninsula. Nasser resigned, only, as happened earlier with Perón, to be recalled by a massive, partly orchestrated demonstration. Three years later Nasser died in office with his power and popularity intact despite Egypt's tremendous material problems.

Nasser and Perón were well equipped to be successful dictators. They were stirring speakers with a flair for the dramatic and intuitively able to judge a crowd. By background and inclination, they were men of the people, educated enough to deal with the wider world but equally able to understand the concerns and emotions of workers and peasants.

"Projecting vigor, good looks, meticulous grooming and charm, Juan Perón cut a dashing figure" in his uniform, one observer recorded. The tall, athletic Perón, flashing his famous smile, stood out in any crowd. Nasser was cut from a similar mold. Egyptian public figures traditionally spoke in classical Arabic. By using Egyptian dialect, Nasser made an immediate populist sensation with his speeches. Perón had an earthy, unpretentious style and an equally charismatic wife, Evita, with a passionate, rousing one.

Yet their public personas and genuine concern for the public's welfare hid cold, detached, and manipulative personalities, eager to accumulate and unwilling to share power. They placed themselves above colleagues by setting themselves away from them. Ambition, determination, ruthlessness when necessary, a deep-seated mistrust of others, and a sense of mission that often excluded compromise were qualities required by their calling.

When it came to any theoretical or philosophical ideology, neither man, like most modern dictators, had much to offer. But their speeches and writings are full of clear explanations on their tactics and objectives. They preached national unity against an internal oligarchy and foreign foes. The party would organize the people; the leader would comprehend the masses' needs and desires. Political cooperation under the leader's baton and state-planned economic harmony would replace the strife of democracy and capitalism. Liberation from outside

71

control and selfish domestic interests would allow the nation to develop without losing its own soul.

Perón's philosophy, *justicialismo*, was vague even by the standards of modern dictators and was redefined at will by Perón. He could combine Fascist ideas (a paranoid anti-Semitism and an advocacy of syndicalism along Mussolini's lines) alongside Marxist ones, including, during the 1960s and 1970s, praise for Castro and Mao. Perón's principle of verticality—a chain of command in which he, as "conductor" stood at the top—meant that Peronists either accepted his orders or left the movement.

Nasser's ideology, built on a foundation of Pan-Arab nationalism, was equally inconsistent in left-right terms. As a patriotic officer and an ambitious power seeker, Nasser was quite willing to tailor his ideology as circumstances demanded. In his book *The Philosophy of the Revolution*, Nasser wrote that success for the revolution and regime required "Unity, solidarity and cooperation of all elements of the nation, and self-denial and self-sacrifice from the individual." Yet all this had to be achieved during a necessary period of change and upheaval that threatened the "disintegration of values . . . dissension and discord among both class and individuals, and the domination of corruption, suspicion . . . egoism."

Nasser originally hoped "that the whole nation . . . only awaited the leaders to storm the strongholds of oppression, to follow them in close orderly ranks on the Holy March to the Great Goal" and that civilian politicians would work together rather than bicker over the spoils. Instead, soon after the coup he realized "that the vanguard's mission did not end at that hour, but it had just begun." Nasser's discovery is reminiscent of Lenin's: A leader was needed to overcome the masses' cynicism and passivity; discipline was needed to unite the activists.

The cult of the dictator's personality helped bridge this gap, thrilling and directing the people and a party that was a conduit for the leader's orders rather than a ruling body in its own right. Nasser's parties—the best known being the Arab Socialist Union—all were virtual shadows; the Peronist hierarchy was peopled with sycophants. The Peronist marching song proclaimed, "Perón, Perón, how great you are!" A first-grade reader during the Peronist regime taught: "Perón is the leader. Everybody loves Perón. Everybody sings 'Viva Perón.' " Nasser was similarly idolized. People supported the dictator because he brought them a vision of the future, a sense of dignity, and real material benefits.

Where for centuries people had feared the government as tax collector and ally of the oligarchy, the dictator created a new identification with the regime. Where no sense of nationhood had existed, identification with the leader proved a simple and powerful way of promoting loyalty to a new identity. But when dictators forget the structures, guns, and subordinates who keep them in power and succumb to megalomania—believing their almost magical link with the people was the only thing necessary to maintain their rule—it is often a sign that the end is near. Perón made this mistake, but Nasser never did.

Most leftists and intellectuals forgave Nasser and, to a lesser extent, Perón for repressing and imprisoning them. The moderate writer Tawfiq al-Hakim spoke for most Egyptian intellectuals describing how, despite the forced conformity, censorship, hypocrisy, and repression of the Nasser era, the regime "bewitched us with the glitter of hopes that had fascinated us for a long time, and they intoxicated us with the wine of 'attainment' and 'glory,' and we got so drunk that we lost consciousness." The intellectuals "had no means and no strength except to stick with [Nasser] because he had stripped us throughout the years of every independent thought and of every strong personality other than his own." After all, how could these "progressive" groups oppose patriotism, anti-imperialism, and reform? Why should they fight against a popular mass movement? How could they miss the opportunity to try hitching a ride on the dictator's popularity, hoping to channel it in their own direction? In addition, anti-Americanism or friendly policies toward the Soviet Union helped a dictator appeal to the left regardless of the content of his domestic policy. The Communists were devoted to Moscow's interests, and Moscow never hesitated to sacrifice local surrogates to consolidate a relationship with a nonaligned or an anti-American dictatorship.

Those who tried to buck the tide were condemned to sterile opposition. During Perón's long years of exile in Spain young revolutionaries preferred to join the Peronist left. When conservative Peronists chanted, "Perón, Evita, la patria Peronista!" radical Peronists responded, "Perón, Evita, la patria socialista!" Both groups saw in Perón exactly what they wanted and helped return him to power in 1973. He died the following year, and his incompetent heirs could not hold the regime together. Another coup deposed the Peronists without tarnishing their founder's continuing mystique.

The Egyptian Communists even dissolved their party to join Nasserist ranks. By providing a form of nationalist radicalism far more comprehensible and appealing to the masses than Marxism, Nasser restricted the Communists' already limited appeal. While the Communists had a special burden in proving they were more loyal to Egypt than to the USSR, intellectuals and artists tried to break down their isolation from the common people and deny subordination to cosmopolitan influences by throwing themselves into the dictatorship's service and the national cause.

In later years Nasser's successor, Anwar al-Sadat, opened the stagnant economy to private enterprise and foreign investment. Western observers were impressed to see shops full of goods and Sadat's moderate foreign policy initiatives. Egyptians were disturbed by open inequality, corruption, and conspicuous consumption. These problems had existed under Nasser but in a more "acceptable," hidden form and alongside a sense of enthusiasm and national mission which Sadat could not rekindle.

While the fruits of Sadat's rapprochement with the United States and Israel were welcome, Nasser's intransigence was much more appealing than the unromantic necessity of compromise. If one had spent years believing, as most Egyptians and Arabs did, that the Arabs should be united, Israel destroyed, and Western influence minimized, then Sadat's moderation was a betrayal of principle and an abandonment of just struggles and potential victories. Sadat saved Egypt from the precipice where Nasser left it, but his assassination in 1981 did not plunge the country into mourning, nor did he leave a legacy of lasting adulation.

Leaders cannot be judged, then, by their objective material achievements alone. Lasting popularity, even love, can come from a reputation, partly made by one's own propaganda machine, for honesty, patriotism, and faithfulness to the people. It was the local, not the international, image that mattered. The shrewd Secretary of State Dean Acheson commented in the 1940s that Perón was "detested by all good men—except Argentinians."

Nasser, however, staged an irreversible change because he destroyed the old ruling elite, redistributed economic power, and remolded the army. The fact that he succeeded politically promoted a series of revolutions and modern dictatorships throughout the Arab world. Perón's failure had equally profound effects on Latin America, a region that remains the stronghold of traditional dictators.

CHAPTER FOUR

The Fall of the Traditional Dictators

The guerrilla "final offensive" against Nicaraguan dictator na-sio Somoza closes in on the capital. One town after another falls even though the regime is willing to kill peasants and destroy houses and factories in revenge for the populace's support for the rebels.

As the noose tightens, the dictator dons military fatigues to inspect the front, declares a state of siege, and blames international communism for the crisis. Cracking under the strain, Somoza reveals the weakness and cynicism behind his strong man facade. "If you're like I am," he tells reporters, "you're just a bunch of shits."

While the dictator's overfed associates revel in unearned wealth and seem totally out of touch with their own country, the rebels are young and popular. "Almost all the kids have joined the guerrillas," says a peasant woman. "We support them. We give them medicine (and) food."

Under the strain of fighting and workers' strikes, the social and economic structures break down. Guerrillas set up barricades in city streets; would-be purchasers form long lines for scarce food and fuel; refugees fill the roads; foreign reporters fill the capital's luxury hotel. It is like the last act of a bullfight, and the old regime is headed inexorably for the sword.

The opposition escalates from hit-and-run raids to stand-up battles against the government's soldiers. The army starts to crumble. Officers desert their men; soldiers flee or surrender in larger and larger numbers. "Liberated zones" are declared amid frantic U.S. efforts to negotiate a resolution of the crisis. Meanwhile, the dictator holes up in his bunker, refusing any compromise. Somoza had such contempt for the opposition, which he had so often outmaneuvered before, that he now cannot take its challenge seriously until it is far too late.

Finally, Somoza flees to Miami in a private jet, ending forty-three years of his family's rule. Picked up by a Cadillac limousine, he is whisked to his huge private estate. From the veranda Somoza blames the U.S. government and everyone else for his downfall. In fact, his own greedy misrule, putting a priority on expanding the multimillion-dollar family fortune, had destroyed his regime.

A few hours after the dictator's plane has left the national airport, the guerrillas enter the capital. There are joyous celebrations; the long night of serfdom has ended. Statues of the dictator are pulled down, and political prisoners are released, blinking at the bright light of the sun, to recount torture and mistreatment. The dictator's estates are seized, his associates run away, and some of his leading collaborators are shot. Everyone hopes that the revolutionary coalition can hold together to inaugurate a new era of democracy and national reconciliation. Unfortunately those aspirations are doomed.

These were the events in Nicaragua in the summer of 1979. A few months earlier, Iran's Shah went into exile under roughly similar circumstances, though the Iranian opposition mobilized in massive peaceful demonstrations rather than guerrilla warfare and was spearheaded by Islamic fundamentalists rather than Marxists. Elsewhere in Latin America—including Argentina, Brazil, Ecuador, Peru, and Uruguay—military juntas simply gave up under civilian pressure and permitted a return to democracy. Elsewhere in the Third World army officers overthrew dictators and formed their own juntas.

Somoza's long rule and steep fall provide an apparent textbook case for the way most Americans think about traditional dictators: corrupt, repressive, standing only for their own aggrandizement, preserving a regressive capitalist economy, out of touch with their own cultures and people, pro-American, and eventually losing power. To talk about politics in Latin America, the remaining center of traditional dictatorship, is to summon up an image of hard, cruel men wearing sunglasses and military uniforms with excessive braid.

Indifferent to the extreme poverty in the rural areas and urban shantytowns, the traditional dictator is thought to want stability even at the price of stagnation. Such men, runs a common perception, may seem helpful to the foreign policy interests of the United States—and may be stout opponents of communism—but they are morally repugnant and historically doomed.

Such regimes still exist, complete with most of these stereotypes, but times have changed. Even a dictator cannot long stay in office unless he learns the skills of a politician. The modernization of the armed forces makes it increasingly difficult for one individual to dominate them politically. There are fewer regimes headed by a caudillo, a single political strong man or by hereditary kings.

This is partly due to the growing complexity of societies—more and more classes and groups militating for some share of power, more highly educated people who will not be satisfied with a cynical transformation of the country into a personal business—and partly due to a more sophisticated opposition. The nature of traditional dictatorships—and how they match or challenge the stereotypes—is illustrated by a look at four dictators and their regimes: Anastasio Somoza in Nicaragua, Shah Muhammad Reza Pahlavi in Iran, Emperor Haile Selassie in Ethiopia, and Ferdinand Marcos in the Philippines.

There are some striking common characteristics among these dictators despite the differences in backgrounds and countries. Marcos was a veteran politician who set up a martial law regime in 1972 after being elected president. The Shah was heir to a parvenu dynasty that had appropriated the historic legitimacy of one of the world's oldest monarchies. Haile Selassie had maneuvered his way onto another historic throne by displacing its heir in the 1920s. Somoza was the third in line of a family dictatorship established by his father in 1936.

Three of the four were overthrown by movements that created modern dictatorships. Haile Selassie was brought down by a military coup in 1974 and was replaced by a junta with a Marxist-populist ideological veneer. Somoza was defeated by an alliance of middle-class moderates and armed Marxist guerrillas in 1979, producing a Marxist-Leninist government with its own local flavor. The Shah fell to an Islamic fundamentalist revolution the same year. Although these revolts came about in different ways and were led by different kinds of ideologies, the resulting systems also have a great deal in common. In contrast, Marcos, who had a background as a democratic politician, was defeated in February 1986 by a moderate, electorally oriented opposition after he had lost control of a large part of the army. This outcome was in large part due to the Philippines' tradition of legalism, pluralism, and a professionalized apolitical army—all factors largely lacking in the other three countries. But even in this case the transition probably was the last chance to head off a growing Marxist-Leninist guerrilla insurgency which, if it had triumphed, would have taken the country down a road similar to that followed by Nicaragua.

The political opposition in a traditional dictatorship has limited options. Obviously it would not be allowed to defeat the regimes in elections. Although some dictatorships, including Nicaragua and the Philippines, provided safety valves for critics to blow off steam—including opposition parties with seats in parliament—attempts to stage public meetings or use the media can lead to arrest, even torture. Marcos arranged for himself to win the 1986 election, but the victory was so costly in terms of domestic and internal support as to force his abdication.

By nature, dictatorships do not yield power gracefully; they must be overthrown by force. The failed or repressed efforts of reformers are taken by many oppositionists to show the need for more drastic tactics. In a sort of Darwinian natural selection, open, moderate critics of the regime are usually easier to identify and arrest. Leaders of workers' and peasants' unions, Christian Democrats, liberal journalists and professors are the easiest victims for the dictator to find. Not only are the moderates vastly reduced in number, but that route comes to seem far more hazardous. At least with gun in hand one can fight back.

For civil servants and professionals the gap between government and people, between the crying needs of the society and its dreams of instant modernization, conflicts with the existing system's passivity. Intellectuals, who play a disproportionately large role as dissidents, receive the dictator's open contempt. He makes no secret of the arbitrariness of his rule.

The traditional dictator's key problem is that the old bonds of patriarchal loyalty are disrupted and he has nothing in his repertory capable of replacing them. Aspects of modern economies and societies in education, communication, and urbanization—even when imported in a limited, piecemeal manner—have a tremendous effect. There are fewer peasants who unquestionably accept an all-powerful landlord's authority. Migration to cities and access to radio or schools give the peasants and middle class new ideas and experiences. The fixed nature of power and the inevitability of existing social arrangements become subject to challenge and doubt.

Hundreds of thousands of people discover that alternatives exist to the order that they once took for granted. They see manufactured goods and different life-styles; the accepted doctrine that status is permanently assigned at birth cannot be maintained as some poor people gain upward mobility. Religion may switch from being a pillar of the regime to liberationist Christianity or Islam; the middle class becomes larger and more restless. The Shah, Somoza, and Haile Selassie thought that they could provide material benefits by becoming sponsors of development, believing that growth could forestall change.

But the more their countries developed, the greater the forces for change became. Nicaragua's relative economic success and Iran's oil boom in the 1970s laid the foundation for revolutions, particularly when these periods of growth were followed by downturns.

Deprived of the historic loyalty and passivity that were taken for granted in the past, traditional dictators had to turn to the other two pillars for their rule: repression and corruption. All dictatorships practice corruption and repression, but these things come in many different forms. It is, of course, immoral to kill and imprison men and women because of political beliefs and peaceful activities or to rob the very subsistence from people and to steal the state's financial lifeblood. But ethical considerations alone do not help much in understanding the political rules of repression and corruption. No amount of religious preaching and no system of ethics have ever eliminated these vices. To understand why corruption and repression flourish in some societies—and to comprehend their effect—a different approach is needed. The useful question to ask is whether the particular types of corruption and repression used by a dictatorial government add to or undermine the regime's stability.

In preindustrial societies repression was exercised mainly against aristocratic conspirators and the occasional peasant revolt. Repression, when successful, worked by being both narrowly focused and comprehensive. The dissidents are completely eliminated; the cruel and terrible punishments meted out discourage others from following their example. At the same time the underlying assumption is that rebels are limited in number and are pushing against the grain of a tightly structured society. They are the occasional drops of water escaping through the dam of traditional relationships that maintain the status quo.

Religious beliefs, hereditary obligations, and the geographic, cultural, and even linguistic barriers that run through and between classes protect the ruler. Merely proclaiming the malfeasants ungrateful rebels against the legitimate authorities is sufficient to remove the threat for a number of years to come. Revolts from within—except on the level of dynastic quarrels among the aristocrats—are widely expected to fail, as demonstrated by ample historic precedent and the popular understanding of the factors that block them.

In modern times, however, traditional dictatorships face a more complex problem: Many of their counterparts have been overthrown, dissidents may be helped from abroad, and their people no longer accept the ruler's permanence or legitimacy. Western countries are more reluctant and less able to save allied Third World dictators. Historically a revolution was the strange anomaly. Now it is the traditional dictatorship's continued survival that seems to run against nature.

Having advanced little in methods of distributing wealth, delegating power, making propaganda, or organizing broader support, the traditional dictatorship's only real advance is better weaponry. Much of this equipment, however, is little help in dealing with internal opposition. In fact, since the officer corps as a whole or individual ambitious officers are often the source of a political challenge, the military's greater strength may be the regime's biggest threat.

In contrast, the revolutionaries reap far more advantages from the changes of the last few decades. They have successful examples to imitate, as well as new forms of organization or tactics (urban and rural guerrilla warfare, terrorism, cell structures, disciplined parties) and modern ideological justifications (Marxism, anti-imperialism, nationalism, Islamic fundamentalism, or Catholic liberation theology). In short, they know that their societies could be different, and they think they should be better. All these factors give them greater staying power. Even if one conspiracy is rooted out, another will spring up. Permanent rather than sporadic subversion must be expected.

The strategy of traditional dictatorships is to meet escalation of opposition by what might be called the "broadcast" method of repression. An unpopular regime's secret police has difficulty finding out about enemies, particularly with widespread discontent and an opposition organized in small, security-minded cells. Secret police and mercenary informers often provide inaccurate information designed to please superiors or settle personal grudges.

The traditional dictatorship's repressive strategy can be more easily understood by comparison with its modern counterparts. Modern dictatorships are just as quick to use torture and paid informers. However, they also may have broader popular bases favoring repression and mass organizations to act as the regimes' eyes and ears throughout society. By controlling communications and education, they portray dissidents as traitors; opponents can easily be denied jobs in a state-controlled economy. Especially important is the fact that repression can be more easily justified by a widely accepted goal, like national sovereignty, economic development, and redistribution of wealth.

Traditional dictatorships have more difficulty sustaining credibility with their own citizens. A Mexican leftist cartoonist ridiculed Latin American dictators' efforts to rally popular support by showing an overweight oligarch in a hammock held up by a tree on one end and a straining peasant on the other. The landlord explains to the campesino, "The Communists want to take away our tree." Since the peasant has neither stake in nor benefit from the existing political order, only the fear of repression and the constraints of tradition keep him quiescent.

Modern dictatorships have conflicting ideas on how to handle publicizing their repression. On the one hand, since the vast majority of the citizens are, by the government's definition of itself as popular, portrayed as being loyal and since regimes are image-conscious, they try to minimize publicity on the extent of their repression. As Aleksandr Solzhenitsyn showed in his remarkable account of Stalin's concentration camps, most Soviets were unaware of the gulag's extent and were unsympathetic toward prisoners. Even the Nazis, openly proud of their brutality, did not publicize the details of its implementation. Modern dictatorships realize that discrediting opponents in the eyes of the people—which includes portraying dissent as rare—is more important than merely punishing them.

On the other hand, repression remains an important pillar of all modern dictatorships, and the rulers want to leave no illusion in the minds of citizens that opposition will go unpunished. The exaggeration of the threat to the government can justify many of its measures and serve to rally people around their leaders. In the 1930s the USSR's show trials, accusing Stalin's opponents of espionage and treason, were the first in a tradition of using repression to eliminate the dictator's leading rivals while, at the same time, using those individuals as scapegoats for the regime's failures and unpopular policies.

To consider Third World revolutions as inevitable reactions against repression and oppression, however, is a conclusion that begs the question. After all, if the level of repression in Iran, South Vietnam, and Nicaragua causes revolution, why do equally or more repressive regimes in Iraq, Syria, North Vietnam, Cuba, and Ethiopia stay in power? One must look at the style, targets, and popular perception of repression—its qualitative as well as quantitative aspects—to understand whether it succeeds or fails in keeping the incumbents in office.

The Shah's Iran provides a good illustration of these principles. Despite widely quoted higher figures, Amnesty International estimated throughout the 1970s that the actual number of political prisoners was "several thousands." While torture was routine, the number of victims was fairly small. On a list of countries holding political prisoners, Iran ranked behind Cuba, Ethiopia, East Germany, Pakistan, Syria, and others. William Butler of the International Commission of Jurists, whose 1976 mission concluded that there was abundant evidence of systematic torture, said that the Shah was "way down the list of tyrants. He would not even make the A-list."

The most reliable estimates are that the Shah's regime killed around 5,000 people during his thirty-seven years in power up to the 1978 revolution. Amnesty International estimated about 300 executions from 1972 to the beginning of the revolution. This is a terrible toll but one certainly comparable to the record of many Third World and most Communist states, not to mention that of the postrevolutionary regime in Iran. Moreover, the Shah's policy was in tune with Iranian historical traditions. Those who sat on the Peacock Throne knew that any sign of weakness could topple them and lead to certain death. The country had always alternated between periods of strong centralization and eras of anarchy depending on the king's ability to destroy court rivals and provincial strong men. Consequently, rulers felt that tolerance and mercy were qualities they could not afford. The Islamic Republic continued the pattern of dehumanizing dissidents, denying fair trials, and invoking the severest penalties.

Obviously, this comparative perspective was not much comfort to Iranians living under the Shah's regime. The intensity of their hatred toward the deposed government after the revolution can be explained by three particular features of his repression. First, prisoners were subjected to horrendous tortures, among the worst ever devised. Jailers regularly used beatings, shock treatment, electric drills, and other instruments that sometimes left prisoners crippled or insane.

Second, the Shah's secret police, SAVAK, deliberately spread fear of its methods and exaggeration of its power as a way of maintaining control by heightening fear. Prisoners were often released only if they, or members of their family, agreed to become informers. Further, in view of the importance of the extended family in Iran, every time one person was arrested the government made a hundred bitter enemies from among his relatives. Since most Iranians, particularly in urban areas, had kin who had suffered from SAVAK's depredations, its methods became their most emotionally expressed complaint.

Finally, and perhaps most important, while SAVAK's direct victims were a small group of active dissidents from a politically conscious minority, its system of repression was designed to frighten the entire population. SAVAK went out of its way to establish a reputation for omnipresence, omnipotence, and arbitrariness. Fear and humiliation left many Iranians with a deep desire for vengeance. Indeed, many of the revolution's leaders were direct victims of SAVAK. Khomeini's oldest son, Mustafa, was killed under mysterious circumstances probably by its agents. Ayatollah Hussein Ali Montazeri, Khomeini's chosen successor, was reportedly tortured, and his eighty-five-year-old father was beaten up. The Shah finally faced a real radical effort to launch urban guerrilla warfare in the mid-1970s; SAVAK, in response, tried to intimidate the entire population.

In 1971 the Shah celebrated with great pomp and lavish expenditure the 2,500th anniversary of the Iranian monarchy. These ceremonies symbolized his desire to identify with the kings of the past who had created and preserved the Persian Empire. His family, the Pahlavis, were parvenus; his father had secured the throne only in the 1920s. The Shah's problems with legitimacy, however, came not from a short tenure but from social changes in the country. The most vocal critics of the 1971 commemoration were the university students, a group that had not even existed in earlier decades.

For centuries the peasantry had looked on the Shah as having almost superhuman power, as a figure of myth and legend yet one not held responsible for the misbehavior of "government," more often identified with the landlord. The pool of potential opposition within the country was relatively small, confined to the aristocracy or, more immediately, members of the royal family. Even if the reign of an individual shah was challenged, the system of having a shah and a small minority of aristocratic oligarchs was accepted. On both psychological and pragmatic grounds, then, the regime was accepted as legitimate. Repression against the court and officials or the mistreatment of individual peasants did not provoke revolt.

The collapse of legitimacy came when authority could be questioned. The middle class, itself largely a product of these changes, was given no political power, worried about repression for itself or its children, and bridled at the limitations on its cultural and individual expression. Some of this group thought the regime insufficiently pious, others considered it insufficiently nationalist. Even high officials feared to criticize policies or use their own initiative, a factor that helped paralyze the regime during the revolution; even those benefiting economically from the government's programs did not feel loyal to it.

At the same time the lower classes were now indifferent to the regime. They had higher expectations of progress and benefits. The disorganization and speed of the modernization program, the growing gap between the elite's cosmopolitan culture and the masses' largely Islamic views, and other factors turned the traditional passive acceptance into a passive rejection. When Ayatollah Khomeini and his followers offered a viable alternative, millions followed them. The Shah had come to be considered not only a bad ruler but also no longer the rightful ruler.

In this context the issue was not that the Shah had a repressive policy but that his kind of strategy no longer fitted the requirements of political survival and even contributed to the consolidation of revolutionary opposition. In South Vietnam, Latin America, and the Philippines the army's mistreatment of civilians pushed many of them into the arms of the guerrillas, who, at least until they came to power, behaved with relative restraint. Trying to win peasant support in the insurgency phase, the rebels enforced discipline against looting, beating, or shooting peasants. Only this way can guerrillas, as Mao Zedong put it, move among the peasantry like fish in the sea.

One story about the guerrilla war in the Philippines in 1985 illustrates the point. A small government patrol set out through villages in Isabela Province, threatening peasants with guns and shooting at their dogs and livestock. Finally the soldiers stopped at a village and took drinks without paying. After sundown Marxist guerrillas attacked and killed them, then emptied their pockets of money to pay for the stolen goods and to buy drinks for bystanders. Such vignettes are common in countries with leftist insurgencies. The guerrillas redistribute land in zones they control, kill unpopular officials, and perform other acts to win popular support.

Brigadier General Dionisio Tan-Gatue, a regional constabulary commander in one of the main areas of insurgency in the Philippines, commented in November 1983, "I often question captured NPA (New People's Army) guerrillas and ask them why they joined. They tell me that either the army killed their brothers or sisters or the government took their land." On the island of Negros falling sugar prices led to a collapse of the plantations and of the historic paternalistic relations between owners and workers. About 200,000 workers and their families faced malnutrition and famine. When some of them tried to plant food on unused plantation lands, estate owners used armed guards to stop them.

In a widely publicized case in March 1984 in the city of Butuan, on the island of Mindanao, seven young men in military custody were murdered, turning residents of the neighborhood into guerrilla sympathizers. As in Nicaragua and other places, the leaders of the armed opposition were Communists, but most of the rank and file joined because they were antagonized by the specific regime in power. Larry Niksch, a Congressional Research Service analyst who carried out extensive interviews in the Philippines in 1985, cites constant popular complaints on the "drunken behavior of troops, checkpoint shakedowns, and stealing from civilians" and the torture or murder of people suspected—though often not accurately—of NPA membership.

Journalists' interviews with Salvadoran guerrillas indicate the motive for many recruits was the death of civilian relatives at the army's hands. People may become convinced that they are safer fighting in the hills than living peacefully at home, subject to the military's indiscriminate killing or bombing.

If the guerrillas can convince people that the regime is vulnerable and that the rebels will dispense order and justice and if the traditional dictatorship can be isolated from foreign support, the insurgency has a good chance of success. But when the guerrillas themselves turn to harsher tactics, they can lose popular support. In El Salvador the Marxist guerrillas forcibly drafted and extorted money from peasants after democratic elections had produced a moderate government more responsive to popular needs. The guerrillas in the Philippines started to intimidate or even murder local leaders or peasants who were neutral or critical. As often as not, though, a traditional dictatorship's repressive strategy plays into its enemy's hands.

Traditional dictatorships know enough in contemporary times to give lip service, particularly when U.S. advisers or journalists are around, to winning the people's hearts and minds, but rarely have such notions been taken seriously. The new conservative rhetoric of the 1970s was that reforms should wait until after any challenge to the regime was crushed. This strategy only gives dictators another excuse to avoid dealing with their regimes' incompetence and isolation. The dictator reasons that U.S. backing is a satisfactory substitute for the support of his own people, a dependency mentality that helped produce the downfalls of Somoza, the Shah, and Marcos and their subsequent attribution of blame exclusively to U.S. policy.

In essence, traditional dictatorships warn the populace: Watch out, terrible punishment can happen to you! Modern dictatorships, in contrast, say they restrict repression to the "other," who is unlike the average citizen. Repression in modern dictatorships cloaks itself in the psychologically satisfying rationalization of the majority's revenge (the people) on the minority (the oppressors), whether the latter be those genuinely responsible for the old regime's abuses, unpopular ethnic or religious communities, the wealthy, advocates of democracy and human rights or even revolutionaries who have fallen from favor.

Just as there are different types of repression, so there are varieties of corruption. Again, the political question is whether corruption contributes to or undermines the stability of a dictatorship. Many people living in Western democracies tend to view all corruption as leading to dissatisfaction and revolt, but this is not accurate.

In most traditional societies redistributive corruption, such as taking wealth from government coffers to share with allies, relatives, and clansmen, is a social duty and a prerequisite for political power. By spreading these benefits, the leader widens his base of supporters and those of the regime as well. Corruption was historically viewed as appropriate: loyalists demanded a share of the spoils of office in exchange for their military and political services.

Many traditionalist regimes continue this system in an effective manner. In Morocco and Jordan, for example, the monarchs give disproportionate benefits to Berber and Bedouin tribesmen, respectively, who furnish the soldiers to keep in line more politicized urban sectors. Officers and government employees use kickbacks to supplement their salaries. While this system wastes resources, penalizes those lacking influential friends, and retards development, a regime which does not offer these perquisites may be even more threatened in the short run. Arab oil-producing states like Saudi Arabia and Kuwait have so much income per person, considering their small populations, that those dynasties can buy off the whole country.

Traditionalist dictatorships err not in allowing corruption but in monopolizing it. The benefits of government contracts, kickbacks, contracts as foreign "middlemen," etc. are confined to a small group around the ruler. Favored "cronies" get franchises for foreign businesses as well as state subsidies, damaging and alienating the mass of businessmen, merchants, and artisans, the class that furnishes most political activists. This pattern prevailed under the Shah, Somoza, Marcos, and Selassie.

Conspicuous waste of resources also turns people against the regime. The Shah's high spending for military equipment, which most Iranians felt the country did not need, particularly stirred anger. Imelda Marcos, wife of the deposed Philippine dictator and a political power in her own right, was once asked, "Why do friends of the Marcos family own everything in the Philippines?" Her answer: "Some people are smarter than others."

Investigators in the Philippines after Marcos's fall found that about two dozen of his friends had amassed assets of between $5 and $10 billion, including castles in Austria, villas in Italy, holdings in over 180 major Philippine companies, and huge Swiss bank accounts. This group included, besides Ferdinand and Imelda, her two brothers, their three children, two sons-in-law, and the armed forces chief of staff. In addition, four close allies came, with government help, to dominate the coconut, sugar, banana, and food-retailing sectors. In some of these cases, the Marcos regime established monopolies, with state-backed low-interest loans or loan guarantees. When many of these businesses lost money, they were bailed out by domestic banks and international borrowing. Other businessmen were forced to grant Marcos stock in their companies or other financial favors.

Under such "crony capitalism" landowners and businessmen are left largely alone unless their businesses or markets draw the envious eyes of the dictator and his friends. The ruler, his relatives, and his allies not only control the government apparatus but scoop up large fees as partners, franchisers, or agents of foreign companies and tend to dominate new areas of business. These actions alienate the middle class, driving many of its members into opposition.

Traditional dictators also tend to favor foreign companies and investments to an extent that antagonizes national patriots. While multinational involvement in Third World economies can be very beneficial if properly managed, the host regime often does not have the structures necessary to bargain very well.

"When investments in Central America were considered," wrote Somoza after his overthrow, "the word on Wall Street and other financial centers was 'place your money in Nicaragua.' This record always gave me a sense of pride." Yet many Nicaraguans had little pride in a situation that indicated their country's weakness, low wages, and inability to tax foreign holdings. While state companies are often mismanaged and inefficient, modern dictatorships have found them a tremendous political asset for assuaging national pride and bringing more of the economy under their own control.

Naturally, this unfair or unmatchable competition antagonizes the existing urban middle class. Its members resent the elevation of crude outsiders who demand admittance to their social circles and clubs; they are humiliated by the dictator's demands for subservience and by their own lack of political power. Their businesses suffer from unfair crony competition or from foreign companies that gain privileges through dealings with the regime. The middle class is also victimized by government shakedowns and sometimes from the regime's economic mismanagement. Even when many of these people do well economically under the system, their displacement from power and the arbitrariness of repression—often against younger members of their own families—embitter them.

Indeed, if radical revolutionaries do not come from military ranks, they usually spring from the children of this sector of wealthy businessmen or middle-class merchants. The Nicaraguan Chamorro family, which produced so many anti-Somoza activists, owned the local General Motors and Toyota dealers and Tona, the country's most popular beer. Bazaar merchants supported, and largely financed, Iran's anti-Shah revolution.

Educated in universities or high schools or through studies abroad about alternative systems, either radical or liberal democratic, young revolutionaries come to see the injustices and inequality of their own countries in terms of shame. In moral, developmental, and patriotic terms, they resent the dictators' domination and organize against it, often risking their lives in that struggle. Such was the case for Iranian, Nicaraguan, and Ethiopian students.

This was what Somoza meant when he said that "if any one thing precipitated" the revolution, "it was an excess of freedom." Despite repression and torture, his regime did not dare dissolve the university's traditional autonomy or arrest too many antiregime priests. Worried about foreign reaction, pressured by the influential parents of young activists, and smugly self-confident in its own permanence, the traditional dictatorship often stops short of the thoroughgoing ruthlessness which one expects of it. The Shah, after all, did not unleash an all-out bloodbath in 1978, though his regime was willing to kill more than 5,000 people.

Furthermore, for traditional dictators, ambition and even self-preservation may be engaged in a losing war with greed.

Haile Selassie mistreated and underpaid his own army. The Shah's family and friends were involved in so much thievery and scandal as to provoke popular anger. When Nicaraguan dictator Somoza was asked his family's wealth, he replied, "I'd start by asking how rich the British Empire is," or, "Without counting the land, $40 million would get you into the ball park." For them and allied families the amount might have reached $1 billion. Their holdings produced sugar, cocoa, tobacco, bananas, and vegetables and included shipping, airline, cement, sugar, and textile companies.

Two turning points in the growing opposition to Somoza's regime came from incidents graphically illustrating the rulers' conspicuous luxury and corruption. The first development was the massive theft of relief supplies and funds after an earthquake in 1972 had leveled most of the capital, Managua. The disaster provided Somoza and cronies with opportunities to buy up resources at low cost. They paid $300,000 for cotton plantations and resold them to the government for $3 million as housing sites. Yet few houses were built; the fields remained planted with cotton. U.S. contributions of cement were purchased by the Somoza-owned National Cement Company at prices set by the regime. A $5 million Brazilian contribution was used to import Mercedes-Benz cars and trucks with a commission paid on each one to the Somoza franchise. Other supplies were sold on the black market; the hangar where they were stored became known in Managua as "Tacho's Supermarket," a reference to Somoza's nickname.

Wealth was flaunted with expensive cars (courtesy of the Somoza's Mercedes-Benz franchise), bejeweled women, and luxurious living. The Sandinista guerrillas crashed one lavish party in December 1974 and held the guests hostage until they were paid a large ransom, freedom for some of the regime's prisoners, and safe passage to Cuba.

While Ethiopians were starving, the emperor had fifteen palaces and made millions of dollars from ownership of the Saint George brewery, the capital's bus company, and other assets. One former courtier poetically explained the elite's attitude to Polish journalist Ryszard Kapuscínski. "In a poor country," he said, "money is a wonderful, thick hedge, dazzling and always blooming, which separates you from everything else. Through that hedge you do not see creeping poverty, you do not smell the stench of misery and you do not hear the voices of the human dregs. But at the same time you know that all exists, and you feel proud because of your hedge. You have money; that means you have wings. You are the bird of paradise that everyone admires."

The Shah tried to alter this situation by using Iran's new-found oil wealth to promote development. Nevertheless, the cronies' disproportionately large share stirred resentment, and huge military spending was interpreted by many people as a way of serving U.S. interests rather than as the expression of the Shah's nationalism. Imports of cheap foreign goods hurt Iranian artisans and merchants while imports of Western culture antagonized the clergy, whose government subsidies were also being cut. The state's economic policies produced social dislocation rather than gratitude, and villagers who moved to the south Tehran slums saw the lavish, "un-Iranian" life-style of the north Tehran elite. On a cultural and psychological level the gap between rulers and ruled had become too wide. On a political and economic level the differences had become too obvious.

The crony class and its repressive apparatus personify the slow pace of development and the great injustices in their societies. The behavior of this class enrages the people and stimulates revolutionary opposition. But this group is often not a pillar for the traditional dictator, who protects and promotes it. By sending their money overseas, its members divorce their wealth from continued possession of political power. Exile is a viable alternative and a much more attractive one than fighting to the death against revolutionaries. As one Ethiopian courtier later explained, instead of trying to avoid revolution, "as the boat started to sink, each one of our magnates stuffed his bag and looked around for a comfortable lifeboat."

For both traditional and modern dictatorships, control of the state apparatus provides new means of enrichment. Foreign aid can be siphoned off, and foreign companies must pay kickbacks to get contracts. International agencies and banks have lent billions of dollars to make up for mismanagement—which prevents funds from being used effectively—and to replace funds diverted into private hands. While the Third World debt crisis is due to a range of factors, corruption plays a significant role.

Preindustrial societies usually had a small oligarchy at the top and a mass of poverty-stricken people at the bottom. A patron-client system made this relationship both more tolerable and less escapable. In Western Europe kings had undermined regional barons in order to build strong nations and centralized states, steps that ultimately opened the way for a democratic challenge to royal authority. Third World traditional dictatorships brought local authorities under their control and replaced them with the crony system that sparked new kinds of opposition.

In the Philippines under Marcos, personal associates of the dictator gained economic benefits and political office by supporting his political machine. Some cronies, like sugar magnate Eduardo Cojuangco and the coconut kings, were given monopolies which allowed them to underpay workers and small farmers. Military commanders made money from large-scale illegal timber cutting and other rackets. Corruption exceeded the usual norms that had, ironically, contributed to stability and began to destroy the economy. Those shut out and hurt by the regime's distribution of favors yearned for its collapse or became actively involved in attempts to overthrow it.

The modern dictatorship neither ends corruption nor discards the tool of having a favored minority. But the new system strengthens itself by making these things less visible and more "democratic." A new ruling class is formed among leaders of the government, party, army, and mass organizations. Control of the national budget and economy allows them to shift money back and forth as they please, while domination of the media and judiciary eliminates the possibility of embarrassing exposés or legal punishment. Under the auspices of the state, a whole chain of vacation homes, special stores, foreign currency accounts, and services is provided for the elite's benefit.

Technically these and other perquisites still belong to the state or, in practice, to the ruling group as a whole. Since these privileges are granted to individuals only in their roles as "servants" of the party and regime, they can be easily withdrawn from those who cause trouble or who are purged. None of these people has access to funds or patronage for any independent power base apart from the regime. To earn their privileges, they must contribute to the functioning of the state. The "idle" rich are discouraged.

Such beneficiaries have no power or standing if they fall from their posts. Rather than create powerful enemies, as happens when traditional dictatorships split, purges in modern dictatorships open opportunities to people eager for advancement. Similarly, members of the elite would lose their perquisites if the regime fell, unlike the traditional wealthy group, which can go into luxurious exile or keep its assets. Rather than the anarchic upper class of crony capitalism—and its complementary antiregime middle class from which most revolutionary leadership comes—the modern dictatorship forges a united ruling group.

The Soviet and Eastern European economies are models for this kind of corruptive system. Their economies would collapse without their pervasive black markets. The most effective advantage of this system is held by the *nomenklatura*, who control the party levers. They get the best jobs, access to foreign goods and travel, and special use of "state-owned" property (limousines, vacation houses, etc.).

Nevertheless, the opportunity for corruption may be somewhat "democratized" in a modern dictatorship. To a greater extent than in traditional dictatorships, the ruling elite is enlarged and opened to those from lower classes. Most important, no one can rise at all without the rulers' tolerance. The political elite is also given a monopoly on wealth, helping prevent the funding of a viable opposition.

Traditional dictators reject such institutionalization partly because of faith in their own personal strength and ability to outfox rivals. During a June 1985 interview, for example, Marcos justified his intention to continue in office because other presidential aspirants were "weaklings" and "lightweights" who could not be trusted to fend off communism or promote economic recovery. Marcos ridiculed even his own supporters. "It will take me several years to build them up," he said, because they talked too much and were too self-indulgent and self-important. If he left power, the country would "suffer more than it has ever suffered."

Yet the dictator's high self-regard was by no means totally misplaced. Marcos and many Latin American dictators were self-made men who showed considerable skill by climbing to absolute power. As Asia expert Robert Manning commented on Marcos, "He had no vision but when it came to staying in power he was a tactical genius." The Shah, Haile Selassie, Somoza, and Marcos brilliantly outmaneuvered rivals and critics on numerous occasions before miscalculating the greatest challenge that finally ended their careers.

This ability to survive and triumph creates a myth of the dictator's omnipotence. For decades he outlasts plots, negative public opinion, peaceful and violent demonstrations, strikes, bombs, armed uprisings, and foreign threats. As Latin American journalist Eduardo Crawley put it, the dictator is seen as master "of the eleventh-hour counter-coup, the last-minute reprieve, the most unexpected political legerdemain."

Such a reputation, in turn, may discourage opposition. Haitian dictator François "Papa Doc" Duvalier sought to enhance this advantage by cultivating his image as an expert voodoo practitioner. He claimed he could predict the future through dialogue with one late rival's head, which he allegedly kept in the presidential palace. In part, these antics are meant to capitalize on or rebuild the popular traditional awe that has been one of the greatest assets of such dictators. His son, Jean-Claude "Baby Doc" Duvalier, inherited his father's luxury-loving ways but not his stainless-steel backbone. As soon as opposition flared up he fled to a European villa in 1986.

The traditional dictator also knew that the public must have no doubt about his willingness to be brutal in stifling opposition, a characteristic often shared by his modern counterparts. Death is always the ultimate sanction for ensuring political quiescence. When a Haitian dictator embraced Dominican dictator Rafael Trujillo during a meeting, their hidden guns clanked together. In countries where violence, torture, assassination, and murder are not aberrations of the moment but deep-seated political traditions, no serious politician can be a pacifist. The Shah used to say that Iran could be governed like Switzerland only when the Iranians behaved like Swiss. The traditional dictator's skill, however, had to go beyond a reputation for magic and raw repression. He who rules by naked force alone often does not rule very long.

Marcos's strength, for example, was his ability to tie up opponents in legalistic knots. In August 1983 the leading opposition figure and likely successor to Marcos, Benigno Aquino, returned home after years in exile. Marcos seemed deathly ill, the economy was going down the drain, Marxist guerrillas were gaining ground in large areas of the countryside. The prognosis was bad for the Marcos regime.

As Aquino's airliner came to a stop outside the terminal building, soldiers boarded and dragged him off the plane. Suddenly shots rang out; Aquino, surrounded by soldiers, was murdered walking down the ramp to the runway. The soldiers, who probably killed Aquino, then shot an alleged civilian assassin.

It was obvious that high government officials had been involved in the killing. Huge, though peaceful, demonstrations and unfavorable international press coverage followed. Marcos tried to defuse the wave of opposition by a complex series of maneuvers. First, he set up one investigating commission loaded with his friends. Then, under international pressure, he chose as head of another commission that had independence and credibility a justice of the Supreme Court known for her integrity. He also removed armed forces commander General Fabian Ver temporarily from power.

About a year later the independent commission reported that there had indeed been a military conspiracy involved in the murder rather than a lone assassin. Its research was hampered by the fact that some key witnesses could not be found;

they had disappeared—voluntarily or otherwise—with the aid of the Philippine military.

By the time the case came to trial, almost two years had gone by and anger had cooled somewhat. A Marcos-appointed three-judge panel then ruled that none of the testimony given to the investigating commission, information sufficient to convict Ver of perjury and involvement in a cover-up, could be used in the trial. In the end no one was punished.

Part of Marcos's strategy was the ability to be flexible when necessary, using small concessions as safety valves. In the 1983 elections Marcos allowed the opposition to win about 30 percent of the seats in order to whitewash an election fixed in favor of Marcos's party. Cardinal Jaime Sin supported the opposition with the slogan "Take the money, but vote your conscience," to cope with the regime's payoffs to voters. Somoza regularly made deals providing legal opposition parties with a quota of parliamentary representation. Both dictators also permitted the presence of some critical media—*La Prensa* in Nicaragua and the church-owned Veritas radio station in the Philippines—as long as Marcos and Somoza continued to control the bulk of news outlets.

When the United States pressured him for reform, Marcos responded with a February 1986 presidential election that he intended to seem just fair enough to win opposition participation while ensuring Marcos's victory. But he was so out of touch with popular sentiment that even after all the campaign fraud, bribery, and propaganda, opposition leader Corazon Aquino received almost 60 percent of the vote. The strain of seeming democratic (in a country where such practices were taken very seriously) brought Marcos down, as the Catholic church, large segments of the army, and even Washington took the side of the opposition.

Although truly trusting only himself, a traditional dictator prefers to choose as helpers his own relatives and friends. The Philippine ambassador to Washington was Imelda Marcos's brother, imperial Iran's last ambassador was the Shah's son-in-law, and Nicaragua's long-serving envoy was related to the

Somozas. Marcos chose his chauffeur as army commander. In Nicaragua the key military unit's commander was the president's half brother, the development bank's president and the editor of the largest newspaper were cousins, and the power company's head was an uncle.

Traditional dictators tend to have a clear idea of what they support (preserving as much of the status quo as possible, accumulating more money, promoting their clan) and what they oppose (communism and revolution). While their practical orientation leads them to place a low priority on developing theories, in recent years the accoutrements of party and ideology have become too fashionable to resist. The Shah was proud of his "White Revolution," which brought some land reform in the early 1960s, and his establishment of a political party, the Rastakhiz. But the land reform was quite limited, and the party remained a somnolent club of dragooned civil servants. He did not credibly present even the shadow of grassroots involvement. To make matters worse, his glorification of Iran's pre-Islamic past to create a specifically Iranian nationalism was condemned by the Islamic clergy as paganism.

Marcos hired a ghostwriter to turn out volumes of philosophy, and Indonesia's military orders that its own philosophy be taught in the schools to compete with Islamic fundamentalism. By the 1960s even many Latin American juntas were codifying their nationalist and developmental views. Nevertheless, there was always something halfhearted about these efforts, as if the regimes were only mechanically imitating what they observed elsewhere.

Similarly, court intellectuals are sometimes purchased to write poems and books glorifying the traditional leader. Still, traditional dictators have not taken very seriously either the importance of propaganda or the political potential of intellectuals. When used at all, the former is directed largely at shoring up Western support more than influencing their own people. The intellectual and cultural circles of the nation are viewed with great mistrust and are often major targets for repression. They have responded by working to undermine the regime's legitimacy and subvert its international image.

Modern dictatorships, in contrast, put a great emphasis on more sophisticated propaganda and public relations techniques to defend their records abroad and mobilize support at home. While modern dictatorships are having problems with their ideologies' diminishing credibility, up to now possession of a coherent world view has given them an advantage over traditional dictatorships. Teachers and writers are given a clear choice between flattery, privileges, and celebrity treatment combined seductively with a feeling of oneness with the masses and the threat of the most severe repression. Either way the intention is to neutralize systematically one of the most potentially active subversive groups, but the modern dictatorship would rather co-opt than silence this sector.

Modern dictatorships loudly proclaim their support for egalitarianism and national culture and their rejection of foreign influences. Traditional dictators tend to be insensitive on these points. They make no effort to hide their attraction to Western culture and material goods. When they attempt to establish credentials as patriots, traditional dictators rarely make a convincing case. The Shah's elaborate celebration of the empire's 2,500th anniversary was more jet-set party than a patriotic pageant appealing to ordinary Iranians. Imelda Marcos's expensive cultural festivals seemed more like contests in conspicuous consumption than politically useful patriotic pageants. Compared to such events, the modern dictators' penchant for building stadiums is practical, providing places to hold mass rallies and entertainments.

While modern dictators may have the same cosmopolitan tastes, they must cultivate a different image for professional purposes. PLO leader Yasir Arafat's chronic three-day beard and disordered kaffiyeh headdress make him look unkempt to Westerners and like a true man of the people to Arabs. Mao Zedong without his "Mao" jacket, Zaire's Mobutu without his leopardskin hat, or Ayatollah Khomeini in a French suit would lose some of their appeal. Military uniforms give the proper touch of revolutionary discipline and austerity to Fidel Castro, Iraq's self-made Field Marshal Saddam Hussein, and others.

The dictator's image and mastery over all the reins of

power, whether he is of the traditional or modern variety, are obviously essential because he is the most important single force sustaining the regime. A junta can usually survive regardless of the fate of an individual general, and even the most charismatically led modern dictatorship (Cuba and Iran, for example) can pass on authority through the party and collective leadership. But a traditional dictatorship and the status of all the relatives and cronies depend on their man's direct hold on power. Their only alternatives are flight to join purloined assets abroad or imprisonment or execution at home. For the king or dictator himself, as King Lear discovered, voluntary retirement is virtually impossible. Caudillos give in only to armed overthrow or mortality.

In view of the system's dependence on one man, his illness—the Shah's cancer, Marcos's kidney problems, Somoza's heart attacks, Haile Selassie's senility, Syrian President Hafez al-Assad's circulatory problems—brings a national crisis and sometimes a change in regime. Without the institutional framework of the modern dictatorship, however, the traditional regime is even more vulnerable to these weaknesses. Even when one man clearly predominates, the secondary leaders in a modern dictatorship seem to have a relatively stronger position in most cases.

By taking all authority and responsibility into his own hands, a traditional dictator enervates his collaborators and prevents the preparation of a successor. By playing off high officials against each other, he sows a distrust and competition for his favors that make it difficult for them to work together. Rather than be welcome, a particularly efficient or popular subordinate would be unpopular and disadvantaged because he can be seen as a threat to the elite's positions and the dictator's preeminence. Dependence on a single individual shows why traditional dictatorships crash so totally and resoundingly. A new dictatorial order may arise, but the old one can never be reassembled. Modern dictatorships also undergo changes in personnel, but the system itself remains more stable.

Similarly, all dictators are susceptible to becoming prisoners of their own propaganda and illusions. Surrounded by courtiers and isolated from the country's realities, the dictator can seriously misread the extent of problems, the erosion of support, and the seriousness of a revolutionary threat. Again, though, the traditional dictator—without the network of party and other organizations—is more likely to be misled. The Shah's behavior during the 1978 Iranian Revolution is a prime example of this problem.

He was baffled by the spread of the conflagration and the hatred of his regime. "Driving through the city of Meshed in an open car only four months before the situation became desperate," he later said, "I was acclaimed by 300,000 people. Just after the troubles in Tabriz (in February 1978) my prime minister went there and had an overwhelming reception. I can recall nothing in the history of the world—not even the French revolution—to compare with what happened subsequently."

As the revolution reached the turning point toward its triumph, in August 1978 the Shah was interviewed by the West German magazine *Stern*. He compared the rebels to the Baader-Meinhof terrorist gang and attributed the upheaval to the fact that "there are people everywhere who are easily instigated. They hear a few words and immediately they are electrified and stop thinking."

When the reporter suggested that "Corruption has grown constantly worse" and that garbagemen, customs inspectors, and others worked only when bribed, the Shah asked, "Do you really have to bribe people?"

"Yes, daily," answered the journalist. Otherwise garbage would pile up in front of the houses. "Believe me, your Majesty, everybody among the people knows that this is so."

"Then," concluded the shocked king, "we will have to talk with the people about it. Perhaps the wages are too low, too. But the salaries we are paying are not so bad after all."

This exchange cannot be viewed as a mere cynical exercise. An inability to visualize the changes his country has undergone is combined with a fundamental disbelief in the possibility of revolutionary discontent. Contemporary traditional dictators can genuinely lose touch with their own societies.

In the Shah's case it was difficult for those bearing accurate information to get through the door of those who were promoted for their subservience and who prospered despite their incompetence. A young officer with good contacts among dissidents, General Nasir Moghadam, sent a report to the Shah early in 1978, outside normal channels, that warned revolution was inevitable unless real reforms were made. The Shah made Moghadam head of the secret police, SAVAK, and then ignored his efforts at compromise with the opposition. Moghadam saw the handwriting on the wall and eventually went over to the revolutionary side.

Somoza was able to speak of the success of agrarian reform when two-thirds of the rural population were landless, and he claimed that few students were revolutionary activists when underground Sandinistas dominated the universities. He was considered so megalomaniacal that when he instituted daylight savings time to conserve electricity, people sarcastically referred to it as "Somoza time."

Perhaps the essential point about the dictator's isolation from society is his inability to understand the effect of his actions in fomenting opposition. He is used to a policy of overawing the masses with his wealth, unbridled authority, military might, ability to make arbitrary decisions, power of life and death over subjects, and international connections. At critical moments, though, this strategy can backfire, alienating the very political base he needs—urban middle class, government bureaucracy, military officers—to stay in power and providing ample grist for opponents in appealing to workers and peasants.

In addition to mishandling ideology and propaganda, traditional dictators fail to promote themselves effectively as patriots. No opposition charge has been more effective than to claim the dictator is a puppet of the Americans who sells out his nation's interests. The revolutionaries present themselves as the true nationalists, seeking to remove foreign political, economic, and cultural influence. This was an important factor in the overthrow of the Shah and of Somoza. It was an effective tactic in South Vietnam and an often used one throughout Latin America. Rare is the radical dissident or political party that does not blame the United States for the existence, maintenance, and policies of the dictatorship against which it is battling.

While U.S. overt and covert aid is often important in helping such regimes, the idea that the rulers are subservient to Washington is less accurate. Indeed, the Shah, Somoza, and Marcos pursued their own self-interest and fiercely resisted U.S. pressures for reform and human rights when such initiatives were made. The Shah, who nationalized the production of Iranian oil in 1973, avidly demanded higher petroleum prices. Marcos was an equally tough bargainer over the rental for U.S. bases in the Philippines. Unlike their radical opponents, however, they lacked the ultimate threat to gain leverage with Washington: a credible willingness to seek Moscow's patronage.

In view of U.S. links with the regimes of the Shah (arms sales, advisers in the country, importation of American films and customs), Somoza (aid, investments), and Marcos (air and naval bases, aid), it was not difficult to make the puppet charge stick. Modern dictatorships make every effort to avoid being placed in this situation. Anti-Western rhetoric, for them, serves an important domestic political function and they often attack the United States in order to gain domestic prestige even if they are seeking U.S. aid and investments.

Radical and Marxist opponents in traditional dictatorships aim to sweep away not only the dictator's regime but the dominant economic classes, not only a historically unequal relationship toward the West but all vestiges of U.S. influence. Even the dictator's establishment opponents, those most likely to take over if elections were held, are considered bound to an economic system that was slow to bring development and a political system that excluded the majority.

Morocco provides a good example of a system in which the ruler and official opposition have linked interests. As a member of this structure explains, "We are all members of a big family. . . . Some call themselves progressives [socialists], others Istiqlalis [traditional nationalists], others monarchists. But we all know one another, and one shouldn't take our public name-calling very seriously." Only when the power of this entire political stratum is destroyed can a lasting modern dictatorship emerge. Such a revolution is most likely to happen when this establishment is already weak and has failed to co-opt the army, most commonly in Africa and in many Arab and Asian states. Where these conditions do not exist, particularly in Latin America, traditional dictatorships follow one another or alternate with civilian parliamentary regimes.

Since many traditional dictatorships' strategies of corruption, repression, modernization, propaganda, and organization do not correspond with changing times and new demands, they tend to be the political equivalent of dinosaurs. A few have adapted, at least temporarily. Middle East monarchies—particularly in Morocco, Jordan, and Saudi Arabia—have learned how to gain nationalist appeal and keep a firm hold on the army. Latin American soldiers have replaced personal dictatorships with the rule of the armed forces as a whole and have tried to implement ambitious economic development strategies.

Nevertheless, the advocates and practitioners of modern dictatorship have far more sophisticated ideas and tools for gaining and holding power and are more difficult to defeat or displace. Faced with these challenges, the traditional dictator is at a serious disadvantage and finds the old responses are no longer adequate. For example, an Ethiopian ex-courtier described the Haile Selassie regime's response to famine in this way: "Death from hunger had existed in our Empire for hundreds of years, an everyday, natural thing, and it never occurred to anyone to make any noise about it. Drought would come and the earth would dry up, the cattle would drop dead, the peasants would starve. Ordinary, in accordance with the laws of nature and the eternal order of things." When foreign countries sent aid, the monarchy taxed it. The regime's behavior was a modern version of Marie Antoinette's response "Let them eat cake."

Alongside famine can be added lack of medical care, unemployment, mistreatment by landlords, lack of opportunity, torture, and a dozen other sufferings of underdevelopment. Where once these things were accepted with passive acquiescence, now there is bitter resentment and a demand for change, particularly among those who know—through education or travel abroad—that something better is possible.

All this is true, but starving people hardly ever make revolutions and never lead them. Haile Selassie was overthrown and replaced by military officers with personal ambitions and an ideology often impervious to suffering. Using the language of Marxism, populism, and nationalism, Ethiopian dictator Mengistu Haile Mariam knew the key to his power was the employment of Soviet military aid, brutal repression, and tightly controlled mass organizations. When famine recurred in the mid-1980s, his regime looted relief efforts, diverted supplies to soldiers and political supporters, forced refugees out of the camps, and resettled them in inhospitable areas. When cholera broke out, officials were told to hide the fact, calling it only "acute dysentery" or the "new disease." Many dictatorial traditions transcend the leap from monarchy to Marxism.

Whether modern dictatorships represent improvement over traditional ones must be considered with the greatest caution on a case-by-case basis. Peruvian novelist Mario Vargas Llosa rightly criticized Westerners who have a "double standard." They advocate a "democratic, reform-minded political system of elections," "representative institutions," and human rights for their own countries. In contrast, they see "revolution, the violent seizure of power, . . . a single state party, forced collectivization, . . . and concentration camps for dissidents" as the sole solution for the Third World. "A Marxist-Leninist dictatorship is no guarantee against hunger," Vargas Llosa concludes, and may make matters worse.

Yet in Cuba and Nicaragua, in Africa's transition from colonialism to independence, in Libya, Egypt, Iraq, Syria, South

Yemen, Iran, South Vietnam, Cambodia, and dozens of other countries, this transition has already taken place. These revolutions were fueled not only by the oppression and failures of the old regime but also by their very success, which had turned against them.

These governments themselves had unleashed powerful forces by expanding universities and giving scholarships to students who would learn about alternative societies and strategies for revolution. They fostered the import of Western ideas that brought subversive dissatisfaction with the old order. Their policies, like the concentration of landownership or mechanization, encouraged peasant migration to urban areas and provided new troops for the opposition. Their better-trained and newly equipped armies began to dream of political power.

Societies, even underdeveloped ones, have become complex enough to make it more difficult to maintain a one-man dictatorship based on personal relationships and the manipulation of favors. The formation of new states, seeking their own identities and trying to consolidate their very existences, spread the gospel of modern dictatorship to whole new areas of the world. The traditional dictatorships died not only because they were evil—though abuses there were in plenty—but because they were outdated.

By the same token, Jeane Kirkpatrick's controversial theory suggesting that conservative "authoritarian" dictatorships may turn into democracies while leftist "totalitarian" regimes are forever lost to pluralism is somewhat beside the point. In the Third World the distinction between "totalitarian" and "authoritarian" or between "leftist" and "rightist" has become increasingly cloudy. The real issues are to explain why dictatorship has become such a pervasive system, how countries with parliamentary systems or traditional dictatorships become transformed into populist dictatorships, and why some dictatorships have greater staying power than others.

CHAPTER FIVE

Latin America: Caudillos and Juntas

By a stairway of El Salvador's presidential palace, just outside the president's office, recounted journalist Christopher Dickey, hangs a huge portrait of the nineteenth-century hero General Manuel José Arce in a beautiful, ornate uniform. He holds a paper carrying the motto "The army shall live as long as the republic shall live." Concluded Dickey: "It might as easily and truthfully say, at least as far as the nation's soldiers are concerned, that the republic is the army and the army is the republic."

For more than 150 years it has been much the same throughout Latin America. The army tolerates civilian rule under certain conditions, particularly when it does not challenge military privileges. Even in nominally free elections officers often sponsor parties or candidates and ensure their victory. An absence of uniforms in the chief executive's office does not in itself mean civilian rule. Julio César Méndez Montenegro, president of Guatemala from 1966 to 1970, later commented that there were really two presidents, himself and the minister of defense, who "kept threatening me with a machine gun." Panama's democratically elected president quickly resigned in 1985, acceding to the army chief of staff's 2:00 A.M. phone call. The crisis took place after the discovery of the mutilated body of a political gadfly who had accused the high command of drug smuggling. He was last seen being dragged off a bus by soldiers. Politicians are often either beholden to the military or unable to escape its power and influence.

Such civilian subordination is remarkably difficult for a country to escape. While the mid-1980s seemed a springtime of democracy in the region, few states could boast of even a decade out from under the shadow of dictatorship. Costa Rica succeeded in maintaining a civilian democratic system by abolishing the army in 1948. Even Chile, long celebrated as the model of consistent, stable civilian rule, succumbed to a 1973 coup which produced—as if in revenge for so many years of army quiescence—the most stubbornly entrenched military regime in South America a decade later. Despite more than 150 years of independence, Latin American countries have been generally unsuccessful at maintaining democracy or avoiding military rule for very long.

To explain the historically enduring fact of dictatorship, in its particular regional variety, is the key issue in understanding Latin American politics. The basis for this peculiar system rests on a Latin American historical experience quite different from the evolution of Western Europe toward democracy. An authoritarian pattern of society emerged early. The bulk of the population in most areas were desperately poor sharecroppers or laborers rather than independent farmers. As the descendants of Indians or black slaves the peasantry in most places was set apart from and below the primarily Creole oligarchy. The urban middle-class businessmen, merchants, and professionals who usually provide the main constituency for parliamentary rule rarely overcame landed interests. The military developed as a largely self-governing institution that only provisionally gave fealty to the state.

The Spanish colonial system did not bestow rights and encourage initiative among its subjects. Rather it was, in the words of political scientist Howard Wiarda, "a hierarchy of despotisms," from the king through his governor down to the plantation owners, who held the powers of life and death over their serfs or slaves. Even after independence, added political scientist Robert Wesson, "class divisions were deep; . . . habits of deference were strong; individualism was weak; and poverty was abysmal."

Under Spanish law, whose influence continued after independence, the military was a special, privileged class the members of which were exempt from the jurisdiction of civil courts. Citizens had no effective redress when soldiers seized goods and land or engaged in lucrative smuggling. Enlisted men and officers owed loyalty to their commanders rather than to the nation. As historian Richard Millett wrote, "In order to win military allegiance, governments had to negotiate with individual officers." Civilian factions eagerly used the military to promote their own interests. While the military became an ally of the oligarchy, it had to be courted "through financial support, cooptation into the elite by marriage or other means and expansion of its role in politics."

During much of the nineteenth and early twentieth centuries, one strong man after another used the armed forces or a private army to rule. Bad as these rulers often were, factional conflict threatened civil war or anarchy in the absence of strong leadership. Some of these regimes survived only a year, others lasted for decades, but all were limited by the health of the individuals on whom they depended.

All the key institutions militated against a strong democracy. The caudillo established a tradition of subordinating the country to his will and sharing out wealth and offices among cronies. The generally powerful Catholic Church defended the inequality of power and property as the natural order of society. Landowners were determined to keep the peasantry dependent and subordinated. The urban middle class was badly factionalized and often feared the poor more than they did military rule. Workers' and peasants' groups in most countries were weak or nonexistent. The army, faced with no credible external enemy, was psychologically prepared to suppress anyone who challenged the status quo at home. U.S. influence, although periodically directed in favor of civilian rule, often favored military regimes and generally created a mentality of dependency in which foreign support could become an acceptable replacement for domestic popularity.

Despite the frequent use of the word "revolution" as a slogan in Latin America, the idea of "rotation" more accurately expresses the course of events. Changes in rulers rarely meant any real shift in the society, much less the march forward and upward sought by radical movements and pledged by modern dictators. Rather, Latin American politics moved in a cycle, with two forces—the military and the civilian "parties"—endlessly taking their turn in power. The failings of civilian regimes produce coups, and the shortcomings of military regimes lead them, voluntarily or under pressure, to permit a return to democracy.

The cycle of alternating civilian and military rule was remarkably consistent across Latin America during the first century of independence. But this pattern also meant that dictatorships repeatedly gave way to elections despite all the factors against parliamentary rule. In addition to the innate internal weaknesses of the caudillo and junta forms of rule, there were countervailing historical forces. The states of South and Central America were born in independence revolts against Spain in the early nineteenth century as part of the age of democratic revolutions. Latin American thought and culture, despite their distinctive nature, belong to the Western political tradition. No matter how frequently it exists, dictatorship is seen as shameful, aberrant, and temporary, an attitude contrasting with prevailing thinking in the rest of the Third World.

Elsewhere in the Third World, coups and army rule have been revolutionary processes, bringing lasting change to a weakly defined social and political order. In contrast, Latin American dictatorships have almost always been conservative and self-consciously antirevolutionary. In general, officers sought to preserve, rather than overthrow, the status quo, although by the 1960s some of them concluded that even this required them to take the lead in fostering modernization.

The factors behind the conservatism of Latin American officers are hardly a secret. These men have links to the oligarchy—either by birth or by an acquired commonality of interests—or use their careers for upward mobility to join this class. They adhere to a reactionary version of Catholicism that stresses order above justice and are hysterically suspicious of anything that smacks of modernism—liberalism, trade unions, women's liberation, intellectuals, and social reform. In recent times they have been obsessed with a communist threat which is not always restricted to their imaginations. As individuals they are often narrow and rigid, with a political vision limited to forcing society to behave and malcontents to shut up.

The militarism of modern dictators in Africa and the Middle East—and in Cuba or Nicaragua as well—is symbolized by the May Day parade. They think in terms of a disciplined nation marching forward under their orders. Traditional dictators, especially in Latin America, are reminiscent of a sentry pacing ceaselessly back and forth, on guard against anything new. Historically, Latin American officers felt no need to be social pioneers or creators of a new order: their countries' national identities and their preferred forms of society were already in existence. Today the old-fashioned personal dictator and military regime have been largely replaced by modernizing juntas that advocate economic development to forestall radical revolution. These juntas still mistrust mass mobilization and the other earmarks of modern dictatorship, but they believe it possible to organize economic growth alongside social and structural continuity. In short, they seek to become conservative managers of change.

Another basic foundation for the rightist, traditional form of most Latin American dictatorships is the structure of the army itself. The Latin American military tends to hold political power collectively while in other parts of the Third World individual officers frequently use the army to achieve power in order to implement their own blueprints for remaking society. But the South American officer corps usually holds the chairman of its junta in check, curbing his wilder schemes and diluting any intention he might have to build a regime based on personal charisma and an appeal to the masses. While there are exceptions, the leader of a coup today is more likely to be a faceless military bureaucrat than a dashing man on a white horse.

When someone more personally ambitious and potentially appealing does appear, the rest of the large officer corps is ready to pull him down, as the Argentinian Army did to Perón. These characteristics explain why it has been harder to institute modern dictatorships in the region. The leader's constituency is his fellow officers rather than the masses, and given the military institution's basic unity, he must seek consensus rather than the violent suppression of other factions. In contrast, successive Syrian rulers, for example, have entrenched themselves in power by purging the army and executing recalcitrant officers.

In Latin America the destruction of the army's hierarchy and its subordination to political authority were most effectively implemented by Marxist revolutionaries in Cuba and Nicaragua who first defeated the soldiers in battle. Knowledge of this fact deepens the anticommunism and concern about revolution of officers in other Latin American countries. In the Middle East, Africa, and even Asia politically minded young men join the army to overturn the government; in Latin America the same type of people join guerrillas to fight the army.

The conservatism of Latin American dictatorships, their social connections, reactionary ideology, historical precedents, and the army's institutional unity and identity have made such regimes loath to adopt the modern dictatorship's innovations. Inasmuch as modern dictatorships rule through nonmilitary channels—single party, mass mobilization—they are anathema to the Latin American coup maker who aims to rule over, rather than with the support of, the civilians.

This does not mean, however, that there has been no change in the style and structure of Latin American dictatorship. Gradually the very consolidation of the military structure has led to a transition from the historic caudillo to the bureaucratic junta more common today. Caudillos arose in the nineteenth century before there were effective national armies. They were men who were able by virtue of their ability—decisiveness, personality, machismo—to hold the loyalty of their troops. Often they were political generals who emerged from the seemingly endless wars between Liberal and Conservative parties that took place in almost every country. Once in power, however, they ruled in their own right. By their constant improvisation, idiosyncratic behavior, and treatment of the country as personal property, they were traditional dictators. Somoza was one of the last survivors of that breed.

This kind of personal dictator has now been replaced almost everywhere by a more sophisticated form of traditional dictatorship: the junta. Juntas are committees of officers who hold power as the directorate of the armed forces rather than as the pawn of an individual leader. The head of the junta might be quite powerful personally, but he is also constrained by his colleagues. Caudillos controlled the army; the junta chairman must maneuver within the framework of the military's interests, internal politics, and personalities. Ultimately he holds power not as a national leader but simply as the man who stands on the top rung of the chain of command. Below him are many younger officers jostling for promotions that can come only when he retires. The most recent Argentinian junta had three chairmen serving four-year terms during its tenure, and its Brazilian counterpart was ruled under a similar system of rotation. Junta leaders, then, are fairly interchangeable, and their rise through the ranks over decades has made them colorless. A caudillo, almost by definition, is indispensable and flamboyantly individualistic.

By the 1970s there were few of the long-ruling strong men who had dominated the region's politics at the turn of the century. The old-fashioned caudillos were restricted to the smallest, least developed countries: Paraguay, Honduras, Haiti, and Guatemala, Bolivia, Nicaragua, El Salvador, and the Dominican Republic. These states not only were under individual rule but often seemed to be the private property of the dictator, his cronies, and a small circle of oligarchic allies. The absolute ruler, as with the Duvaliers in Haiti or Trujillo in the Dominican Republic, can be a modern-day Caligula or, in the

115

case of the revolving-door Central American dictators, a man determined to accumulate as much loot as possible in his brief tenure. As of the mid-1980s Alfredo Stroesner of Paraguay was the only one left.

One reason for the decline of the individual strong man, in common with traditional dictators elsewhere, was the precarious nature of his balancing act. He must tirelessly and with great delicacy outmaneuver cronies and henchmen while personally overseeing a perpetually dangerous military. The elite must be kept satisfied and relatively powerless at the same time. It must be plied with privilege while kept divided in factions quarreling over the caudillo's attentions and favors. He can allow no rival to emerge and so can rarely dare to name a successor unless he has a hereditary heir, as with the Somozas and Duvaliers. But even sons, like Baby Doc Duvalier, are rarely up to the level of cunning and ferocity of their fathers. When faced with rioting, "Baby Doc" fled Haiti for the pleasures of a luxurious retirement. The dynasty ended on that day.

In contrast, the contemporary Latin American junta can build on a ready-made chain of command respected by the officers. The armed forces serve as a surrogate political party. Consequently, the junta has become a more common basis for rule in Latin America than has the individual strong man, even one who tries to develop a populist appeal. The situation in Africa and the Middle East is the exact opposite. There the armed forces are often riven by factional splits over ideology and ethnicity, forcing a coup leader to look elsewhere for support. He has an incentive to broaden his links with the civilian masses, build political institutions, and smash competing groups in the officer corps. A drive toward modern dictatorship, which would produce a revolt within Latin American militaries and scant support from civilians, becomes in other parts of the Third World not only an attractive alternative but a necessity for survival.

In view of conditions in Latin America, then, the contemporary junta is the highest form of traditional dictatorship, and that region is its last stronghold. In the most developed countries, particularly Brazil and Argentina but also places like Peru, Chile, and Uruguay, juntas have tried to show that they can more effectively promote economic development than can their civilian antagonists. Toward this end they copy some of the methods tried elsewhere in the Third World—though their inspiration is more likely to be South Korea and Japan than the Soviet Union or China—installing civilian technocrats who claim to have free market or mildly corporate state answers to the mysteries of industrialization and controlling inflation.

Yet although these juntas represent a real departure from their predecessors, they have made no serious effort to base their power on mass support, having an old-fashioned contempt for systematic ideology or political parties. They are more likely to use death squads for wiping out opponents than to combine repression with a populist drive to expand the ranks of their own supporters. At most, they hope that prosperity will produce civilian gratitude, but in no case have they been able either to deliver the former or to reap the latter. They remain traditional dictatorships.

Furthermore, while the junta may be better adjusted than an individual caudillo for governing a complex modern society, it is not a very stable form of government. The very factors that made it harder for a caudillo to rule—the rise of middle and working classes, economic improvements, population shifts from countryside to city, and higher educational levels—also gradually subvert the junta's hold on power. Once the public gets over its demoralization over the failings of past civilian rule, it begins to demand an end to the army's control. Even the oligarchs who are closest to the officers will not indefinitely tolerate a loss of direct political power as soon as they feel that any threat of leftist revolution is past. As Richard Millett wrote about the Guatemalan junta's return to the barracks, "The right had promised the military that an alliance would produce order, stability, and prosperity. Instead, it had produced conflict, international isolation, and economic col-

117

lapse." Fearful that continued military rule would jeopardize their own position, the officers ordered a return to civilian government despite the oligarchy's misgivings.

The seeds of the junta's end are always sown internally as well. Senior officers may find it difficult to work out arrangements among themselves as they jostle for personal power. Rivalry among the army, navy, and air force over political authority also heightens friction. A large number of senior generals and colonels see themselves as professional soldiers and are eager to get out of the governing business. Other officers, particularly the junior generals and the colonels, seek the commanders' retirement in order to gain promotion into positions of political and military authority. There is also some inevitable factionalism around personalities and over decision making. Some officers favor more repressions, others more concessions to civilians; soldiers also start to argue over spending priorities, economic strategy, and division of the military budget. Like a political party, the armed forces conduct their own primaries and elections, with the counting of guns and units that support each side replacing the adding up of ballots.

The result is that the process of ruling together threatens the military's unity and the sanctity of the command structure. This makes officers nervous about the possibility of violent conflict. The armed forces took power in the first place to protect their position, now the continued exercise of political power threatens the institution. Unavoidable unpopularity arising from their repressive activities and failed policies also demoralizes many officers. If the conflicts become too threatening, the military will leave power rather than engage in internal battles. The decision to return to the barracks is almost always made collectively and peacefully. Richard Millett recalled a satirical pamphlet published while Guatemala's constituent assembly was drafting that nation's new constitution. It suggested including an article specifying that "civilians would take power whenever the military totally fouled things up, the military would take power whenever the civilians totally fouled things up, etc., etc." In short, the frequency of appearance and relative conservatism of Latin American dictatorships are deeply rooted, but so are the transient tenure of individual dictators and juntas and their persistent alternation with civilian parliamentary regimes.

Generally, coups are launched when generals conclude that the normal political process is deadlocked, the civilian parties and politicians have failed, and only the army can save the country from collapse. If internal subversion or disintegration is the main threat to the nation's survival, they reason, the military is only carrying out its patriotic mission by seizing power. Since the high command does not want politics to jeopardize the army's unity, it must await a consensus on the need for a takeover.

To point out the officers' hesitation to seize power is not to justify their behavior. Their discomfort with politics and their obsession with maintaining consensus within the military do help explain, however, why military rule is always seen as being transient (even if it lasts twenty years) and is reluctant to entrench itself as a modern dictatorship. Latin American officers act to save what they see as a threatened social order; African and Middle Eastern officers act to overturn what they perceive as an unjust social order.

In contrast with caudillos, most juntas often claim merely to be preparing conditions for the return of civilian rule. This attitude, even when hypocritical, often proves ultimately to be a self-fulfilling prophecy. Military attempts to stave off a return to civilian control by legitimizing the junta's rule through elections usually end in defeat. Perón twice outmaneuvered the Argentinian military at the polls to gain power. Brazil's junta set up a two-party system in which the opposition constantly won; Uruguay's military regime had to yield power in 1980 after losing a plebiscite it had organized to prove its own popularity.

In power, the military tries to force its own values of order, discipline, traditional morality, and hierarchy on society. But unlike modern dictatorships, it does not try to change the existing patterns of family, religion, education, class relations, or ideology because it is not that unhappy with what already

119

exists. Obsessed with their separation from civil society, the officers still cannot reconcile themselves to any effort for systematically cultivating popularity or civilian support. Juntas have learned to be fatalistic even while following the same old pattern. Argentine junta leader General Jorge Videla prophetically complained in 1976, "The civilians will simply take everything we do and turn it around 180 degrees after we return to the barracks." His regime still went forward with its suicidal policies that ruined the economy, spread hatred of military repression, and led Argentina to a humiliating defeat in the Falklands War.

Some civilians, however, also agree that their own failures lead to the military's taking power. Jose Sarney, later Brazil's first postjunta president, commented on the 1964 to 1984 junta, "Democracy is in difficult circumstances in Brazil because there is a conspiracy of radicals teaching people to unlearn it." He admitted that civilian incompetence and radical disruption helped produce the coup. When an opposition senator attacked the junta, Sarney had defended it for allowing some measure of free speech: "What dictatorship is this that permits such criticism?" Finally, although he had advocated expropriation of large landholdings in his poor northeastern state, Sarney went to court to expel peasants who took over his own property. It is no accident that "Order and progress," in that order, is Brazil's national slogan. Argentinian newspaper publisher Jacobo Timerman, who suffered harrowing torture in a junta prison, had originally been an enthusiastic supporter of the coup as a means of ending the anarchy into which his country had fallen. These events and statements demonstrate three reasons why many middle- and upper-class civilians are often willing to accept military rule: their fear of communism and instability, the likelihood that repression will leave them untouched, and the fact that conservative dictatorships protect their properties and positions.

When Socialist President Salvador Allende ruled Chile, conservative women threw chicken feed at officers and called them cowards for not seizing power. The Chilean military did not move against the government until it was convinced that much of the middle class supported a coup. Many Argentinian civilians saw the military as their protector against Peronism and mounting terrorist violence. In many cases the military takes power with wide, if minority, civilian backing, particularly among the urban middle class. Equally, when a junta so mismanages the economy as to threaten its future or when repression is so extensive as to endanger too many people, the military loses whatever civilian support it has. There is an increasing clamor for a return to civilian rule.

Military regimes have demonstrated that they can run the economy as well as do civilians, but in Latin America this is not necessarily a compliment. Hyperinflation and recession produce coups when civilians are in office and democratization when juntas are in power. The same rule applies to civil unrest. Soldiers who do not hesitate to respond to guerrillas with repression and death squads find mass protest far more perplexing. Most of the time the army simply gives up, though the process can take several years and cost many lives.

This pattern has continued in the last fifty years, beginning with a wave of coups reflecting the economic catastrophe and political instability of the Great Depression in the 1930s. European Fascist regimes helped inspire the military to patriotic posturing and belief in its own ability to rule, but the motivation for coups and the subsequent regimes were strictly based on local traditions. Military leaders conspired within the ranks of the armed forces against weak civilian regimes in Argentina, El Salvador, Nicaragua, Chile, Cuba, and other states. They had no interest in mass movements, demagogic oratory or fancy new ideologies, although a civilian politician, Getulio Vargas, experimented in Brazil with some of the new techniques and corporate rhetoric. Perón was educating himself for his later effort by observing Mussolini.

Events in Nicaragua and El Salvador illustrate the traditional style of regional politics and the ways in which caudillos establish themselves. In Nicaragua the Liberal and Conservative parties had long contested political power. Both groups were factions of the urban and landowning elite, each with its own private armies. Coups and warfare, torture and killing, martial law and rigged elections were merely extensions of this contest for control of the country. There was no institutionalized national army that stood apart from this battle.

After a series of coups in the 1920s a U.S. Marine contingent landed to enforce order. One Liberal general, Augusto Sandino, refused to accept a U.S.-imposed compromise between the parties and launched a guerrilla war from the hills. Sandino became a folk hero and a symbol of resistance to U.S. power. Nevertheless, he enjoyed little military success at the time. Washington's policy was aimed at producing a democratic solution rather than at imposing a dictatorship. When the Liberal candidate won U.S.-supervised elections in 1932, the marines withdrew, and Sandino laid down his arms.

But U.S. intervention had added a new factor to the political equation. To preserve stability after their departure, the marines had helped organize and train a National Guard. In Nicaragua—as in Haiti and the Dominican Republic where a similar organization was established—the guard commander had a base of power outside the party system that could be used for gaining political control.

Here was the basis for a long-lived caudillo system. The army was the instrument of one man rather than the arbiter of political power. Thus, Anastasio Somoza, the National Guard commander, arrested and executed Sandino in 1934. Two years later he seized the presidency and "won" election by a vote of 107,000 to 169. Thus began the Somoza dynasty. Somoza ensured his control over the military and the country as a whole by using his position as president to take over a large amount of Nicaragua's land and commerce. This gave him a huge fund for rewarding cronies, distributing patronage, and paying off officers.

Neighboring El Salvador, with a military establishment already in place, developed a method for rotating caudillos. The *tanda* system linked together students in each graduating class from the national military academy. As one rank of the officers' group enriched itself under its leader, it was pressed from behind by those more junior who wanted their turn.

While working together to defeat civilian reformers or

revolutionaries, the Salvadoran military found it difficult to assemble a lasting formula for rule. The events of the 1930s temporarily solved this problem by producing a powerful threat to the status quo and a strong leader at the same time. Typically, however, the appeal of this military establishment caudillo, General Maximiliano Hernández Martínez, grew among his fellow officers in direct proportion to his ruthlessness against the civilians. When El Salvador collapsed economically from the worldwide depression, he overthrew the staggering civilian cabinet in 1930. When the Communist party organized a peasant revolt two years later, he massacred tens of thousands of people, an event known in Salvadoran history as *La Matanza* ("the slaughter").

The political fallout of World War II ended the 1930s era of dictatorships and turned the cycle back toward the civilians. The Allies, in desperate need of Latin American raw materials, paid premium prices that brought prosperity throughout the region. Argentina, for example, found high-profit markets for all the wheat and beef it could export. The anti-Fascist struggle made U.S. leaders suspicious of the loyalties of Latin American dictators while encouraging Latin American intellectuals, professionals, and politicians to attack their own dictators.

In country after country the military was pressed to return to the barracks while liberal reformers swept into office. In Argentina Perón used the popular demand for higher living standards and hatred of the oligarchy to transform a traditional junta into a modern dictatorship. If economic depression brought military regimes to power, recovery threw them out again. While disillusion with parliamentary dithering and party bickering encouraged civilian passivity and indifference, hope for renewed freedom made the population impatient with the stifling reign of those in uniform.

Almost all of Central and South America went through a new turn in the cycle. Hernandez Martínez was overthrown by a short-lived democratic upsurge in El Salvador in 1944. A few weeks later some young Guatemalan officers staged a coup and held free elections, which were won by liberal reformists. The new regime instituted universal suffrage, spent one-third of the budget on social welfare, raised workers' wages by 30 percent, and outlawed forced labor. In Costa Rica a 1948 revolution brought land reform and ensured civilian government by disbanding the army.

Once again, however, the military did not stay out of the presidential palaces very long. The next round of military takeovers grew out of the usual factors along with a particularly intensified fear that reformist civilian governments were paving the way for communism. The onset of the Cold War brought a decisive shift in U.S. policy toward Latin America. Almost any regime became eligible for U.S. aid and support if it took sides against the USSR. Repression and coup making were overlooked if they could be portrayed in anti-Communist terms. Latin American officers were quite willing to exploit this new attitude; in fact, they were the firmest believers in the identity of liberal or social democratic reform with Marxism and Soviet subversion. U.S. influence and the knowledge that Washington would back them often encouraged Latin American generals to seize power.

As early as 1954 Washington's concern over the progressive Guatemalan regime led it to orchestrate a coup there. But the main wave of military seizures of power came in the mid-1960s as a reaction to the Cuban Revolution and the guerrilla movements it inspired and promoted. Castro's takeover in Cuba made credible the possibility of similar upheavals elsewhere. While Moscow had played no role whatsoever in his rise to power, Castro's active support of insurgencies throughout the region now made real the concern about international subversion. The colonels and generals judged the dominant civilian politicians even more harshly and watched more carefully for any hint of a political breakdown.

Regeared for domestic counterinsurgency and concerned with the possible spread of Marxist revolt, the military also became even more suspicious of civilian reformers. This era began with the overthrow of Presidents Arturo Frondizi in Argentina in 1962 and Joao Goulart in Brazil in 1964 and ended with the bloody coup against President Salvador Allende of Chile in 1973. Ironically, where radicals themselves failed to overthrow existing regimes, their efforts inspired the officers to do so. In Uruguay the Tupamaro guerrillas set out to undermine that country's long democratic tradition, erroneously believing they could more easily organize a revolt against a military dictatorship than against an elected civilian regime. But the armed forces turned this analysis on its head; by seizing power and throwing off both parliamentary and legal restraints, the army found it easier to wipe out both armed radicals and liberal critics.

Modernization of military training politicized officers, who were introduced to ideas about a greater role for the military in national development and social welfare. Successfully combating the "subversives," they believed, required both unapologetic toughness and a willingness to cope with some of the conditions that produced revolutionary movements. Whole groups—teachers, journalists, militant trade unionists, even priests—were classified as likely enemies. Luxuries like civil liberties, which might themselves encourage disrespect and antigovernment activity, had to be eliminated. Torture or the deniable murders by death squads were considered a low price to pay in order to obliterate the radicals.

Increasingly sophisticated officers knew, however, that repression alone was insufficient. A strong economy and political stability were vital to undercut the appeal of leftist revolution, they learned in U.S. training sessions and at their own staff colleges. Aware of the growing demands by peasants, workers, and dissatisfied middle-class elements, the soldiers concluded that unless the armed forces took the lead in ensuring economic progress, poverty and stagnation would produce social upheaval. At the same time these conclusions made them only more doubtful about the civilians' ability to maintain stability. Without military rule to impose discipline and political order, bumbling and quarreling civilian politicians would bring anarchy.

Yet while more and more officers knew that something new was needed to avoid revolution, they were still suspicious of the techniques of modern dictatorship, which they identified with communism, even though these strategies were used by many non-Communist regimes in Africa and the Middle East. The fact that Cuba, their preeminent enemy and the embodiment of communism, had a single party, land reform, and other earmarks of a modern dictatorship tainted these institutions with Marxism.

As the armed forces took power in one country after another in the 1960s, they tried to deal with these contradictions by developing a new kind of junta—a "modernizing junta"—that could strengthen the fatherland and undermine the appeal of radicalism and revolution through state planning, the fostering of domestic industry, and new jobs. Since political turmoil had slowed development, the soldiers believed, only their firm control plus responsible fiscal and social conservatism could ensure growth. To accelerate economic growth, military dictatorships brought state planning to Brazil, land reform and nationalization of foreign-owned businesses to Peru, and a large public sector to Argentina. This economic nationalism sometimes led to friction with the United States although relations were generally quite friendly.

Despite these innovations, the overall conservative tenor of the juntas was preserved. A well-entrenched chain of command and high standard of professionalism in the region's armed forces meant that radical junior officers could not split the army and unseat their superiors, a frequent pattern elsewhere in the Third World. At the same time the most powerful conservative officers identified the instruments of political mobilization with their leftist enemies. Mass organization, for example, was seen more as a threat than as an idea that military dictatorships might co-opt for their own purposes. Concessions to workers were seen as the kinds of programs usually urged by irresponsible populist politicians to the detriment of the economy. As in the past, the generals were paternalistic rather than populistic although, in contrast with earlier caudillos and juntas, the juntas from the 1960s to the 1980s put a high priority on economic development.

Each junta had a different view, based on its country's traditions and recent history, of exactly how best to achieve economic progress. Peru's junta of the late 1960s instituted land reform and other left-nationalist policies, with a greater emphasis on undercutting the country's strong left-of-center parties than on organizing the peasantry. General Augusto Pinochet's Chilean regime reacted against the actions of over-thrown leftist President Salvador Allende with conservative free-market policies, including the return to private hands of state companies. The Brazilian junta supported massive in-vestments in projects for export promotion in the 1960s, pro-ducing what was then called an "economic miracle." Argentina, with a strong state economic sector ever since Perón's rule, lifted capital controls, price controls, and subsidies.

By the 1980s, though, Peru, Brazil, Chile, and Argentina were deep in debt. Since the Argentinian military refused to cut spending on itself and its pet industries, the free-market economic package made for runaway inflation. Brazil and Chile found that the lower prices of the raw materials they produced and the rising cost of imports battered their economies. None of these regimes came close to matching South Korea, the most successful combination of junta rule and economic mobiliza-tion.

The military regimes are willing, even eager to use repres-sion to suppress radical forces, threats to their own rule, and complaints about their policies. The Argentinian junta's "dirty wars" of the 1960s began with a thirst for revenge against the guerrilla left's kidnappings of officers and armed attacks on army installations. After the revolutionaries had been deci-sively defeated, the junta's campaign only widened into indis-criminate torture, killing, kidnapping, and "disappearance" of anyone who was outspoken against—or might conceivably op-pose—military rule.

The result was a more extensive and systematic repression than had ever been seen before in Argentina. All institutions responsible for "indiscipline"—peasant and trade union or-ganizations, civilian reformers, critical journalists and profes-sors, and anyone suspected of sympathy with these groups—could become targets. More than 9,000 people disappeared, and can be presumed murdered by the military, between 1976 and 1983. The torturers' sadism seemed to feed on itself, producing a viciousness that mounted as the threat to the regime declined.

Nevertheless, this violence was far less "effective" than the modern dictatorships' campaign to destroy or drive out whole classes and political groups. Latin American traditional dictatorships are still able only to impose themselves on society temporarily rather than be capable of transforming it. The very real reign of terror that went on under the Argentinian junta made no apparent lasting change in Argentinian society. Many people were left untouched by the violence, and afterward the country emerged with far fewer scars than might have been expected.

It is revealing that in chronically junta-ruled states like Ecuador, Peru, and Argentina the same political parties that existed before the coup were revived after civilian rule had returned. When the Brazilian military took over in 1964, it was trying to ensure the political destruction of reformist, populist politicians like Jañio Quadros and Leonel Brizola. Twenty years later Quadros was elected mayor of Saõ Paulo, and Brizola was elected governor of Rio de Janeiro, the country's two largest cities.

The nature of the civilian-military cycle and of the limits of traditionalist military dictatorships can be most clearly seen in Chile, the country that so long held it at bay, and in Argentina, a nation whose level of development would seem to make it a viable democracy. Chile's large middle class and democratic traditions sustained a parliamentary system for many decades before it finally collapsed in civil strife over President Allende's government. Allende came to office by a vote in Congress after none of the three candidates could win a majority vote from the electorate. His Socialist-Communist united front's attempt to move Chile to the left within a legal framework was opposed by conservative forces and by the United States.

The Nixon administration saw the Allende regime as intent on establishing a permanent Marxist regime in Chile and, hence, as a geopolitical threat. Chilean conservatives opposed Allende's policies. The armed forces commander at the time of Allende's inauguration, who supported the military's traditional apolitical stance, was murdered by rightist plotters associated with the CIA. Chile's economy declined as the result of Allende's actions and Washington's sanctions. As society broke down, disrupted both by the anti-Allende right and by leftists who thought the president was moving too slowly, the military, encouraged by conservative civilians, decided to step in and take over.

Considering the high ideological passions involved, the coup was a very repressive one. Having concluded that democracy had almost led to communism, the regime of General Augusto Pinochet was determined to avoid any return to the old pluralist system. It promulgated a new constitution to ensure the continuation of military rule into the distant future. Beyond that, Pinochet's prescription was for "protected democracy," with the left excluded and the armed forces as the protector.

Faced with growing opposition pressure—even many conservative civilians wanted to end military rule—Pinochet gave little ground. He attacked political parties as factions useful only to ambitious, self-serving politicians, and the division of the opposition made it much easier for the army to stay in power. Gradually Pinochet overrode other members of the junta who were more willing to compromise, and his control of promotions assured that he could count on the loyalty of most officers. He assumed supreme power as president in 1980.

The Chilean experience demonstrated some of the main weaknesses that lead to the fragility of democracy in Latin America. Both conservatives and leftist radicals claim that reformist politicians—men like Perón, Frondizi, and Arturo Illia in Argentina or like Goulart in Brazil and Allende in Chile— make changes conducive to political instability. The moderates' policies fall short of a thoroughgoing revolution that would smash the old order, but their innovations are extensive enough to convince defenders of the status quo that they are in a battle for survival. From that point, extremists on both sides agree, the country must go either "forward" to modern dictatorship involving some version of Marxism or "back" to a rightist junta. Such is the strength of Latin America's political gravity that there are very few cases in which the military is foiled. Moderate democrats who oppose both extremes triumph momentarily only to see the cycle swing around again.

As in other Latin American countries, the position of the army in Chile was so central and intertwined with politics that it could not long stand aloof from the turmoil around it. Similarly, the economic and political leverage of the United States also destabilized democracy. Economic swings, whether genuine or artificially augmented, were hard to contain within a parliamentary system. The gap between the wealthy and the poor created demands and antagonisms on both sides that could not be mediated by legalistic structures. The rich would not make even the kinds of concessions to trade unions, social welfare, and redistribution of land taken for granted in the United States or Western Europe. The poor would no longer remain indefinitely patient; much of the middle class, fearing anarchy and radical revolution, preferred at least temporary military rule.

There were some signs of success for these modernizing juntas—the revolutionary movements of the 1960s were smashed in virtually every country; financial and economic changes seemed to be producing results at first, too, most notably the Brazilian "economic miracle"—but the ultimate results were disappointing.

So once again, by the late 1970s, the cycle was ready to take another turn. The soldiers had worn out their welcome. Mismanagement created too many problems; the accumulation of victims drove civilians to mounting protests. The leftist challenge had receded, and politically unsophisticated juntas quickly lost control of experiments with tame political parties and limited elections. Rising foreign debt and economic slowdowns made staying in power less attractive for the officers. Even U.S. policy shifted against them, as President Jimmy Carter pressed the issue of human rights.

In Argentina the military regime's foolish provocation and incompetent handling of the Falklands War against Britain humiliated a junta already under increasing civilian criticism for its torture and murder of dissidents. Free elections returned civilian governments to power in Argentina (1983), Bolivia (1982), Brazil (1985), Ecuador (1979), Peru (1980), and Uruguay (1985), among other countries. Although the return to democracy is welcome, there is no reason to think that the cycle is ended.

As traditional dictators, Latin American military rulers may solve short-term problems of instability, economic collapse, political deadlock, or revolutionary threat, but they do not put their countries on different courses. Yet the preoccupation with economic development, nationalism, and even some inklings of social consciousness have made these modernizing juntas take on certain aspects of modern dictatorships as well.

Peru is the most interesting, if a rather atypical, example of these regimes. Officers, many of them from poor peasant backgrounds, were trained at the Center for Advanced Military Studies and at the National Planning Institute to think about the social structure's shortcomings. With civilian rule at a dead end and Marxist guerrillas in the mountains, the military took power in 1968. Reform-minded officers won the struggle within the army. The junta took over the sugar plantations, set up cooperatives, and nationalized several foreign mining firms. More conservative officers eventually regained the upper hand and moved toward a more traditional system. Faced with economic difficulties and mounting opposition, they finally gave up power in 1980. The developments in Peru show how Latin American juntas were changing and how they fell far short of the African or Middle Eastern style of modern dictatorship.

The fact that the modernizing juntas were viciously repressive does not, in itself, distinguish them from modern dictatorships. But while the Brazilian junta originally rationalized its violence as preventing Communist revolution, once in power it claimed that dissidents would sabotage the military's own top-down revolution. Concluded a banker allied to the junta in 1973: "We need to grow fast or we'll lose the development war." Repression, censorship, even torture were permissible means of preserving security, reasoned the generals and their friends, but a failure to bring economic growth would undermine the entire society. "Development with security" was their motto since tight control was the necessary concomitant to development. Strikes and collective bargaining were outlawed, wages were held down, and opponents of every kind were rounded up.

The junta chose a four-star general as president every four years. Politics were not abolished, said one Brazilian writer, but were simply transferred to the army. The military had its own party and permitted a relatively tame opposition party. The electoral college that formally selected the president was controlled by the junta through appointees and fixed elections. Thus, General Ernesto Geisel, a retired officer and industrial administrator and whose brother was defense minister, became president in 1974.

The Brazilian economy was turned over to technocrats. The powerful minister of finance between 1967 and 1974 was a former economics professor, the planning minister was the head of an economic research institution, and the minister of mines and energy was president of a state mining company and a trained economist as well. They recommended a program of maximum government investment and international borrowing, claiming they could avoid inflation by indexing wages and prices.

During the Brazilian junta's first decade this strategy seemed to be producing an economic miracle. Annual growth was at around 10 percent, and there was more industry, exports, and consumer goods. Brazil's economy was under as much state control as any other economy outside the Soviet bloc. Under the authority of the modernization-minded junta, 70 percent of investment came from the government. In 1971 state-owned firms held 82 percent of the assets, 32 percent of the sales, and 51 percent of the jobs among the largest Brazilian companies.

The regime promoted nationalist slogans like "Nothing will stop Brazil," "Brazil has teeth," and even "If you don't love Brazil, leave it." The censored newspapers explained that development required a "strong, pure and tough" state. Businessmen, landowners, and a large segment of the urban middle class supported the regime. This attitude was not surprising since the regime's philosophy, as expressed by Minister of Planning Antoñio Delfim Netto, was that "no one can achieve rapid development without concentrating wealth. You've got to make the cake bigger before you can start slicing it up."

But this growth-oriented strategy also overheated the economy. The turning point for the economy was in 1974, when inflation hit 35 percent. The poor were hit hard, rising oil prices destroyed Brazil's balance of payments, international recession depressed its markets, and debt reached new heights.

The faster the economy deteriorated, the quicker the military moved toward restoring democracy and the more people voted for the opposition party. Geisel promised a greater degree of freedom but warned that the junta would not allow "turbulent or errant minorities, which upset national life." He faced down military hard-liners, particularly in the air force, who held the allegiance of fewer divisions than he did. But Geisel could not entirely restrain the interest groups that had developed around maintaining the repression and that feared retribution if civilian rule was renewed.

It took a full decade for the military to return to the barracks. Its development plan had failed, having come close to wrecking Brazil's economy, and civilian support for the junta was long dissipated. On the other hand, it had lasted twenty years, a not inconsiderable span. Perhaps future frustration with civilian rule will lend that era a certain air of nostalgia. At any rate, the modernizing junta had shown itself to be a very different kind of regime from its less activist predecessors.

Argentina underwent a similar, though even more traumatic, experience. But even after its horrendous period under a discredited and defeated military junta, Argentina cannot be considered immune to another swing of the cycle. Its return to democracy in December 1983 gave rise to celebration at home and among foreign well-wishers. Yet the elected regime of President Raúl Alfonsín was very much constrained by the country's economic problems, the continuing threatening power of the military, and the political attitudes of most Argentinians.

Robert Cox, veteran editor of the *Buenos Aires Herald* who had fled in 1979, when death squads threatened his family, returned to attend Alfonsín's inaugural. "We sang the Argentine national anthem. Its florid rhetorical stanzas, made meaningless by a half-century of military coups, had suddenly become stirring, 'Listen, mortals, the sacred cry: Liberty, liberty, liberty! Hear the sound of chains breaking!' " Amid wild enthusiasm and high hopes, Alfonsín took his oath of office not from the presidential palace balcony, defiled by Perón and so many junta leaders, but from the building where independence had been declared in 1810.

The immediate changes were dramatic. The Ford Falcons without license plates used by the military to transport kidnap victims disappeared from the streets. Police smilingly offered directions instead of demanding identity papers. Yet in the midst of such joy Cox felt the "bleak realization that democracy was no miracle after all, that it was no more likely than the military coups of the past to cure Argentina's ills." The calls threatening Cox's life started again; the officers would let civilians try only the nine junta members for human rights violations. Lower-ranking torturers could not be tried or imprisoned—the military rejected the jurisdiction of civilian courts—lest punishment provoke another coup.

During the era of military rule between 1976 and 1983, repression could not have been more severe for those urban professionals, students, journalists, or others labeled, on the flimsiest grounds, likely "subversives." Death squads operating with junta backing kidnapped parents or children in front of their families. Thousands murdered by the military disappeared, never to be heard from again. Torture became routine in scores of secret, small-scale concentration camps, sometimes decorated with swastikas by the jailers.

The army's rampage was partly a response to the killings, kidnappings, and robberies of the Peronist and Marxist left which had convulsed the country in the 1970s. But by any measure the junta's "dirty war" went beyond any rational bounds. Once armed opposition had been crushed, the soldiers convulsively sought to destroy the roots of dissidence, which they identified with any left-of-center political or modernist cultural views.

By 1983 the peso had shrunk to a one-millionth of its 1959 value. The junta twice created a new peso, first by adding two zeros and then by printing four more zeros on the existing currency. The Argentinian military attacked and easily occupied the Falkland Islands but ultimately found the British a better-armed foe than its own civilians. Perhaps the military thought that a dose of patriotism would excuse its poor economic performance, but the junta was also genuinely drunk on its own macho and chauvinist rhetoric. The war turned into a humiliating disaster that probably cut several years off the junta's longevity.

While Alfonsín instantly ended the repression, he had no easy answers to inflation. Rising prices sparked disruptive strikes, a strict austerity program equally produced discontent. The middle class began to complain, "So they call this democracy!" Memories of repression faded, and those of economic insecurity increased, just as the military had before been first decried, then welcomed back to power.

In turn, the military's arrogance proved unquenchable. Former Air Force Commander Brigadier Cayo Antonio Alsina told a 1985 officers' club banquet, "We are living in times of absolute confusion in which it is said that we have passed from authoritarian repression to marvelous liberty. Nothing of the sort. Let us be clear . . . and say no to libertinage, to the corruption of undisguised pornography, to the questioning of our elders, to the deformation of our youth through foreign music and drugs, to the dissolution of the family, and to the subordination of the natural order and divine origin." In its idea of order this statement could have come from a hundred other dictators or would-be dictators of the left or right. Another Argentinian general commented that the military merely did the dirty work for the civilians.

President Alfonsín responded at the armed forces' annual

banquet in July 1985 by arguing that the military had dishonored itself by violating constitutional order and becoming a prime source of instability in its own right. The only answer to "our current state of prostration" was to avoid "dramatic extremes" and build a society free of fear, blessed with tolerance, and able to safeguard civil rights. "All of this is called democracy," he concluded. As part of this effort Alfonsín managed to try the nine junta members for their human rights abuses, including the disappearances of 9,000 people who must be presumed dead. Most of the tried junta members were convicted.

Alfonsín's struggle is a noble but a very difficult one. It will not be easy to break the alternation of civilian and military rule. The replacement of caudillos by modernizing juntas is a stronger trend. The techniques of modern dictatorship may come to Latin America via this new style of junta or through Marxist regimes, as has already happened in Cuba and Nicaragua.

While traditional societies have produced traditional dictatorships, it seems likely that changing societies will produce modernizing juntas or modern dictatorships. Asia has produced both kinds of regime, with countries like Singapore, Indonesia, Pakistan, and South Korea, for example, following something like the Latin American pattern.

The prospects for traditional dictatorship, or for the democratic system Alfonsín would build, are worse elsewhere in the Third World. Africa, a continent in search of political identity and economic development, is full of countries that are being both wooed and controlled by a new type of charismatic dictator.

CHAPTER SIX

Africa: Founders and Survivors

No two men could be more different than Amilcar Cabral, leader of tiny Portuguese Guinea's independence movement, and Idi Amin, Ugandan dictator from 1971 to 1979. Yet comparing the ideals on which their countries were founded with the tragic fates that befell them provides vivid insight into the course of dictatorship in Africa.

In most countries the prestige and charisma of the man who led the independence struggle assured him a long rule as a modern dictator. Where the leader proved inadequate for the job or where the internal pressure of economic disaster or ethnic conflict proved too great, the army took over. These leaders varied greatly in their personalities, capabilities, and ideologies, yet in virtually every case the same kinds of problem and solution proved necessary for those who would seize and hold power.

The African ruler had to find a way to impose unity on the nation by marshaling nationalism while building a cohesive party or tribe or both as a reliable base of support. He had to ensure government control of the economy to finance his regime, reward supporters, and prevent the rise of any alternative ruling group. But at the same time there were often no nongovernment forces within the country that were capable of developing the economy. Self-interest and necessity often seemed to merge. Many politicians and intellectuals argued that the new states required an enforced unity to survive and develop. A radical (or radical-sounding) ideology legitimized these measures. In short, African states became more or less repressive and more or less successful modern dictatorships.

In 1960 alone, seventeen African states became independent. Twenty years after Ghana had celebrated its sovereignty in 1957, Africa had fifty-one functioning states with 455 million people, half of them under fifteen years of age. Things went very badly for most of these countries. Military coups seemed to follow one another in endless succession. Almost every state became a food importer, dependent on foreign aid and deep in debt. Living standards actually declined in many places. By the mid-1980s per capita income averaged only $365 a year.

Other statistics were equally gloomy. The terms of trade for sub-Saharan Africa declined by approximately 13 percent between 1977 and 1985, with each percentage point costing about $200 million in lost export earnings. Population grew at the rate of 3 percent a year, fastest of all the world's continents. External medium- and long-term debt rose from $14 to $66 billion between 1973 and 1983; average per capita gross domestic product declined 4.5 percent between 1970 and 1985. The number of noneconomic refugees climbed from 400,000 in 1965 to 2.5 million in 1985, 1 out of every 200 Africans. Despite some bright spots—higher school enrollments, better health facilities, improved transport and communications—Africa remained far behind even the rest of the Third World in almost every category.

Virtually all the new states started with democratic institutions and nearly all dismantled them in less than a decade. By 1965 there were sixteen one-party states. Once the original electoral systems had been abandoned, the military began to seize power for itself. In 1965 alone there were five coups.

Many of these difficulties were inevitable in view of the region's innate problems. But particularly crippling was the political paradox of Africa: Regimes either were unstable or were modern dictatorships purchasing a modicum of political stability with economically counterproductive practices and policies.

Cabral was the kind of leader who embodied political philosopher Fanon's idea that revolutionary struggle brought forth a nation's best elements. Although his country was one of the smallest, poorest nations on a continent of tiny, pauper states, this agricultural engineer organized a party and guerrilla army that successfully waged war on the Portuguese for a decade before his assassination in January 1973.

To meet Cabral was to recognize a rare man combining modesty, sensitivity, and charisma. Well grounded in his country's social structure and in revolutionary theory, he was alert to the pitfalls suffered by earlier revolutions and clear-eyed about what he wanted to achieve. His goal was to adapt Marxism to his own country, and Cabral worked tirelessly to ensure the triumph of a humane socialism with honest, democratic-minded leaders.

But when independence came a few months after Cabral's death, all his labor and theory evaporated. The new state of Guinea-Bissau quickly degenerated into a typical despotism ruled by a venal, incompetent elite of which Cabral's own brother was one of the main villains. Finally the military took power and settled down into ruling a ramshackle and stagnating country.

What were Cabral's teachings? In his speeches and writings he argued that the country's very backwardness could be turned into a beneficial inheritance. Homogeneity enhanced the nation's chances for unity; shared poverty and an absence of class conflict eased the way for socialism and egalitarianism. But the people also had to guard against the rise of a new set of rulers who wanted to "exploit their own people, . . . to have all the diamonds, all the gold, . . . to do as one pleases, to live well, to have all the women one wants in Africa or in Europe." Such leaders were mainly interested in "touring Europe, being received as presidents, wearing expensive clothes—a morning

coat or even [traditional dress] to pretend they are Africans"—
while they were really "lapdogs of whites."

Independence could be gained only by a "struggle of the
people, by the people, for the people . . . to satisfy the aspirations, dreams and desires of our people: to lead a decent
and worthy life, . . . to have peace in order to build progress
in their land [and] happiness for their children." To achieve
development without despotism required "an organization such
that even if some want to divert the conquests of the struggle
to their own advantage, our people will not let them."

Already in the course of the independence struggle, Cabral argued, this bright future was being shaped and protected
by the cadre of his African Party for the Independence of
Guinea and Cape Verde (PAIGC) with its guerrilla fighters,
supportive peasants, and the children being educated in the
party's liberation schools. In short, the anticolonial struggle
would be waged in conditions that would also incubate a close,
cooperative relationship between leaders and people. Only the
best could join the party; anyone who lied or abused the people
would be purged. Even those making great sacrifices should
not expect to have "a fine motorcar, servants, several wives,"
or other privileges. "Authority must be based on real work,
on the accomplishment of duty and on conduct . . . which is
an example to everyone."

Cabral's views were paralleled by those of fellow anti-
Portuguese revolutionaries in Angola and Mozambique, the
left-nationalist regimes in Tanzania, Zimbabwe, and Zambia,
and other African leaders. The result in Guinea-Bissau and
elsewhere, however, was a modern dictatorship which used
these symbols to perpetuate its rule. Political elites selfishly
exploited the new ideology and structures while failing to deliver much social or economic progress.

Uganda provides an example of a state where a "progressive" nationalist modern dictatorship not only failed to
counter the forces making for anarchy but actually helped
create the conditions for a breakdown. A country rich in resources as well as natural beauty, Uganda could have become
prosperous and peaceful but fell victim to persistent misrule—

the kind of leaders characterized by Fanon as "nationalizing the robbery of the nation"—and internal conflict.

When Uganda gained independence, President Milton Obote seemed an attractive leader, typical of the first generation of African heads of state. Yet Obote bears a major responsibility for Uganda's despoliation, the death of so many citizens, and its possibly irreversible economic and political degeneration. He ruled from independence in 1962 until his own hatchet man, Idi Amin, overthrew him in 1971. When Amin, in turn, was tossed out in 1979, Obote eventually returned to power. At first Ugandans were jubilant at being liberated from a mad dictator whose regime had killed up to 300,000 of them, tortured and robbed additional thousands, and left the nation impoverished. Soon, however, they found that years of exile had not mellowed Obote. Conditions improved only marginally, and in 1985 Obote was booted out by another coup, which was itself set aside a few months later.

Cabral's liberation movement had soon converted itself into an unresponsive ruling class. Obote's political institutions performed the same function almost from the start. Obote's rule rested on his own party, security police, and the Acholi and Langi tribes that made up half the army. He abolished parliament and made himself president for life, jailed thousands, and used the army to suppress the powerful Buganda tribe. His domestic authoritarianism was coupled with a vocal radicalism in foreign affairs. A sizable section of the population was genuinely represented by the governing group and gained a share of the benefits, the rest were forced into line.

Obote's great error was to neglect the army's political potential. A civilian himself, he employed the military to suppress enemies but neither integrated the generals into his patronage system nor successfully indoctrinated them with an ideology that might cement their loyalty. No doubt Obote believed that the large Acholi presence in the ranks would ensure his rule. He ignored warnings about Amin's ambitions and unstable character, remembering how Amin had saved him from an early coup attempt.

When an overconfident Obote finally accused Amin of

embezzlement and then foolishly left for an overseas visit, Amin seized power. The new ruler quickly destroyed Obote's political base by banning the party, destroying the security police, and purging Acholi soldiers. Of 4,500 Acholi in the army, 3,000 were killed and the rest fled. Amin then put into place his own support structure by enlisting and promoting Nubian mercenaries and members of his own small tribe.

As an added incentive for loyalists, Amin seized the property of Uganda's 40,000 Asians and gave their homes, cars, shops, and businesses to followers, who in turn divided the new wealth with their own friends and relatives. A whole group of officers, officials, and tribesmen was thus given a vested interest in Amin's rule. Moreover, Amin's expulsion of Europeans and Asians, insults aimed at the West, and orientation toward the USSR, Libya, and the PLO made him seem a strong "anti-imperialist" nationalist. The Ugandan leader had a good reputation throughout Africa.

If Amin had stopped there, he might still be in power today, but his mentally unbalanced excesses led to his downfall. A modern dictator who eliminates his own supporters when they cannot be replaced and systematically wrecks his own country's economy cannot long survive. Even the most determined opportunists would not long devote themselves to a mercurial six-foot-four-inch, 240-pound general who ordered the execution of his own cabinet ministers on a whim. Endless rounds of beatings, arrests, executions, and looting disrupted society to the point of a breakdown.

In the end Amin made the same kind of mistake as his idol Adolf Hitler. Drunk on his own rhetoric, Amin invaded Tanzania in October 1978, giving that country the opportunity to counterattack. Ugandans, sickened by the reign of terror, would not defend the country; Amin's own men had fallen out over dividing the spoils. Libyan troops and PLO bodyguards could not save Amin, who fled to refuge in Saudi Arabia.

Amin's rise showed that civilian dictators like Obote had to figure out a way to control the military if they wanted to stay in power. But Amin's fate also showed that repression alone could sustain a regime for only so long, particularly if it was indiscriminate. Further, while demagogic foreign policy talk might contribute greatly to a leader's popularity, adventurous action could spell ruination, as it almost did even to the mighty Nasser in 1967.

After Amin had run away and the exiles from his reign of terror had returned home, Uganda embarked on an experiment in pluralism that showed the poor prospects for that sort of government. The attempt to establish a cabinet incorporating all sectors of political opinion broke down in the face of Uganda's ethnic, religious, ideological, and personal splits. Initial enthusiasm quickly bogged down in disastrous paralysis. Obote's earlier manipulation of tribal differences had left too much bitterness and mistrust; Amin's destruction of the civil service, provincial administration, and military discipline meant that the capital's decrees remained mere words on paper. Law and order and national unity proved impossible to rebuild.

The economy stagnated as politicians fought for months about power, policies, and whose followers would receive the ex-Asian businesses now seized from Amin's supporters. When the interim president tried to dismiss the new army commander, the general removed the politician instead and returned former President Obote to office. But the would-be populist dictator could neither govern competently nor unite the country. Five years later Obote was overthrown by officers from an allied tribe. He had never really learned how to control the army or build a multitribe political base and a more viable party structure. His political skill was effective enough to rule Uganda for fourteen years, but it left him in exile and the country in ruins.

The leader of Guinea-Bissau sought a different course. While himself a Marxist, Cabral was conscious of the danger that all the fine talk about people's rule, socialism, liberation, and nationalism could end by becoming a self-justifying apologia for a small ruling class. He tried to ensure that these institutions would have enough democratic life in them to ensure a real "say" for the common people.

But Cabral's intended safeguards could not turn his party

and mass organizations into pillars of democracy and grass-roots participation because once the party and state had eliminated pluralism and subordinated everything else, it created a system custom-made for abuse by leaders. These very institutions then became effective instruments of a dictatorial regime. In the case of Uganda, such a regime produced the conditions in which a murderous monster like Idi Amin could take power. Elsewhere it paved the way for chronic instability or, where rulers were skilled and conditions were right, modern dictatorships.

These tragic developments were a far cry from the expectations of both Africans and foreign well-wishers during the early period of independence in the 1960s. At that time "moderate" nationalists held that foreign rule was Africa's primary problem. The end of colonialism could not resolve all difficulties but would at least allow new states to begin the battle for development with a fair prospect of success. The leaders of former French colonies like Senegal and the Ivory Coast and ex-British possessions like Kenya and Nigeria began with this premise.

While imposing a large degree of state control on the economy, the political elite used its power to seize some of the best land, franchises, and commercial opportunities. These states' economies did grow faster, but they also produced sharp disparities in wealth, with the large number of landless or impoverished peasants disguised by aggregate positive statistics on development. Tanzanian President Julius Nyerere called them "man eat man" societies. Responding to the economic failures of Nyerere's government, a Kenyan leader retorted that the radical model made "man eat nothing" societies.

The "radicals" claimed, along the lines of Fanon and Cabral, that a social and economic revolution must accompany formal, legal independence. Otherwise, colonialism would live on as neocolonialism; the oppressed/oppressor dichotomy would be reborn in an unequal division of wealth and power between a colonialist-imitating elite and the large majority of peasants and workers. The gift of independence installed ready-made was worthless if it merely put in place parliaments and poli-

144

ticians chosen as acceptable stand-ins by the departing Europeans.

Ironically, by advocating the concentration of power in a state without any real restraint, the radicals also created a new elite empowered by its permanent hold on government. Nyerere defined a capitalist as a "man who uses wealth for the purpose of dominating any of his fellows," but a simple semantic change from "wealth" to "control of wealth" describes the situation in the radical states. Even their relative egalitarianism compared to the "capitalist" regimes was largely neutralized by the fact that failed economic policies produced far less wealth to distribute.

While "moderates" and "radicals" criticized each other and academics strained to define the differences between them, the two systems had much in common. Almost all African regimes subordinated the legislatures, trade unions, and media to a single party, which in turn is tightly controlled by the ruling elite. Socialism and nonalignment are proclaimed national policy as the state takes a large economic role and proclaims neutrality between the United States and the USSR. The president builds a cult of adoration; rivals are silenced or driven into exile. But because of the regime's dependence on one man, a leader's fall or failure means the military is likely to seize power.

Yet there are not many viable alternatives. Politically, electoral democracy hardly ever worked well or long survived except in a handful of countries. Economically, governments were often desperate to avoid famine, much less make progress. Socially, the task of knitting together disparate groups into one nation was extremely difficult. Underlying everything is what Nyerere called "the greatest evil of colonialism: the destruction of the self-confidence of the people." There can be no heavier responsibility than to direct a nation in its search for identity, to make a people believe in themselves, their country, and their leaders.

As if these problems were not daunting enough, African regimes must address these problems at the same time as they face great social change and psychological upheaval. There are high birthrates, a shortage of educated people, a lack of infrastructure, growing foreign debt, and an unfavorable trade balance for the producers of raw materials, who must pay more and more of their crops and minerals in exchange for the same amount of imports.

Urban migration, for example, disrupts attempts to cope with unemployment and the uncontrolled growth of cities. In Tanzania 66 percent of those living in towns were born in rural areas. Stable villages, the cooperation and hospitality of which display the finest aspects of African traditional society, are made politically irrelevant or are disrupted by urban dominance. Mutual family support allows people to survive in the cities, but this asset is transformed into the basis for corruption as officials put their own families and tribal relations first. Contact with city ways, which implies more influence from Western ideas and culture, raises popular demands for faster progress and new kinds of goods, particularly among those born there. All this puts added pressure on the country's political and social structure.

Since the cities are mainly administrative and commercial, rather than industrial, centers, they provide fewer jobs than are needed. They soak up foreign aid and domestic taxes rather than add to the nation's wealth. Many of the nation's talented and educated citizens are employed in an unproductive bureaucracy that comes to view the government as its own property and the citizenry as its subjects.

This relationship is generally reinforced by a socialist development strategy which exploits agriculture by paying the peasants low prices for crops and instituting government control over export earnings. City people benefit from low food prices and get imported goods bought with foreign loans and export income. Not only do urban dwellers make up most of the political, professional, and bureaucratic elite, but they can also influence the regime through riots or strikes. Since the rural areas have no political leverage in a modern dictatorship, their problems can be ignored. The peasants can retaliate only by themselves moving to the city, a step that damages rural productivity and undermines the whole system.

Indian economists suggest their country has increased agricultural productivity and virtually eliminated famine because politicians in a democracy must listen to peasant demands to win their votes. In an African modern dictatorship, however, control of the capital, army, and radio station replaces any need to heed rural demands. The ideas of men like Cabral for combining Marxist rule with grass-roots democracy are not put into practice. Rather, the ruler uses the new ideologies and party organizations for more effective control, not for more effective participation.

Outside of the dictator and the organizational channels he authorizes, many of these countries have no institutional backbone. If Latin America is paralyzed by its heavy historical legacy of entrenched oligarchy and reactionary officer class, Africa is weakened by the lack of national identity and the strength of ethnic friction. While class interests and entrenched struggles between interest groups limit change in Latin America, the stable alignments needed for political constancy are absent in Africa. The only reliably cohesive institutions have been the tribe and the army.

Tribes are simply an African equivalent of national and ethnic groups. They enjoy the loyalty of members, and each is differentiated from other tribes by linguistic, regional, religious, cultural, historical, and even occupational differences. In view of the weakness of countrywide patriotism and the lack of other strong institutional loyalties, tribal membership assumes a particular importance in forming political blocs.

"When the word government was mentioned," explained Nyerere, "the African thought of the chief, he did not, [like] the Briton, think of a grand building in which a debate was taking place." So the African leader would try to become the new chief, but one standing above an individual tribe. Nyerere rejected the multiparty system, which would "reduce politics to the level of a football match." The party and national ideology would be substitutes for tribal localism. Leaders like Obote and Amin, who essentially based themselves on one tribe, were far more vulnerable than those who could assemble a broader coalition of supporters.

All regimes must strive to convince their subjects to be good citizens, and in Africa the local concept of socialism has often been used for this objective. Again, Nyerere proves to be most articulate in explaining this objective: "The question 'What profit would I myself get?' must be . . . replaced by the question 'What benefit, and what loss, will be obtained by the people who make up this society?' " As in the West, practice often falls short of idealism, and leaders do not set a good example.

Still, the Third World desperately needs to encourage such behavior because the old society, where individualism was submerged for the sake of family and community, is rapidly being destroyed. In Western capitalist countries these bonds were gradually supplemented by civic consciousness and the regulatory state. In Communist countries the coercive state and propaganda take over. Citizens are told, and allowed, only what the rulers believe will serve the regime's needs. Sincere patriotism and desire to contribute to national development will always stimulate an idealistic minority. But African states cannot afford the patience to await such an evolutionary process. The techniques of modern dictatorship, providing citizens with a choice between being persuaded and being repressed, will inevitably seem swifter and surer to most leaders.

Africa's problems have been intensified by arbitrary borders drawn by nineteenth-century colonial powers which knew little and cared less about how these lines affected the tribes. Nevertheless, the problem is not so much that tribes are divided by borders as that diverse ones are necessarily thrown together by them since most tribes are too small to sustain a national state of their own.

The variety of tribal mix affects the politics of African countries in different ways. A few lucky states like Tanzania have so many small tribes that the problem largely disappears. Where there are two major tribes, as in Zimbabwe, or three, as in Nigeria, their battle for predominance threatens to preoccupy national politics. Similarly, where one large tribe confronts several smaller ones, the former may win the upper hand, as in Kenya, or the latter may form inherently unstable alliances to rule, as in Uganda. Other kinds of divisions include the more modernized coast against the less developed interior (most of West Africa), farmer versus nomad tribes, Muslim against Christian, or even Catholic against Protestant.

The result is that battles for power are rarely based on ideology or party alignments, although these may become the tools of different interest groups. Almost every African state is fragile because it lacks a national identity or patriotism that can bind the country together. The one advantage of this weakness is that there are few wars between states.

Contrary to Western experience, African states exist before nations have been built. The accumulation of a common experience as citizens of one country—political history, economic patterns, the influence of leaders, and the power of the state bureaucracy—may produce national integration over time, as they have in the Arab world. But trends that resist this development are also set in motion. The likelihood that each internal conflict, election, or open debate could turn into civil war makes a multiparty parliamentary system seem quite dangerous, threatening the country's survival in one piece. Civilian democratic politicians find it difficult to build a base that is both national and cohesive; modern dictators justify their rule as necessary to avoid chronic anarchy or even the dissolution of the country. Only the caution of these leaders has kept the number of coups and civil wars from being even more numerous.

To build a viable country able to maintain its unity and to develop economically was the objective of each of the independence movements and the leaders who became their countries' first presidents.

Three of the most influential of these men were Kwame Nkrumah in Ghana, Sékou Touré in Guinea, and Julius Nyerere in Tanzania. Each became president when his country attained independence in 1957, 1958, and 1961 respectively. All three implemented their ideas in creating somewhat different versions of modern dictatorships and setting the political patterns that dominate the continent.

No one was more influential in the founding generation

that struggled to resolve these problems than Ghana's first president, Kwame Nkrumah. In the 1930s, when few Ghanians even finished the first grade, Nkrumah become a secondary school teacher. He studied in the United States from 1935 to 1945 and then spent two years in London. Nkrumah's experience with American racism and segregation inevitably made a deeper impression on him than did his observations of an imperfect American democracy.

Returning home in 1947, he put into practice his new ideas: Independence required a movement for organizing, politically educating, and uniting the people. If Britain and France did not want to give up their empires, Africans would have to force them to do so. Europe yielded independence only when it was credibly demanded, a lesson Third World leaders were to remember in future dealings with the West.

While still in Britain, Nkrumah had been offered the leadership of Ghana's nationalist Convention People's party (CPP) which advocated independence and leadership by young, Western-educated activists instead of by the traditionalist tribal chiefs. In the decade after his return home Nkrumah wrote the party's platform, set up branches, organized a central office, and spoke at meetings around the country. He built alliances with the trade unions and cooperatives while creating veterans', farmers', and women's organizations. At a showdown meeting with the chiefs in 1949 Nkrumah asked thousands of cheering followers if he should pack his bags and leave the country. "No," his supporters loudly chorused. As with many other modern dictators, a threatened resignation had settled the issue.

The CPP called for peaceful demonstrations, breaking with the old elite's timidity. What seemed radical soon became mainstream positions, and the British began a series of concessions leading to internal self-rule. After a general strike and boycott of the colonial regime, London finally decided the colony was more trouble and expense than it was worth. Ghana became the first black African country in modern times to achieve independence.

Of course, as Nkrumah recognized, this was only the beginning of a new stage of struggle. "Slums and squalor in our towns, superstitions and ancient rites in our villages," unfarmed land, nutritional diseases, and a lack of roads or railroads meant the new country had "much ignorance and few skills." There was no industry, and there were too few teachers; trade and commerce were mostly in foreign hands. The new government's task would be to solve problems great enough to defeat even the bravest and most innovative leader.

Nkrumah described himself at the time as "a nondenominational Christian and a Marxist socialist," yet he was above all a modern dictator. The unions, civil service, and media were subordinated to his direction. To break tribal loyalties and transfer popular allegiance away from the chiefs, Nkrumah encouraged a campaign to glorify himself. Projecting himself as the national symbol might have promoted unity, but it also meant that national identity was dependent on his permanent rule.

Addressing the one-party National Assembly, Nkrumah explained, "The multi-party system which exists in Western countries is in fact a reflection of a social cleavage and the kind of class system which does not exist in African countries. A multi-party system introduced into Africa results in the perpetuation of feudalism, tribalism, and regionalism, and an inordinate power struggle and rivalry." Nkrumah warned against the power of an economic "petty bourgeoisie," an idea taken more from Marxist texts than from Ghana's reality. Cabral, a far more consistent Marxist than Nkrumah, had realized that the real threat to the country came from those who used the control of government and party to their own advantage rather than from small traders or shopkeepers who barely stood above the peasantry.

Nkrumah's goal as dictator was to prevent individuals from possessing enough wealth, popularity, or independent organization to stand outside the control of government or party. But the real danger to stability came from what the regime did to itself and the country. Nkrumah created a political class thriving on a socialism that monopolized power and wealth in the state they controlled while eliminating competition from other groups, criticism from the media, or punishment from the courts.

Nkrumah admitted that unless the CPP expressed the "will of the masses [it] can quickly develop into the most dangerous form of tyranny," but he never used his power to prevent this development. Behind the fine rhetoric were corruption and mismanagement. The CPP leaders enjoyed loot at home and prestige abroad as courageous radical nationalists. When Nkrumah spoke to parliament about punishing officials who held funds in overseas banks—the main way of hiding ill-gotten gains—the chamber rocked with laughter and the president himself smiled. Under such conditions the country's fine civil service, perhaps its best inheritance from colonial days, was demoralized and joined in the division of spoils.

Graft used up the limited national resources. When the chairman of the farmers' cooperative asked for money to import tractors, a senior civil servant discovered that the last shipment ordered was still sitting in storage, rusting in the rain. Nkrumah called in the man responsible, who quickly fell on his knees before the president and said, "If I ever let you down, you may hang me in the public square!" The matter was forgotten. After all, Nkrumah had his own priorities: Political loyalty came first. Honesty could be "objectively" disloyal since it meant making accusations against party leaders and undermining the system that ensured their support. The cost of this system was high. A 10 percent kickback on each tractor purchased did not interfere with development statistics, but the people or aid donors had to pay for the overpriced and useless equipment as well as for the commission itself.

Similarly, projects like stadiums, fancy government buildings, unneeded military weapons, or roads and factories sited for political benefit rather than economic efficiency could serve a constructive political purpose. National pride would be augmented, and important constituencies appeased, thus protecting the leader's base of support. Such spending priorities are common in Western democracies, but they can afford the waste better than Ghana and have self-correcting mechanisms—legislatures, newspaper exposés, honest courts, even competing interest groups—to limit the damage.

In Ghana, however, the only way the system could be challenged was by its overthrow. If control of the state was merely a means of self-enrichment, there was no reason why others would not grab it to gain their share. The falling price of cocoa, Ghana's staple export, when added to Nkrumah's misrule and inexperience in maintaining his regime's security, led to trouble. Military officers were particularly incensed at Nkrumah's increasing use of foreigners in the presidential guard, a move they considered a step toward the army's dissolution. While Nkrumah was abroad in February 1966, the military staged a coup. His once-adoring public did nothing, welcoming the regime's fall because they had painfully experienced its mismanagement.

Nkrumah's apologists see the army takeover as an isolated event caused only by foreign intrigue. They remain confident that the people could never reject socialism, the party, and the leader who loved them and protected their interests. Exiled in Guinea, as guest of its more "successful" modern dictator, Sékou Touré, Nkrumah himself promoted this explanation. In increasingly abstract tracts he attributed defeat to insufficient firmness in stamping out opposition and opposing foreign imperialism. If only he had more relentlessly applied Marxist analysis, Nkrumah said, he could have detected and wiped out his enemies. In a sense, this conclusion was accurate: A tougher party structure, a more reliable police apparatus, and a more thoroughgoing purge of the army might have allowed Nkrumah to stay in power longer. But Nkrumah also missed the point: The abuse of the state and of one-party rule was as much the cause of his defeat—and even more the source of his declining popularity.

Nkrumah's conclusions at the end of his life about the political course he should have followed were no doubt influenced by the policies of his host, Sékou Touré, whose Guinea followed Ghana into independence.

Touré was much tougher than Nkrumah had been in

stamping out opposition, and he stayed in office for twenty-five years compared to Nkrumah's nine-year tenure. Clearly the Guinean dictator developed a much more sophisticated type of modern dictatorship, with institutions that were strong at least as long as the leader was there to provide a focal point for decision making. Guinea paid a high cost for sovereignty. When Touré was the only leader of a French colony to refuse Paris's offer of delayed independence, an angry French President Charles de Gaulle ordered out French technicians, removed equipment, and cut off aid. Guinea was economically devastated, but Touré's defiance made him a hero. At independence Touré declared that the Guinean people preferred poverty in freedom to riches in slavery. Unfortunately Touré gave them both poverty and slavery.

Partly because of his fear of foreign intervention, Touré maintained a high level of internal repression. Members of the elite who fell under his suspicion were tortured to extract confessions, imprisoned, killed, or forced into exile. Tight political and economic controls maintained the regime but could not deliver much development. The economy grew an average of only 1.5 percent annually during his reign. Between 1970 and 1982 debt doubled and food production fell. Conditions became so bad that an estimated 1 million Guineans went abroad for political or economic reasons. There were many parallels with other African countries and modern dictatorships.

Touré's international reputation and domestic support, however, remained fairly strong. Keeping out the foreign media and controlling dissent prevented any contradiction to official exhortations and announcements of successes. Moreover, the regime created an elaborate network of institutions for its protection. Touré had learned well from his years of experience allied with the French Communist party, on which he apparently modeled the Democratic Party of Guinea (PDG). In addition, there was the PDG-controlled Youth of the African Democratic Revolution, Local Revolutionary Authorities, Women's Wing of the PDG, and National Confederation of Guinean Workers. In contrast with Marxist models, however, all Guineans were party members (dues were paid as part of their taxes), and as many as 20 percent of Guineans were elected party officials.

Despite this pantomime of participation, the party was ruled along democratic centralist lines—i.e., from the top down—and Touré rejected any decentralization of authority. After all, he argued ingenuously, since the government was in the people's hands, to give any special authority to, say, the judiciary or the press would simply rob the masses of control. It was a neat justification for the concentration of power in his own hands. The regime allowed shortcomings to be discussed only either when it announced measures to combat them or when it blamed the difficulties on recently purged officials.

There was, however, a real popular reservoir of gratitude to Touré's regime for bringing some improvement in living conditions and the only independence Guineans had ever known. The regime was also successful in maintaining control because 90 percent of the population was illiterate peasants or young people. They had no experience with palatable alternatives. The regime was the sole source of information, patriotism, and rewards ranging from career opportunities to educational and sporting facilities. Those still unhappy could always emigrate, as hundreds of thousands did.

The other 10 percent consisted of traders, intellectuals, bureaucrats, and soldiers who had more knowledge about the regime's failings and about possible alternatives. They found it easier to envision their future apart from, even enhanced by, the regime's demise. This group was at the same time the system's main beneficiary (if it worked for the party or government) and the main target of its surveillance and repression. Thousands of them left the country.

But Touré also had them politically stymied with his ideology as much as with his secret police and party network. If these people felt alienated from the regime, he was able to brand them as unpatriotic, procapitalist, and proimperialist, disruptive of national unity. In his quasi-Marxist approach Touré (like Nkrumah) warned against the unreliable nature of the intellectuals and petty bourgeoisie. The subordination of this group's independence and initiative damaged the development process since it sapped the energy or excluded altogether many of those people most qualified to lead the development effort and to correct or implement policies better. It bred and encouraged the worst characteristics: sycophancy, dishonesty, refusal to take responsibility or initiative, decisions made on erroneous information or ideological dogmatism, and the paralysis of lower levels afraid to point out errors and shortcomings.

This structure also enhanced the regime's control. As in Communist countries, class analysis was in the service of a ruling class that entrenched itself under the pretext of serving the people. The more it talked of socialism and the rule of the masses, the tinier became the circle of those with power. By playing on real needs—unity against foreign threats and tribal conflicts, cooperation in the difficult process of development—the government could impose unanimity of opinion and eliminate any power centers outside itself. Socialism had proved tailor-made for modern dictators. It is not surprising that the system did not work well, but equally, there are good reasons why it sustained itself for so many years.

Yet while the leaders frequently changed in many of these states, the demand for unanimity and the appeal of nationalism remained constant themes that often succeeded in rallying support. When a new leader rose to power, the old regime might be more skeptically viewed, but an incumbent could always claim loyalty by dint of being national leader and through the patronage he could distribute.

Guinea amply illustrates this point. When Touré called on the people to vote for independence from France in 1958, 98 percent had supported him. And he was quite sincere in his determination to reduce foreign influence, allowing no one else to take France's place. The USSR's ambassador was expelled in 1961 for interference in internal politics. Youth group members were organized to attack U.S. cultural centers in 1966. By attributing all problems to past colonialism and to current "imperialist and neocolonialist machinations," the regime sometimes cynically manipulated popular fears. But these attitudes were also sincerely held and had a basis in reality. Guineans knew how the French had tried to sabotage independence; in 1970 the country was attacked by Portuguese mercenaries.

Such powerlessness produced an injured patriotism—"How easy it is to inflame an insulted people," comments Nyerere—and the Third World's efforts to create a nonaligned movement. There is anger at the former colonial states for past mistreatment and at the West for its wealth and power. International trade and debt often take more capital from the developing countries than aid and investment return. African leaders fear that the gap between rich and poor countries is growing, that much of the Third World is sliding backward.

The weakness of the African states makes them fearful because they know how easy it is for foreigners to buy or overthrow political leaders and to play on internal divisions. "The question is still being asked," notes Nyerere, 'Who is going to control Africa?' Those who are asking it do not expect the answer to be: 'The Africans.' " Usually the Third World's only way to retaliate is with heated anti-Western or anti-American rhetoric, which also wins the ruler popular support.

Nasser's pattern of playing off the two great powers was closely followed by Touré as well as other Third World leaders. The story is told that Tanzanian President Julius Nyerere and Singapore Prime Minister Lee Kuan Yew once met at a summit meeting of the nonaligned nations. "According to an old Swahili proverb," said Nyerere, "when the elephants fight, the grass gets trampled." "Yes," answered Lee, "but when the elephants make love, the grass also gets trampled."

So Touré set out to derive the most benefit from foreign powers' jockeying for influence while mistrusting all of them. The government preached that there was a "permanent plot" against the country's independence, a conspiracy in which anyone might be involved, although France was a sentimental favorite. There was the teachers' plot and the traders' plot and the military plot, all of which were dealt with by summary arrests, torture to obtain confessions, and long prison sentences.

These groups, though usually innocent of treason, were not chosen at random. They were the sectors of the population most critical of Touré: intellectuals who thought the regime was not Marxist enough; small merchants and marketwomen who thought it was too economically inefficient; military officers who sought power in their own right. The modern dictatorship's response is to talk of "class struggle." Critics, charged with having selfish motives, are threatened with the loss of their privileges unless they accept the regime's primacy.

The government's proudest claim was that it transcended tribal and religious conflicts and forged a basis for national unity. Ironically, Touré argued that counterrevolutionaries thought in tribal terms, but those he accused of this crime—his critics—came from the most cosmopolitan, detribalized sectors. Touré used "ethnic arithmetic," a type of affirmative action, in distributing posts. When Guinea had its first military coup, the junta was multiethnic.

The more important fact, of course, was that Guinea finally did have its coup, albeit only after Touré's death in 1984 on an operating table in Cleveland, Ohio. The quarter century of party, ideology, mobilization, political education, and battalions of committees did not prevent the battalions of soldiers from taking over. The PDG disappeared overnight, and a Military Committee of National Recovery took over.

The apparatus had served Touré's purpose, enabling him to become black Africa's longest-reigning ruler, but the modern dictatorship system did not guarantee continued rule by the dictator's designated successor. It did, however, ensure that the new ruler would keep the established pattern even if he changed the names of the institutions and the faces of their masters.

In traditional terms, Nkrumah and Touré seem like men of the left. The distinction between "left" and "right," however, has little application to their policies and tactics. Nationalism, statism, a ruling party, ideology, and the rest of these political techniques were as useful for Stalin as for Hitler and as much employed by Khomeini as by Castro. To divide Africa—or the Third World—into progressives and reactionaries or between Communists and pro-Western leaders only masks the striking similarities of these regimes.

The third of Africa's "radical" founding fathers was Julius Nyerere. Like Cabral, Nyerere tried to create a modern dictatorship that would also be profoundly democratic. Although his system was milder than that of Nkrumah or Touré, it did no better at development and only somewhat better at fostering pluralism. Tanzania's relative flexibility helped preserve the system but, ironically, in no small part because it made the country such an appealing client for Western aid givers.

In a part of the world where institutions and national political cultures are so weak, a dictator's personality can have a tremendous role in shaping his country. There are few, if any, innate reasons why Uganda did not have the good fortune to produce a Nyerere or Tanzania did not just happen to have an Idi Amin instead. Because Nyerere was Tanzania's leader, though, he tried to ensure that the country would never produce an Idi Amin. He sought to make the country's single party, the Tanzanian African National Union (TANU), a representative national organization that policed itself against corruption and abuses. He tried to create guarantees of rights and political checks and balances similar to the pluralism that protects Western democracies from becoming tyrannies.

Can a modern dictatorship also inspire autonomous popular participation and criticism? Nyerere tried to do so by ensuring inner-party democracy in TANU. He mandated a network of elected village development committees and a party cell for every ten houses in the country. Rather than serve as a mere conduit for his decrees, these institutions were to provide, in Nyerere's words, a "two-way all-weather road" linking the rulers to the ruled, the capital's center with the rural periphery. After all, Africa's really exploitative "capital-ism" is a system in which the capital exploits the peasantry. Cabral once told French journalist Gérard Chaliand that it would be better not to have a capital city at all. As they stood in a forest clearing,

159

Cabral explained, "You know, after independence this wouldn't make a bad capital—a tree in a clearing to rest under, after making the rounds of the villages."

Ruling a country, however, required a trained bureaucracy that easily made itself into a privileged elite which was not accountable to the people. The concentration of power in the leadership was a constant temptation for self-aggrandizement and the abuse of prerogatives. Faced with such unpleasant realities, Nyerere often ignored the practice and took refuge in his theories.

But he persevered with charm, energy, and imagination, if not always with effectiveness. To retard development of a permanent political ruling class, he ordered that TANU members compete in elections for parliamentary seats. It is an interesting example of the parallelism among African modern dictatorships to note that "conservative" Kenya has this same system. In contrast with Kenyan leaders, however, Nyerere set a good example with his modest life-style. His charisma and image as a progressive but humane leader were the country's greatest single asset, attracting $3 billion in Western aid during the 1970s to cover two-thirds of the development budget. Relative to other Third World modern dictatorships, Nyerere did create a populist dictatorship with a human face.

The theory behind Nyerere's economic strategy was *ujamaa*: self-reliance, grass-roots democracy, and an emphasis on agriculture rather than the usually disastrous Third World leftist stress on heavy industry. *Ujamaa* villages concentrated the peasants into larger living units which could be more easily supplied with schools, health centers, and other services. But Tanzania's image was damaged when the outside world discovered that many peasants had been forcibly resettled and that a number of the consultative structures were frauds. Meanwhile, government-owned companies, the workers and managers of which lacked incentives or competition for greater efficiency, were in ruins, and Tanzania did not have enough foreign exchange to buy bags for shipping its export crops.

Nyerere's system must be judged a failure on two counts: It did not provide successful economic development, even relative to other African states, and it did not lay the foundation for a lasting democratic society even in terms of a single-party socialist state. While Nyerere was a largely benevolent dictator, there was nothing to stop his successors from using the mechanisms in the brutal ways familiar from Ghana, Guinea, and elsewhere.

Where Nyerere was undeniably successful was in subordinating the army to the party and avoiding the coups that plagued so much of Africa. Other regimes, whether originally civilian or led by officers who had put aside their uniforms, tried to buy off officers with economic privileges or to keep the army professionally apolitical. In modern dictatorships as diversely "socialist" as Tanzania, Zambia, and Zimbabwe or as variously "capitalist" as Zaire, Kenya, and the Ivory Coast, officers have been held in check for two decades or more. These countries each had a strong charismatic modern dictator who attracted enough loyalty, spread enough fear, and established a solid enough alliance of benefiting groups to stay in power. Other states, lacking such a strong man, trying multiparty democracy, or bereft of even a minimal base for national unity, faced one coup after another.

It should be clear that some of the "moderates" who came to power at independence or through a coup can build modern dictatorships that have both the strengths and weaknesses of their "radical" counterparts: well-entrenched regimes coupling economic failure with political strength yet unlikely to outlive the dictator himself. Perhaps the most notorious of these regimes is that of Mobutu Sese Seko, by some reports the world's wealthiest man, in Zaire. Once a noncommissioned officer in the Belgian Congo, Joseph Mobutu gained quick promotion after his country's strife-torn independence in 1960. The wealthiest province tried to secede with backing from a Belgian mining company, the first president, Patrice Lumumba, a Touré-like figure, was murdered, and UN troops had to be called in to restore order. Mobutu emerged, with U.S. support, as dictator in 1965 and for the next twenty years managed to hold together his complex country.

Precisely because he had come to power with questionable

credentials, Mobutu worked hard to emphasize his authenticity. He wore a leopardskin hat and carried the staff of a chief. Political scientist Manfred Halperin has suggested that an African leader must act somewhat like the Wizard of Oz, presenting himself as a miracle worker by busily "working smoke-machines and amplifying his voice." Mobutu, like his colleagues, has a terrific grasp of political symbolism. He Africanized place-names and personal names and made his murdered predecessor Lumumba a national hero (as Ghana's later military rulers did for Nkrumah). After a visit to China and North Korea, Mobutu copied for himself the titles of Helmsman and Guide held by his Communist modern dictator hosts.

The cult of personality was reinforced by gimmicks like showing Mobutu emerging from the clouds and descending to earth at the beginning of television programming. Western business suits are banned, and officials must wear "Mobutu suits." This is an interesting reflection on the reversal of sartorial symbolism since Kemal Atatürk made Western dress mandatory as a sign of modernization. Again, many other countries have decrees similar to those of Zaire to promote what is designated as "the national costume," usually with limited success in keeping out foreign fashion. Such actions were marks not of craziness but of political shrewdness as leaders sought to manipulate traditional social, mythical, and religious imagery. The extent of Mobutu's regime's corruption necessitated some psychological and political countermeasures, particularly since the weak army could not maintain order very effectively through repression.

Mobutu's party, the Popular Movement of the Revolution (MPR), is an extension of the government bureaucracy, and every Zairian is a party member, a pattern familiar from Touré's "progressive" Guinea. Mobutu explains, "In our traditional societies . . . there has never been two chiefs in the same village, the true chief and the opposition chief. There have perhaps been conflicts between villages. . . . But once they were unified, only one chief emerged democratically: the chief of all. That is African authenticity." And that is the ideology of Mobutu and the MPR, widely paralleled elsewhere in Africa.

Political conformity, like cultural homogeneity, is seen as an essential form of loyalty and patriotism. Participation in the party and mouthing the official line, as in Communist states, are a precondition for temporal success. Those who do so are admitted to what is called the "helper class." Mobutu's corruption is so extreme even by African standards that it is counterproductive in the pattern of traditional dictatorships. But while undermining the economy, it still plays a role in shoring up the regime.

Mobutu also is more extreme in that the extent of his rewards to the elite and its helpers allows them to treat the people as prey. A former interior minister comments, "Most administrators treat their charges as conquering occupiers." Abuses include accepting bribes to remove files; demanding payments for office visits and letters of recommendation; the sale of the government's gasoline and misuse of its vehicles; taking kickbacks from poachers, job seekers, and ivory smugglers; officials' neglect of their duties to run private businesses; embezzlement; tax fraud; shakedowns by the military and police; and kickbacks for hiring. All these activities go on in states ruled by Mobutu's "radical" counterparts as well. In Tanzania or the Marxist states, however, the regime's sense of acceptable limits and self-preservation forces officials to be more cautious and restrained in their depredations to escape possible punishment.

Yet if Mobutu had ever ignored his populist side, he would not have survived so long in power. When state transport workers called a wildcat strike, Mobutu personally discussed grievances with their leaders and fired the company's Belgian expatriate director on television. Mobutu is, in the words of a perceptive journalist, "Part actor, part statesman, part gangster."

The experience of the only African leader to experiment with traditional dictatorship will probably discourage others from following his example. Jean Bokassa showed his nostalgia for the old style by crowning himself emperor of the Central African Republic in 1977, complete with throne and a celebration that cost $22 million, one-fourth of the annual national revenue. Two years later he had several dozen schoolchildren murdered after they had protested being forced to buy uniforms supplied by a Bokassa crony. France, which supplied half his budget, engineered a coup. Those dependent on foreign support are more easily removed by foreigners, a lesson that Touré, Nyerere, and their counterparts well understood.

The effectiveness of a modern dictator cannot, then, be judged by superficial measurements of popularity or legitimacy. Nkrumah, after all, had a better international image than Mobutu. The Ghanaian leader was considered a heroic pioneer, a man of integrity and imagination; Mobutu, in comparison, seems a thug. Still, Mobutu, although he was more personally corrupt, proved a better survivor—and probably not a worse ruler—than Nkrumah.

To judge political virtue by economic policy is equally problematic. Modern dictatorships firmly believe in Mao's dictum of "politics in command," meaning that the regime's requirements for staying in power should never be subordinated to strictly economic considerations. Socialism in the Third World does not necessarily mean a rigid refusal to deal with foreign companies. A modern dictatorship's two key objectives are to avoid any concentration of domestic economic power outside the government and to keep any foreign multinational corporation or corporations from being able to undermine national independence.

As rigid state planning and autarchy failed, many modern dictatorships adopted more flexible economic policies while carefully preserving their tight control over their economies. In fact, these reforms are designed to protect the political status quo, not alter it, as can be seen in China's post-Mao use of market mechanisms, material incentives, small-scale private initiative, and offering opportunities for foreign investment. Capitalist companies, accustomed to wholly owned investments and subsidiaries, fought against nationalization or any challenge to their power to do as they pleased. Used to paying low prices and wages to government and workers, the multi-nationals were spoiled. Anything less than subservience to United Fruit, ITT, Kennicott Copper, Standard Oil, or other such companies in the 1940s and 1950s would earn a regime the epithet of "Communistic" and inspire U.S. sanctions or even a covertly sponsored coup.

Yet when nationalistic Third World governments were able to take over their own resources and survive, most companies quickly adjusted. Now there was plenty of money to be made within the framework of contracts, partnerships, or joint ventures with the "radical" governments. Businesses found many of these regimes to be reliable in their dealings, and the new contractual relationships lessened the danger of dispossession by local instability. Modern dictatorships even ensured that labor would remain docile.

Ironically, trade unions are one of the main targets for control and subjugation by modern dictatorships, particularly leftist ones. Since unions represent workers, they conflict with the regime's claim to embody the working class's interests. Any labor demands against state industry pose a direct challenge to the state's determination to set economic priorities and contradicts the leader's alleged objective of improving workers' conditions. Trade union independence is totally unacceptable to the modern dictatorship. In Tanzania, as well as in Guinea and other such states, the unions are amalgamated into a national federation under the party's control and are forced to put increasing production ahead of improving wages or conditions.

In Zambia, where founding father President Kenneth Kaunda's modern dictatorship has been unable to gain complete control of the unions, the government has not hesitated to attack them. It arrested and held union leaders for several months in 1981, charging that strikes were a conspiracy to overthrow the government. High inflation and empty treasuries also mean that workers' pay lags behind price increases.

The regimes' priority on efficiency and discipline does not leave much room for workers' autonomy. Further, since foreign-managed projects are often the country's sole source of foreign exchange, protecting them from any threat is of vital importance. Thus, there is the apparent paradox of Cuban soldiers, called in to preserve the Angolan government, guarding the Gulf Oil Corporation's installations there from pro-Western guerrillas and even from South African saboteurs.

The dictatorship's economic policy is designed to maximize the government's income and to keep wealth or control out of the hands of potential rivals. The state must take the lead in economic development because there are too few native entrepreneurs with too little experience and capital. By the same token, only the state can negotiate on an equal basis with foreign multinationals. This does not mean, though, that the ruling elite and its relatives do not themselves become rich through political power, accumulating wealth through the misappropriation of government assets or, where permitted, by accumulating land and business ownership.

Like governments elsewhere, African regimes differ in the quality of their leadership, the degree of open debate permitted in their single parties, the heights of violent repression, the extent of openness toward foreign companies, the amount of conflict or cooperation among tribes, and other ways.

Yet what is far more striking are their similarities: the one-party state; the regime's large (though far from total) degree of control over the economy and society; the ideology of consensus and nationalism; the priority on development and the limited success in gaining it. Dictators experimented with instruments and ideas for staying in power, discouraging coups, fostering development, and building popular support. Military officers, having made a coup, had to learn how to use the techniques of modern dictatorship to legitimize their rule. The lessons of Atatürk, Nasser, and Perón—as well as those of Marx—were adapted to African and Third World conditions. This road was followed both by military men and by the more doctrinaire Marxist revolutionaries among the second wave of African modern dictators who came to power during the 1970s and 1980s.

CHAPTER SEVEN

Africa: Soldiers and Radicals

Captain Thomas Sankara, chairman of the National Council of the Revolution and head of state of Burkina Faso, is an obscure dictator running an equally obscure country. He changed the name from the more prosaic Upper Volta to its new moniker meaning "Country of Incorruptible Men." The new name is an example both of the wish fulfillment that so commonly colors Third World rhetoric and of the importance of symbolism in shaping the consciousness of the people. Sankara's political ideas are also typical of the military and radical-sounding regimes that have come to dominate Africa.

Speaking in his capital, Ouagadougou, on the second anniversary of the "Popular and Democratic Revolution" in August 1985, Sankara explained: "The aim of our revolution [is] the constant search for the happiness of our people . . . the continual, eventful transformation and departure from the present which has kept us prisoner."

The desire to escape from underdevelopment and weakness is a powerful incentive; the rejection of an unhappy present is a rationale for revolution. Explains Sankara, referring to the wasted postindependence era: "What does going too fast mean when we still have 23 years to catch up [on]!" Modern dictators not only rail at the country's underdevelopment but also reject the efforts of their predecessors in trying to cope with it. Many citizens, whose own lives have not been visibly improved by the preceding regimes, are ready to agree that too much time has been lost in bickering and that something new is needed.

In and of itself, Burkina Faso is one of the least important countries in Africa, but its history provides a good case study for the appeal of modern dictators and their ideas. Sankara's radical Third World ideology includes such ingredients as Marxism, Qaddafi's influence, Maoism, African socialism, and French leftism.

Burkina Faso has only 7 million people, almost all of them poor peasants. Its infrastructure was only slightly improved by the French colonial rulers. Exports of beef, peanuts, and cotton bring in little money, and many workers have emigrated to the relatively booming Ivory Coast. Inevitably the country has been dependent on foreign assistance, and aid agencies from abroad compete for scarce office space in the capital.

The government put into place by the departing French did not last very long, and a military regime took power in 1968 under General Sangoulé Lamizana. The junta made no major changes in the country and a decade later held elections under a new constitution promising civil liberties, the right to work, health care, and education. These three stages were seen in other African countries where no strong leader emerged to become a modern dictator:

> The original regime rules without any real effort to win popular allegiance or to guarantee control of the military. It lasts only until the army realizes its own political strength.

*   *   *

The military seizes power but does not know what to do with it. The costume of the ruler but not the system itself has been changed.

Finally, the dictator returns to a familiar civilian model, either keeping power himself or turning it over to the older generation of politicians.

These all were fairly minimalist types of government, content with the issuing of orders in the capital city and control of the national treasury. On one level this approach is realistic. A five-year development plan can be more easily drawn up than funded. Universal primary education may be pledged, but by 1975 Burkina Faso had been able to enroll only 14 percent of school-age children.

Given the inevitable disappointment with the government's performance and the ambitions of officers, the elected government lasted only two years before it was overthrown by the Military Committee for the Recovery of National Progress in 1980. The new junta's name shows the soldiers' belief that the country was stagnating. Having observed the outcome when Lamizana stepped down, this military regime was determined to be tougher. It arrested trade unionists and student leaders, outlawed strikes, and banned meetings of independent organizations. But the Military Committee did not take the additional step of creating its own supportive groups.

So in 1982 the Military Committee in turn was overthrown by the People's Salvation Council, from which emerged Captain Sankara, already distinguished as a hero of earlier border skirmishes with Mali. The colorful Sankara, then in his mid-thirties, enjoyed some support from Libyan dictator Qaddafi and composed his own "revolutionary music" on his guitar. Regardless of how long Sankara personally will rule Burkina Faso, the political and ideological underpinnings of his regime take the country to the level of modern dictatorship.

While Sankara can attract some Libyan and Soviet bloc aid, his takeover hardly solves the country's shortage of resources. His first step is to argue that underdevelopment is an artificial situation created by the local elite's selfishness and incompetence and by the domination of foreign imperialists. In contrast with previous regimes that were content to cultivate popular passivity, Sankara argued that development can arise only from the willpower of a highly organized and motivated people.

Radical ideology is supposed to be the key to unleashing this great effort. It provides an explanation for the failures to date—the obstructionism and exploitation of foreign imperialists and domestic class enemies—and a method for defeating them. It glorifies the people and rationalizes the dictatorship. When leaders cannot cope with their tremendous problems, the ideology of modern dictatorship provides ways to turn rivals into scapegoats and to keep the masses enthusiastic and in line. Even if a given dictator is discredited and overthrown, his successor can use the same arguments and the same system. The people, who yesterday abandoned the old dictator, will cheer the new one out of fear, opportunism, conformity, conviction, and patriotism—or some mixture of all these factors. Just as the structure of populistic dictatorship can survive, its ideology becomes a new opiate of the people, easing their pain and sorrows at their current sad state.

The Chinese approach to ideology, unlike the Soviet one, offered an unbounded belief in the creative power of the people. Mao's "foolish old man who removed the mountain" did it little by little with his patient labor. He did not need a bulldozer or dump truck. This was, of course, the philosophy of the Cultural Revolution, before Peking decided that modern technology, expertise, and material incentives were necessary. The African ideologists who embraced or duplicated such views in the 1970s and 1980s were simply taking and adapting what most fitted their needs.

To provide an appearance of progress, keep the masses busy, stir the enthusiasm of a long-passive people, and tie them to the government, radical modern dictatorships pursue one campaign after another. There have been Stalin's dams and canals, Cuba's pursuit of a 10-million-ton harvest, Iran's crusade against Iraq, Nicaragua's literacy campaign, and so on.

Sankara recalls Burkina Faso's "crash vaccination campaign as a successful gigantic effort to check diseases. Along with the battle for a railroad, the campaigns are achievements that only the revolution can make possible." Other innovations include the Revolutionary People's Tribunals and efforts to make prisoners productive: "At Baporo and Yelkoto, 40 prisoners are successfully exploiting 50 hectares of land, thus confirming that it is possible to instill . . . the ethic of progress when a man is determined to earn forgiveness from the people."

As in Sankara's prison reform, campaigns are intended to develop resources and train the "new man," whose ethic is cooperation, self-sacrifice, dedication, and reliability. Some of the goals are deemed good in most societies. For example, Sankara advocates the fair treatment of women and children in a historically male-dominated society of polygamy in which wives are turned "into maid servants." The state mandates laws guaranteeing wives "reasonable financial support" from husbands. This is the kind of social program—along with public education, unemployment insurance, old-age pensions, and so on—common in countries thinking of themselves as developed but rarely available in Third World countries.

Lacking organized social reform movements or lobbies and lacking the time for a long, slow process of progress, the state must become the principal innovator of and educator toward change. In terms of Third World rhetoric, this role of the state is what is most often behind the word "socialism."

Building a nation and national identity is the state's most important single task. Sankara claims, "Our society is becoming mature and united and the [people] are beginning to understand and agree on the need for solidarity beyond the small family, tribal, or village cells. When the children from Ouagadougou and the women from Orodara raise funds to assist the victims of the Gorom-Gorom disaster . . . this is surely an eloquent sign. . . . When militants of the Revolutionary Defense Committees . . . from various provinces come together to build the Sourou canal or lay the rails for the Sahel railroads . . . they think of the whole of Burkina Faso."

Some of this boosterism is trying to talk away real problems. "In spite of the mobilization of our masses to move mountains [a paraphrase of Mao] we felt that we were still moving in lukewarm semidarkness," complains Sankara. It is often difficult to tell whether the "militants" are really volunteers or sullen victims of forced labor or if the prisoners being allegedly rehabilitated through work are actually being starved and tortured. Such realities often—but by no means always—stand behind the slogans and billboards of modern dictatorships.

Training people for national loyalty and responsibility is a necessary and desirable duty of the state. The people must become socially conscious and nationally conscious, able to look beyond their families, tribes, and regions to the needs of the nation as a whole. Thus, Sankara trumpets his revolution's social and psychological function: "Progress, true progress, would not have been achieved as long as man himself remained unchanged."

But the modern dictatorship wants to foster only activism that it closely directs. The regime's subjects frequently see their ruler's double standards and hypocrisy. Even criticism of the society can become a government monopoly: The state media may publicize abuses of power in order to purge individual officials and provide scapegoats. All such shortcomings are transmuted into propaganda for the regime since they are labeled as counterrevolutionary and temporary phenomena that will be eliminated by changing consciousness.

"We must root out . . . impersonators, opportunists, and hypocrites incapable of leading a consistent struggle," says Sankara. "It is among them that we find neofeudal . . . elements with base ambitions. . . . We must emphatically tell our military and paramilitary law enforcement forces that [they] cannot behave like the drunken, barbaric, repressive, and cruel agents of bygone times." We must "rid our forces of law and order of their repulsive image without harming their firmness and their vigilance."

Such talk and the action it sometimes—though not always—entails serve several purposes. The regime's misdeeds are rationalized since those who behave badly are by definition not true revolutionaries. There is an element of sincere effort to set up a self-correcting mechanism. Since there is no opposition, independent judiciary, or free press, the government tries to police itself. Such efforts almost always fail to end dictatorship's innate abuses—Khomeini's endless preaching of Islamic morality could not root out even clerical corruption—though they may curb the unbridled looting and humiliation of common people that wreck so many traditional dictatorships.

The leader thus faces a major paradox. He is attempting to convince the people to step forward, become active, complain when things go wrong, and refuse to become cynical about the revolution. Yet a citizen unprotected from powerful officials and liable to be called a traitor for the mildest deviation is likely to remain silent and passive. Most peasants will not complain if agents of the secret police are rude to them. But the tamed conformist participation that the regime seeks in order to mobilize support for itself is easier to organize. When leaders and policies are periodically denounced for failures, lose in factional battles or become victims of new coups, the masses are allowed some officially sanctioned revenge against some of their rulers.

The dictator's life is a dangerous, insecure one, and it is not surprising that he is obsessed with discovering and denouncing enemies. Sankara even anticipates criticism of paranoia and repression by charging that foreign conspirators "finance and arm counterrevolutionaries to attack us and then invoke human rights considerations."

The claim that critics are tools of imperialism fulfills both domestic and international purposes. Western leftists and many intellectuals remain silent lest they help the reactionary forces against the progressives. Some foreign journalists and scholars whitewash repressive and incompetent Third World regimes to avoid charges of racism. These groups often accept the governments' claims to represent the people's will.

Within the country itself the regime's cries of subversive conspiracies may be believed by many and sometimes are even true. Aside from fear and national pride, the regime's warn-

173

ings of subversion strike a responsive popular chord for another reason. It is easy to believe that undermining the current rulers is more likely to produce anarchy than improvement. The understandable fear of average people that things could be worse, in view of the destructiveness of civil war or constant changes in government, makes the incumbents' survival more acceptable if their rule is at all tolerable. In many cases the alternative leaders would not act any better if they actually gained power.

The dictator, of course, has no difficulty in choosing repression in order to survive. If political rivals or dissidents—in Sankara's words, "plotters and assassins"—are not crushed, "they would persist and threaten to overthrow our regime." So faintheartedness or half measures are unacceptable. The personal and collective, selfish and idealistic costs of defeat—death, exile, the loss of privileges, a reversal of the regime's achievements, the forfeiture of national independence—are too high to risk. "Comrades," concluded Sankara in his anniversary speech, "as you know, it is a matter of winning."

What Sankara is preaching—and the same sentiments can be found more or less articulately expressed by several dozen African and other Third World rulers like Qaddafi and Khomeini—is a hybrid philosophy adapted to the needs of developing countries and the requirements of modern dictators. It provides not only a set of words and symbols for speeches on revolutionary anniversaries but also a guide for the regimes' cadres and an inspiration for its citizens. The fact that the ideology is imposed does not necessarily vitiate its appeal. If the new ideas provide an interpretation of reality in accord with the population's experience and prior culture and belief, they may be widely accepted. In the dizzying progression of change and novelty brought on by even the smallest doses of modernization, many people are desperately seeking to understand what is happening to them.

The Third World radicalism of modern dictatorships tries to meet this demand by blending traditional loyalties with "scientific" interpretations of international relations and the prob-

174

lems of development. It tries to combine the ideas of immediate survival, progress in development, and a utopian goal.

First, the regime claims that only centralization, mobilization, and obedience to its directives can save the country. Otherwise, the state will be riven with civil strife; foreigners will destroy the nation's sovereignty and turn its culture into a pale imitation of the West. The leader is the symbol of national unity at home and the champion of the people standing up to powerful enemies abroad.

Second, unless all the national resources are organized and properly directed, there can be no hope of progress. An immediate dividend is won by expropriating the homegrown elite or foreign interests. For the long haul, however, the economy must be directed by the state (socialism).

Third, if this political and ideological road is properly followed, the result will be a powerful nation, respected (and feared) abroad; blessed and happy at home. Materially the people will enjoy the highest benefits; ethically the nation will be superior to the West and—depending on the specific country—the Soviet bloc as well. Culturally it will raise the existing mores to a higher level rather than abandon them.

The fact that such ideologies have not produced the promised results has by no means discredited them. Even if the regime's campaigns fizzle, large sectors of the people remain cynical, and economic mismanagement brings disaster, such politically useful ideas are not easily abandoned. The appeal of self-interest and idealism dictate continued efforts. Outsiders can often underestimate the effects of partial successes like slow but steady improvements in living standards, the promotions achieved by individuals, or the psychological benefits of pride and national self-respect.

If the USSR remains a Communist modern dictatorship after seventy years, one should not underestimate the strength of a roughly and theoretically comparable system in states like Mozambique, Angola, Zimbabwe, Benin, Burkina Faso, Ethiopia, and others. If it has done nothing else, the technique of modern dictatorship has taught how to gain and retain power, and for the leaders who use it, this is a great enough achievement to justify it.

In Africa modern dictators have come to power as founding fathers of new countries, as commanders of armed liberation movements against colonialism, or as leaders of coups. African military takeovers have differed in several ways from the Latin American pattern. Latin American militaries are professional, officers' loyalties are primarily to the institution and to the chain of command. African armies are often divided by ideology, ethnicity, and personal ambitions. In Africa and the Middle East colonial powers tended to recruit from smaller, marginal tribes and communities. Such soldiers had grievances against the indigenous ruling establishment and were tempted to use their guns to advance group interests. Officers who saw their elders quickly promoted after independence were impatient for advancement to the higher ranks. Consequently, they were willing and able to stage coups against each other.

When Flight Lieutenant Jerry Rawlings staged his 1979 coup in Ghana, for example, he executed several senior military officers, three of them former heads of state. Most of the takeovers in coup-ridden Nigeria have been against fellow soldiers. A would-be modern dictator can be somewhat less dependent on the army by becoming a civilian and seeking popular support as an alternative. But he must still keep a firm hold on the officer corps to avoid another coup.

The formula, perfected by Ethiopia's military regime, which took power in 1974, combined a revolutionary social policy (nationalization of land and industry, liquidation of the old ruling class), an ethnic base (Amhara tribe), an imitation of Marxism-Leninism, a close-knit group of officers (the Dergue junta), a charismatic leader (Colonel Mengistu Haile Mariam), the repression of all competitors (secessionist ethnic groups, leftist students), and tightly controlled party, media, and economy. In Ethiopia's case the regime's political survival also entailed its stealing foreign food aid from starving people during the famines of the 1980s to give soldiers, civil servants, and supporters.

No dictator can long forget that his principal problem is not how to bring overnight progress or democracy but how to survive the inevitable and tremendous social and economic problems. Usually no swift and satisfactory solution exists. The key issue for the Ethiopian rulers, for example, is to solve the problem of power, not starvation. African militaries all may rule by virtue of their weaponry and relatively disciplined organization, but the life span of an individual leader or junta depends on skill in holding on to power.

Economic disarray by itself does not cause a military coup or a dictator's fall; many African countries are in such dire straits most of the time. More important in triggering a coup is the failure of any one leader or political force to gain national hegemony. The independence leaders almost universally tried to use their broad popularity to establish modern dictatorships. Offsetting their advantages, however, was a lack of experience in controlling the military. They were most vulnerable in the early years, when a few hundred, even a few dozen, troops could catch them off guard. Mobutu took Zaire with 200 men; the anti-Nkrumah plotters had 500 reliable troops in an army of 10,000.

Another superficially appealing but ultimately erroneous expectation is that a junta is more likely to provide stable control than is a single leader. African militaries usually lack the cohesion to make a junta work very long. Ironically, this situation reinforces the chances of a modern dictator rather than a traditional one. An individual is hard put to control an African army without a communal and organizational base to inspire fear and loyalty in a larger group. Nigeria, so much bigger and more complex than Burkina Faso, shows how difficult it is to assemble a stable and legitimate ruling group under either a parliamentary democracy or a military junta.

Nigeria has 100 million people, 20 percent of the continent's population. On independence in 1960—before the discovery of extensive petroleum reserves—it had few developed resources but at least was able to feed itself. Apart from economic underdevelopment, tribal friction was its biggest problem. Among Nigeria's 400 linguistic groups, three major ethnic factions disputed power: the Muslim Hausa-Fulani in the north, the Ibo in the southeast, and the Yoruba in the southwest.

For the first six years after independence Nigeria retained the parliamentary system organized by the British. The era did not produce fond memories of electoral politics; it was a time of rigged elections, endless legal battles, bewildering shifts in political coalitions, sporadic violence, and revelations of corruption at every level. The three regions were each dominated by a tribal-based party that ran its domain like an ethnic ministate. The politicians were not only greedy but more localist than nationalist. Since the party system functioned in a divisive way—just as the advocates of one-party states charge—it was impossible to assemble a strong, widely accepted central government.

In January 1966 Nigeria's first coup, initiated by lower-ranking officers but quickly co-opted by the high command, occurred after the murder of many leading politicians. Although greeted with popular enthusiasm, the junta squandered this support because it had not yet learned how to rule and, far worse, was considered an Ibo front. A second coup led by northerners in July—they called it a "return match"—murdered the junta and put General Yakubu Gowon in power. The politically inexperienced Gowon could not bring the regional governors under control. About 20,000 Ibo were killed in massacres and the Ibo area seceded as the state of Biafra in May 1967.

In short, during its first political phase the army was the tool of battling ethnic groups (as in Uganda) and only further divided the country. The politically inexperienced officers understood little about how to rule and stay in power. By the time Biafra surrendered in 1970, an estimated 600,000 people, mostly civilians, had died. Thereafter, experience with the war's horror helped deter ethnic strife, the military's role in saving the nation legitimized its rule, and Nigeria's oil production strengthened the economy.

Gowon made many serious errors. His governors, many of them officers, were notoriously corrupt. After Gowon's fall almost all were convicted of embezzlement and bribe taking; nine of them were ordered to return loot totaling $16 million. Oil earnings brought inflation, expensive imported goods, and a breakdown in the harbor and transport systems. A controversial census to determine the size of tribal groups was bungled, and the regime broke its promise to return to civilian rule.

As the country became impatient with mismanagement, officers felt their reputations were damaged by the regime's poor performance. Still another coup overthrew Gowon in July 1975 and purged the civil service and military. The army had now learned to act decisively, in contrast with the two earlier juntas, but it also accepted the legitimacy of civilian rule. The generals allowed the formation of new parties and of a carefully crafted constitution combining a U.S.-style system with Nigerian guarantees against ethnic and regional strife. The new parliament convened in December 1976, and national elections brought to power a civilian president.

There was a bicameral legislature, an independent judiciary, elected state governors and assemblies, and thirteen daily newspapers to watch over the system. But there were also five parties, none of which enjoyed a majority. The difficult task of development was worsened by Nigeria's declining oil income and mounting debts. President Alhaji Shehu Shagari warned against expecting miracles, but Nigerians and foreign well-wishers at least thought the country would settle down under a beneficial democratic regime.

Honest men were increasingly hard to find as the poison of corruption permeated the society and paralyzed the civil service. Contracts cost the taxpayers twice as much as they should have to cover the cost of kickbacks to officials. Consequently, the number of development projects was drastically reduced, and hospitals, housing projects, and roads were left unfinished. Ironically, the free press increased popular disgust by showing the extent of fraud: illegal import-export transactions exceeding $6 billion, the mysterious disappearance of $2.5 billion allocated for import licenses, scandals surrounding construction of a new capital city, the disappearance of build-

ing supplies from warehouses, payments for nonexistent workers on government payrolls, fires that destroyed records, and
so on. Having more elected officials meant more people to be
paid off and more money to be skimmed off.

Family loyalty, personal greed, and the need of underpaid
civil servants to supplement their incomes had always resulted
in officials' pocketing a certain proportion of the national wealth.
Now the centralized state's control of vast resources and its
regulation of the economy provided vast new opportunities
for corruption. The influx of large amounts of oil money and
the presence of foreign companies willing to offer or required
to pay huge bribes transformed traditional, small-scale corruption into a paralyzing sickness. A democratic civilian government lacked the will or ability to prosecute thousands of
people in its bureaucracy and political coalition. New values
and controls did not exist to deter such overwhelming criminal
behavior, which weakens and discredits parliamentary democracies and traditional dictatorships alike at a particular
stage of development.

Shagari's reelection in 1983 was marred by widespread
accusations of fraud and police intimidation. Once again, in
December 1983, the army took over. This event marked a
third phase in Nigerian political history. Each coup had lowered the threshold for the next one. The army was no longer
hesitant about ruling—as were the earlier juntas—nor did it
see a return to civilian rule as the right and necessary step.
Two factors also strengthened the staying power of the military in government, if not the prospects of any particular junta.
Officers had reduced the problem of ethnic conflict within the
military by carefully balancing the distribution of power in the
juntas. The central government now had more power over
the regions because it controlled oil money.

These new attitudes were reflected by Major General Ibrahim Babangida, a key organizer of the 1983 coup who took
power himself two years later. "I think that each and every
one of us," he said of the junta members, "is quite conversant
with the way governments are run." Babangida made clear his
disgust with civilian rule: "The history of our nation had never

Kamal Ataturk, leader of
Turkey, 1922–1938.

President Gamal Abdel Nasser (right) meets fellow dictator, Indonesia's President
Sukarno, and China's Premier Chou en-Lai in 1965.

President Juan and Eva
Perón in 1951.

Emperor Haile Selassie of
Ethiopia as he promises
reform in a rare press
conference in 1974.

The Shah of Iran, pictured in full uniform, 1972.

Nicaraguan dictator President Anastasio Somoza in his role as hard-working plantation owner. Nicaragua was his plantation, 1955.

Philippines President Ferdinand Marcos gives an independence day speech in 1969.

Ugandan dictator President Idi
Amin.

Ghana's President Kwame Nkrumah (right) and Guinean President Sekou Toure at
a 1965 conference.

The personable Tanzanian President Julius Nyerere on the eve of his retirement in 1985.

Syrian President Hafez al-Assad.

Leader in the independence struggle and dictator of Mozambique, President Samora Machel, inveighs against bureaucracy and corruption, 1980.

Muammar al-Qaddafi at the
center of media attention in a
bedouin tent.

Ayatollah Ruhollah Khomeini of
Iran.

recorded the degree of indiscipline and corruption as in the period between October 1979 and December 1983."

In short, Nigeria seemed on the road to becoming a modern dictatorship. Yet the country was also something of a special case, since it had never produced an exceptionally charismatic leader or ideology. The armed forces are too large to be brought under control without massive battle and bloodshed. The complex tribal balance, mirrored by interest groups in the army, has required shaky coalitions within the military. Political parties have been so discredited as to make officers unwilling to establish a party of their own.

During the early years of Shagari's civilian rule, many commentators claimed the military's willingness to restore civilian control demonstrated that representative democracy is deeply ingrained in Nigerian society. But the Nigerian juntas show that electoral systems are not necessarily better—or even more popular—governors than are juntas. As one expert on the country, Larry Diamond, commented after the republic's fall, "What caused the coup was not the ambitions of the soldiers but the decay of the country under four and a quarter years of civilian rule."

There are no simple answers for Nigerians contemplating the relative advantages of civilian and military rule or comparing electoral democracy and the army's dictatorship. Neither system has worked well, but popular bitterness toward civilian politicians and parties made army rule seem preferable to anarchy. No one could easily argue that the military had run the country worse than the civilians, that civilian rule was the proper state of affairs, or that an electoral multiparty system would work in Nigeria. As one highly respected Nigerian intellectual put it, "At least the military limits its own corruption. The politicians seemed to be competing to see who could more thoroughly betray their sacred trust." Nigeria's history makes this kind of attitude understandable and explains why many Third World people find military rule and dictatorship as plausible as parliamentary government.

This growing self-assertion by the Nigerian military was matched and exceeded by the attitude of officers in other countries who found it easier than their Nigerian colleagues to rationalize their rule and maintain solidarity. The 1985 Nigerian coup was Africa's seventy-third since Ghana attained independence in 1957. Thirteen heads of state had been assassinated. As one of Babangida's fellow coup makers said in his broadcast announcing the Nigerian coup, "No nation has ever achieved meaningful strides in its development where there is absence of cohesion in the hierarchy of government." Without unity at the top, stability is impossible; without stability, increases in productivity and living standards are impossible.

The officers' answer to the problem of conflict among the political leadership is not to stop making coups but to consolidate their own unity so as to preserve military regimes. Whether the dictator dominates the army or is only first among equals, he must always watch over and extend the soldiers' privileges.

Samuel Doe, who led the coup in Liberia, speaking at the country's 1985 National Day celebration, called on Liberians to "become fully committed to all that is true, good, and beautiful. We must care for and sustain our spirit of national identity and togetherness." Doe had overturned a corrupt, oppressive civilian regime, dominated by the descendants of American slaves who had returned to Africa, and executed its leaders. He added, "This administration has maintained a commitment for the development of this country. . . . Consistent with this commitment, we had the occasion yesterday to dedicate the first communal home of our national police force. . . . We also look forward for the time when our men and women of the Armed Forces of Liberia will be beneficiaries of similar facilities." He would not repeat his predecessors' mistake of underpaying and mistreating soldiers, conditions that spurred Sergeant Doe himself to revolt.

While the junta's leadership is engaged in reshaping the armed forces, it also seeks to be recognized as the true defender of the state's sovereignty. Nationalism is the natural ideology for African military regimes. As soldiers they have built their careers on preserving the country from enemies, foreign and domestic. As rulers they want to make the decisions governing the state rather than bend to powerful foreigners. As an elite they want development to enrich the country and, thus, themselves. As leaders faced with a difficult and dangerous task they want unity and a sense of national identity to make their jobs easier and their tenures longer. As administrators they detest outside pressures, which frequently come from multinational institutions like the International Monetary Fund, to adopt fiscally sound but unpopular and disruptive economic policies. Moreover, nationalism has a tremendous appeal to the urban and rural masses. Even socialism is largely presented as a way of strengthening national unity and promoting progress.

In contrast with Middle Eastern dictatorships, however, this radical nationalism is directed toward domestic change rather than used as an excuse for expansionism. Africans are too busy with development to think seriously about aggression against neighbors. The two examples in which troops were sent across borders for such purposes—Idi Amin's invasion of Tanzania and Somalia's attempt to conquer portions of Ethiopia—ended in such disasters as to discourage imitation.

Social radicalism, like nationalism, is also shaped by domestic requirements. The style and rhetoric of Marxist militancy suit the basic objectives of those like Sankara or Rawlings who are in no way Communists. It provides a theory of governance, a route for development, and a set of symbols. The imitations can be seen in the Ethiopian junta's self-conscious modeling on the Bolshevik Revolution, the renaming of Congo-Brazzaville as the People's Republic of the Congo, Ghana's Committee for the Defense of the Revolution, the hammer and sickle and AK-47 assault rifle that adorns Mozambique's flag, and the profusion of ruling workers' parties in countries with tiny or nonexistent proletariats. Marx's theory and the USSR's Leninist-Stalinist institutions are a treasure chest through which African leaders can rummage for useful tools and weapons to consolidate and justify their rule.

This pattern gives rise to the ironic development that such regimes' left wings, usually Marxist intellectuals, have the biggest aversion to democratic participation since they accept the Leninist idea that top-down rule is necessary. Militants in Tanzania, for example, argued in the 1960s that any competitive elections, even with TANU members as the sole candidates, threatened domestic security.

The TANU militants' underlying idea—rejected by Nyerere but central to most modern dictatorships—is to replace any shred of real consultation of the people themselves with the party hierarchy's decisions. This is the deeper significance of the term so often used by quasi-Marxist Third World regimes, "scientific socialism." If Marxism—or the local regime's ideology—is a science for directing government and society, then it is as necessary for modernization as any other type of science or technology. In such circumstances, public opinion is no more useful than would be taking a vote to solve some problem in chemistry or physics.

Marx and Lenin even warned that the ballot box had a negative effect on revolutionary progress. To Marx, most people failed to understand the true nature of their society because of false consciousness. Lenin predicted that workers would always choose "economism," an improvement in their wages and conditions, rather than revolution unless prodded, organized, and led by a vanguard party. His Third World successors argued that peasants and others would choose economic development without social transformation. The masses must be told, not asked, what they required. These Third World leaders not only believed that social revolution was preferable but also considered it a precondition for successful economic development or even true national independence.

By the 1980s the economic argument of radicalism had been badly battered. Some states, most notably China, decided that dramatic internal reforms were needed to unleash the initiative and creativity of the people. More concluded that a greater receptivity to Western investment and technology would be sufficient. But none of them was willing to abandon either the political power that radical ideology justified centralizing in their hands or the institutions that helped guarantee their continued rule.

Mozambique provides an interesting example of these developments. Stretched along the southeast edge of Africa, Mozambique was a Portuguese colony for 400 years. Its beautiful port cities flourished for the hundreds of thousands of Portuguese settlers, but the interior was left undeveloped. The black Africans fought a ten-year guerrilla war, gaining control of large numbers of villages and rural areas. Finally, a coup by Portugal's exhausted army produced a government in Lisbon eager to divest itself of the costly, troublesome colonies.

On June 24, 1975, came Mozambique's epiphany. At Machava Stadium in Laurenço Marques people embraced as the country's flag was officially raised for the first time. Veteran militants, the widows of national martyrs, and representatives of other movements who dreamed of their own independence day marched in review. Receptions, street theater, and celebrations turned the modern city into a festival. Eyes filled with tears as the new president, Samora Machel, intoned the revolution's motto, *La Lutta continua* ("The struggle continues").

From the very beginning the leaders of Frelimo, the Mozambique Liberation Front, had known that while the guerrilla struggle against the Portuguese was the first part of the battle, the problems of independence were its continuation. In 1971 Marcelino dos Santos, vice-president of Frelimo (and later vice-president of Mozambique), explained, "Our goal from the beginning has been to achieve victory in the struggle for national liberation . . . but [one] which at the same time would enable us to create a really new society."

In this two-front war, liberation was a way station to creating a "new man" and a successfully developing, egalitarian state. Continued dos Santos: "We have to create relationships of perfect identification between the fighters and the population, and between the leaders and the guerrillas." The liberated zones would be the new state in embryo.

But there was a profound difference between the way Frelimo governed the areas it controlled during the independence war and how it behaved afterward. In the first stage, rule was decentralized and participatory. Villages chose their own councils, which had a great deal of autonomy from the

Frelimo leadership. Of course, the movement—the single party in embryo—lacked the time and personnel to institute tight control and needed the peasants' support against the Portuguese.

In 1977, at Frelimo's third congress, it adopted scientific socialism as the guiding ideology and condemned the idea that Mozambique might have its own interpretation of Marxism. Now "dynamizing groups" of party supporters were established to mobilize the villages, and these cells were soon to take over control of their local areas. Not only were nonparty people and democratic decision making excluded, but even the party cadre lacked any independent role. Their job was to implement the policy made from above.

At the top, Samora Machel, Mozambique's president until his death in an October 1986 plane crash, introduced centralized planning modeled on Cuban and Eastern European practices. State farms replaced the communal cooperatives that gave peasants more control and benefits. "Commandism" replaced populist democracy; the theory was, as in so many other places, that the state would give orders and the people would produce the results.

Obviously only the government could run the industrial and service enterprises abandoned by Portuguese settlers since there was no other organization capable of doing so. But the destruction of the independent peasantry or small-business sector—which the regime's Marxist ideology distrusted as petty bourgeois— mangled the already hard-pressed economy. As has frequently been observed in the USSR and China as well as in the Third World, peasants will work harder and produce more for themselves than as employees of the state. Decisions made by bureaucrats in the capital will be less effective than those of the experienced farmers on the scene.

Within a few years the combination of the inefficient system, drought, a guerrilla war launched by South African-aided dissidents, and Moscow's unwillingness to provide more aid and military support brought the regime to serious straits. Debts grew, the state-owned "people's stores" were empty, tourism disappeared, and red tape blocked corrective action.

The country moved away from strict import substitution. "Our government doesn't have to make match boxes," said Machel.

In 1982, the government moved toward a rapprochement with the West in order to obtain aid. Frelimo's fourth congress, in April 1983, decided to decentralize economic planning and to put more emphasis on family farming rather than on state farms. A new investment code offered foreign companies safeguards against nationalization and guaranteed their right to transfer profits abroad in hard currency. To handle its debt situation, Mozambique became a member of the International Monetary Fund. In an effort to stop the disruptive guerrillas, it even went so far as to make a deal with South Africa, the political equivalent of the devil.

The economic evolution was both promising and surprisingly easy. Mozambique has extensive mineral resources and agricultural potential. Multinational companies, which once would have been frightened off by the regime's rhetoric, were now hesitant only because they questioned its ability to repress opposition. They had learned that joint ventures or contracts with the government could be as lucrative as any old-style wholly owned mine, plantation, or factory.

Machel turned himself into a salesman for Mozambique with the same drive and enthusiasm that had made him such a successful guerrilla leader. He dined with Ronald Reagan and harangued, teased, encouraged, and even embraced corporate executives. In turn, businessmen already involved in Mozambique treated him with a deference, flattery, and submissive bearing that reversed the traditional relationship between colonizer and colonized.

The government's special inducement was low-cost, cooperative labor (no strikes allowed). But companies did not invest since Mozambique could not provide another prerequisite—a stable security situation—as a result of the operations of South African-backed guerrillas. In general, however, corporations were discovering that doing business under socialism could be even better than dealing with a less predictable capitalist system. The Third World host's independence would be safeguarded by the regime's own power, share in the enterprises, and option to play off a variety of investing companies.

By the 1980s, then, some modern dictatorships adjusted their economic policies when radical theories of economic development did not work. Those like Zambia (copper) or Ghana (cacao), which were dependent on a single export product (except for oil, the price of which, though falling, could be somewhat buoyed by the producers' cartel, OPEC), and those which stubbornly clung to the "pure" socialist system, like Tanzania, did badly. Other countries made an economic opening to the West with varying degrees of success.

The essential point is that these economic decisions had limited or no effect on the political structures of Third World modern dictatorships. As Mao Zedong had said, they would keep "politics in command." To show that economic policy would not be deterministic, these regimes resisted pluralism, free speech, or any detraction from the power of the leader, single party, and government.

In fact, they argued that allowing some greater role in economic decision making to foreign corporations and to managers or peasants at home required renewed vigilance on the political front. An influx of Western fashions or music was allowed, though often limited, but any deeper contamination would be fought. These regimes were making a wager: For the sake of development (or to avoid economic collapse), they would bet that private agricultural plots, small private urban enterprises, and foreign participation would not undermine their own systems.

Although in the long run these governments might prove to be wrong, economic changes have so far not produced political shifts in countries like Mozambique. One of Machel's aides, at an international conference, gave a Marxist political speech in the country's lingua franca, Portuguese, and then shifted to English for a talk on the economy. He explained, "Our [Marxist] ideology governs our country, English is the language of international capitalism." The modern dictators' regimes believe the separation can be maintained, and their chances of doing so should not be underestimated.

In the days when it was still called Dahomey, the country now known as the People's Republic of Benin was probably Africa's most chronically unstable country. A 1972 coup brought to power Ahmed Mathieu Kerekou, who established a modern dictatorship complete with a People's Revolutionary party. In the 1980s he began reversing his earlier nationalizations. "A pilot can land his plane from any direction, east or west," Kerekou told a party congress, "and there are different ways of maneuvering a plane towards the airfield." He certainly intends to remain at the controls. Similarly, the People's Republic of the Congo, led by Denis Sassou-Nguesso and his Congolese Workers' party, adopted Marxism as its official ideology. In the face of slumping growth, the regime rebuilt relations with France; most of its oil was sold to U.S. companies. But foreign investment and a mixed economy did not erode the rule of the regime's politburo. The sloganeering billboards in red lining the road to the capital—"The five-year plan is everyone's business"; "Earn your daily bread through work"—probably do not inspire much idealism. Nevertheless, the regime's ideology and institutions are all that transcend the country's quilt of tribes and local loyalties.

Nationalism is a vital and constant factor in the definition of the modern dictatorships' foreign policies. It is genuinely felt by the leaders themselves and is usually the one really effective ideology in their countries. One day Mozambicans, Syrians, and Nicaraguans may see themselves as Marxists, but now the average government supporter defines himself as a patriot. Even if the people have no say in choosing the regime, it remains "their" government in a passionate sense, particularly when memories of foreign rule are still fresh.

Thus, despite its Marxism and imitation of Soviet institutions, Frelimo's nationalism made it refuse Moscow permanent military facilities. Soviet bloc advisers are more acceptable than bases because the regime believes that it can control them. Mozambique—and Angola, Nicaragua, Ethiopia, South Yemen, Libya, and other left-oriented modern dictatorships—welcome thousands of Soviet, Cuban, and East German soldiers and secret police technicians. When local pilots are lacking, Soviet bloc substitutes can fill in. If the leader does not completely trust his own colleagues to refrain from staging a coup, foreigners can be sprinkled through the intelligence apparatus to keep an eye on them.

Obviously precautions are taken to keep these outsiders from dictating which coups triumph or who succeeds to the leadership, but such checks are not necessarily dependable. Secret internal political leverage is a real danger posed by Soviet involvement in Third World states, but as the United States has learned, this strategy can sometimes backfire. Moscow did not endear itself to Anwar al-Sadat, for example, by sponsoring a rival leadership faction. The KGB recruits agents among the local cadre, providing money to the venal and promises of political support to the ambitious. Modern dictators are aware of these dangers and have expelled Russian influence—in Egypt, Somalia, Sudan, Guinea—or kept it strictly limited—in Syria, Libya, and radical African states—when the occasion required.

Still, while the economic gamble opens up the door to Western influence, the security gamble can make modern dictatorships dangerously subject to Soviet manipulation. It is not easy to decide which of these two types of leverage is more powerful, and perhaps the answer depends on whether a regime is more worried about economic collapse or military disintegration.

Soviet bloc assistance has saved a number of regimes from the latter fate. It enabled Ethiopia to defeat a Somalian invasion and to hold off internal insurgencies, and it maintains the Angolan modern dictatorship against highly motivated rebels. Moscow is the primary arms supplier for Syria and Libya, gives Cuba security guarantees against U.S. pressure, exercises impressive leverage over South Yemen, and actually invaded Afghanistan to save the Marxist government there from its own people.

The Soviets are not personally popular even in the most closely allied Third World states. Unlike the Cubans, they are thought to be arrogant and racist. They do not mix well, if they mix at all, with the local people. Still, the need for Soviet help to survive and to some extent the links provided by parallel ideologies mean that modern dictatorships' relationships with the USSR are not based on personalities. Mozambique, Iraq, and other countries will seek Western aid and superior technology, but they generally will be unwilling to compromise their politically and strategically valuable ties with the Soviets to do so.

Economically the Soviet bloc is certainly a disappointment. Despite all the talk of fraternity and cooperation against imperialism, Soviet behavior is often blatantly imperialist. It grabs Ethiopian coffee, Somalian meat, Mozambican fish at low prices—even reselling them on international markets for hard currency—and overcharges for its oil and arms. Advisers sometimes have to be paid by the host states. These countries find themselves increasingly in debt to Moscow. One factor in Egyptian President Sadat's 1972 decision to break with Moscow was the neat escape it gave him from repaying these massive debts.

At first glance, then, if the Soviets sell Ethiopia arms and the Americans give food to its starving people, the Ethiopian regime should be more grateful to the United States. In the framework of a modern dictatorship, however, this is not at all logical. The regime views the arms as a higher priority to keep itself in power. The people are not consulted; much of the famine relief is diverted to ensure the loyalty of the military and the bureaucracy. Sometimes the masses are not even told that the food aid, in fact, comes from the United States.

Ethiopia is, indeed, a fascinating example, showing how modern dictatorships are formed and the factors shaping their foreign and internal policies. Like Iran, Ethiopia underwent a deep and thoroughgoing revolution that destroyed an entrenched system of traditional dictatorship and replaced it with a modern dictatorship. The army played the principal role in this process, and Mengistu Haile Mariam, son of an enlisted man and a servant, shot his way into its leadership.

After overthrowing Emperor Haile Selassie in 1974, the military went through the "onion-peel" politics that so often characterizes Third World political struggles. One after another, the factions belonging to the original coalition of armed forces' and civilian groups were defeated and discarded until a single leader had assembled a base of power. The dictator then had to protect his own support from this erosion principle—the falling out of personalities, ethnic groups, classes, and ideologies—by institutionalizing it.

The arena in which the battle for control was fought out was the Dergue, the junta that took over in 1974. Its first chairman, General Aman Andom, was murdered after a majority of the Dergue decided his policies were too soft. Over the next few years Mariam similarly eliminated other rivals as the Dergue was reduced in size by the purges. Marxism, adapted to African conditions and military rule, was his organizing tool and rationale for seizing control.

The junta launched a "national democratic revolution"— in Marxist theory a transitional stage to the "dictatorship of the proletariat," in which the Communist vanguard makes a temporary alliance with the peasants and middle class. True to this blueprint, the junta seized large enterprises and the property of the aristocracy while distributing land to the peasantry.

The regime neutralized the old ruling classes through its nationalization and repression. Some members of the aristocracy were executed; many more fled the country. Those who stayed were deprived of their wealth. While the National Resources and Development Ministry, formed to manage the businesses taken over, did not do a very effective job, it certainly guaranteed that control of those resources stayed in government hands.

To reward, mobilize, and monitor the urban population, the Dergue established neighborhood committees called the *kebeles*. The value of this type of arrangement for a modern dictatorship is shown by its widespread use in countries as diverse as Iran (*Komitehs*), Cuba (Committees for the Defense of the Revolution), Iraq, Nicaragua, and elsewhere. Like these other groups, the *kebeles* collect rent on nationalized homes, provide local justice and police services, and run stores. The leader of each committee is a specially trained cadre (given courses in Marxism-Leninism), and the lower committees elect higher *kebeles* up to the level of a mayor. While there is some elective function, choice of the officials is firmly in the regime's hands.

Kebeles can punish their constituents—they furnish the rulers' eyes and ears in every neighborhood—and their patrols have license to shoot curfew violators or lawbreakers. But these groups also award compliance and build loyalty for the regime. If farmers do not provide enough food, the *kebeles* send trucks into the countryside to seize crops. In the face of shortages and long lines, the *kebeles* supply activists with necessities and luxuries and carry out social welfare programs. Bringing a sense of solidarity and cooperation among the urban poor, the *kebele* and other mass organizations give them a sense that they can improve their lot and control their destiny—at least as long as they accept the regime's overall authority and directives. Inculcating these attitudes, in turn, is a prerequisite for both economic development and political mobilization.

The *kebele* may maintain playgrounds and kindergartens while teaching the children military drill and the government's ideology. It forces shopkeepers to keep prices down and punishes hoarding. In short, it is the microcosm of the modern dictatorship, mixing repression and rewards to ensure the regime's control and survival. It is an institution beyond the imagination of a traditional dictatorship and far more effective than even the most lavishly financed old-fashioned secret police organization.

The regime was particularly successful in winning support from the peasantry with its land reform program. Sharecroppers who formerly paid most of their crops as rent gained their lifelong dream of having their own land, particularly in the southern part of Ethiopia. Government policies canceled the peasants' debts and set higher prices for their produce. More than 24,000 peasant associations, slightly more democratic than the *kebeles*, were formed to administer rural life and local cooperatives. Reluctantly, though wisely, the regime limited attempts at forced collectivization, which would have met strong resistance. Those forced to migrate from famine areas were bitter but were also too weak and desperate to protest.

High school and college students were sent into the countryside to implement a literacy campaign, build schools and health clinics and dig wells. Such programs not only provided material benefits for the peasants but also allowed the idealism of young people to be used in a socially constructive way from the standpoint of the regime.

Those students and intellectuals who had their own ideas about the revolution's direction, however, were another matter entirely. The soldiers needed their organizational and technical skill, even their mastery of the approved ideology, but were not eager to share power. Fortunately for the Dergue the Marxist groups, many of whose members returned from abroad after the revolution, were divided.

One such group, the Ethiopian People's Revolutionary party (EPRP), opposed the Dergue, launched an urban guerrilla warfare campaign, and was violently repressed in an orgy of mutual killings. Its rival, the All-Ethiopian Socialist Movement, worked with the Dergue, running the Provisional Office for Mass Organizational Affairs, which helped create the *kebeles*, peasant associations, and the ruling Marxist party. When this work was completed, and the EPRP eliminated, the regime also arrested, tortured, and killed many of the Socialist Movement's leaders.

One of the collaborating Marxists' most important tasks was the subordination of the trade union movement. When union federation leaders called for a people's republic, civil liberties, and the right to demonstrate and strike, they were arrested and their organizations were dissolved. A new All-Ethiopia Labor Union, subservient to the government, was created.

Thus, while the Ethiopian regime faced a number of serious problems—famine, regional revolt, serious debt, a virtual freeze on economic development, and others—an irreversible revolution had been carried through and a powerful modern dictatorship had been established. Even if Mariam himself were overthrown, the regime's style and structure would likely continue. The revolution had entrenched a new type of system and set Ethiopia on a different course.

The Ethiopian regime is far more rigid and brutal than the postindependence government in Zimbabwe, which still has a nominally parliamentary system. Nevertheless, the political and intellectual frameworks of the two states come from the same mold. After the white settlers in the British colony of Rhodesia had issued a unilateral declaration of independence in 1965, a guerrilla war gradually developed, particularly after 1973, between the white minority and the black nationalist movements. The conflict was finally resolved by a British-brokered agreement, and Rhodesia became independent Zimbabwe in 1978. While the Portuguese fled Mozambique and Angola, a majority of whites—including the highly productive commercial farmers—stayed on in newly independent Zimbabwe, where their rights were safeguarded by a constitution reserving 20 percent of the seats in parliament for them.

Zimbabwe's leader, Prime Minister Robert Mugabe, was a fascinating blend of characteristics. In contrast with the murderous Mengistu Haile Mariam, Mugabe had a legalistic side. Compared to the flamboyant Machel, he was introspective, even cold. Like both of them, Mugabe was a type of Marxist, but he was also a practicing Catholic.

While Zimbabwe's flag was almost identical to Mozambique's, it had a bird in place of Machel's AK-47. Observing neighboring Mozambique's economic disaster, Mugabe was cautious about implementing revolutionary changes and wanted to avoid driving out the economically useful whites. Mugabe's armed struggle had been diverted to the ballot box and council chamber by British mediation. But the resulting constitutional restraints—parliamentary representation for the tribal and white minorities—also brought him some unique constraints for an African leader.

Zimbabwe took so long to gain its independence because the white settlers were willing to fight a prolonged war for their own continued rule and because of deep divisions among the black Africans themselves. The two liberation movements—Mugabe's Zimbabwean African National Union (ZANU) and Joshua Nkomo's Zimbabwean African People's Union (ZAPU)—were unable to unite primarily because of tribal divisions. ZANU had overwhelming support among the majority Shona people of the north and east; ZAPU held the loyalty of the Ndebele tribe of the south and west. In elections, ZANU was bound to gain a large parliamentary majority, but ZAPU won all the Ndebele seats. The political role of the Ndebele and whites did not stop Mugabe from ruling but made it difficult for him to impose one-party rule.

Although ZANU predominance was beyond question, Mugabe and his party did not feel secure but only more determined to institutionalize their political monopoly. Instead of seeking a compromise with the Ndebele, the ZANU regime appointed its own men—usually Shona—to posts in the Ndebele regions. A relentless pressure was kept up on ZAPU, with Nkomo constantly in danger of arrest and many of his colleagues thrown into prison. The result was the return of many ZAPU fighters to the bush and a consequent escalation by the government side. Troops in pursuit of the guerrillas brutalized Ndebele villagers.

After the July 1985 parliamentary elections, when ZANU won almost all the black seats (63) except for 15 in the Ndebele region, members of its youth league beat up, clubbed, and expelled opposition supporters from the capital, Harare. One ZANU activist explained, "These people must not stay here any more. Their parties have been beaten and beaten well. There is no space for them in the one-party state." Here was the real tribalist sentiment lying behind the rhetoric of a united people. Having "lost" the struggle, the Ndebele had no rights, though fortunately Mugabe was mild-mannered enough not to kill or long imprison many of their leaders.

Zimbabwe prospered economically. By allowing white family farms to go on earning foreign exchange, Mugabe had to go more slowly on land reform, but there was still a good deal of land and plenty of jobs in the bureaucracy to give supporters. Psychologically the joy of national independence and black rule provided an impressive political dividend as well.

It was still surprising how quickly ZANU officials, despite their reference to each other as comrade and their radical rhetoric, formed a new privileged elite. As elsewhere in the Third World, the Mercedes-Benz was their symbol. They bought up the houses and farms of departing whites, often using government funds for the purpose. Mugabe denounced those who "preach socialism by day and practice capitalism by night." Like most modern dictators, Mugabe was not personally corrupt, but he needed the support of many men who were less fastidious or less easily satisfied with the exercise of power as an end in itself. Despite a leadership code which, as in Tanzania, prohibited officials from having outside business interests or income-earning property, no one was forced to quit office or sell his assets.

In a major July 1985 speech, Mugabe amplified his philosophy of government, an archetypal one for modern dictatorships. "We are one family, one country with one nation, one government. And so we must have one party. It's that simple. . . . We believe in the inexorable law of unity: You must be united or else you can be divided and perish."

The continued existence of an organized opposition, Mugabe declared, only encouraged resistance to the regime. "Without ZAPU, without the dissident elements, they [the Ndebele] will fall in line." In short, the way to eliminate conflict within the country was to repress those voicing complaints— a philosophy basic to all dictatorships and abhorrent to the democratic viewpoint.

Mugabe's refusal to seek unity through compromise and concessions to the minority threatens Zimbabwe with future bloodshed. Yet he was acting within the political framework of modern dictatorship under the assumption that given the opportunity, the opposition would be equally merciless. There was a populist side to his policy as well: Dividing the spoils with another group would reduce the resources he could distribute to his own followers. Thus, Mugabe was also right. Either he would break the Ndebele's power or the Ndebele (or rival Shona politicians who would take a more chauvinistic anti-Ndebele line) would displace him.

Radical African regimes were based on just such a manipulation of popular sentiments and distribution of resources. Since these regimes were still very much in the building stage, their dictators had to mobilize supporters among both the elite and masses through bribery, organization, ideology, nationalism, and fear. Since the problems faced were so difficult, even insurmountable, the extravagant promises of demagoguery and the cruel victimization of scapegoats often seemed a necessity for political survival.

All else failing, the revolutionaries' deep belief in the power of words and theories hypnotized them into believing in their own success. In the regime's rhetoric, everything up to independence or the rise of the new regime was one long night of exploitation and oppression; everything since is glorious. Each success is due to the revolution; every failure is the fault of its enemies. New laws promise freedoms never delivered; the leader's speeches pledge benefits never to materialize. Yet this role-playing serves a real political purpose particularly since the other side of the story is edited out of the regime's statistics, schools, and media. In the best tradition of George Orwell's novel *Nineteen Eighty-four*, the Ministry of National Guidance becomes one of the most powerful government agencies. The modern dictatorships have, in fact, guided their countries to national independence and relatively improved the lot of some of their people. Patriotism, desire for stability and fear of anarchy, traditional attitudes toward the sacrosanct nature of leaders and unity, the focusing of repression and corruption, demagoguery and overspending, plus the feeling that the nation is marching toward progress, help cement support for the regime. The laxness of regulations, the extent of nepotism, corruption, and the central government's weak control in the outlying provinces all provide citizens with a great deal of breathing space that would not exist in a "totalitarian" state.

Similar considerations apply for the Middle Eastern modern dictatorships, to which we now turn. In no other part of the world is the institution so widespread and deeply entrenched to the point that any other form of government has become almost unimaginable.

198

CHAPTER EIGHT

Middle East: System Makers and World Shakers

The terrible sun, far redder than in more temperate climes, rises all at once, and in a moment the heat is everywhere. The land it illuminates with razor-sharp light is some of the most desolate on earth. A broad, lazy river, the Shatt al Arab, produces little that is green or prosperous, even though this area along the Iran-Iraq border forms one tip of the Fertile Crescent.

Although there are date palm plantations on both sides of the river—their unharvested fruit squishes underfoot as you walk—they soon give way on the eastern, Iranian shore to long-dried, cracked mud. On the western, Iraqi side are reed swamps, flooded by the Iraqis in an attempt to block an Iranian advance. Fighting over this seemingly forsaken land has killed or maimed more than 1 million people since the Iran-Iraq War began in the autumn of 1980, including teen-aged Iranian volunteers who marched forward through mine-fields to clear them.

The passionate hatred and iron commitment among both Iranians and Iraqis have a number of causes, including centuries-old Arab-Persian suspicions and the inflammable friction between the Shiite branch of Islam, which dominates Iran, and the Sunni branch, to which Iraq's rulers belong. Ethnic and nationalist patriotism grows from their clashing histories, identities, and cultural differences. Yet patriotism and religious passions are intertwined with support for their leaders and governments. Rulers in Baghdad and Tehran have built an ideology, proregime institutions, and achievements to reinforce loyalty, with a certainty of punishment when popular support wears thin. Ayatollah Ruhollah Khomeini's Islamic Republic of Iran and President Saddam Hussein's Baath party state in Iraq have shown themselves equally capable of harnessing mass support and destroying dissenters.

The contemporary Middle East is a stronghold of modern dictators, men whose energy, cleverness, and ruthlessness have enabled them to master their countries. Muammar al-Qaddafi in Libya, Khomeini in Iran, Hussein in Iraq, and Hafez al-Assad in Syria constructed populist, repressive regimes able to tame some of the world's most turbulent and violent political systems. To stay atop the tiger, they must have an ideology acceptable to their cultures, a party and mass organizations furnishing a wide base of supporters, and an energetic secret police to break up antigovernment conspiracies. To ensure its financial and military power, the regime must also dominate the economy and control the army. Anyone who can accomplish this Herculean task must be a tough political realist. The Middle East dictators are even more ambitious since they claim to have discovered a proper ethical and political system for the entire region or even the whole world.

With his eclectic philosophy, aggressive foreign policy, and subsidies for terrorism, Qaddafi has made himself an international figure far beyond Libya's tiny population of only 2 million people. Khomeini ridiculed the idea that the Iranian Revolution was conducted for material advantage—in his contemptuous words, "to lower the price of housing or watermelons"—but rather attributed it to an effort to fulfill Islamic values and to show the way to the oppressed throughout the world. The Baath party, the quarreling factions of which rule in Syria and Iraq, and Nasser had only slightly more modest goals. They wanted to promote revolutions to unite all the Arabs, from Morocco's Atlantic shore to far Oman on the Indian Ocean. If these leaders are brutal as well as visionary, it is because they are simply acting on their own experience of the Middle East's unusual political framework.

The very first anecdote usually told to students of the Middle East is the story of the scorpion and the frog that one day find themselves on a riverbank. The scorpion asks the frog to carry him across to the other shore.

"Don't be ridiculous," answers the frog. "If I let you on my back, you'll sting me."

But the scorpion points out that he cannot swim and if he were to sting the frog in midriver, "we both would drown."

So the frog, persuaded by the logic of the argument, allows the scorpion to climb on his back, and they set out into the river. When they reach the middle, however, the scorpion stings the frog and the paralyzed amphibian starts to sink beneath the water. "Why did you do that?" he croaks. "Now we'll both die."

"Oh, well"—the scorpion sighs, shrugging his carapace—"after all, this is the Middle East."

Middle East politics are, as the fable suggests, violent and vengeful, but they are not so irrational. In the regional context, realpolitik requires something quite different from Western practice. Foreign policy functions to consolidate internal support by playing on populist themes. The behavior of Arab leaders has been shaped by a set of powerful ruling values. They are supposed to be militant Arab nationalists, supportive of Islam, and opposed to Western influence and to Israel. Even terrorism is accepted widely as a reasonable weapon to use in these causes. When a crazed Egyptian soldier in the Sinai murdered seven Israeli tourists, mostly children, in cold blood in 1985, a number of governments and movements were ready to proclaim him a hero. On the level of high policy Nasser marched into a disastrous defeat in 1967 and Saddam Hussein made his ruinous invasion of Iran in 1980 as the result of considerations of internal and regional politics. Both leaders were trying to prove to domestic audiences and rivals alike their strength and determination in combating the enemies of Islam and Arabism.

Yet most of these dictators temper ideology with caution. When Muammar al-Qaddafi took over Libya in 1969, Egyptian President Gamal Abdel Nasser dispatched a confidant, the famous journalist Mohamed Heikal, to Libya. Heikal returned with startling news. "It's a catastrophe," he told his president. Why? asked Nasser. Is he against us? No, much worse, retorted Heikal, he's for us! But Qaddafi's naïveté made him far more dangerous than if he were an enemy. He was "shockingly innocent—scandalously pure." These are not characteristics usually ascribed to Qaddafi, but Heikal's point was that the Libyan leader's true belief in Pan-Arabism and regionwide revolution would make him take too many risks to be helpful in achieving these goals or in pursuing Egypt's interests.

Heikal's possibly apocryphal story is partly cynical and partly admiring. Dictators in the Arab world (and in Iran) act rationally most of the time—if one understands the structure of their rationality. They act in accord with domestic and regional political needs rather than behave as the West might think proper. These modern dictators face very exacting demands from Islam and from Arab nationalism and are simultaneously manipulators and prisoners of the powerful symbols of these politics. Heikal disdains Qaddafi as a fanatic who is more the slave than the master of these principles, but he also recognizes that the Libyan leader's very extremism allows him to use Arab and Islamic symbols against more moderate Egypt.

For most of the last 1,300 years much of the Middle East has been at least nominally united under one Islamic ruler or another. Division, brought on by internal decay and external intervention (the Crusades, European imperialism), means decline, weakness, and foreign domination. To overcome this problem requires unity under a great political and military leader. Saladin defeated the Crusaders; the modern Arab nationalists hoped to drive out the West and its influence. Arabs also sought models in romantic nationalist movements that united fragmented countries (Germany and Italy) and in ideologies (Marxism and fascism) believed to have built strong states.

New concepts were called upon to revive old dreams. If the unity of Muslims as one people and of Arabs as one nation were essential elements of the golden age when Arab culture, science, and military power had been in advance of Europe, then perhaps their renewal was the missing ingredient needed to revive the Arabs' power and superiority. Twentieth-century anti-imperialism blended smoothly with Muslims' profound suspicion to non-Islamic societies and resentment at their power; modern nationalism reinforced their existing belief in Arab and Islamic superiority. In short, the newly imported ideas were all the more quickly accepted and adapted because they matched existing needs and traditions.

Islam, the religion of the overwhelming majority of people in the Arab states and Iran, is not merely a set of beliefs about God but also a very specific program for individual behavior and social organization. It sets high standards, demanding a state that promotes social justice and promulgates laws in accord with the Islamic code. Although some of its precepts constrain development, Islam has generally adopted itself to dealing with new technology and industrialization as long as they can be fitted into its rules of conduct and society. The Muslim clergy once denounced radio and movies; now they want to make Islamic films and programs.

Beginning in the 1930s and reaching its apex with Nasserism, Arab nationalism played a more important role than did Islam in defining political identity and options. It demanded a struggle for Arab unity, the removal of non-Arab influences and Israel's destruction, economic progress, and military might.

But there is, in all this, an inherent contradiction: reality does not match expectation. Walid Khalidi, professor and political activist, wrote, "The manifest failure even to approximate unity does not negate the empirical reality of the Arab Nation. The Arab Nation both is, and should be one." But in fact, the theoretically fraternal Arab leaders and states struggle against one another as often as against anyone else. If Arab states are merely, in Khalidi's words, "interim caretakers" for the Arab nation and if the existing frontiers are "illusory and permeable," being the ruler of one of these fragments in and of itself accumulates only limited respect.

Consequently, those in power in Arab countries faced a complex, delicate series of decisions. In daily practice their primary concern was to be for their own territories. Egypt and Iraq, Jordan and Saudi Arabia, Syria and Libya had to operate in regard to different kinds of capacities and problems. Pragmatic considerations often potentially violated Islamic and Arab nationalist precepts. For example, a regime might need Western support to counter the aggression of another Arab state. These necessities, however, had no explicit legitimacy within the framework of Arab politics and ideology.

Thus were set the rules of regional relations, internal politics, and intellectual debate: Everyone had to be in favor of greater inter-Arab cooperation and had at least to give lip service to Islamic values. Each Arab country had the right to interfere in the affairs of the other states but always under the rationale of promoting Arab unity. Every Arab government could try to impose its will on the others but only under the guise of seeking Arab leadership and struggling against traitors. No compromise was permitted on the Arab-Israeli conflict; Western influence was always under a cloud of suspicion. Militancy and radicalism in the name of Arabism or Islam could not be challenged but might only be outbid. Beginning with Nasser, the rhetoric of revolution, socialism, and anti-imperialism were enshrined as the only politically proper or effective routes to development and independence.

Thus, Pan-Arabism and Islam represented for the incumbents a dangerous weapon in the hands of the opposition, a force in public opinion that could not be neglected, and a marvelous banner around which to rally support for rulers and their policies. Of course, under the surface all the usual forces of politics were in operation: ambition and localism; competition and calculation; pragmatism and realpolitik; greed and idealism. To gain power, politicians had to be able to exploit the prevailing tides; to stay in power, they could not stray too far from the mainstream. More often than not they even shared these popular sentiments.

In highly stable, democratic societies politics is usually a race for moderation. Each politician attempts to preempt the vast political center. Where strong ideological postulates of what constitutes right and wrong are passionately accepted and where politics is a life-and-death battle between competitors, it becomes a race to militancy. In short, the principle of Arab politics is in accord with Barry Goldwater's dictum "Extremism in the defense of liberty is no vice. And . . . moderation in the pursuit of justice is no virtue." Subversion, aggression, and terrorism are justified by this intellectual framework. In short, Arab politicians seek the same end as Western counterparts—maximizing their popular support—but they do so in the opposite manner.

Nonetheless, the Arab political outlook and the viewpoint of the individual dictators are marked by a curious combination of overweening self-confidence and deep self-doubt. After all, the rise of modern dictatorships in the Arab world and Iran is the product of past failures and humiliations. Earlier regimes fell—and current ones are challenged—because of the contrast between their promises and performances. Opponents are able to pose difficult, critical questions: Why haven't the Arabs been able to unite? Why have Islamic values failed to prevail? Why are their states still behind the West, and why is the West able to intervene so easily in their regional affairs? Why has Israel been able to defeat repeatedly its more populous Arab opponents? Because the regime follows the wrong policy! It strays too far from Islam or from Arab nationalism; it is servile toward the West and afraid to fight Israel. The rulers must credibly respond that they are pursuing these goals. The governments' vulnerability to such attacks makes them all the more strict in silencing potential critics.

Aside from their subversive capacity, these questions also have some psychologically disquieting implications. Imperialist machinations can be blamed for many setbacks, but if the enemy is so omnipotent and so successfully devious, perhaps it cannot be beaten at all. Often the lack of self-confidence can be glimpsed behind the belligerent rhetoric. Khomeini repeatedly proclaimed that the United States "cannot do a damn thing" about the hostages in Iran, yet most Iranians believed Washington could destroy the revolution. In the words of President Abol Hassan Bani Sadr, one could see among the Iranian leaders, "A whole generation's fear that the revolution could fail." Antagonism to the West became enshrined as a basic requirement for legitimacy. Yet as political philosopher Hisham Sharabi noted, the Arab nationalist awakening "was haunted by a sense of impotence and fear." Fear of the West fueled a continued need to "prove" one's political "manhood" by confronting it.

The Middle East landscape from the 1930s through the 1960s was strewn with overthrown regimes and murdered politicians. Governments that were too flexible in the Western sense were often destroyed in the unforgiving Darwinian process of Middle East politics, and the idea that the Arab world could advance by imitating the West was discredited. History had disproved the claims of intellectuals and "democratic" politicians alike (from the 1850s into the 1940s) that constitutionalism and political independence would in themselves foster the growth of strong, prosperous states. An extremely small elite continued to rule with a remarkable amount of corruption and incompetence. The rulers of the old regimes had been from families that had been wealthy and powerful for centuries, as merchants or officials of the old empires, or had been Ottoman officers who had joined the Allied side in World War I. They held the traditional elite's aristocratic contempt for the mostly peasant masses, seeing them as uncivilized animals whose only political functions were to pay taxes and furnish soldiers. As chief beneficiaries of the social order they found change threatening once it went beyond removing foreign rule. Their parties were small cliques united by a lust for office and fragmented by personality conflicts. They had no interest in drawing in or harnessing the energies of the new professional and urban groups that sought a share of power.

On matters of international politics, the old elites were

much affected by their ability to gain independence through diplomatic bargaining. Dependent on aid and using foreign leverage to protect their hold on power, the rulers were careful to maintain good relations with London. On issues of Arab nationalism—like the Palestine conflict—these governments competed in militant posturing and demagogic threats but were constrained by a rational assessment of their own lack of power to alter events.

The generation of the 1930s and 1940s had a very different approach to politics. They were revolutionaries who wanted rapid progress toward Arab union and modernization along the lines seen in Germany and Italy. If subservience to Britain was "rational," then they rejected the idea of being "sensible" and moderate. No longer should politics consist of visits to the British Embassy in order to gain London's covert support for one's political ambitions. The first step toward overcoming the foreigners' power was to reject it, the second was to organize mass support, and the third was to find new foreign allies to counter Anglo-French economic and military superiority. While revolutionaries in Iraq, Iran, Palestine, Syria, and Egypt turned toward Nazi Germany for help, Berlin's defeat set back their cause by several years.

But wasting this respite, the old regimes, the landed elites and old-fashioned politicians in Syria, Egypt, and Iraq, could not survive the demands of politics and change. They failed the test of Arabism and Islam when Israel gained its independence and administered a humiliating defeat to them in 1948. Constantine Zurayk, in an influential contemporary book, expressed the despair and questioning of many Arabs: "Declarations fall like bombs from the mouths of officials . . . but when action becomes necessary, the fire is still and quiet, and steel and iron are rusted and twisted, quick to bend and disintegrate." The disaster prompted officers at the front to argue, as Nasser did, that the real battle was at home. Their guns were turned against their own governments in coups. Some of the coup makers turned themselves into modern dictators; the coups became revolutions.

The conflict with Israel, then, was not the cause but merely a catalyst for the operation of deeply rooted domestic trends. If 1948 showed the breakdown of the old regimes, 1956 appeared to demonstrate the power of the new type of modern dictatorship. Nasser nationalized the Suez Canal company and then weathered an invasion by British, French, and Israeli troops. Political success was not endangered by military disaster. Nasser had shown how the West was a "paper tiger." Cairo Radio spread the message of nationalist revolution; Egyptian intelligence operatives financed subversion in other countries. Foreign holdings were taken over, and land was distributed to the peasantry. Truly, Nasser had achieved what seemed impossible: social change at home; political power internationally. Nasser was a dictator, yet he could have won a fair election in Egypt or anywhere in the Arab world.

While Nasser's charisma and Egypt's social structure provided continuity in Cairo, his would-be imitators in other countries found the going more difficult. The 1950s and 1960s were periods of learning and experimentation in the Arab world, not conducive to stability. Syria, for example, had successful coups in 1949 (two) and 1954. In 1958 it united with Egypt, and in 1961—after another coup—it broke away. More coups followed in 1962, 1963, 1968, and 1970. Iraq had successive coups in 1958, 1963, and 1968. And for each military takeover, there were dozens of foiled plots, assassinations, and acts of political violence.

The new regimes were run by military men who blamed Western imperialism and domestic capitalism for the Arabs' failures to achieve international equality and domestic development. They willingly turned to the Soviets for help without ever becoming puppets of Moscow. Nasser bought arms from the USSR when the Americans refused to make them available. Since the West supported the old regimes and the Soviets backed the new modern dictators, the foreign policy orientation of the latter was not surprising.

But for these regimes to last very long, they had to fulfill two tasks. First, they had to build a base of support among civilians to uproot the old elite, disperse competing groups, and avoid dependence on a politically ambitious officer corps that might make a new coup. Second, they needed to cement together the ruling group against perceived Western pressure and the constant threat of internal schism.

Strong leaders could, at the same time, appeal to the general population while intimidating or persuading their fellow coup makers on the Revolutionary Command Councils of Egypt and Libya and in the Baath party in Syria and Iraq. Personal charisma and a cult of personality spread by public relations techniques were mutually reinforcing in seizing the number one spot. Around this new leader the regime's inner core was reinforced by kinship or regional or communal ties. Most of the Syrians were members of the Alawite Muslim minority; the key Iraqi leaders came from the Sunni Muslim minority there, often from a set of villages around Tikrit. Qaddafi also used men from his region and tribe as a primary loyalty group, and Khomeini could call on his former theology students and many—though by no means all—of his fellow clerics.

Techniques were also perfected for controlling the army. It was purged of all officers loyal to the old regime or to competing political factions. The new ruling group exercised tight control over promotions and ensured frequent transfers so that no officer could depend on his troops' loyalty if he tried to stage a coup. It placed trusted officers in key positions and set up intelligence groups to watch each other and the military. These efforts were reinforced by the ruling party's monopoly on recruitment among officers. Saddam Hussein suppressed the Iraqi Communist party and killed many of its leaders on discovering its secret cells in the military. Khomeini repeatedly purged the armed forces, first of monarchist elements and later of proleftists. Political leaders of the Iranian Communist party (Tudeh) were merely imprisoned, but soldiers who were members were executed. The Iranians also built an alternative, loyalist force, the Revolutionary Guards, and placed Islamic "commissars" in the regular army.

Another central element in these modern dictatorships was the ruling political party. The Baath in Syria and Iraq, the Islamic Republican party in Iran, and the people's committees in Libya brought together in all parts of the country and from all sectors of society a "vanguard" of loyalists who enjoyed special power and privileges. Party control of jobs in the government, industry, unions, media, military, schools, and elsewhere was a key factor in winning the active support of tens of thousands of people for whom proregime activism was the key to a successful career and a comfortable life. Opposition, of course, was more likely to lead to an early grave.

The effectiveness of this system is proved by its ability to survive mistakes. By the 1980s these radical regimes had fallen short of their promises. Nasser lost the 1967 war, and the Syrian Baath the 1973 war with Israel. Arab unity still failed to appear. The new governments actually exacerbated differences as they followed their own state interests. Algeria and Syria supported Persian Iran against Arab Iraq in their war; Lebanese Maronites allied themselves with Israel; Egypt signed the Camp David accords with Jerusalem. While the regimes delivered an improvement in the living standards of many people—higher oil prices helped this process a great deal—the prosperity was uneven, and many groups were dissatisfied with their lots. But even when an individual dictator fell, he was simply replaced by another who followed similar policies.

A new wave of Islamic fundamentalist revolutionaries tried to exploit these failures. They argued that political radicalism, social reform, and economic nationalization had not solved the essential problem. On the contrary, Arab defeats were due to secularism and deviation from Islamic principles. But while such ideas smashed the Shah's traditional dictatorship in Iran— where Arab nationalism did not provide an alternative to Islamic politics—it failed to displace the Arab regimes that had mastered the techniques of modern dictatorship.

These skills of Middle East modern dictators and dictatorships explain why the number of coups and political upheavals in their countries had declined from the unstable 1950s and 1960s. By 1986, excluding the Afro-Arab Sudan, the last real regime change in the Arab world was Qaddafi's 1969 coup in Libya. Elsewhere there had been some transitions to new leaders without disrupting the system.

The modern history of the Arab world shows that as in

Africa or Latin America, there were values and issues that most people believed far more important than democracy. A regime was considered representative if it was properly Arab nationalist and stood basically (if not perfectly) in accord with Islam. The people's judgment was not made on the basis of the number of votes received by the rulers. Unpopular governments had often been elected, and predictatorship elections were usually of questionable fairness. The politically valid question is the "rightness" of the government in terms of nationalism, distribution of benefits, and handling of popular causes. If it was proper, 100 percent of the people might support it, but if it was not acceptably militant, nationalist, free of Western influence, and pious, it did not matter how it came into office. The same criterion applies to the surviving monarchies in Jordan, Morocco, and Saudi Arabia, which must be especially careful to stress their allegiance to populism, independence from the West, Arab nationalism and Islam.

As in other Third World cultures, conformity is considered a prime social responsibility the absence of which threatens the whole society. Muslims are supposed to form a harmonious community (*umma*) and Muhammad is often quoted as saying that the believer should "not separate himself from the community." Truth must be in accord with God's laws, but consensus is a sign of correctness. In Muhammad's words, "God will not allow my people to agree on an error."

The majority Sunni branch of Islam went so far as to accept the idea that "tyranny is better than anarchy." The Shiites continued to maintain a right of rebellion against unjust regimes—a factor important in the Iranian Revolution. But once pious rulers were in control, the duty to obey them became just as strong as among the Sunnis.

In the Arab context, leaders and intellectuals constantly preached that disunity was a major cause of weakness and that dissenters were conscious agents of foreign powers or, at best, objectively helped the nation's enemies. Thus, political opponents are quickly branded as American or Israeli puppets.

Healthy pluralism does not develop when the dominant world view defines every act as one of patriotism or treason;

211

democracy cannot flourish where there is no acceptance of the idea that debate is legitimate and can be peacefully resolved. Generally the modern dictator has the power to define what is patriotic and what is treasonous, telling the people that "he who is not with me is against you." But the roots of this black-and-white distinction stem from the group solidarity of Islam and of the tribe reinforced by modern nationalism and a sometimes accurate, usually fanciful paranoia about foreign conspiracies.

The constant competition among the regimes also puts an edge on all claims of ideology and performance. The Cairo Islamic university Al Azhar, for example, issued a declaration during Sadat's rule: "We are proud that the true Islam is here in Egypt. Egypt is the island of freedom, democracy, and man's dignity as desired by Islam. . . . There isn't in Egypt a ruler who spends money on gambling tables while Muslims in many parts of the world are suffering. There isn't in Egypt a ruler who spends the money of Muslims on plotting, bribery, and baseness just to build an imaginary leadership." In short, Egypt was claiming to be more properly Islamic than either Saudi Arabia or Iran.

Nasser never had much use for Islam in public life. He survived an assassination attempt by the fundamentalist Muslim Brotherhood and broke up the organization in the mid-1950s at a time when it had as many as 2 million supporters. So overwhelming were Nasser's control and charisma that he never had to demonstrate any Islamic credentials. During his reign, from 1952 to his death in 1970, radical Arab nationalism, mixed in various proportions with Marxism, attracted the activists and revolutionaries. Islam was seen as a conservative, traditionalist tool exploited by Saudi Arabia to protect the status quo.

Like Nasser, Sadat had been a youthful activist who had entered the military to conspire for revolution and political power rather than as a professional career. During World War II, along with other young officers, Sadat believed that Egypt's first priority must be to throw off British influence. In 1941 he was arrested twice after attempting to spy for the Germans. Sadat was not a Fascist but, like other future modern dictators, found attractive aspects and a useful ally in Hitler's system.

Within a few months of his release he became involved in the murder of a pro-British politician. Once more imprisoned, Sadat threw the prosecution's case into disorder by falsely charging that he had been tortured. After thirty-one months in jail he was again found not guilty and, in 1950, was reinstated in the army.

Clearly Sadat was neither a good conspirator nor an able organizer. While Sadat founded the Free Officers, it was the dour Nasser who built up the organization to overthrow the decadent monarchy. Obviously Sadat resented his own reduction to a secondary role, complaining that his fellow members of the Revolutionary Command Council had "never known what homelessness and destitution meant, never served time in jail, . . . never gone through the chastening cycle of hope-expectation-frustration." This is partly the pose of a man of the people and man of action confronted with latecoming opportunists, but in Sadat's case such statements have a certain validity.

Sadat's most important characteristic, however, was an ability to learn from his observations. Nasser took credit for defeating the invading armies in 1956, the event that made him the most celebrated Arab leader. Sadat knew that it had been U.S. diplomatic intervention that had turned the Suez crisis from a "military defeat into political victory" for Egypt. Nasser's baiting of the United States in the 1960s strengthened his position as the valiant knight of Egyptian sovereignty and Arab interests. Sadat saw that it also led to the loss of desperately needed economic aid and pushed the country deeper into dependency on Moscow. Nasser's regional and domestic popularity continued to ride high after the disastrous defeat in the 1967 war. Sadat, as a political insider, saw that Egypt had been pushed to the brink of ruin. "Nasser was smart enough," quipped an Egyptian journalist, "to put the conservatives in charge of the economy and the radicals in charge of propaganda." But on the economic front as well, Sadat thought, such extreme populist policies could no longer be afforded.

The role of successor in an established modern dictatorship is sometimes more difficult than that of the founder, who can blame all problems on a vanquished prerevolutionary regime. Until or unless he can eliminate his colleagues, the successor must be more of a conciliator and consolidator than a commander. Sadat's preparation for this task came from two decades' experience as an understudy. He was the only member of the original coup-making group who avoided an open break with Nasser. For years he was shunted aside and laughed at as a yes-man, only to emerge at the end as the sole potential president who could appeal to all factions, partly because they wrongly believed he would be easy to control.

This was the staggering negative legacy that Sadat inherited. He countered it by using the novelty of his personality, redistribution of booty, and cautious criticism of Nasser's errors to "refinance" his rule. Once firmly ensconced as the president, bloodlessly eliminating potential rivals along the way, he used the tremendous power of incumbency to put Egypt back on a solid, if inevitably precarious, footing. In such a centralized system Sadat simply gave the orders, and the country's policy—if not society—obeyed the helmsman.

When Sadat succeeded Nasser, he projected an image as a pious president. Although Sadat tried to manipulate Islamic groups, particularly to counter his opponents, the image reflected his character as well. Inheriting a country facing disaster on all fronts, Sadat sought to revise downward Egypt's ambitions and to repair its fortunes at home. He contrasted himself with Nasser, whom he described as "suspicious, extremely bitter and highly strung."

In order to deal with Egypt's economic deficits, Sadat needed to attract Western aid and (if possible) investment, reopen the Suez Canal, and regain the Israeli-occupied Sinai oil fields. He waged the 1973 war against Israel in large part to strengthen his diplomatic position and negotiated the Camp David accords to end the conflict with Israel. These policies of peace, realignment with the United States, and an economic opening greatly improved Egypt's fiscal and global position. But pragmatism did not make for popularity. By violating the Arab and Islamic injunction against making peace with Israel, Sadat was ostracized by the Arab world and criticized by radicals at home. Nasser's economic policies might have brought stagnation, but Sadat's were politically more problematic because they created more visible inequalities. His friendly attitude toward the United States and criticism of the Soviets made him popular in America but to some Egyptians smacked of old-fashioned submissiveness. In short, every step taken toward moderation conflicted with the militant attitudes of Arab nationalism, Islam, and Third World thinking.

When Sadat was assassinated in October 1981 his martyrdom was useful for his successors. It was not that Sadat became, in death, a hero. Rather, the needed changes he had made could now be taken for granted as established facts without any of his successors' being held responsible for them. To this day the hero of Egypt remains Nasser, who was, in Western terms, a "failure." Nasser was unable to win victories at war or to make peace. He created a repressive regime that closely regulated intellectuals and destroyed trade unions. His economic policies led to dead ends. In retrospect, however, this negative side is less important for Egyptians than is the positive: Nasser restored Egypt's dignity in the world, made it leader of the Arab world and a leader of the Third World, improved the lot of many peasants and allowed some of their children to rise in the world, and so on. With Sadat, on the contrary, Shakespeare's dictum holds accurate that "The evil that men do lives after them,/The good is oft interred with their bones."

Yet the political significance of Sadat's assassination can be easily overstated: A small radical fundamentalist group was merely able to prove its ability to carry out a killing. No revolution took place, and Sadat's chosen successor, Hosni Mubarak, dealt with the challenge not by ceding any real power but by talking with the left and Islamic oppositions and avoiding any steps that would inflame tensions. As the Egyptian

215

joke goes, when Mubarak came to a crossroads, he asked his chauffeur, "What did Nasser do when he came here?" The driver said he turned to the left. "And what did Sadat do?" He turned to the right. Mubarak replied: "Signal left, signal right, then park."

And even given all this, Egypt is the most secure and homogeneous of the Arab states. Its long history provides an identity relatively independent of Islam and Pan-Arabism. The fact that almost all of Egypt's people live in the narrow Nile Valley and its small river delta has made them used to bureaucratic, centralized rule.

Other Arab modern dictators cannot, however, afford the luxury of relative passivity because they rule countries that are even more complex and volatile than Egypt. In contrast with Egypt, they need to create much stronger parties and institutional structures since loyalty and centralism can never be taken for granted. Syria, it has been said, is a country where 60 percent of the people think they are leaders, 30 percent consider themselves prophets, and 10 percent believe they are gods. Questions of national character aside, the difficulty of ruling Syria and Iraq is due to their regional and demographic diversity and their short, violent histories.

Syria gained independence from France's mandate after World War II, and its politics were remarkably unstable in the following years. Once the thin layer of political legitimacy had been broken, there was no stable coalition or hegemonic group capable of consistent control. Syrian politics was like an onion, with endless layers of skin and no core. In communal terms there were Sunni Muslims, Alawites, Druzes, and Ismailis, all represented in the officer corps. On a political level there were Nasserists, Communists, Baathists, Islamic fundamentalists, and conservatives. Coups and purges during the years of strife eliminated one group after another from both government and army. After 1963 only the Baathists remained, and by 1970 this group had been narrowed to one predominantly Alawite faction of the party around General Hafez al-Assad.

Assad was born in 1928 to a poor Alawite peasant family in the backward northwest region. He went to Latakia to attend high school and joined the Baath party at age fourteen, becoming involved in underground activities against the French. His official biography claims that he was a volunteer in the 1948 war against Israel and afterward joined the air force, becoming a pilot in 1954. While in semiexile in Cairo during the period of Egypt-Syria union, he helped form a military committee, which staged the 1963 Baathist coup. Three years later, as air force commander, he helped his friend—and fellow Alawite—Salah Jadid—take over the leadership. Assad served as defense minister and as prime minister. But the Jadid regime's adventurism and Assad's own ambition led him to arrest Jadid and take over power himself in 1970. Jadid is still in prison today.

The Baath party's ideology can most simply be described as Marxism heavily adapted to Arab nationalism. Each Arab state is considered only a part of the Arab nation, and thus, the party's "regional" branch in each country is only a part of the "National Command." In practice, however, as with communism, the international aspect quickly became subordinated to the interests of the rival Baathist regimes in Syria and Iraq.

Otherwise, Baathism provides an ideal ideology and structural basis for a modern dictatorship. It defines itself as scientific and modernizing, anti-Western, and populist democratic. Like Marxism, it calls on the lower classes to play a central role in building a new, nonexploitative society. But in Baathist terms "freedom" refers not to individual rights but to national sovereignty, nonalignment, and the exclusion of imperialism. Party cadres are supposed to serve the people, be accessible to the masses, carry out self-criticism, and be models of integrity.

The system is designed to give at least a large proportion of the population both a psychological and material vested interest in the regime's continuation. Coupled with the party's disciplined organization in the military, which its rivals could never equal, this is the key to the regime's staying power. The cadre is given personal benefits in exchange for strengthening the regime; young people are encouraged to strive to become cadre for reasons combining idealism and self-interest. The regime tries to give itself a monopoly on patriotism; dissenters know they face swift and severe punishment.

The national appeal is also underpinned with the strong traditional forces of family ties, regional loyalties, and confessional solidarity. In both Syria and Iraq the leadership is reinforced by kinship and marriage connections. Assad's brother Rifaat is one of three vice-presidents and commander of his own military units. Cousin Adnan is head of another part of the praetorian guard. Those who rule Damascus come disproportionately from the Latakia region; those who rule Baghdad from the Tikrit area. Assad's supporters are from the Alawite minority, which includes only about 11 percent of Syria's population; Saddam Hussein's men are from the Sunni Muslim minority. But enough members of the larger groups—Sunni Muslims in Syria, Shiite Muslims in Iraq—are included to hold a base of support in those sectors as well. Rifaat al-Assad, incidentally, has two Sunni and two Alawite wives. The party becomes, in a sense, a new tribe trying to instill overarching loyalties.

Although radicalism is the stock-in-trade of these regimes—and Libya and Iran as well—it is important to know where to stop short of straining the country's resources, creating unnecessary internal antagonisms, or attracting enough foreign intervention to overthrow the regime. All four of these regimes have good relations with the Soviets, but all are careful to keep Communists under control. One of the reasons why Assad moved against Jadid is the latter's errors: Excessive nationalization at home had endangered the economy and alienated the urban mercantile Sunnis. Jadid's strong secularism—including the elimination of Islam as the state religion—had stirred up the fundamentalists and underlined the Alawites' questionable credentials as true Muslims. Jadid's adventurous foreign policy—supporting a Maoist-style "people's war," which in practice meant terrorism against Israel—had helped bring Syria to its disastrous defeat in the 1967 war.

There is a clear, if unspoken, contract between the dictator and the party-military elite. The leader makes the key decisions but takes into account the views of his colleagues.

218

The latter, in exchange, cooperate in purging their own institutions of anyone who does not show personal loyalty to the dictator. Assad is the head of the government, army, and the party's National and Regional Commands. He chooses the judges, cabinet members, military commanders, security and intelligence chiefs, party officials, leaders of the mass organizations, heads of state economic organs, and newspaper editors. The key group is the twenty-one-member Regional Command. Under it are organized the branch, district, sub-district, and village commands which spread the party's eyes, ears, and voice throughout the country, creating a whole stratum of dependable loyalists. These channels are more important than official governing bodies like the People's Assembly, the members of which are screened by the party and are regularly "elected" with 99 percent of the vote.

Other conveyor belts of support and control are the mass membership Revolutionary Youth Organization, Union of Students (only the Baath can legally recruit members in the universities), Women's Organization, Peasant Federation, General Federation of Trade Unions, and Union of Writers. These all are headed by reliable people and will not deviate from the regime's directives. The unions, for example, represent the government's economic directives rather than the workers' demands, a position rationalized by the need to mobilize all resources for development and national welfare rather than selfish particularism. Needless to say, such unions are not likely to call strikes, although each can do some lobbying for its interest group.

The youth organization holds mandatory summer training camps where children from five to twenty years old are indoctrinated with Baathist ideology and loyalty to the regime. They may be sent to help peasants with the harvest. School texts have been rewritten; teachers must convey government-approved facts; cadres pass on party songs and ideology; young people participate in parades and meetings. Entry to professional schools and travel abroad are based on loyalty. Poor youths can follow this path to advancement. Everything they have will be owed to the party and leader, and if they fall from grace, it all can be taken away from them. As a source of benefits and punishments the party can function somewhat like an old-fashioned American political machine. The fact that loyalty is born of expedience as well as sincere belief only strengthens its hold. Armed force may be the single most important pillar of the regime, but as has already been seen, it is far from the only one.

These observations are not contradicted by the centrality of the regime's continued control of the armed forces. The Baath party has a monopoly on recruitment in the military, which itself is a privileged sector of society. Pay and benefits are high by Syrian standards and often include invisible perquisites, like the army's lucrative smuggling from Lebanon of stolen cars, hashish, and other goods.

Officers know that on retirement they can start or join companies that enjoy the regime's favor. The armed forces receive more than 30 percent of the country's budget and almost 60 percent of current spending. This priority on military spending, legitimized by the conflict with Israel and kept acceptable by the regime's constant claim that it is surrounded by enemies, does not become a cause for resentment, as happened under traditional dictatorships like that of the Shah.

The Syrian government conducts centralized economic planning and controls about 85 percent of the economy. These two factors, not any implication of workers' control, generally define socialism in Third World modern dictatorships. The private sector is still quite active but is limited particularly to commerce, retail distribution, and small-scale production. Even if the private sector is more efficient, political requirements demand some loss in efficiency in favor of protecting the regime. Ideologically any major expansion of the private sector would mean a growing bourgeoisie which might challenge the party-military apparatus. Historically the prerevolutionary elite's lack of social consciousness, inability to develop the country, and open pragmatism rather than militant patriotism persuade many that capitalism is an unacceptable system. Pragmatically, contraction of the state sector would cut into government finances, the military budget, and officials' perquisites. In populist terms socialism is a powerful image. Why, Nasser long ago asked, should one man live in a palace and another in a mud hut? If the modern dictatorship does not ensure equality, many Arabs and Africans believe, it at least limits the gap.

Many Syrians have benefited from Baathist rule. The expansion of rural electrification and the party's distribution of seeds, fertilizer, insecticide, water, and credit help the peasants while expanding their gratitude and dependence on the regime. The Baathists never tried to impose collectivization. Hafez al-Assad's liberalization of the economy after unseating Jadid pleased the business community. Even merchants and manufacturers critical of the regime came to like government contracts and officials' flexible attitude toward bribery. They also fear the competition of foreign multinational companies if economic controls were to be further loosened.

Repression, too, is an important pillar of the regime, and no chance is taken with security. Executions and torture are routine. One man who had been sentenced to death in Syria under a very different regime some thirty years earlier refused to return, saying, "They hold on to all the old lists." There are multiple security and intelligence agencies, keeping an eye on one another as well as on the opposition and potential coup makers. Special military formations considered ideologically reliable are created and stationed to block any action by regular troops. In Syria these have included Rifaat al-Assad's 50,000-man Defense Companies, stationed strategically near Damascus with their own tanks, missiles, intelligence, and prisons, as well as General Ali Haydar's 15,000-man Special Forces.

Corruption is more a privilege than a crime so long as it is kept within reasonable bounds. The extent of Rifaat al-Assad's unrestrained criminal activity made him personally unpopular with most of the elite and seriously damaged his prospects for succeeding to the presidency. The regime will periodically dismiss even Alawite loyalists for poor performance. An anticorruption commission was launched in 1977 to investigate illegal profits, kickbacks, collusion in awarding state contracts, and the pilfering of government supplies. But the small fry have more to fear than the large violators.

The greatest domestic threat to the regime came from Islamic fundamentalists who resent it as godless, Alawite, and socialistic. To reduce such antagonisms, Hafez al-Assad introduced a new constitution specifying that only a Muslim could be president (after first inducing top Sunni clerics to classify the Alawites as true Muslims) and published a new printing of the Koran with his picture in it. The president began going to mosque on Friday and talked about making the pilgrimage to Mecca. The continued prominence of Sunni Muslims in the hierarchy—like Defense Minister Mustafa Tlas and Foreign Minister (later Vice-President) Abdel Halim Khaddam—was also supposed to help. The fundamentalist terrorism consolidated the solidarity of the threatened, interlocking Alawite and Baathist communities.

Hard-core fundamentalists, however, were not impressed. They assassinated members of the Alawite elite whenever possible. In February 1982 they began a poorly coordinated uprising in the city of Hama. The regime sent in the army, whose house-to-house attacks and indiscriminate shelling wrecked the city's downtown area and killed as many as 20,000 people. But the regime never stopped to moralize or ask whether repression would be effective. Instead, it wanted to persuade the citizens that armed opposition or revolutionary activity would surely bring death. The lesson was effective; thereafter the fundamentalists were decimated and demoralized.

Internal dissension in the ruling group was a bit harder to contain. When Hafez al-Assad suffered a heart attack on top of other medical problems in November 1983, would-be successors began maneuvering for control. Rifaat al-Assad's Defense Companies promoted his candidacy with military maneuvers and propaganda. They were opposed by Haydar's Special Forces and by General Shafid Fayyad's 3d Armored Division. When Hafez al-Assad recovered his faculties, he sent all three men abroad for several months. His brother was the last to be recalled home but was rewarded with a vice-presidential post.

A showdown was avoided by leaving the succession vague. Syria, however, is ruled by an institutionalized dictatorship as well as a personalized one. When Hafez al-Assad dies, the fact that there may be a struggle and some new faces at the top does not mean that the regime itself will be dismantled. No one is likely to throw away such a widespread, prefabricated political-military-economic-ideological structure. Indeed, the successor will likely owe his elevation to those very institutions and interests. Modern dictatorship has a continuity even if the specific dictator changes.

Syria's foreign policy rests on a combination of national interests—objectives that transcend individual leaders—and regime interests. The idea that Syria is a steadfast promoter of Arab nationalism, an important power in the Arab world, and a country that stands up to the Americans, Israelis, and other enemies is bound to inspire pride and patriotism. The predominance of the suspect Alawite minority in the leadership makes it all the more necessary for it to prove its Arab nationalist credentials. A regime that stays in power at home by using bazookas against Hama apartment buildings will view intimidation as a very effective tool abroad as well. Thus, tough power politics, including sponsorship of terrorism against others, is seen as a legitimate pursuit of Arab and Islamic duty and of Syrian interests. The general domestic acceptability of a modern dictatorship's foreign policy applies to Syria's intervention in Lebanon, Iraq's invasion of Iran, and Qaddafi's foreign adventures.

The object for sponsors of international terrorism, as for masterminds in other forms of criminal activity, is not notoriety but success. By that standard Libya's Muammar al-Qaddafi is a bumbler. Syria, in contrast, has used terrorism with remarkable acumen to attain its goals.

Reluctant as they have been to publicize or react to Libya's role in promoting terrorism, West European governments are more horrified at the idea of tackling Syria and the West is not likely to apply sanctions against Damascus. Syria's strategic and military posture makes such actions too politically costly. Syria is the state, after all, that President Ronald Reagan profusely thanked for helping free the TWA hostages in 1985, despite U.S. intelligence showing Syrian involvement in Beirut car bombings that killed close to 300 Americans and U.S. embassy employees.

Syria uses terrorism more effectively and with less risk than the other major purveyors of international terrorism—Libya, the PLO, and Iran—because it follows several important rules:

—Employ terrorism for limited, well-defined goals rather than as a means of sparking revolutions. For Syria, this has meant maximizing its influence in Lebanon, destroying U.S. and Israeli leverage there, discouraging Jordan from making peace with Israel, weakening any PLO independent of Syrian domination, and blackmailing wealthy Arab oil-producing states.

—Deploy terrorism in conjunction with diplomatic and military instruments and strategy. For example, terrorism, combined with Syrian Army's occupation of parts of Lebanon and Assad's clever manipulation of internal politics there, allowed Damascus to outmaneuver the United States and maintain its hegemony there.

—Avoid publicity and refrain from boasting about involvement in terrorism—which is difficult to prove otherwise—to protect your image and gain sympathy. Organize sporadic incidents rather than a continuous offensive to avoid provoking sanctions.

—Be strong enough in your own right and close enough to the USSR to deter military retaliation.

Syria learned these lessons from hard experience. President Assad's adventurous predecessor's open, energetic support for Palestinian terrorism was a major factor leading to the disastrous 1967 war with Israel and to weakening Syria's regional position. Assad, who took full power in early 1971, would be more careful and selective.

Lebanon provided the first test for Syria's strategic use of state-sponsored terrorism. The Syrian Army entered Lebanon in 1975 and easily overpowered the indigenous militias engaged in civil war. But Assad realized that the conflict in Lebanon was too complex to be resolved and that the country was too fragmented to permit total Syrian control except at a very high cost.

Instead, Damascus's policy was to maintain strong enough relations of alliance and intimidation with each faction in Lebanon so as to be able to play them off against each other. Thus, Christian, Druze, or Sunni and Shiite Muslim groups were subsidized or punished depending on Syria's immediate goals. Syria sought to prevent any faction from winning the civil war.

Damascus apparently organized the murder in 1976 of Kemal Jumblatt, the most impressive and independent of the "radical" side's leaders, because he was seeking a total victory. Similarly, Syria was behind the killing of President Bashir Gemayel in 1982 because of his dynamism, determination to produce a Christian military triumph, and connections with Israel.

In addition to assassinating leading Lebanese figures and controlling local groups for terrorist actions, including the Lebanese Syrian Social National party (SSNP), the Tripoli Alawite militia, etc., the Syrian Army systematically looted Lebanese property and threatened citizens. As one Beirut witticism put it, a man went to the police to complain, "A Swiss soldier just stole my Syrian watch." "Don't you mean," asked a police sergeant, "a Syrian soldier stole your Swiss watch?" The victim answered, "You said it, I didn't."

To avoid coverage of Syrian corruption and repression, at home as well as in Lebanon, Damascus also used terrorist attacks against Arab and Western journalists. Already in 1977, seven Lebanese newspapers had been closed down. In 1980 one of the most outspoken editors, Salim Lawzi, was kidnapped and murdered during a visit to Beirut in 1980. He had moved his newspaper, *Al-Hawadess*, to London to escape the censorship, and its columns had been critical of Syrian leaders. His body showed signs of horrible torture. Other unsolved killings and threats also seem to have emanated from Syria.

The most important use of Syrian-sponsored terrorism within Lebanon was to force the withdrawal of Israeli troops and U.S. marines. At the least the Islamic fundamentalist suicide bombers who attacked the U.S. forces and Embassy in 1982 and 1983 were allowed a free hand to train and mount their operations through Syrian-held territory. American hostages were also held in areas occupied by the Syrian Army. Despite the anarchic conditions in Lebanon, it would have been impossible for these operations to have been mounted without Syrian knowledge and assistance.

Having forced a U.S. pullout, Syrian intelligence then turned its attention to southern Lebanon. Certainly much of the guerrilla and terrorist activity there was organized by Shiite extremist groups, some of them tied to Iran. At the same time, however, Damascus assisted some factions, particularly those of Syrian-controlled Palestinians as a way both of striking against Israel and of showing that the pro-Syrian groups were more successful than those of Yasir Arafat. Syria was also determined to destroy the May 1983 Lebanon-Israel peace agreement.

Some suicide bombers were even more closely tied to Syria. In July 1985, for example, a twenty-three-year-old Lebanese blew himself and his car up at a checkpoint of the Israeli-backed South Lebanese Army. The day before he did so, Abbas gave a television interview, greeting Assad (whose picture could be seen on the table and the wall) and calling him "the symbol of resistance in the Arab homeland and the first struggler." He was a member of the Lebanese branch of Syria's ruling Baath party. Other terrorists were members of the Syrian-controlled SSNP.

After the relatively successful series of operations in Lebanon, Syria's main goal was to wipe out those few PLO members who advocated serious negotiations with Israel or alliance with Jordan. Syria itself rejects Arab-Israeli negotiations not at all because it wants to ensure return of the Golan Heights or seeks better terms. Damascus's rejectionism runs very deep. Any solution is likely to strengthen Jordan's hand over the Palestinian question, make the PLO free of Syrian influence, allow Israel to be a recognized state in the region (and hence a rival to Syria), defuse tensions and turn Syria into a second-rate power, and increase U.S. prestige. Since Damascus views Palestine as "southern Syria," Assad has explained that Arafat has no right to make any decisions that contradict Syria's views. In short, almost any conceivable solution is anathema to the Syrian government. Although it is often argued that an increased stress on pressing Arab-Israeli negotiations would decrease terrorism, common sense shows that the three terrorist-supporting states—Iran, Syria, and Libya—and the most actively terroristic Palestinian groups as well all oppose any serious negotiations. Terrorism then, is not a cry of outrage against a Western failure to pursue peace but an attempt to block diplomacy altogether. Sadly, the more strongly the United States pushes for peace, the more terrorism will increase. During the last few years whenever King Hussein of Jordan has considered the possibility of negotiating with Israel these efforts broke down in part because of Syrian pressure through terrorism. In April 1983 PLO moderate Issam Sartawi was murdered in Portugal by Syrian agents. In October the Jordanian ambassadors to India and Italy were wounded and a Jordanian security man in Athens was killed. In December an attack in Spain killed one and wounded another diplomat. The Jordanian charge d'affairs in Romania was killed in December 1984.

In December 1984 former West Bank mayor and PLO Executive Committee member Fahd Kawasmeh was killed in Amman, eliminating a man considered friendly to King Hussein, showing that Jordan could not protect the Palestinian leaders, and serving as a warning to others. In April 1985 a rocket was fired at a Jordanian airliner taking off from Athens. In July the Jordanian airline's office in Madrid was attacked and a diplomat was killed in Ankara. In September a Jordanian publisher was murdered in Athens. The ensuing murders of Palestinian moderate Aziz Shehadeh in Ramallah and of Nablus Mayor Zahir al-Masri could also be traced to Syrian surrogates.

These events were carried out through Syrian links with

two sets of Palestinian terrorist groups: those of Abu Nidal and the Syrian-sponsored PLO faction led by Abu Musa. From the beginning Syria sponsored the original Palestinian terrorist groups of the 1960s, like Heroes of the Return, during the PLO's pre-Arafat days. It directly controlled Al-Saiqa, at one time the second-largest PLO group until Syria's anti-Palestinian actions in Lebanon discredited it. Al-Saiqa's leader, Zuhair Muhsein, was killed in 1979 while on a gambling trip in southern France.

To strengthen its terrorist capacity, Assad recruited Abu Nidal when he was forced to leave Baghdad in 1980. Although Abu Nidal had earlier staged operations against Syria, he was willing to accept the job. Many of the anti-Jordanian actions listed above were carried out by his men. In the middle of 1985 Abu Nidal moved on to Libya but continued to cooperate with Syria. Damascus has also been involved in supporting terrorist attacks against Turkey (through Armenian groups) and Iraq.

Syria's long history of supporting terrorism against Israel is due to a number of factors. Obviously Damascus views itself as an Arab nationalist state playing a leading role in an anti-Zionist struggle. But in practical terms Syria is also a regional power desirous of undercutting Israeli strength without, most of the time, becoming involved in a direct confrontation with Israel that it could not win. Consequently, Syria has been careful never to strike directly against Israel through the Golan Heights—an act that might prompt direct Israeli retaliation. Instead, it has routed operations through Lebanese, Jordanian, and even European territory.

As in the cases of the Iranian and Libyan modern dictorships, then, Syria's rulers have combined brutality, terrorism, and radical rhetoric with a certain amount of caution in preserving the regime's existence. While Assad has perfected much of the modern dictator's repertoire and added a few original touches of his own, the basic pattern is repeated elsewhere in the Arab world.

The structural foundations for the Assad regime in Syria are paralleled in Baathist Iraq, the National Liberation Front government in Algeria, the more explicitly Marxist Yemen Socialist party in South Yemen, Qaddafi and his network of people's committees in Libya, and variations for more moderate Egypt and for non-Arab, Islamic fundamentalist Iran.

In Iraq, compared to Syria, the civilian party apparatus is even more important vis-à-vis the military. The 1968 Baathist coup there was led by civilian Baathist revolutionary Saddam Hussein, though for a decade thereafter he preferred to remain as vice-president with a respected military officer as figurehead. Despite his lack of army career, Hussein later made himself a general and was often pictured in uniform.

Saddam Hussein's experiences as an underground fighter—he carried a machine gun in an unsuccessful assassination attempt on a non-Baathist predecessor and had to flee the country—have been reflected in his own regime's toughness. He has never hesitated to execute factional opponents, and there have been periodic purges in the party's ranks. On one famous occasion a repentant informant pointed out "traitors" in a televised meeting of high party officials. The unfortunate individuals fingered were dragged out of the hall and never seen again.

As with Assad, Hussein's face is everywhere in the land. One local joke has it that the population of Iraq is 28 million: 14 million people and 14 million pictures of Hussein. He is omnipresent on television—often visiting villages or neighborhoods to chat with the local people—and in the press. His speeches and writings are published in quantity. Again, the narrowness of any distinction between personal and party loyalty does not weaken the value of the Baathist organization.

Iraq, like Syria, has enough credible enemies to keep the core group of rulers and beneficiaries together. A long rebellion by the non-Arab Kurds in the north was put down by a mixture of ruthlessness and co-optation. The more dangerous threat was from the Shiites, a traditionally neglected and poorer group, who form the largest sector of the population. This problem was accentuated by pro-Khomeini agitation among the Shiites after the 1979 Iranian Revolution. The Iraqi regime murdered such respected Shiite leaders as Ayatollah Bakr Sadr and his sister and expelled tens of thousands of Iraqis of Persian descent. At the same time, however, some Shiites were incorporated into the leadership and party; others saw their living standards improved by the Baghdad government.

Most of these gains were made possible by Iraq's oil boom. The higher price of petroleum—and in 1980 Iraq was the region's second largest producer—paid for billions of dollars in economic development, higher wages, new jobs, better housing, health and social security payments. Although this new money came easily, the government did a good job of distribution and limiting waste, at least until the war with Iran ate up the resources.

As it happens in modern dictatorships, the benefits were accompanied by repressive terror. The slightest criticism could be punished with the greatest severity. When asked the greatest problem of Iraq's economy, an industrial expert replied that the managers and bureaucrats were afraid to make decisions lest these lead to their downfall or imprisonment. The party and secret police apparatus was more widespread even than in Syria. Officials in all sectors were selected by the party hierarchy. Professors, teachers, journalists, and writers all were strictly controlled.

The war with Iran brought heavy costs and seemed capable of wrecking the gains of earlier years. But patriotism and a genuine hatred of the Iranians (and fear of fundamentalism—Baathist Iraq is a relatively secular regime) inspired the populace as much as intimidation frightened them. The army was watched carefully lest officers turn their criticisms of the war's conduct into an attempt to take over. Despite a number of early pessimistic appraisals from observers, the regime showed impressive staying power.

As elsewhere in the Third World, these societies have a long record of hierarchical, top-down organizations in which the citizen had little redress or protection against the state. Family, clan, religion, and state all demanded loyalty. Political power has repeatedly grown out of a gun barrel; parliaments have always been rubber stamps. The modern dictatorship keeps the structure of authority but modernizes it and opens up rewards and a chance for power to a much wider group. As political scientist Adeed Dawisha has written: "Just as the process of modernization proved to be a curse for the (traditional) rulers, it ended up being a curse for the ruled. For with modernization came technological advancement, and that placed in the hands of the ruler's methods of social and coercive suppression that made earlier means of population control pale into insignificance. . . . A two-pronged maxim was followed: put fear in people's hearts but also try to win their support, no matter how grudgingly given. On the other side of the fence, the ruled realized very quickly through bitter experience the futility of demanding genuine and full political participation." All that is promised never comes true, but part—for at least part of the people—usually does.

CHAPTER NINE

Middle East: Khomeini and Qaddafi

The eyes of millions of Iranians were on the Air France plane as it taxied to a stop at Mahrabad Airport on February 1, 1979. Out stepped an elderly black-clad clergyman. Thousands of his supporters kept the crowd under control as it chanted allegiance. It was an outpouring of political passion rarely equaled in modern history. The Shah had just fled the country, marking the end of the 2,500-year-old Iranian monarchy. Ayatollah Ruhollah Khomeini had returned home from Paris to establish the Islamic Republic.

Not content merely to make a revolution and rule their own countries, Khomeini and Libya's Colonel Muammar al-Qaddafi sought a new world order. This wider ambition often overshadowed the fact, impressive enough in itself, that they had achieved total power at home. The relationship between internal triumph and external aggressiveness rested on two ideas in the minds of these often dissimilar dictators: a belief that their victory against all odds proved their cause was divinely inspired or ideologically correct and the conviction that

Islamic fundamentalism or a Green Revolution in one country was under all-out attack from foreign powers.

The young colonel and the aged cleric had very different political philosophies, but they had much more in common than first met the eye. Their air of recklessness and apparent fanaticism could not hide a keen sense of the limit of acceptable risk, although their range went beyond that of countrymen and colleagues. The ability to be so daring and still survive added to their legends. Each had an inborn sense of drama and a personality able to inspire great loyalty, persuading people to follow him and to persecute those who would not. Both had great organizational ability.

In short, each had a split personality combining tough realism and dreamy idealism. They were true believers whose sincerity inspired others and clever operators whose coldly calculating minds saved them from being naïve idealists. This duality is a key secret of the most effective modern dictators who can base themselves on easily recognizable, emotionally powerful ideas close to their audience's hearts—Arab nationalism, national dignity, indigenous culture, Islam—at the same time as they develop something new and different enough to galvanize these sentiments into action by credibly promising their fulfillment.

Thus, while Qaddafi claims to be a follower of Nasser, his thinking and behavior are his own. Libya has little of Egypt's prestige and only one-twentieth of its population; Qaddafi must cope with a distinctive set of problems. Equally, Khomeini's claim that he is only copying the early Islamic polity of 1,200 years ago is even more misleading. Muhammad did not fly in from Paris on a jet plane, mesmerize the nation via television and radio broadcasts, or finance his state on the international oil market.

Another paradox about the rise of Qaddafi and Khomeini is that their revolutions flourished from the very failure and degeneration of their traditions. Qaddafi came on the scene when the principle of unity was being treated with increasing cynicism by other Arab regimes. Independence and Arab socialism had not lived up to expectations. Nasser's manipulation of Arab nationalism as an instrument of Egyptian national interest raised suspicions; Cairo's failure to promote Arab unity increased skepticism. Khomeini's revolution was made possible by a rapid social transformation that had been pushing Islam into an increasingly smaller corner of Iranian life. The fact that the clergy was besieged by the Shah-instituted changes yet was seen as maintaining its purity in an otherwise corrupted society was Islam's greatest asset. In the Arab world Islamic fundamentalism had suffered greatly by being seen in the 1950s as a tool of reaction against the rising wave of Arab nationalism. Khomeini refashioned it as a revolutionary instrument.

There is an additional clue in the demonstrative, even psychologically insecure boasting of these two regimes. Iran and Libya were latecomers and loners. Lacking anything equivalent to Arab nationalism, Iran had no strong ideology to compete with Islam as an alternative to the Shah's traditional dictatorship. The Shah's efforts to promote Iranian nationalism had never taken root, and his regime had also kept Iranians insulated from the ideas of Marxism and radical, secularist nationalism that had gained hegemony among the Arabs and elsewhere in the Third World. Thus, Iranians were neither disillusioned with the untried force of Islam nor sufficiently attracted by some other ideology.

Libya gained independence later than the core Arab states and only experienced secondhand the tumultuous course of Arab nationalist politics during the 1940s, 1950s, and 1960s. Consequently, it never fully comprehended the lowered expectations of other Arab countries after Nasser's failures, defeats by Israel, and the growing fragmentation in the Arab world. Kept in a pristine state by their own traditional dictatorships, Libya and Iran emerged after their revolutions with all the zeal of the newly converted. They peddled as universal ideologies and movements that were really the particular products of their own distinctive histories and societies. Qaddafi, outwardly a Pan-Arabist, actually functioned as a Libyan nationalist conducting a particularly Libyan revolution. Similarly, although Khomeini's Islamic fundamentalism rejects Iranian nationalism, he, too, had a truly national function and appeal.

Spreading the revolution has been a major priority of both Khomeini and Qaddafi. Despite periodic Western hysteria about alleged waves of Islamic fundamentalist revolt or Libyan domination of neighbors, the foreign policy record of Libya and Islamic Iran is one of unbroken failure. Miscalculations were due to their erroneous view of all opposition as U.S.-inspired, their misreading of international politics, and their underestimation of the strength of local nationalism. It is not so easy to spread revolution. Tunisia, Morocco, Chad, Sudan, and Egypt all rejected Qaddafi's threats, bribes, and covert operations. His behavior made him unpopular in the Organization of African Unity and a laughingstock in Arab circles. His supporters were almost completely restricted to isolated groups that he rented with oil earnings. If the Arab states publicly opposed any Western intervention to overthrow Qaddafi, it was only a matter of regional political etiquette and concern that such an event could create a precedent for actions against themselves. One might conclude that a prophet was without honor except in his own country. This proverb certainly fitted Qaddafi's situation.

Iran's revolution briefly inspired a wide range of Islamic fundamentalist movements, but most of its direct followers, too, were leased. Loyalty to Tehran was limited to a minority of Shiite Muslims and even among them primarily to people of Persian descent. When Iran began to have some influence among militant Shiites in Lebanon, Syria moved quickly to counter this drive, supporting the far larger Al-Amal group. In Iraq Saddam Hussein used repression and material benefits to ensure that his large Shiite population did not support Khomeini in the Iran-Iraq War.

This is why their appeal abroad is limited. When Qaddafi told an audience of Egyptian women in Cairo about their impending lower status in a new, merged Egypt-Libya, they were aghast. When merger is suggested to Syrian leaders, they remember the debacle of the 1958–1961 Syria-Egypt union, which President Assad saw firsthand. When an all-out assault against Israel is demanded, the Egyptians and Jordanians contemplate their costly defeats in previous wars. Similarly, most Iraqis rejected Khomeini's bid to turn them into Islamic fundamentalists, considering this a step backward. Overseas the political missionary efforts and theatrical effects of Khomeini and Qaddafi often seem clownish because they are out of touch with their own region even as they project values—maximalist Arab nationalism in Qaddafi's case; pious Islam in Khomeini's case—which their neighbors must accept in public but have ambiguous feelings about in private. Qaddafi and Khomeini are confused and frustrated by failures that are not supposed to happen. Khomeini complains, "We have lost faith in many of the so-called Islamic countries, and we do not have any hope of being able to guide them unless God Almighty brings about a change in them."

Yet this very friction with other states and peoples that should theoretically welcome them as liberators also reveals their essentially national characters. Qaddafi and Khomeini are in step with their own countries' political and psychological needs. Libya is led by a man from a tent-dwelling pastoral nomadic tribe—the stereotype of Arabs in the West but the only Arab leader from such a background. Having barely achieved its own unity, Libya is more willing than better-established societies to immerse its weak identity within the wider Arab world. Qaddafi views his success in welding together Libya as a model of how easily the Arabs could unite. Libyans are flattered by the idea that they could leap so quickly from being the most backward Arab state to becoming a regional, even a world leader. Having been subjected to the especially brutal colonialism of Fascist Italy, Libyan political culture views the West as irredeemably rapacious. Given a more limited and negative contact with Western culture, Libyans reject it more thoroughly and see this attitude as self-evident. Having achieved quick, painless wealth through oil at the very moment of their revolution, they underestimate the difficulty of development and believe that determination and ideological steadfastness will solve all problems.

Khomeini warned continually about foreign threats and

sincerely believed that aggression and subversion were taking place. Functionally, however, these positions reinforced the unity of the elite and the allegiance of the populace. Some of Khomeini's specific citations of Western misdeeds and double standards were accurate; others were imaginary. His view of the West was secondhand at best, replete with remarkable misconceptions, and he grossly overestimated U.S. influence on the Shah. But right or wrong, it was a conception of the world that many other Iranians—and people elsewhere in the Third World—were willing to accept from their leaders.

Both Khomeini and Qaddafi consistently followed a pattern which corresponds to a timeworn anecdote. A man is standing on the sidewalk, snapping his fingers over and over again. A bystander comes up and asks him to explain this behavior.

"I'm snapping my fingers to keep the elephants away," replies the first man.

"But there aren't any elephants within thousands of miles of here!" exclaims the confused observer.

"You see!" triumphantly answers the finger snapper. "It works!"

The overbearing interference of a great power is not merely an imaginary figment in the mind of a Khomeini or a Qaddafi. Each of them can cite examples from his country's history on this point. "So much adverse propaganda has been spread by foreign sources for hundreds of years," Khomeini said on the seventh anniversary of the revolution in February 1986, "it has made all of us believe that it is impossible to resist these powers. . . . Whenever anything happened it would suffice for one foreigner serving in that country to say that such things would not happen and that would be it. . . . If, for instance, the British ambassador were to say something, even the sultan would not go against it."

Yet the two charismatic dictators repeatedly and deliberately baited the United States: Khomeini by seizing American hostages, Qaddafi by his open sponsorship of terrorism. They each proclaimed that the United States was doing everything possible to subvert their regimes and predicted repeatedly that an American invasion would soon take place. But when the United States acted more moderately or when the alleged subversion did not overthrow them, the two leaders boasted that their defiance had neutralized U.S. plans and transformed a superpower into a paper tiger. When the United States did bomb Libya in retaliation for its aid to terrorism, Qaddafi rallied nationalist sentiments.

What makes this tactic particularly potent is that even top colleagues trembled at the dangers only to have their faith in the leader's genius reinforced when the feared retribution did not come. America's ability to overturn so easily the nationalist Mohammed Mossadegh government in 1953 had convinced many Iranian political figures that it would never "allow" the fundamentalists to take power or remain in office. In Bani Sadr's words, a whole generation feared that the revolution could fail. After all, Iran was the kind of country where high officials in the Islamic regime would routinely denounce the United States in meetings with American diplomats and then request U.S. visas for their friends.

Khomeini tried to break this inferiority complex, saying repeatedly "Our youth should be confident that America cannot do a damn thing." In reality, President Carter spent the months after the Iranian Revolution trying to patch up relations with Khomeini's Iran. During the hostage crisis he only reluctantly dispatched an abortive rescue mission when negotiations failed, and even then it was purely aimed at saving the kidnapped Americans. Thus, the hostage seizure was justified in the first place by a perceived American threat; the failure of that alleged threat to materialize after the hostage taking was portrayed by Khomeini as an Iranian victory. America, though still dangerous, had been defeated. Washington's failure to fit the aggressive, imperialistic image painted by Khomeini did not lead Iranians to question the whole theory of U.S. conspiracy. Instead, they attributed the American lack of success to Khomeini's effectiveness in anticipating and countering it.

If Iran blamed all prerevolutionary problems on the United States, Qaddafi took the same attitude on the Arab world's difficulties. No American leader would have been inflamed by Qaddafi's domestic activities in the absence of his foreign adventures. Nevertheless, the dictator could demonstrate his own power by keeping off the elephants. Qaddafi, like Khomeini, argued that if other leaders only acted as he did, the illusory bonds of their states would drop away. And the failure of other leaders to take a similar revolutionary attitude only proved that they were hopeless American puppets.

While Islamic Iran seems a unique, exotic state, an examination of its workings reveals adherence to a worldwide pattern of modern dictatorship. Most important is the rule of a charismatic leader. The long-lived ayatollah himself is a figure of such dimensions that if it were not so alien to his religious belief, he could be called a political demigod. Architect and goad of the revolution, he seems to have almost singlehandedly directed the demolition of the Shah's seemingly allpowerful regime. When others believed it impossible to overthrow the Shah and that the Americans would not allow the fundamentalists to gain power, Khomeini remained resolute. He enjoyed the support of massive crowds willing to risk their lives in Iran's streets and the support of skillful organizers (many of them also clerics). By directing and inspiring these people, Khomeini's uncompromising willpower ensured the revolution's success and Islamic fundamentalist rule.

The 1978–1979 Iranian Revolution was not only a revolt against the Shah's modernization and development program but also an upsurge of forces and attitudes created by those very same policies. The rise of both Khomeini and Qaddafi challenges the widely held Western view that the Third World would change in a linear progression from "traditional" to "modern" society. The former represented historical customs and attitudes—the primacy of family and clan ties, rural and subsistence agriculture, hereditary status, and a strong religious orientation—that would inevitably give way before the forces of industry, improved communications and transport, science, and secularism. The growth of new classes, ideas, and institutions would change the form of government. The West expected a trend toward democracy while Soviet bloc ideologists predicted the spread of communism. Both schools of thought arose out of an intrinsic belief in technological determinism.

As oil revenues built up, particularly after the 1973 petroleum price increases, the Shah fulfilled long-held ambitions and plunged into gigantic economic and military spending programs. Billions of dollars of new arms were purchased, Western manufactured products and machinery poured into the country, extensive construction projects were begun, and tens of thousands of Iranians studied abroad. The Shah and his associates wanted to do everything at once.

By the late 1970s, however, their plans faced three basic problems. First, while many Iranians benefited from these programs or were intimidated into silence, few felt strong loyalty to the regime. Some groups were left behind in the drive for progress; others were unable to compete with Western imports or subsidized court favorites who monopolized the fruits of government contracts and corruption. The Shah's perhaps inevitable political failure was not so much an absence of progress toward democracy as an equal inability to transform himself into a modern dictator. Efforts to institute a White Revolution or to establish a single party turned into public relations campaigns largely aimed at the outside world.

Second, by the late 1970s, as the government overspent its revenue, Iran went into a recession. Projects were cut back, unemployment rose, and inflation became serious. Wages in the construction industry—the main source of jobs for the unskilled—fell by as much as 30 percent. University graduates found few opportunities. To save money, the government reduced subsidies of the religious establishment from $80 million to $30 million a year. Thus, the Shah's rule made new enemies by appearing incompetent and unable to meet the people's needs—some of which the regime itself had created.

Third, the modernization process uprooted the old society and left the people without a psychological anchor. Peasants moving from countryside to city found their new environment incomprehensible. The rules of the new urban society, increasingly secular, technological, and Westernized, were contrary to what they had been taught was right and just. The vacuum demanded fresh ideas, preferably rooted in familiar symbols and values, to explain what was going wrong in the country and how it could be put on the right track.

In these circumstances Khomeini and his followers provided the most acceptable answers. They reinterpreted Islam, the central element in the popular world view, to explain the problem and the solution. The problem was defined as "Westoxification," an excess of foreign influence poisoning Iranian society and manifesting itself through an unpatriotic regime. The solution Khomeini proffered was a clergy-led Islamic republic.

By offering this analysis and remedy, Khomeini himself was an innovator whose ideology conflicted with historic Iranian Islamic thought. He had always been an ideologue and a political mullah rather than a scholar explicating Islamic law and practice. There was no real tradition in Iranian Islam for clerical rule. After the revolution Khomeini's followers admitted that their views represented a sharp break with the past. As a 1985 editorial in the proregime newspaper *Kayhan* explained, "Mainstream Islam had developed a sense of inherent and almost unalterable inferiority before the West." Ideas and attitudes toward life were imported wholesale because they were seen as "items of universally valid knowledge." But Khomeini, and Qaddafi for that matter, tried to show how Islam could present its own alternative and indigenous version of "modern" society. In the same manner other modern dictators tried to produce their own national solutions to these problems.

Khomeini was consciously seeking to institute a dramatically new order in Iran. He sought an "inner revolution of the nation," not just "a transfer of power from one hand to another without any change in the condition of the people." It would be a government that came from the masses—"whose prime minister was a bazaar tradesman, whose officials were farmers"—and that listened to their demands. Such a populist, even representative dictatorship had nothing in common with traditional regimes. Khomeini and Qaddafi are not antimodern throwbacks to some earlier century. They adapt contemporary ideas for their own purposes. Their movements succeed because they embody an acceptable approach to the problems of modernization. Khomeini sought to use rather than suppress altogether radio, television, films, and recordings—all objects of horror to believing Muslims fifty years ago. Similarly, Qaddafi not only avidly sought the most modern weapons but also employed contemporary public relations techniques to a degree equal to that of any American politician. Khomeini and Qaddafi were wagering that technology is value-neutral, that a radio can broadcast readings from the Koran just as easily as it can be used to play rock music.

While charisma often seems like a magical quality, it is also a marketable one. The leader is popularized by his picture's constant appearance on billboards, on posters, in newspapers, and on television. He is praised in the media and the schools; his sympathy and concern for the common people are communicated in meetings and speeches. Success, of course, is not automatic—the Shah tried many of these techniques as well—but must also arise from the content of the leader's ideology and policies as well as his advantage in being new, lacking responsibility for the past and existing society.

Khomeini uses his power to be more of an arbitrator and guide than a ruler. No factional dispute can tear the regime apart because everyone knows that Khomeini's word is final. As *velayat-e faqih*, an office he wrote into the new constitution and one of questionable theological legitimacy, Khomeini is the supreme authority on all social, political, and religious matters. He dictates overall policy while the government hierarchy takes care of daily decision making.

The Islamic regime's survival was never left to Khomeini's personal popularity alone. The government's power was institutionalized to a remarkable extent through a wide variety of organizations and groups to maintain the Islamic Republic. In fact, while the whole structure had an Islamic flavor, its underpinnings were typical of modern dictatorship. There were neighborhood Komitehs, reminiscent of equivalent local watchdogs in Cuba, Nicaragua, Libya, and Ethiopia. To some extent the network of loyal local clerics replaced that of a deeply rooted party. The mosques became centers for military recruitment, administration of the rationing system, indoctrination, and control. The regime's Islamic Republican party (IRP), more a collection of factions claiming allegiance to Khomeini than a centralized cadre party, still performed the function of organizing supporters and choosing leaders.

Motivated by idealism, opportunism, or even conformity, many young people of varied social backgrounds continue to support passionately the new order. The regime also retains strong loyalty from the Islamic movement's historical backbone—poor urban slum dwellers who are financially subsidized with Iran's petroleum earnings and who gain a sense of self-importance and identity from the government's propaganda. A new web of agencies—from state-financed charitable foundations to neighborhood committees—provides benefits to Iran's poor.

Many of the approximately 80,000 Iranian clerics are active as local political agents of the IRP. Mullahs serve as president and as speaker of parliament and hold about half the seats in the legislature. By constitutional provision, they occupy six of twelve positions on the Council of Guardians, which can veto parliament passed laws, and dominate the Assembly of Experts, which chose another cleric, Ayatollah Hussein Ali Montazeri, to be Khomeini's successor as *velayat-e faqih*. Many mosques have their own sources of income. Mass-membership Islamic Associations pervade the villages and factories.

Every province and city has a cleric who serves as Khomeini's personal representative. Mullahs lead the Crusade for Reconstruction, which organizes volunteers for building roads, schools, and houses (its achievements are among the revolution's proudest boasts), and the Foundation of the Dispossessed, a powerful money-disbursing agency. The Ministry of Islamic Guidance, headed by a cleric, controls censorship and publishing, and local mosques give clearances to students wishing to attend a university. Political loyalty is a major criterion in determining who can teach or study in higher educational institutions. Such a large apparatus will not be easily dismantled or overthrown.

The IRP clergy also form a coherent group of men united by long collaboration, friendships, and even marriage. Montazeri studied under Khomeini in the 1940s and later served as the exiled leader's personal representative in Iran. President Sayyed Ali Khamenei, who is also general secretary of the IRP, was a student of Khomeini's as well. Other key leaders were prominent supporters of Khomeini before and during the revolution. Thus, the revolutionary clerics should not be seen primarily as theologians but as a political group analogous to Syria's Alawite-Baathist officers or Iraq's Sunni-Tikriti-Baathists. Khomeini can depend on a loyal in-group of old associates who will stick together against all outsiders.

The forces of repression are no less organized than those of leadership and of mobilization, The Shah's secret police (SAVAK) was refurbished, renamed, and streamlined. Even though it retained some of the Shah-era personnel, the institution was relegitimatized. Street gangs of loosely organized Hizbollah, the party of God, which are also directed by some of Khomeini's lieutenants, strong-armed opponents, broke up opposition rallies, and harassed women who did not properly cover up, paralleled the Nicaraguan Sandinistas' *turbas*, the Syrian special militias, the youth associations of many African ruling parties, and other groups practicing what was purported to be populist repression.

The officer corps was thoroughly and repeatedly purged after the revolution. Senior officers were retired, imprisoned, executed or fled the country. Those officers who remained owed their rapid promotions to the new government. The regime organized its own parallel military establishment, the Revolutionary Guard (Pasdaran), with its own naval and armored units. The government also placed Islamic political commissars in regular military units to check on and intensify loyalty.

Khomeini's disdain for traditional dictatorship, under which "people could not reach the government" and officials "relied on the power of the bayonet," was reflected by his emphasis on mass organizations, the integrity of leaders, and repeated elections for president and parliament. Although only proregime candidates could run, the regime clearly had confidence in its broad base of support. The parliament has been no mere rubber stamp, fiercely debating and sometimes rejecting government policies and nominations for high offices. Disputes resulted from differing views on several major issues. The clergy and IRP were divided between those favoring state control of industry and distribution of land to smallholders and those defending the existing property arrangements.

There were, of course, many dissatisfied groups. A great deal of land was distributed to—or seized by—peasants in the revolution's aftermath, but the Islamic government failed to establish a national land reform policy. Peasants also lost income because of the slowdown from the economic boom of the Shah's era. Bazaar merchants—who make as well as sell goods—had been major supporters and financiers of the revolution. They, too, had some grievances with the Islamic regime's sporadic attempts to control foreign trade and conduct antiprofiteering campaigns.

Most dissatisfied of all were large elements of the wealthy urban middle class, whose privileges, jobs, and Western cultural orientation had tied them to the Shah or at least alienated them from his Islamic successors. Middle-class women faced special problems because their Western dress and liberated ways were now regarded as treasonous. Those who appeared in public wearing cosmetics or without the black all-encompassing chador were subjected to harassment. Women were also forced out of a wide variety of jobs.

Yet the regime could counter or limit all these conflicts. Many peasants did receive land or benefits from the revolution, and they were particularly responsive to Khomeini's personal appeal and the guidance of local imams. Bazaar merchants successfully lobbied against radical policies and were the most ideologically supportive of all nonclerical groups. Lower-class women, who retained a traditional life-style and wore the chador anyway, were not affected by the antifeminist policies.

Well over 1 million Iranians, mostly business and professional families, emigrated. The migration or passivity of those middle-class elements opposed to the Islamic Republic removes them as potential rivals. Khomeini welcomed their departure: "Let these moribund brains drain away; these brains have worked for the aliens [and] were part and parcel of [SAVAK]—let them flee the country." Even the loss of initial enthusiasm for the regime does not threaten its survival inasmuch as the atmosphere among the disgruntled is one of cynicism or fear. The ability to export as little as 1 million barrels of oil a day makes possible the reasonable functioning of even a badly mismanaged economy.

Organized opposition groups were demoralized, disorganized, divided, and forced into exile from 1979 to 1984, beginning with the anti-Shah democrats and continuing through the supporters of President Abol Hassan Bani Sadr, the new left, dissident clerics, and the Tudeh (Communist) party. Along the way Kurdish nationalists and anti-Khomeini clergy were defeated or neutralized. These groups were destroyed because they were blamed for internal disturbances, linked with foreign powers, and defined as being in opposition to Khomeini's teachings. The hostage crisis was particularly useful in this respect, allowing the regime to declare Iran as being under attack from America. Khomeini said in 1979, for example, "We suspect that those who pose as leftists and who think they are supporting the people are agents of the United States." By such means repression was made popularly acceptable.

The revolution also refused to be judged on its material accomplishments alone. Said Khomeini: "I do not accept that any prudent individual can believe that the purpose of all these sacrifices was to have less expensive melons, that we sacrificed our young men to have less expensive housing. No one would give his life for better agriculture." A Tehran radio commentary added, "For [the West] politics is nothing but a mathematical process." But for Iranians "dignity is better than full bellies."

After defeating the Shah's regime and rival political groups, Khomeini had to ensure that the regime would not destroy itself from within. He did this by allowing some freedom of debate within the ruling circles while settling disputes by his own unchallengeable decrees. He tried to maintain high standards among the ruling group. "If one single clergyman takes a wrong step," he said in a May 1985 sermon, "then the entire clerical class will be blamed." There is a long tradition in Iran of anticlericalism based on the view that mullahs are corrupt and hypocritical. As one story has it, a woman in a store loudly criticizes the regime because there is no soap powder available. "You should not complain," says a mullah standing nearby. "Fatima [the prophet Muhammad's daughter] never had soap powder." "Yes," replies the woman, "but Muhammad never rode around in a Mercedes either."

The ayatollah also warned Iran's leaders to restrain their individual ambitions. "To seek power, whoever might seek it, would lead to one's fall." Satan knows that the best way to manipulate a person is to convince him of his own importance. Khomeini even sought to curtail his own cult of personality by insisting that the media limit the number of stories and pictures about him. He constantly urged unity on his followers, and he threatened to destroy anyone who threatened their collective rule.

Like other modern dictatorships, Khomeini's regime sought to redefine freedom to justify its control over the population. Liberty, to the West and Iran's Westernized intellectuals, said Khomeini, meant hedonism, taverns, houses of prostitution, and coeducational bathing. Such imported thinking was "freedom designed for us by the West, rather than a freedom planned by us [and] would lead our country to destruction." Indeed, the Western style of freedom was a conspiracy by those "who plan to plunder our wealth."

Similarly, Khomeini challenged the morality of the international order and the standards used to criticize Iran. "Let them erect a wall around Iran and confine us inside this wall," he said at a "Crimes of America" rally in June 1980. "We prefer this to the doors being open and plunderers pouring into our country. Why should we want to achieve a civilization which is worse than savagery?"

Qaddafi would agree. He was born in the most backwater region of what was then just about the most backwater country in the Arab world, but he had wonderful credentials for a man who would unite Libya and preach Arab nationalism. The politics of Libya had long been marked by rivalry between the Cyrenaica and Tripolitania regions. Qaddafi's family were nomads belonging to a small tribe living along the border, and he received his early education in the third province, Fezzan. His poor family saved money to send him to school, where he was looked down upon as a Bedouin.

These simple facts point to many factors that shaped Qaddafi's character. Coming from a poor family, a weak tribe, an undeveloped region, and an unprestigious Bedouin background, Qaddafi suffered oppression several times over. Yet his family's pastoral way of life had been the wellspring of Islam and of the great Arab conquests, culture, and prized virtues. Qaddafi must have seen the disdain shown toward him by city people as a symbol of their rejection of traditional ways. Just as Khomeini saw himself, and was seen by others, as the paladin of pious Islam, Qaddafi qualified as the representative of heroic Arabism.

After the Italian conquest in 1911 and under twenty years of Mussolini's rule, the Libyans were treated far worse than were Arabs under any other European regime. Up to half the population died under terrible conditions of war and famine. Italy did nothing to develop education or the economic infrastructure. The resulting bitterness accounts for Qaddafi's view of a ravaging Western imperialism and his obsession with a full-scale U.S. invasion of Libya today, providing a parallel with Iran's psychological fixation on the U.S.-backed coup of 1953.

When Libya finally achieved independence in 1951, it was a poor country, artificially created by the merger of the three regions and ruled by a newly created monarchy. The elderly king had a long record of nationalist struggle against the Italians, but his base as head of the Senusi religious brotherhood was restricted to Cyrenaica. King Idris lacked the roots and legitimacy that allowed the Saudi and other Persian Gulf monarchies to survive and never had the time needed to gain momentum and credit from the oil wealth that began to flow into the country in the 1960s. Oil money proved as destabilizing as it did in Iran. Urbanization disrupted society while prosperity did not spread widely enough to solve the problems created. Politics remained the private property of a small elite. Parties and trade unions were banned; elections were corrupt contests between clans. As in Iran—and Egypt, Iraq, and Syria as well—new groups arose to protest this monopoly of power. The failure of the old regime to mobilize successfully the masses' loyalty made it vulnerable. The manipulation of elections and parliaments discredited those institutions.

Meanwhile, Qaddafi and his fellows, including Abdul Salam Jalloud, his boyhood friend and later number two man, were being stirred by the Arab nationalism of Nasser and Cairo's radio Voice of the Arabs. Expelled from high school for leading a student demonstration and failed out of the university, Qaddafi intensified his secret political activities. In 1963 he entered the military academy, like Nasser in Egypt and Assad in Syria, to prepare a coup rather than to seek a career.

Qaddafi's group copied Nasser even to the extent of calling itself the Free Officers. In September 1969, with Qaddafi not yet thirty years old, the conspirators took power in a bloodless coup. The story is told that when the Libyan leader met his idol, Nasser commented, "You remind me of my youth." Qaddafi took this as praise, but in the spirit of Heikal's story, the implication of Qaddafi's inflexibility and naïveté also had a hidden sting. At any rate, the Egyptian president had only a few months to live and could not serve as Qaddafi's mentor.

Qaddafi imposed his own personal style on the regime. After Nasser's death Qaddafi considered himself the best candidate for leadership in the Arab world. Tripoli began to open up relations with the USSR. An Arab Socialist Union (the same name as Nasser's party) was organized as the sole political party; Communists, Muslim Brotherhood members, and other dissidents were imprisoned. Up to this point, Libya's regime was similar to other radical Arab military governments, but, rather than emphasize consolidation of his rule at home, Qaddafi was frustrated that the quick and easy Arab unity he expected did not materialize. The inconclusive nature of the 1973 Arab-Israeli War and Egypt's decision to make peace with Israel at Camp David further radicalized him.

Qaddafi, like Khomeini in later years, condemned the breakdown of traditional values. But interested as both men were in social and cultural continuity, they sought technological and political change, economic development, and military strength. In Libya, as in Iran, the revolution's first stage was aimed at rooting out the old regime, consolidating the new government's power, removing foreign influences, and ensuring national control of valuable resources. Qaddafi demanded the closure of British and U.S. air bases, and the two countries quickly complied. He nationalized British Petroleum's share of Libyan oil production and began to pressure the U.S. companies as well. Libya was a weak link for the international oil cartel since coming on-line relatively late, it was drilled by small companies that would make far more concessions to keep their holdings.

From being one of the world's poorest countries—for many years its leading export had been scrap steel from World War II battlefields—Libya became the recipient of billions of dollars in oil revenue each year. Qaddafi used some of this money to make tremendous strides in raising the nation's literacy rate and standard of living, and these benefits also increased support for his rule.

The nature of this kind of economic boom has tremendous implications on the direction and politics of Libya and other petroleum welfare states. Development is fragile since it rests on no agricultural or industrial base. Unless the rate of income to population is very high, as it is in Saudi Arabia and Kuwait, imports can quickly eat up surpluses. The government has tremendous power in its hands since, from the start, it controls what is overwhelmingly the main source of income. The oil industry needs very few employees, so on the one hand, it does not solve the problem of employment, but on the other, it creates no discontented proletariat. The influx of foreign technicians can create tremendous antagonisms, but if the oil money allows the nation as a whole to benefit from the import of service and domestic workers to do the dirty work, it turns the relatively small local population into a sort of Athenian aristocracy.

The quick and easy rise of income can also lead to a dangerous arrogance, underestimating the limits of willpower and the difficulty of solving economic problems. Saudi Arabia and Kuwait, bound by tradition, are cautious about change. The Westernized Shah and modern dictatorships are more prone to such dangerous hubris. Iraq spent its oil money on grand development schemes until the war with Iran derailed its progress and, in both combatants, reduced petroleum production and soaked up much of the remaining oil income.

As the oil glut appeared in the 1980s, prosperity faded. The sale of petroleum made Libya $19.5 billion in 1980 but only $10.4 billion in 1984 and even less thereafter. External debt rose to $7 billion; financial reserves fell to the lowest levels in a decade. The economic situation was worsened by Qaddafi's political decisions. His pet project, the "Great Man-Made River" to irrigate large tracts of Libya, may cost as much as $25 billion and could well end in breaking the country. In 1980 he nationalized commerce, explaining, "Trade is a form of exploitation." Foreign merchants were also expelled. Combined with Libya's lower oil income, this meant that shops became emptied because of the mismanagement of distribution. Taking over retail trade is—along with underpaying peasant producers—the worst economic mistake made by modern dictatorships. Syria and Iran rejected this option, partly because such a step would turn disenchanted merchants and artisans into new political enemies. Libya's tiny middle class, however, could mount no such opposition although the inefficiency disenchanted hard-hit consumers. In the best Bedouin tradition Qaddafi proclaimed, "Land is no man's property," and supporters burned property registries in many places. Similarly, Qaddafi did not have to cope with a large peasant class whose dearest ambition was to own its own land. The country's unusual social structure allowed him to be more flighty, having escaped the gravitational pull of class and interest group demands.

251

These factors, combined with Qaddafi's whimsical style, also had some disadvantages, however. The regime continued to have a narrower political base than governments in hierarchy-oriented Egypt and the better organized Baathist dictatorships in Syria and Iraq. The original Revolutionary Command Council broke up in 1975, when two of its members, outraged at Qaddafi's lavish spending, organized an unsuccessful coup. The two men fled, and other relative moderates were imprisoned or executed. But the increased amounts of oil money were also Qaddafi's greatest asset. He could spend as much as he wanted on military equipment, development, imports of consumer goods that filled Libya's stores, and foreign activities for many years without coming close to exhausting revenues.

"Needs and demands are two different things," says one of Qaddafi's slogans, which, like many aphorisms of modern dictators, give unintended insights into their underlying philosophies. The people demand what they want, but the leader decides what they need. The average Libyan may remain concerned about his personal and family's well-being; Qaddafi determines that the Libyan people are going to get more spending for arms and for promoting foreign revolutions. All political leaders must decide how to divide limited resources among competing social sectors. Dictators can ignore the requests from below, but a shrewd modern dictator will at least modify his policy by listening to the sectors represented in the party, mass organizations, and key advisers. The more Qaddafi talked about the masses and about how to involve them in decision making, the more he became out of touch with them. Qaddafi did not have to take account of their wishes since he assumed that he already represented their will. As the Libyan slogan puts it, "The Libyan people are Muammar al-Qaddafi."

Attempting to mobilize Libyans was particularly frustrating because the people lacked experience of political life. Their inferiority complex over the country's unimportance in the Arab world and in the world at large was assuaged by Qaddafi's flamboyant internationalism. But since the regime had a weaker base than counterparts, it needed to threaten a larger proportion of its own people. At home, as abroad, Qaddafi adopted extreme measures to attain his goals.

Qaddafi's organizational structure is based on the idea of direct democracy. He has proclaimed Libya a *jamahiriyah*, a state of the masses, rather than a *jamhouriya*, a republic. A central part of his cultural revolution was the establishment of about 1,400 people's committees, combining the equivalent of party cells with the local groups charged with punishment and reward seen in so many other modern dictatorships. The basic people's congresses chose delegates to regional congresses, who, in turn, chose representatives to a general congress. In theory, Qaddafi had no power; in practice he had tremendous but not total power. For example, socially conservative Libyans blocked his proposal to give women compulsory military training.

On the national level Libyan politics centered on factions battling for Qaddafi's attention. The veterans of the regime and army are represented by Jalloud, the government apparatus by Foreign Minister Ali Taraki, and the people's congress activists by a third group. Each faction tried to prove itself more faithful to Qaddafi, with the most militant group having an inherent advantage since it had no inhibitions about backing everything he did. Qaddafi's informal style of governing encouraged this kind of competition. Thus, there were five different intelligence agencies, which watch one another. Behind Qaddafi's showy female bodyguard stood his real inner bodyguard of tribal kinsmen. Qaddafi demotes, promotes, and rotates high officials at regular intervals. There is a great deal more improvisation than there is institutionalization.

Qaddafi's government by whim is dangerous to himself. The lack of institutions deprives him of the protective cushion enjoyed by the modern dictatorships in Iran, Iraq, Syria, and Egypt, where institutions, ideology, and proregime loyalties are wider and deeper. If Qaddafi were to die, Libya would still be an Arab nationalist dictatorship, but it would be a very different kind of state in many respects.

While Qaddafi maintains a close watch on the army, the lack of a party structure has made it more difficult to ensure the military's loyalty. Indeed, he has gone out of his way to bait the officers, saying in January 1986, "The masses must replace the Army. The regular Army will disappear, and armed citizens will replace it." But he has neither built any parallel military force, as has Khomeini, nor developed bonds of party loyalty, as have the Syrian, Iraqi, Algerian, and South Yemeni regimes. "It would be difficult to have a coup," says Qaddafi, "because the authority is in the hands of the people and they would refuse." It is one thing for a ruler to make statements like this and another to act as if he believed them.

If Qaddafi's attempts to assassinate dissidents abroad represents, once again, an extreme position, his attitude toward opposition is typical for a modern dictator. Since his theory and system are properly Islamic, Arab, and nationalist, Qaddafi argues, opposition to it is un-Islamic, un-Arab, and antinational. Hence dissent is by definition treasonous collaboration with foreign imperialists. He calls opponents "stray dogs," a far nastier characterization to Arab than to Western ears.

Qaddafi proclaimed in February 1980, "Physical liquidation is the final stage in the dialectic conflict between the revolution and its enemies, when all other means of liquidation (social, economic, and political) have failed." Regimes that owe more of their ideology to Marxism are usually content to eliminate opponents as a class, but Qaddafi's and Khomeini's systems are also oriented to punishment and revenge. At a conference in New York Islamic Iran's ambassador to the United Nations was being heckled by exiled Iranian students. He smiled broadly and explained that "our enemies can certainly try to kill us but we have a right to kill them first." He made the prospect seem more a matter of pleasure than of political necessity.

As an ideologist and leader Qaddafi believes in reshaping reality. Again, this is a common theme among Third World modern dictators, but again he takes it to an extreme. The arguments are impressive: The current situation is too unpleasant to accept, other countries have developed, and the experience can be duplicated; the regime has shown in the past its success in altering seemingly inevitable facts—overthrowing the king, expelling the U.S. and British bases, taking over control of oil resources, and even confronting superpowers in head-on confrontations. Like economic decision making, ideological and foreign policy choices can be made on the basis of excessive confidence.

Thus, Qaddafi claims his ideology is superior to communism and capitalism. Like other modern dictators, he sees the Third World as an oppressed equivalent of what the proletariat is for Marxism and sees nationalism as the substitute for class struggle. The idea of development as a technical problem is rejected in the same way that Lenin attacked trade union demands. These leaders argue that a qualitative, not just a quantitative, change is needed: an internal revolution against those blocking progress; an external struggle against imperialism.

Despite such "mainstream" aspects to his thinking, Qaddafi introduces some highly unusual features. He takes the universal aspect of his theory more seriously than do those who mainly confine their concerns to one country. His ideology is more synthetic and idiosyncratic. Khomeini is a universalist, but he gives credit to Islam, not himself, for Iran's ruling ideology. The Syrian and Iraqi Baathists restrict their attentions to the Arab world and borrow more self-consciously from Marxism.

Finally, Qaddafi's proposed solution is a combination of tribal-style democracy, anarcho-syndicalism, and the corporate state. All this is presented in Qaddafi's three-volume *Green Book*. Many of its themes are common ones in contemporary Third World modern dictatorships and even in the seminal European dictatorships. "Democracy means popular rule, not popular expression," is a very revealing notion. The theoretical hegemony of all the masses replaces majority rule. Since the people are in control, there is no need for any free speech or other rights to criticize or oppose the government. "Representation is a falsification of democracy" is another common theme. But where most modern dictatorships would go on to extol the party and charismatic leader as true carriers of the people's will, Qaddafi's solution is the committee system, which seeks to empower everyone yet produces less real involvement than a cadre party. The greatest freedom is the right to support the righteous leader, who, by definition, represents the people.

Qaddafi's choice of green as his symbol embodies the belief in his own monopoly on political and theological virtue. Green is the color of Islam—the hue of Muhammad's banner. It also represents prosperity and development, the Bedouins' ideal of the oasis. Yet while everything possible is painted green in Libya, Qaddafi's relation to Islam is somewhat ambiguous. North African Islam has always been somewhat of a deviation to the classical tradition as viewed from Cairo and points east. Qaddafi has taken such a negative attitude toward clerical hierarchies and some commonly held Islamic beliefs that he almost seems like a Middle Eastern Martin Luther. Not only has his behavior put him at odds with Libyan mullahs, but he has also forfeited much of the cohesive value that Islam provides for Iran, Saudi Arabia, and other countries. Qaddafi has banned alcohol and instituted proper dress codes. Women are allotted a limited public role. But essentially Qaddafi's view is that Islam is what he says it is, and even compared to Khomeini, there are few outside Libya who would accept his interpretation.

Terrorism, as noted in Iran's case, is as much Qaddafi's weapon of desperation as of choice. Terrorism is a substitute for, not a means of, making revolutions. He does not have thousands of followers or powerful political movements willing to follow him. On the contrary, he must hire or subsidize small bands of a few hundred. He cannot successfully invade or organize coups in targeted countries, so he resorts to assassinations and spectacular attacks to neutralize enemies and intimidate bystanders. Further, by hosting terrorist training camps and supporting a range of groups, Qaddafi claims to be doing his Arab and Islamic duty to "liberate" Palestine, overthrow "reactionary" regimes, and bring true Muslims to power.

The most salient point about Qaddafi's foreign policy is its remarkably consistent failure. Qaddafi's desire to cause international turmoil should be taken seriously, but his capacity for doing so has repeatedly proved quite limited. One of the main reasons for this reality is his inability to make and sustain alliances. In view of his unreliability—Libya does not even deliver on most of its promised financial aid—he has alienated all of Libya's neighbors and made himself increasingly unpopular among black African states. Again, however, if he is too clumsy and ultraradical, the themes he keeps before the world—aiming to destroy Israel, blame Third World problems on the West, assert equality with the superpowers, and demand Arab unity—are widely accepted among Libyans and Arabs in general.

Essentially Qaddafi, like Khomeini, demands equality with the great powers by acting like a superpower. When the United States pressures him, he threatens to attack it. Qaddafi's efforts to obtain nuclear weapons is part of this search for equality. In all of the Middle Eastern modern dictatorships, there is a curious ambiguity in attitudes toward the United States. Qaddafi, the most outspoken critic, wants U.S. recognition and acceptance. He seeks to punish America for failing to treat him as an equal and recognizing his importance. Like the United States and USSR, Qaddafi, too, will be active everywhere in the world: He plans assassinations of foreign leaders, coups in Sudan, covert operations against Tunisia. He has virtually annexed the desert area of northern Chad and given money to the Eritrean Liberation Front, Muslims in the southern Philippines, black Muslims in the United States, and even the Irish Republican Army. He builds mosques and distributes bribes in Africa, organizes a unity march of 50,000 on the border with Egypt, and permits terrorist training bases on his own soil. Of course, Libya's capabilities do not match up to these ambitions, and attempts to convince the rest of the Third World to follow his example are, consequently, unpersuasive except when they are intimidating.

To make up for his weakness, Qaddafi uses the magnifying and transforming qualities of the media. At home the television weather map omits Egypt, Israel, and the United States. For foreign consumption and his own ego, he dons beautiful costumes, arranges press conferences and photo opportunities, even supervises the positioning of cameras. After all, Qaddafi was a communications officer, not an infantryman. It is not surprising that he is a better actor than strategist.

All modern dictatorships are proficient in using the media, but it serves them far better at home, where they have full control and know how the message will be received. During the hostage crisis Iranian leaders genuinely believed that the American people would be supportive if only they heard Tehran's message. Instead, the kidnapping of U.S. diplomats only heightened American antagonism toward Iran, dissipating the sympathy accumulated in the struggle against the Shah's traditional dictatorship. Images do not travel well across cultural barriers, but resonances within the country work far better. Khomeini was a master speaker and manipulator of symbols among Iranians; Saddam Hussein and a number of African counterparts were equally successful in projecting positive images and building direct links with the people.

Qaddafi is the most preoccupied of them all with foreign affairs. Like the regimes in Syria, Iran, Iraq, Algeria, and South Yemen, he maintains good relations with the Soviets (who are his main source of arms) but is neither their puppet nor their reliable ally. Common enemies and interests consolidate cooperation but do not undermine the Arab regimes' nationalism and priority on independence.

While other Arab governments pursue state interests, however, the Libyan dictator is obsessed with duplicating Nasser's relative mastery of the Arab world. Qaddafi courts confrontation with the United States, hoping to reproduce the 1956 Suez crisis, when Egypt, invaded by Britain, France, and Israel, emerged politically victorious against tremendous odds. Nasser became a godlike figure at home and the Arabs' hero. Qaddafi credits the miracle of Suez to Nasser's steadfastness and Arab support; a more accurate account, ironically, would point to a U.S. refusal to see Nasser overthrown. Nevertheless, Nasser once wrote that leadership in the Arab world was a role in search of an actor. As Qaddafi issues his broadsides against America, supports anti-American terrorism, or sails

off in cape and naval uniform to confront U.S. military maneuvers near his self-proclaimed "line of death," he is in search
of his own Suez crisis. On the one hand, any combination of
U.S. bluster and relative restraint would play perfectly into his
hands by giving him this chance. It would be more effective
for the West to ridicule his failures than to exaggerate his
successes. On the other hand, Qaddafi's misunderstanding of
contemporary regional politics means that he gains nothing
from these opportunities. He receives world attention but not
respect, not even among the Africans and Arabs.

To understand Qaddafi's theory of foreign policy, it is
necessary only to analyze his own words. While his practice is
more adventurous than that of other modern dictators, once
more his ideas reflect common concepts among those regimes.
Speaking at the graduation of military cadets at a ceremony
held on the former U.S. airfield in August 1985, Qaddafi
revealed some essential aspects of his thought. "We have smashed
the sign bearing the name Wheelus Field with our feet, and
have replaced it with Mi'itiqah Base . . . and the national flag
was hoisted over this base in spite of America." This echoes
the thesis that the modern dictator has reversed the power
equation, vindicating nationalism, slaying the imperialist dragon.
The change of names symbolizes this new order; the occur-
rence of one miracle—the ejection of foreign bases—attrib-
utable to good leadership and national willpower, shows that
other great deeds are possible through these qualities.

Qaddafi continued, "We are convinced . . . that force alone
has kept the peace for 40 years [between the United States
and USSR] during which time they began to manufacture
nuclear weapons and set up nuclear bases everywhere. . . .
This means that peace itself depends on force. As for the calls
we hear from them to stop any buildup of force, this is a
deception aimed to keep small peoples weak, spheres of influence influential." The centrality of force in the world and
the conspiracy against Third World sovereignty necessitate a
high degree of unity, a strong central government, and an
emphasis on military power. This requires an "armed people

259

where millions are organized [for] battle . . . so that the Arab nation, armed by the masses, will rise up and crush Zionist injustice and finish off imperialist haughtiness. . . ."

But why has this not been done already? Qaddafi's answer cannot be, as Arabs said a century ago, that their weakness is due to a lack of constitutionalism or democracy. He will not argue, like a technocrat, that a change in circumstances requires a long period of development and stability. Instead, he traces the problem to treachery: "The Arab rulers surrendered in an unprecedented manner, prostrating themselves and begging in humiliation." Even these measures, however, will bring them nothing, he claims. Qaddafi, of course, has not paid the price or accumulated the sad lessons of those states that once tried to do as he now advises.

He continues with the "finger-snapping" paradigm, claiming success in keeping the elephants far away. The only thing holding back American aggression, even occupation, is the U.S. fear of the Libya's military force. Portraying an American eagerness to invade Libya—as Khomeini does with regard to Iran—Qaddafi warns that all true nationalists must now support his leadership in this moment of crisis. Anyone who opposes his regime "is a crook and hireling," an American agent. Still, Libya will not remain on the defensive, because "unity can only be achieved with force. Thus we as revolutionaries . . . feel that from now on the sanctity of all the artificial borders should be dropped," and the rulers imposed by colonialism overthrown. Now he is no longer speaking the language of Pan-Arabism so much as he is implying—again in terms parallel to those of Islamic Iran—that those who resist will be conquered by his own state. These issues are all "internal matters, . . . like the unity of Italy . . . Germany . . . China, and . . . America. All these nations have achieved their unity by force and the international community did not interfere. Anything that happens inside the Arab homeland from the Atlantic Ocean to the [Persian] Gulf, we must consider as an internal action," a view that expresses the widely accepted idea of the Middle East as a zone that should be dominated by the Arabs or Muslims, off limits to anyone else.

Here, too, is Qaddafi's version of Third World political existentialism. So threatened is the existence of the nation that survival must take priority over everything else, but the battle for survival will inevitably allow a much higher stage of development. National existence precedes essence, willpower will shape the nature of the state and society, and the modern dictator will inspire and channel the necessary determination and organization.

Invoking equality with the West is only a stride toward the argument of proclaiming superiority. "We have to prove that this is not Grenada," continues Qaddafi. But Libya is "a nation which is greater than America. The material force of America does not make it better than the great Arab nation which created civilization."

In the end Qaddafi is both shrewd manipulator and true believer. Within his own country he can be extremely effective; in foreign policy his naïve fanaticism often gains the upper hand, and his inability to understand other people becomes a handicap. To Western ears Qaddafi is out of tune; in the regional context he plays the right notes but in a manner too strident to be ultimately appealing. Within Libya he may be less effective than comparable modern dictators, but his popularity and achievements should not be underestimated.

Modern dictators must take postures suitable to their conditions. Qaddafi is the courageous, flamboyant hero; Khomeini is the ascetic, honest, and stern servant of God; Saddam Hussein and Assad are the no-nonsense, radical-pragmatic men of the people; Mubarak is the paternalistic conciliator. Each of them will eventually die, and their immediate supporters may lose out in the ensuing power struggles. Still, each of their countries is liable to retain a style of government very much like the one they built.

CHAPTER TEN

At the Controls

Modern dictatorships are fearsome but rarely flawless. In the discussion of such topics as repression, economic control, mobilization of support, and creation of a loyal ruling group, the results should be seen in terms of relative rather than of absolute success. Some modern dictatorships, particularly in Africa, are quite ramshackle, and a regime's rhetorical claims always outstrip its successes.

All dictatorships have ways of controlling their people. The mechanisms used by modern dictatorships are more sophisticated than those used by traditional regimes. This does not imply, however, that these methods come near to the perfect totalitarian state envisioned in George Orwell's *Nineteen Eighty-four*, Aldous Huxley's *Brave New World*, or other accounts of "antiutopias." Opposing groups and individuals are never fully rooted out; repression does not catch or discourage all dissidents, nor education and tame media convince all the people. Government authority does not reach every corner of society or each of its objectives. There are always many people to cheer the dictator's fall, and not a few to help bring it about, although the result is often a similar type of regime.

Analyzing dictatorships may seem an exercise in comparative evil, but there are more hard questions than easy answers. On the "positive" side, modern dictatorships occasionally provide stability and internal peace, nationalist pride and self-respect for previously downtrodden people and groups, faster development and better conditions than predecessors, a wider distribution of benefits, and new opportunities for many individuals. Representative democracy might well do better but is not necessarily possible—or, at least, in existence—in a given country or set of political and historical circumstances.

Modern dictatorships claim to have improved their citizens' lot compared to the overthrown traditional dictatorships. If a Western critic were to call the modern dictatorship worse, its defenders would ask, "Worse for whom?" In Iran, Cuba, or Ethiopia one would be told that it is certainly now worse for those who were privileged but that they are a minority. Obviously these governments draw strength not from their victims but from supporters and beneficiaries who perceive their interests as diametrically opposed to those of the victims.

Yet modern dictators most often continue or intensify injustice, fear, torture, discrimination, lack of liberty, pervasive material and spiritual corruption, poisonous propaganda, violent hatred, xenophobia, economic decay, and aggression. The tragedy of the modern dictatorship is not so much that it worsens conditions in the short run as that it undermines evolution toward the freedom and material well-being it so energetically promises. The regime's relative strength and durability block the evolution necessary for a viable democracy. There is no sense in people's sacrificing for a future that never comes or for a better way of life for which the basis is never prepared.

At the same time the modern dictatorship has discovered, although its leaders may not consciously realize, that revolt arises not so much from poverty or repression but from a simultaneous incompetence of government and the organization of opposition groups that can challenge the regime. To counter this threat, the modern dictatorship finds new ways to discredit and repress alternative elites; monopolize military, political, and ideological power and resources in its own hands; and maximize the ruling elite's unity and popular support.

This structure does not require a totalistic state controlling every aspect of life, but it does need a regime with far more power and scope than a traditional dictatorship. The rulers can focus their attention on urban areas, particularly the capital, where the people most capable of seeking, seizing, or assisting in the exercise of state power are concentrated. The government must not be openly opposed in the villages, but its direct influence and full program need not be present, nor its ideology understood, in the nation's remotest hamlets.

The modern dictatorship's expanded authority is due in no small part to necessity. The traditional regime did not have to interfere with the country's culture, values, family structure, religion, and education, among other characteristics, because they were generally acceptable to it. Those who seek to change society, however, must transform all these aspects of life to achieve their developmental and political ends. Failure to use the new techniques and ideas will leave a vacuum that others might fill, a lesson the rulers usually discovered in their struggle against the old regime.

Part of the West went through a parallel period in the eighteenth and nineteenth centuries, but the world was then at a much lower level of technology and self-consciousness. Individual freedom was defended as a set of inalienable rights endowed by the Creator or as provisions of a social pact arrived at by individual assent. Science was defined as the right of free inquiry. In short, democratic ideology was based on not only the right to life, liberty, and the pursuit of happiness but also the chance to seek these goals in an atmosphere of pluralism and tolerance.

But the modern dictatorship believes it possesses absolute truth, as symbolized by the phrase "scientific socialism" to describe a popular variant of its ideology. This attitude is integrally related to the ideas—accepted by non-Marxist modern dictatorships as well—that freedom is the recognition of necessity and that social structures must be judged on a class basis. Capitalist repression was bad; proletarian dictatorship is good. Such thinking also opened the door to making distinctions among "progressive" and "reactionary" torture, censorship, or terrorism.

The rulers' power expanded as the citizens' rights contracted, and in its voyage from theory to ruling ideology Marxism-Leninism helped create a new class distinction between ruler and ruled. Leaders claimed superiority because their correct ideology and social background gave them a scientific understanding of social laws and history's course. This provides the perfect grounds for rising Third World elites, overturning tradition and the existing social rules, to legitimize their right to rule. As George Orwell noted in *Animal Farm*, some would be more equal than others in the new order. Once-powerful classes could be dissolved as bourgeois and antipatriotic. If workers resisted, they would be crushed by the "proletarian" regime; if intellectuals, artists, or scientists contradicted the ruling political line, they would be put down according to its "scientific" ideology.

This innovative claim of a "right" to suppress is one of the main distinctions between the traditional and modern dictatorships' attitude toward repression: the latter's attempt to create what can be called "credible" or "popular" repression. Of course, individual modern dictatorships differ greatly to the degree that they hold political prisoners, punish arbitrarily defined crimes, rig trials, mete out extreme punishments and torture, establish concentration camps, have omnipresent secret police, or exert effective control.

Perhaps the best sense of the despair wrought by this type of repression was given in 1938 by a drunken German major in occupied Prague. "To live under terrorism," he told a Hungarian journalist, "is not only a question of courage. Most acts of resistance lead to sudden arrest. To resist is generally nothing but committing an isolated suicide." The apparent hopelessness of dissent and a belief in the inevitability of retribution encourage passivity and collaboration. The dissident is deprived of publicity or, conversely, is discredited in the controlled media. Either way his message does not get out. Unless he is part of a community at odds with the regime (Soviet Jews, Sunni Syrians, an oppressed African tribe), he can be easily isolated. He is far more likely to find fellow citizens angry rather than grateful, considering him an unpatriotic scoundrel in league with foreign enemies, a troublemaker who may bring repression down on them, a reactionary favoring an unpopular former regime, or a member of a despised group. In short, the dissident not only finds himself at the mercy of the ruler's power but is also outshouted by arguments acceptable to a large portion of society.

All dictatorships use repression to intimidate dissidents and to discover their plans and activities. Brutality may also result from individual leaders' sadism or prejudice. A modern dictatorship has two additional uses for repression: purging other elite members or groups that are rivals and fabricating antigovernment plots to eliminate targeted classes and consolidate its own base of support. Traditional dictatorships prefer to paint a picture of universal serenity; modern dictatorships often benefit by stimulating a siege mentality.

While a modernizing junta benefits from the unity of the whole armed forces, modern dictatorships must build a disciplined ruling group from scratch. Purges eliminate leaders or factions that might challenge the current rulers while also providing a way to settle disputes and apportion blame for failed policies. Ironically, Friedrich Engels, Marx's coauthor and close collaborator, ridiculed this practice, writing in 1851, "When you inquire into the causes of the counterrevolutionary successes you are met on every hand with the ready reply that it was Mr. This, or Citizen That, who had 'betrayed' the people. . . . Under no circumstances does it explain . . . how it came to pass that the 'people' allowed themselves to be thus betrayed. And what a poor chance a political party stands whose entire stock in trade consists in a knowledge of the solitary fact that Citizen So-and-So is not to be trusted."

Nevertheless, Stalin's purges of the 1930s, which he extended two decades later to satellite Eastern Europe, showed that powerful political figures could be simultaneously discredited as traitors and used as scapegoats. As in those efficient factories that profitably employ every waste product, the liquidated victims are at the same time used to show how the infallible system went wrong without its being at fault. The dictator's ambitions are fulfilled while his reputation is preserved.

Losers in the battle for power suffer bodily and endure character assassination. In Ethiopia members of the ruling military council who advocated more moderate policies were murdered, sometimes in gun battles between officers. In South Yemen personal and tribal antagonisms were masked by Marxist rhetoric; the defeated clans were said to be counterrevolutionaries. In Afghanistan competing Communist parties engaged in a blood feud that would not stop at Moscow's behest. Even the threat from opposition guerrillas could not bring the factions together. Nor did sincere patriotism make the victim immune. A Syrian officer, who fled abroad when his faction was defeated, returned in 1967 to fight against Israel. He was arrested and executed.

Mexican writer Gabriel Zaid's comments on Central American revolutionaries apply to these situations. "Any combatant who is not content to be simple cannon fodder is a contender in the internal struggle for power—whether by hook (distinguishing oneself, winning over the leaders, the rank and file) or by crook. And who's right? How do you settle what's to be done (which in the final analysis is to settle who commands)? . . . It is hardly surprising that those who renounce the force of arguments and choose the arguments of force in confronting oppression should use the same arguments in settling their differences."

Such conflicts occur most often when there is no generally respected arbiter who can settle disputes. When a powerful dictator emerges, the struggle shifts to a competition for his approval. He has the power to determine who is a true, sanctified representative of the people and who is a vile traitor. When Fidel Castro said, "Everything within the revolution, nothing outside it," he retained the power to define the acceptable limits or even to change them without notice.

The goal must be total power for a single faction usually under the leadership of a single individual. There can, after all, be just one legitimate representative of the people, only one possessor of scientific ideology. All coalitions with other forces are merely transient tactical arrangements. Iran's revolution was made by a united front including moderate dem-

267

ocrats, several ethnic groups, a variety of clerical leaders, Islamic-Marxists, and Marxists. All were eliminated by Khomeini and his followers. The Syrian and Iraqi Baathists allied themselves with Nasserists, Islamic fundamentalists, Communists, and other groups, all of whom were similarly destroyed or tamed. African nationalist movements strove for independence with unanimous popular support, but while many called for freedom, few were chosen to exercise it.

The process of repression is most effective when those representing opposition political parties or advocating other economic or political systems can be portrayed as selfish minorities. In Nicaragua the Sandinista National Liberation Front (FSLN) labels anyone opposing its dictatorship as "bourgeois" and hence incapable of ever articulating the views of the majority, the workers and peasants. FSLN leaders, almost all of whom are the highly educated children of the elite, claim a monopoly on meeting the needs of the masses. History is even rewritten to portray a revolution made by a coalition or the people as a whole (as in Iran, the Arab world, or many African countries) as the sole achievement of the surviving ruling group. The Sandinistas try to omit the key role played by the moderate parties and the Catholic Church in overthrowing Somoza at a time when the FSLN was a small and isolated (though respected) group. The mass uprising began in reaction to the assassination of courageous journalist and "bourgeois" opposition leader Pedro Joaquín Chamorro. But the FSLN later banned meetings commemorating the anniversary of this murder.

Shortly after the revolution, in November 1979, Nicaragua's Catholic bishops proclaimed, "If socialism stands for power wielded in the interests of the great masses and increasingly shared by the organized people in such a manner that there is progress toward a true transfer of power to the popular classes, it will find" the church supportive. But if "it usurps the people's role as free masters of their own history, if it seeks to force people to submit to the manipulation and dictates of those who arbitrarily and unlawfully seize power, we would be unable to accept such a dubious or false socialism."

At that very moment, however, the FSLN was secretly formulating a dictatorial strategy. A December 1979 internal document explained that alliances were merely tactics "to isolate Somozaism" and expand its own forces. Now the FSLN would put its partners in their proper subordinate place. Even if the majority of the people supported the regime, their role was to applaud, not to direct, the government. "The FSLN has exercised power on behalf of the workers and other oppressed segments of society, or to put it another way, the workers exercise power through the FSLN." But how did the workers exercise this power? By following the FSLN's orders, of course.

On one level the FSLN promised to use mass mobilization as a form of democracy. "For the Sandinista Front," said the group's 1980 statement on elections, "democracy is not measured only in political terms" but by popular participation in all aspects of life. This involvement had clear limits: "The revolutionary process taking place in our country cannot go backward." The FSLN was "the true vanguard and leader of the Nicaraguan people"; no fundamental criticism of its rule and policies was permissible.

FSLN leader Humberto Ortega added, "The elections that we are talking about are very different from the elections sought by the oligarchs and traitors, the conservatives and liberals, the reactionaries and the imperialists. . . . They are not a raffle to see who has power, because the people have the power through their vanguard, the Sandinista National Liberation Front and its National Directorate." In other words, the only valid elections would be those that merely confirmed the FSLN's leadership.

This was, then, the common pattern of a two-phase revolution. The first part was the overthrow of the traditional dictatorship and the system it represented. The second stage would be the erection of a new modern dictatorship, justified as patriotic, socialistic, and more truly democratic and based on the destruction of the power of the "bourgeoisie." It was not the Sandinistas' fault, said FSLN leader Sergio Ramírez in 1981, if the middle class "misinterpreted" the situation by expecting to be a real partner in the post-Somoza era, whereas it was merely the next victim. Of course, the FSLN expected that this class would struggle against extinction; resistance only made the government's repression preemptive and defensive.

Modernizing juntas in Argentina, Brazil, and Chile also became more cogent in justifying and systematizing repression, but the junta's bloodshed and brutality reflected a frustrated inability to destroy dissent and a self-defeating dependence on violence rather than on more subtle means of base building and social control. As José Zalaquett, a Chilean human rights lawyer, describes the rationale of these Latin American regimes, "Since the war on Marxism is an insidious one, unorthodox methods are called for, including torture and extermination of irredeemable political activists. . . . Communism is to be [defeated] by decisively waging unconventional war and, at the same time, through economic policies . . . that are expected to benefit most of the population, thus curing or immunizing them from Marxism." This doctrine foresees "a democracy 'protected' by the vigilance of the armed forces, the custodians of long-term national objectives and the watchdogs of national security." The army tries but cannot play the part of FSLN, Islamic Republican party, Baath, Zimbabwe African National Union, Ethiopian Dergue, and other such "true vanguards and representatives of the people."

Thus in Latin America the modernizing juntas lack enough legitimacy, impetus for social change, or economic success to stay in power. Their more sophisticated and developmentally successful versions in such Asian countries as South Korea, Indonesia, and Pakistan survive better but fall short of the modern dictatorship's impressive hegemony.

Modern juntas' insecurities enhance their psychological need for repression; their inadequate use of ideology and institutions to build a mass base guarantees that they will have enough enemies to give them someone to punish. They invoke emergency rule or a state of siege, suspend citizens' rights and remedies, and extend the power of detention. The modernizing juntas display the first primitive signs of a sense of public relations: instead of being executed, people "disappear"; instead of being arbitrarily held in government custody, they are spirited away by mysterious death squads. Yet these are not the methods of a confident, calculating repression but the hysterical reflexes of rulers who are convinced that they have enemies everywhere but have no idea how to root out the problem.

Far more impressive is the ex-revolutionary's or coup maker's knowledge of how to stop new revolutions or coups. Milovan Djilas, the honest chronicler of Yugoslavia's Communist regime, recounts how the new rulers decided to build a modern prison. Knowing firsthand that inmates were heartened when they could communicate between cells by tapping on walls or pushing messages through drainpipes, the authorities eliminated these possibilities. The brand-new prison appeared more humane and was also more effective in demoralizing dissidents. Similarly, modern dictators understand how important it is for opponents to feel they are heard and well regarded by the people. The regime responds with slander—a dissident becomes an "enemy of the people"—and silence. International public opinion, particularly that of intellectuals, will often believe the regime's propaganda where they would never accept that of a traditional dictatorship. How else could a Nicaraguan official responsible for prisons, secret police, and censorship be lionized at a 1985 PEN writers' conference the theme of which was the abuses of state authority?

The techniques of repressive political control are well known. They include identity cards, travel restrictions, and the tying of job security to loyalty. Meetings or demonstrations must be approved by the government. A network of informers is recruited through bribery, fear, opportunism, or blackmail. The omnipresence of the regime's ears not only gives the rulers information but also sows distrust among would-be dissidents, who never know if one of their number may betray them. The terrible creativity of torturers has been amply documented. The tools of Brazil's military junta in the 1970s included electric shocks; submersion in water; beating with wooden paddles, wet ropes, plastic hose, and rubber or leather whips; steel tourniquets; burning by cigars and cigarettes; intense light; loud noise; suspension from hooks; deprivation of food and water; rape; and incarceration in tiny cells.

Syria uses such methods and variations, including beating prisoners hanging from suspended tires or upside down from the ceiling, beating the soles of the feet (painful but leaving no mark), pulling out hair or nails, pouring on boiling or icy water, torturing or sexually abusing relatives in the presence of prisoners. In Mozambique dissidents or those suspected of aiding them may be whipped or have their arms bound tightly behind their backs for hours or days. If the ropes are soaked with salt water, they contract and dig into the flesh as they dry.

Yet while torture is the most horrible means of repression, it is always applied to a limited number of people. Once the poor were the "torturable class"; today it is political activists— those whose public skills or posts make them threatening— who are so treated. Workers or peasants are more likely to be murdered without much ado. Torture knows no ideological bounds, however. The Shah's use of it against opponents made him bitterly hated by Iranians; torture continued, however, under the Islamic Republic. It was simply a matter of different people's being the victims. In both cases the psychological basis for torture was a dehumanization of dissenters, but its function was to deter those who were not imprisoned.

The "educational" role of repression on the majority is as important as its use to remove and intimidate actual opponents. For example, since state and government deserve citizens' total loyalty, other bonds can be shown as secondary. Both Khomeini and Saddam Hussein went on national television to praise fathers who had turned in their sons for execution. In Iran the boy was a leftist; in Iraq he was a draft dodger. "We have fathers and mothers denouncing their children knowing they will be tried and executed if found guilty," explained Iranian Intelligence Minister Mohammad Mohammadi Reyshahri in September 1985. These kinds of incidents occur rarely, but the publicity given them indicates the message the regime would send its citizens.

The ideas of absolute loyalty and the regime's sure ability

272

to punish enemies are meant to teach the inadmissibility of criticism and the inevitability of retribution. Qaddafi's murders of exiles overseas is an extreme but illustrative case. Equally interesting are the arrest and trial of Liberian economist Ellen Johnson-Sirleaf in 1985. Her crime was to make a speech in Philadelphia calling for less government intervention in the economy and for more spending on rural development than on large government buildings. After all, as is often explained by modern dictatorships, only constructive criticism is allowed. Johnson-Sirleaf was sentenced to ten years in a prison camp but was released as the result of U.S. pressure.

A dictatorship's top priority is to discourage, detain, or eliminate active opponents. Modern dictatorships are more likely than traditional ones to define whole groups—business, intellectual, ethnic, etc.—as objects for suppression. The technique must be adjusted to the threat and target. Infinite and never resting are the ways of repression. Thousands of refugees are expelled, the movement of citizens is controlled within the country, or citizens are barred from going abroad. Other peoples are forcibly resettled. Mozambique and Iran have public flogging, South Africa and Zaire practice "banning," a form of house arrest which stops activists from meeting with other people or speaking publicly. Every dictatorship has political prisoners, and most have laws permitting, to quote Tanzania's statute, the arrest of anyone "considered dangerous to public order or national security." Journalists and teachers lose their jobs for saying or writing the wrong ideas or facts. Nigeria's military regime issued an order allowing imprisonment of up to two years for publishing anything "calculated to bring the Federal Military Government . . . or a public officer to ridicule or disrepute."

The police and other services charged with destroying opposition are given special privileges in all dictatorships. In Haiti Duvalier's Tonton's Macoute, with their trademark sunglasses, provoked tremendous fear by their mere presence and such hatred that they were killed on sight after the dictatorship's fall. In Iran the police are limited to traffic control, building security, and criminal investigation; special Islamic groups have authority over religious, counterrevolutionary, and drug crimes. Modernizing juntas or traditional dictatorships may respond to revolutionary threats by semiofficial death squads; modern dictatorships prefer more disciplined methods.

If the army has to be called out against dissidents, the situation has already degenerated seriously. In Iran and the Philippines large segments of the military refused to defend traditional dictatorships. There is always the chance, as happened to Zulfikar Ali Bhutto in Pakistan, that soldiers mustered to suppress opponents might themselves seize power. And an army racked by corruption, with officers promoted for loyalty rather than competence and with soldiers reluctant to fight, is not necessarily a bulwark against determined revolutionaries. Many African armies are so poorly equipped and disciplined that they are more a danger to than a protector for civilian rulers.

Every regime must blend its own mix of repressive institutions. The important point is that these instruments of control be effective. George Orwell's novel *Nineteen Eighty-four* was misleading in creating the "perfect" repressive state, just as it proved unenlightening to designate Nazi Germany and Stalinist Russia as "model" totalitarian states. There is no such thing as a completely secure and successful system of repression, as there is no truly perfect crime, because people living in the society witness the evidence and some will understand the system's nature. From the dictator's point of view the proper amount of repression is not the maximum possible but simply the amount needed to retain control. The most repression is required when the regime is first consolidating power or facing a serious crisis.

Dissidents, at least cautious ones, will always exist, but when they are afraid or unable to organize and propagandize, they do not endanger the regime. Traditional dictatorships have proved far more vulnerable, despite their brutality and priority on violence, because they are overly dependent on repression and yet find it difficult to carry out systematically.

They can kill, imprison, torture, or intimidate intellectuals, but they have a hard time gaining their loyalty. Modern dictatorships are quite willing to use repression when necessary, but they can also win a significant portion of this key social group. These regimes are equally capable, unlike traditional dictatorships, of completely uprooting troublesome sectors.

A modern dictatorship that uses ideology, patriotism, revolutionary chic to make opposition seem abhorrent and that succeeds (or appears to try to help) in ameliorating the poor's suffering and the nation's underdevelopment will gain the backing of teachers, writers, journalists, and others who can help it control the media, education, and culture. Repression and material rewards, the same techniques used by the traditional dictatorship, still have great supplemental value but are so justified as to be less embarrassing for those who would rationalize service to the regime. As in any other group, many intellectuals are opportunists or cowards, but they are determined never to appear this way. Traditional dictatorships invite opposition since collaboration can be motivated only by fear or careerism.

By developing a clear sense of strategy and tactics plus a way of defining friends and enemies, the modern dictatorship gains confidence and a way of indoctrinating supporters. Ideology, a systematic set of ideas explaining how the world works and how it can be changed, is a tool giving the modern dictatorship a great advantage over a traditional one. The entirety of the revolution's and dictator's rhetoric can be seen as a text which (when combined with their political practice) reveals the new system. A caudillo or even a modernizing junta rarely worries much about ideas and, at any rate, takes its assumptions for granted. The modern dictator's theory is seen as objective truth—indeed, the sole objective truth—it is commonly described as "scientific." It is used to predict the behavior of classes and the steps needed to make and secure a revolution. These ideas are not mere rationalizations. They are themselves a source of strength, capable of cementing loyalties within the ruling group and between the people and

275

leaders, and a set of instructions for keeping power. No more are these regimes, to use a popular Latin American phrase, gorillas in power.

During the monarchical era in Western, Islamic, and Asian civilizations religion was taken as explaining the meaning of life. Courtiers like Machiavelli penned guides for princes on managing political affairs. Ideology now performs both functions. But while earlier practical guides to the art of politics and governing were intended for a small group, the new doctrines are composed for a large body of cadre, organizational, and local leaders, even ordinary citizens. Mao Zedong's *Red Book*, a collection of his sayings and extracts from his works, is a case in point. The small volume, published in tens of millions of copies, served as a modernizing agent. By teaching Chinese peasants and workers that they could change the world through their own actions, it undermined a traditional philosophy that rested on repetition of old patterns of behavior, fear of change, and submission to gods, rulers, and natural forces. The *Red Book* provided ethical guidelines (placing society rather than family first), methods for pragmatically reasoning out problems (truth came from analyzing experience and from scientific experiment), and ways to organize people to achieve common ends. At the same time the regime used the book—and traditional thinking transformed it—as a quasi-religious document to symbolize and inspire reflexive support for the government.

While slogans and simpler concepts are needed to motivate or manipulate the masses, highly educated people require more sophisticated treatment. Fanon gives an important clue to this process, noting that "individualism is the first to disappear" among intellectuals who join the struggle and trade their egoism for the joy of merging themselves into the people. Many of them willingly accede to a system that grants absolution for their guilt about privileges and promises an escape from lonely alienation. Having a cause to believe in, such individuals accordingly redefine their values. "Truth," wrote Fanon, "is the property of the national cause. . . . Truth is that which hurries on the break-up of the colonialist regime, . . .

promotes the emergence of the nation, . . . protects the natives, and ruins the foreigners."

For those who accept the doctrine, whatever promotes the revolution or regime is good, and that which threatens it is immoral. Propaganda and misinformation, something these people railed against under the traditional dictatorship, now become sanctified. This kind of thinking also infects "progressive," sympathetic intellectuals abroad. Facts must be treated warily if they can be used to further the cause of "reactionaries." One should not criticize Nicaragua, for example, since to do so might aid the Reagan administration policy of attacking that country.

Roque Dalton, a Salvadoran poet who joined the guerrillas in his country, expressed this eagerness of the intellectual for self-transformation. "We cannot, without . . . a useless measure of vanity that can only amount to impotence," he wrote, "assume the defeat of Nazism, for example, and not assume the Stalin of the concentration camps. Or insist on emphasizing the conditions I as a lily-white intellectual attach to supporting the Cuban Revolution. Who are we to go putting conditions on the power of the people, when this power never . . . summoned us to support it! It has allowed us to support it, at any rate, and I for one feel grateful. The revolutionary's support of a revolution is, in essence, unconditional." Unfortunately some of his comrades concluded that the "power of the people" required branding Dalton a petty bourgeois CIA agent and executed him after a mock trial.

Exchanging independent judgment for the promise of a populist utopia, then, is a dangerous practice. Marx explained that philosophers only analyzed the world; the point was to change it. Yet, he added, "Even the educator must be educated." Someone is going to do the defining of what is good and evil, what is revolutionary and reactionary. In modern dictatorships and the movements that spawn them, leaders—not the "people"—perform this function, and to surrender oneself to the "popular will" is usually to yield one's autonomy to the dictatorship.

Consequently, says radical French writer Gérard Chaliand, "Intellectuals all too rarely fulfill their main function, which is to provide criticism. Most of the time, in the Third World, intellectuals are nothing but bootblacks, hack propagandists for whoever is in power." Even in Western countries "snobbishness and fashion all too often prevail over critical analysis. And too often intellectuals make themselves the unconditional spokesmen and promoters of ruling powers and ideology by actively lending a hand—often in good faith—to the upkeep of mystifications, simplifications, and sectarian dogmas."

Mexico, the mild polity of which might be called a democracy where the ruling party almost always wins, has institutionalized this relationship. Intellectuals there are a privileged elite, promoted, financed, and tolerated by the government. As journalist Alan Riding wrote, "It is a strangely incestuous relationship, rich in posturing and ritual, obscured by radical language, frequently denied by both sides and long ago determined to be mutually convenient."

In more virulent specimens the game becomes serious, even deadly. The modern dictatorship's ideology soothes those who must bridge the gap between truth and falsehood into a willingness to cover up contradictions, what Orwell called "double-think." As Jean-Paul Sartre said of Stalinism, "In the name of realism, we were forbidden to depict reality; in the name of the cult of youth, we were prevented from being young; in the name of socialist joy, joyousness was repressed." As long as Communist intellectuals believed in the system, "at least as the thankless and painful way that leads to true socialism. . . . First they resigned themselves to Evil because they saw in it the one way to attain Good, then . . . they saw in it Good itself, and took their own resistance to the process of petrification to be Evil."

Accepting the party's view as the right view, the outlook of the working class and nation by whom they passionately desired to be accepted as full members, they adopted a faith both blind and expedient. "Cement poured . . . through their eyes and ears," added Sartre, "and they considered the protests of their simple good sense to be the residue of a bourgeois ideology that cut them off from the people." What better acknowledgment of this pattern's power than the fact that Sartre, who so brilliantly diagnosed the malady, was afflicted by it to the end of his life?

The formative era in a new modern dictatorship's drive for ideological and cultural hegemony is well illustrated in Sandinista-ruled Nicaragua. Pablo Antonio Cuadra, a leading writer, explains that his country's long rule by traditional dictators fed a yearning for democracy that played the main role in the anti-Somoza revolution, a movement taken over by the Sandinistas who "brought us back to our point of departure—from dictatorship to dictatorship." In the Marxist dialectic's spirit, it was a much higher level of dictatorship.

The Sandinistas present Marxism as the sole path for modernization but find it expedient to deny their objectives in order to maintain the support of foreign democrats. Attempts to point out the reality behind the rhetoric are censored ("The Communists disdain to conceal their aims," Marx's famous declaration in his *Communist Manifesto*, has been made hollow by history). "Hypocrisy, false labels, can create slogans but not poems; propaganda but not life," complains Cuadra. But he misses the point: The regime wants propaganda, particularly the type that convinces people it is something else.

The Sandinista minister of culture, Ernesto Cardenal, a fine poet in his own right, promised absolute cultural freedom after the revolution. But the First Convention of Cultural Workers in February 1980 formulated the new, narrow definition of proper revolutionary culture. Cuadra says, "By virtue of possessing power, [Sandinista leaders] were converted into supermen, individuals of extraordinary talent . . . qualified to send all of the intellectuals and artists to a ramshackle schoolhouse, where they would be taught how . . . they ought to work. . . ."

Sandinista leader Bayardo Arce explained, "We should not like to see culture ever again assume the decadent forms it has taken in the past. . . . We want to retain artistic quality, but remember, please, that art is of no value if it is not understood by workers and peasants. We want a situation where, every time someone paints a picture or writes a poem, publishes a book or arranges a song, [he] asks himself, first, to what degree is it going to assist our people in the process of self-transformation." Fellow Comandante Sergio Ramírez, himself a novelist, added, "We never thought to admit the existence of a culture isolated from the revolutionary process." The traditional dictatorship condemned anything that seemed to criticize its treatment of the masses or to defend their rights. Now, in the name of those masses' well-being and rights, the modern dictatorship prohibits the very same kinds of criticisms. It is still censorship but of an apparently more attractive sort—"democratic" and "socialist" censorship—for intellectuals at home and observers abroad. Punishment was no longer for advocating pluralism and social change—ideas the traditional dictatorship labeled "revolutionary" and "communistic"—but for being selfish and reactionary in opposing them or denying that they already existed.

To ensure the incumbents' monopoly on truth, justice, and progress is to deny any alternative. Ramírez called all Nicaraguan culture prior to the revolution "a failure," despite the fact that Nicaragua was known in the region as the "country of poets." And, he explained in another speech, "Revolutionary culture, just because it is revolutionary, cannot fail to be authentic." It is no accident that one of the regime's slogans is "Nicaraguan history begins with the Sandinista Front." Everything else is either Somocista or "bourgeois."

As Cuadra comments, "In one fell swoop literature and art were converted into branches of the bureaucracy." First came threats, then a ban on publishing or even citing the work of those deemed uncooperative. The Union of Cultural Workers, a government-controlled group armed with privileges and punishments, threatened similar treatment to anyone writing for the opposition newspaper. Artists backed down or used pen names to avoid reprisals. The Ministry of Culture held workshops to develop proletarian writers whose gratitude and lack of experience would ensure their reliability. As one of these apprentices explained on state television, "Before now I was in error: I went about writing love poems. In the work-

280

shop I have learned why my poetry was bad—it had no political message." Needless to say, it was not merely a matter of having a political message but of having the right political message.

But, a liberationist clergyman or intellectual might quickly reply, the treatment of pampered artists is of little import if the lot of the people is being improved. Many of these same pampered artists would agree, particularly given the irony that agreement—and hence collaboration—ensures their privileges. It is a paradox easily grasped, and after all, depending on the country, the modern dictatorship's policies may genuinely benefit many of the hitherto downtrodden common people.

Whether or not this is true, the regime tirelessly claims it as so. Bayardo Arce shows why Nicaraguan workers do not require independent trade unions or the right to strike and why all criticisms of their condition are, by definition, false. These workers "now have class consciousness," which means a lack of interest in "salary increases, a reduction of the work week, or an increase in vacations. . . . Payment for overtime has been replaced by the revolutionary concept of voluntary work and other necessary sacrifices for the defense of the revolution."

Again, in some cases—particularly in the earlier stages, when hope and spontaneous enthusiasm run high—people are willing to make personal sacrifices. Arce's phrase "defense of the revolution" is central to this context. The greatest motivation for supporting the Sandinistas is fear that the clock will be turned back, combined with a patriotic rejection of foreign interference. These are key elements in the modern dictatorship's ideology and may or may not reflect real threats. Patriotism may be the "last refuge of scoundrels," but it is also the strongest ally of modern dictators.

Problems and dissension are externalized, pinned on imperialism and its agents. The Communists took over in North Vietnam by gaining hegemony in the nationalist movement. Their comrades elsewhere usually failed because they were distracted by other issues, including protecting Moscow's interests, from being guided by such indigenous considerations.

After Vietnam had gained independence from France, Hanoi welded the state together in a struggle to reunite the nation, drive out the Americans, and conquer Laos and Cambodia.

In Ethiopia the United States gave hundreds of thousands of tons of food (paying $28 million for port fees in 1984 for the privilege of doing so). The Soviet Union contributed little—even charging for its truck drivers' services and overcharging for the oil it sold. But on May Day the posters showed Marx, Engels, and Lenin, and the slogans accused Western imperialists of waging "psychological warfare" against the country. Said dictator Mengistu: "They vilify and oppose all our positive efforts [against famine] and pretend to sympathize with our people."

Meanwhile, seven-year-olds are trained in military drill, chanting, "Hit, stab, kick, kill!" A guide told visiting American writers, "We are not militarists, you understand, but we must involve even the youngest in the defense of our revolutionary motherland." And how can those not devoted to the nation be unmasked as reactionaries and obstructionists? A young commissar explains, "Usually they give themselves away by asking the same question over and over in discussions."

There are, then, many common themes in modern dictatorships' ideology: The people rule the nation, and the government represents the people. Since the leader responds to the people's requests, elections and limits on the state's power not only are unnecessary but would actually damage the people's interests. Surrounded by enemies, pinned down by underdevelopment, the nation requires absolute unity. Unity means supporting the regime. Those who demand more rights, call for change, or criticize policies break that unity. They are traitors who objectively help the nation's enemies. By repressing them, the regime is protecting the people. Perhaps nobody believes all of this, but many citizens believe some of it.

By mobilizing nationalist sentiments, a leader like Khomeini or Qaddafi tells his people: The United States is not attacking me, it is attacking you. By controlling education, a modern dictatorship also seeks to inculcate identification with the regime. In many individual cases the effort will fail; in many others it will have some real effect. The "philosophy program" for teacher training in Nicaragua says, "Our education has as its objective the training of new generations in the scientific, political, ideological, and moral principles enunciated by our national leadership, the FSLN, turning them into convictions and habits of daily life." Children practice handwriting in first grade with the slogan "The FSLN guided and guides the struggles of the people." A reading text explains, "The Yankees will always be defeated in our country," and the "symbols of the revolution" are the FSLN flag and hymn. Obviously, even though other parties are still permitted, they are not accorded much legitimacy and will certainly never be allowed to take power.

As the modern dictatorship's ideology recognizes, power springs from controlling and using a wide variety of institutions and channels, including the military, repression, culture, education, ideology, youth and professional organizations, and the media. As the regime's property they are denied independence or any critical content.

Political censorship is a form of cowardice, an admission that the existing system cannot face criticism and emerge unscathed. By refusing to allow the contradiction of official ideology and description of events, the regime outlaws nonconformity. Yet criticism can also be a safety net. Cuadra comments, "As I have told my Sandinista friends and former friends until I am blue in the face: any revolution which denies the right to criticize is bound to wallow in stagnation and backwardness." This is not difficult to prove. In Czechoslovakia the brief period of "socialism with a human face" revealed, Sartre said, "ruins, the ravaged economy threatened to collapse; the factories, now many years old, were spewing out products of mediocre quality, and no attention was being paid to the real needs . . . the level of technical and professional skills was falling day by day . . . since official lies and the faking of statistics had not only destroyed what knowledge there had once been but also completely halted surveys and socioeconomic research on the realities of the situation."

Nevertheless, the modern dictatorship portrays as virtue

what democrats see as vice. The newspapers, radio, and television will be changed from an instrument of decadence and commercialism into a tool for development and education. Instead of commercials for soap and cars, news and culture sell the state itself. The positive side of this can be mobilization for modernization and an appeal to the audience's finer motives—patriotism and social service—instead of its desire for money and material goods. Having limited resources and much experience with media sensationalism, Third World states can argue that "developmental journalism" is both necessary and more responsible than the alternative. The negative side, of course, is that the media are totally subject to government manipulation. Different views are not permitted; the gap between reportage and reality may be quite wide.

Radio, rather than newspapers or television, is the ideal media for modern dictatorships. Compared to newspapers, radio involves a large, complex, and expensive apparatus, which limits the number of potential proprietors. When such regimes came to power in past decades, radio was just being started and lacked the traditions and established private ownership of the print media. The limited number of stations that could be established and the precedent of government ownership in Europe also helped justify a state monopoly on radio in Africa and the Middle East.

The newspaper requires literacy, a fast distribution system, employment of many journalists, and people willing and able to pay its daily price. More easily established, newspapers tend to multiply and, if not state controlled, to represent a diversity of opinions and parties. Television, too expensive both for the consumer and the broadcaster to be widely used in Third World states, also requires electricity, often lacking in rural areas. Television's demand for high-cost, visually engaging programs makes it tempting to use cheap Western imported material, which the modern dictatorship seeks to avoid or at least to limit.

Radio more easily carries the emotional, rhetorical appeals of the rulers, which can be stirring when heard but boring in print. When not broadcasting state-controlled news, it can play music, less politically threatening than television's entertainment programs from alien cultures or the newspapers' filler items of foreign news or prying information about domestic developments. But the modern dictatorship's philosophy justifies directing, controlling, and censoring all types of media.

An official Somalian decree, reported by journalist David Lamb, provides a good sense of the modern dictatorship's role for the media: "It is the function of the nation's mass communications media to weld the entire community into a single entity, a people of the same mind and possessed of the same determination to safeguard the national interests." The state has many sanctions to achieve this goal. The Ivory Coast's president, Félix Houphouët-Boigny, a relatively benign dictator, explained that he never sent journalists "to prison, but to do their military service in order that they may not engage in fruitless agitation. I put them in direct contact with the army. They had affirmed that the army was not on my side. I could not offer them a better opportunity to win the army to their side."

The ruler of Sierra Leone, Major General Joseph Momoh, told a rally in August 1985 that the press enjoyed absolute freedom but that this did not constitute a right to attack the state, engage in character assassination, or circulate gossip and rumors. Responsible journalism must be patriotic, promote peace and stability, and help eliminate tribalism. This meant refraining from publishing items that undermined the security of the state or portrayed the country in a poor light. A 1985 law passed by Iran's parliament forbade stories that promote atheism; support prostitution or are contrary to public decency; publicize extravagance and waste; provoke acts harmful to society; reveal military secrets or speeches from closed sessions of parliament; insult the "true religion of Islam"; involve plagiarism; or imply "calumny, vilification, and insults to the country's authorities, establishments, organs and individuals, even by publishing photographs or caricatures." Publication of this law is, strange as it may seem, a mark of relative openness; many states keep the parameters of censorship themselves quite secret.

285

Sometimes journalists are intimidated and repressed by the government, but many are genuine loyalists—an attitude which may explain how they gain and keep their jobs—or patriots who agree that criticism is embarrassing. Ridiculing those who wrote critically of the Ivory Coast, the newspaper *Fraternité Matin*, responded, "We have made our national identity blossom. And we are all voluntarily committed to its protection [so] that . . . like our president, we defy those who—on their own—have alienated themselves from our country. But . . . what really can a bird do against the tree which held its nest and shelters it as an adult?"

Ayatollah Khomeini told employees of the Tehran newspaper *Kayhan*: "The press must write what the nation wants, not that which runs counter to the nation's courses. . . . If the press still wants to write anything in support of criminals and traitors, this will not be our press—this will be treachery."

Given this philosophy, it was logical for Khomeini's followers to assume the same system prevailed in other countries—if not openly, then behind the scenes—and that the U.S. media was, in the words of Radio Tehran, controlled by "imperialism, American intelligence," and other hostile forces conducting psychological warfare against Iran.

Just as certain cultures view opposition or criticism as divisive ingratitude, many Third World leaders are genuinely incapable of comprehending the functioning of a free press. Twenty years before anyone ever heard of "developmental journalism," Nasser could not believe that articles in U.S. newspapers did not necessarily reflect government views. Yet many dictatorial elites also understand their own need to obtain reliable information. In China a series of secret publications provide accurate information on domestic problems, real popular attitudes, natural disasters, and translations of articles from the foreign press. The higher-ranking the official, the more data he receives. These publications' very existence is rarely mentioned. A Chinese leader commented in 1956, "Something that has happened may be true, but if open reporting about it serves the enemy and not our own cause, then

286

we cannot allow it to be openly reported, but should rather write about it internally."

Leaders are particularly worried, as the Iranian law cited above indicates, about news on corruption. The modern dictatorship does not eliminate corruption but makes certain qualitative changes in it, "democratizing" opportunities for enrichment to reward a much larger group of regime loyalists and officials. By turning much of the economy into state property, by promulgating unworkable regulations, and by its own mismanagement, the modern dictatorship may force citizens to become corrupt in order to carry on daily life. At the same time this situation gives the regime another form of leverage over individuals since almost anyone could be tried for illegal activities.

As in a traditional dictatorship, however, if corruption gets out of hand, the regime can break down entirely. Ghana's Cocoa Marketing Board, for example, was unable to account for half of its foreign exchange earnings from 1975 to 1979. Some of the money must have gone to pay for the Mercedes-Benz cars flown into the country (estimated cost plus shipping: $110,000) by the ruling junta's members. A high Nigerian official serving a military government, however, said of civilian regimes, "It's as if they take some sort of delight in violating their sacred trust. At least," he added in frustration, "the military ethic keeps their corruption manageable."

The Nicaraguan Communist party, often critical of the Sandinistas, complained in March 1985 that "the fundamental cause of corruption is the ruling party's concept of . . . public funds as private property," an attitude that is not, however, unknown in Moscow. Leaders' salaries are secret; they are given cars and exempted from paying for rent, telephone, electricity, or water. They also have access to U.S. dollars for use in buying imported luxuries at special stores, a common practice in Third World dictatorships.

When accused of mismanagement, the regime lashes back. Nicaraguan President Daniel Ortega laid, with some justification, the source of economic problems on U.S. policy but he

287

also blamed "a few of its accomplices in this country." Their real complaint, he said, was that the revolution granted workers too much "participation and liberty . . . and that these workers require a millionaire employer in order to produce well." The kind of efficiency they allegedly preferred was that of the Somoza regime. These last points are tendentious—the state, not the workers, now ran the economy; Somoza or the Sandinistas were not the sole conceivable alternatives—but can nonetheless be quite effective in discrediting criticism and in rallying support.

The new elites justify their privileges by past services and current importance but are careful not to flaunt their lifestyles. Sandinista leader Tomás Borge tried to trick foreign journalists into believing that he actually lived in the modest bungalow where he received them. Both the illusion and the reality still contrasted sharply with the opulence of a Somoza, Marcos, or Shah who seemed to be personally trying to consume the country's entire wealth. After the revolutions against all three traditional dictators their material gluttony provoked international astonishment and disgust.

But what is rejected is the gluttony, not materialism itself. While Western romantics have sometimes seen Third World modern dictatorships as attractively ascetic, the rulers and their people want higher living standards and modern manufactured goods and services. Complaints about Western cultural imperialism unabashedly coexist with demands for Western products. The most inconsistent behavior is seen on the part of the leaders themselves, who are usually—Iran being an exception—among the most cosmopolitan or Westernized elements.

To meet the needs of the people—survival in the case of the majority, consumer goods for the urban, better-off sectors—the government must be able to show some economic success and progress. After all, development is a central goal of the regime, which claims to be implementing the necessary strategy and imposed discipline for achieving it. Obviously no government wishes to take responsibility for shortcomings in these efforts, preferring to blame predecessors or externalize the problem by attributing it to foreign imperialists. Since the Soviets did not rule Third World countries in the colonial era and tended to play a relatively small part in providing trade or investment, the West is usually the target of such criticism.

This approach is as common as it is appealing to Third World leaders and intellectuals who have adapted parts of the Marxist analysis. Typically, a reporter for the relatively moderate magazine *Jeune Afrique* interviewing Ivory Coast President Houphouët-Boigny in August 1985, said, "Your Western friends, short of plundering the raw materials, do not do anything to get the Third World countries out of their predicaments. . . ." The president interrupted. "Africans are the first to be held responsible." The frustrated reporter asked if the country's past economic crisis "made Ivorians at least more vigilant and more conscious?" Houphouët-Boigny responded, "It has taught us not to live beyond our means anymore."

The Ivory Coast's president, however, is very old and is widely viewed as a lapdog of the West. Few other leaders would take such primary responsibility for the roots or consequences of their problems. Yet, perhaps not by coincidence, Houphouët-Boigny is also leader of what is perhaps the most economically successful country in sub-Saharan Africa.

By their nature, modern dictatorships want to be in control of the economy, but they have a choice of whether or not to seek direct command of it. Some, particularly the more Marxist among them, take over all industry and set out on a course of "class struggle" to destroy any independent middle class. In most cases, however, they have wisely refrained from turning land into state farms—peasants' land hunger being so great—although the countryside may be organized into cooperatives. Other states have been content simply to control the economy's commanding heights—bargaining with foreign multinationals, purchasing and exporting domestically produced crops and minerals, directing major projects, nationalizing banks and overseas trade—while permitting a significant private sector to continue as long as it keeps its place.

This was, for example, Nasser's course after he'd taken power in Egypt in 1952. He carried out an agrarian reform, nationalized foreign property, expanded the state bureaucracy to provide jobs, and improved health and education in the impoverished rural areas. So great was the psychological impact that his popularity twenty years later could still be traced to these programs.

The modern dictatorship's power is so broad that the rulers begin to believe they can do anything; ideology and propaganda persuade them that they know the right choice. A regime can easily confuse ordering a certain social or economic change with the ability—or value—of implementing it.

In 1973 Tanzania's ruling party decreed that all farmers—11 to 12 million people—should form collective villages within three years. The regime believed that concentrating the peasantry would improve productivity and allow the more effective delivery of schools, clinics, and running water. President Julius Nyerere went into the countryside for some symbolic hoeing. The picture was posted around the country and published in the foreign press.

Independent-minded farmers, including the most productive, were reluctant to leave their ancestral lands and private plots. Local officials, pressured by superiors and eager to show their zeal in implementing orders, forced peasants at gunpoint to go to the new sites. Some of them were dumped in the bush and told to build villages; others were sent to places with incomplete houses and no available water. Production levels fell sharply; low official prices encouraged farmers to smuggle their remaining crops across the border to Kenya. Tanzania's economy collapsed.

National weakness and poverty force many unpalatable choices on Third World leaders. In Kenya peasants can migrate freely to the city, creating giant slums and bad conditions; in Tanzania would-be urbanites are loaded into trucks and returned to the villages. The first system involves more suffering; the second requires more compulsion. Kenya's choice is based on rural overpopulation and a fairly laissez-faire ideology. Tanzania's policy is a response to having so much uncultivated land and an ideology that justifies such measures.

Nyerere's popularity and control allowed him to survive

the collectivization mess, just as a repressive Ethiopian regime could spend $4 billion for arms and only 3 percent of its budget for famine relief during its first ten years in power. It is better not to court disaster, but where there are neither political alternatives to threaten the regime nor clear solutions to rescue the people, many governments can survive mistakes for a long time. If they do fall, the successors are usually similar regimes that can say they represent a fresh start.

The most successful industrialization policies in the Third World have been practiced by South Korea's modernizing junta and by modern dictatorships in Taiwan and Singapore. They combined high government spending, a low-paid and disciplined work force, and ability to absorb new technology in order to produce manufactured goods for export. Modernizing juntas in Argentina and Brazil have tried unsuccessfully to copy this pattern.

African societies cannot hope to finance or organize industrialization outside the government. The Ivory Coast became the most successful of black African countries in agricultural development by giving private farmers good prices and a free hand. It became a leading coffee and cacao exporter, expanded food production faster than the population growth, and diversified with new crops.

But there are reasons why other countries find it difficult to copy a South Korea or an Ivory Coast. Third World producers of raw materials or cheap manufactured goods compete with each other. Success for one saturates the other's potential markets; increased production of bauxite, tin, cocoa, or coffee means lower international prices. The industrialized countries may put up protective customs barriers against cheap Third World manufactured goods. Only the oil-producing cartel managed to escape this trap even partly, and its ability to control production and raise prices spelled economic disaster for dozens of Third World oil-importing states. By the mid-1980s even OPEC was unable to stave off the oil glut's downward effect on prices.

At about the same time economic problems forced many countries, notably China, to experiment with reforms, including decentralized decision making, market forces, material incentives to encourage workers and peasants, joint projects with foreign multinationals, and additional private farm plots. These steps might help individuals or the economy for a whole, but they are not allowed to challenge the ruling party's control. As Mao Zedong indicated, politics—not efficiency or development—must be in command. The contrary, pragmatic view was articulated by Deng Xiaoping, Mao's eventual successor: "It doesn't matter whether a cat is black or white, as long as it catches mice." This is all right, some modern dictators could add, as long as the cat—businessman, professional, intellectual—doesn't eat them.

Clearly, then, there is no one foolproof strategy for development. In Third World countries, however, the state's role in the economy—even in relatively laissez-faire states— is going to be much greater than is common in the West. This situation is due partly to necessity, partly to the modern dictatorship's determination to use the economy for its own purposes.

Repression, ideology, and control of the culture, media, and economy are factors through which the modern dictatorship rules its society. This system goes far beyond a regime based only on fear and torture in its attempts both to dominate society and to build a positive base of support. Effective repression clears the field of rivals who are deprived of their livelihood, audience, legitimacy, and freedom. The regime's message is broadcast everywhere while alternative or opposition views are kept out of schools or the media. The economy is reorganized to control or eliminate any independent class outside the ruling group while giving the government funds and jobs to attract supporters. Other techniques and relationships go even further in allowing the modern dictatorship to mobilize supporters, loyalty, and legitimacy.

In fact, indoctrination does work to considerable extent, particularly on a younger generation whose experience is totally within the framework of such a regime. Obviously, the success rate is never close to 100 percent except in the imaginary dictatorships of novels. There are always brave individuals who dissent but they are a minority. Most of those who

292

oppose the regime remain silent and most of those who speak out are not effective in undermining the type of government under which they live. The majority is either supportive or passive, willing perhaps to celebrate the modern dictator's fall but unlikely to help bring it about. Even such courageous critics as Aleksandr Solzhenitsyn and Anatoly Shcharansky were passionate true believers before their disillusionment. Such pessimism gives one no pleasure and it would be far preferable to speak of the heroic human spirit refusing to submit to the chains of tyranny, but this is not the main experience of history when it comes to modern dictatorships.

CHAPTER ELEVEN

The Ruler's Rules

Modern dictatorships rely on control (of the economy, military, media, and culture) and fear (repression). They also develop a nationalism and ideology—Sandinism, Islamic fundamentalism, Nyerere's *ujaama*, Nasserism, Qaddafi's "third way," Baath socialism, scientific socialism, Marxism, and all the local variants—and they create groups—a party and mass organizations—that build links within the elite and with the masses. The dictator himself embodies the regime as a whole, inspiring fear and confidence, pride and hope.

He must be tough, self-confident, and decisive, daring but balanced. Whether as a vigorous young revolutionary or as a respected, wise elder, he must be capable of imposing his will on others. He must awe the masses to command respect but also needs to appear as one of them to work his populist magic. The purpose of my rule, he tells his people, is to elevate you. "China has brought forth Mao Zedong," according to the words of "The East Is Red," anthem of the Chinese Cultural Revolution. "He works for the people's happiness. . . . He's the people's savior." The idea of the servant/savior, not unknown to religion, reflects the dictator's need to balance ambition with image. Asceticism is a good posture. There are none of the sybaritic tendencies of conspicuous consumption, at least not witnessed by the public.

Dictators seek power and glory rather than wealth, but

unlimited control can turn the modern dictator into a mega-lomaniac. Kim Il Sung, the Communist leader of North Korea, had a fifty-six-story tower built to mark his seventieth birthday, with one piece of granite for each day of his life. North Korean literature is largely devoted to his worship. He made his son political heir. Kim Il Sung's version of Marxism, *juche*, studied in mandatory after-work classes, stresses national self-reliance and is more reminiscent of Third World ideology than of Moscovite orthodoxy. There is no unemployment, no private cars, and no freedom. People are even marched out of their workplaces in formation at the end of the day.

Most modern dictators prefer to keep their cult of personality under some control. Syria's Assad does not drink, has only one wife, and gave up chain-smoking overnight for health reasons. Ayatollah Khomeini ordered his photo removed from mosques and asked the media to reduce the space devoted to him. But the dictator must also be a public figure, the country's leading celebrity and rock star. Japan's emperor was considered a god, and the highest honor was to give up one's life for him. Yet until he announced Japan's surrender on radio in 1945, the public had never heard his voice, whose high-pitched tone and mere mortal sound surprised them.

Today dictators like Fidel Castro, Saddam Hussein, or Samora Machel are constantly on television and radio, greeting delegations, making long speeches, visiting schools and farms around the country. Qaddafi is a master of the media: dressing in peasant garb to drive a tractor or a navy uniform to patrol Libyan waters. The African leader creates the image of himself as chief of a nation that is one big family, one big village. Zaire's Mobutu and Togo's president took the title of Guide, Nyerere, The Teacher, Malawi's dictator Hastings Banda, Chief of Chiefs, and Kenya's Jomo Kenyatta, Wise Old Man.

So widely known has the style of behavior become that it almost seems subject to self-parody. On first taking office, Liberian dictator Samuel Doe wore his military camouflage fatigues, a gold pin saying "Chairman," yellow sunglasses, and an army beret or cowboy hat, and he carried a machine gun or two-way radio. Qaddafi often appears to be playing a stage role as dictator, though actors are not unknown among world leaders elsewhere today.

When Kenya's leader Kenyatta died, his successor as president, Daniel Arap Moi, announced he would call himself Nyayo, Swahili for "footsteps," to show his intention of following Kenyatta's policies. While pledging loyalty to the late leader, however, he made it clear that the ruling group should show him equal submission: "I would like ministers, assistant ministers and others to sing like a parrot after me. That is how we can progress." To knit together and expand the elite, he ordered all civil servants to join the ruling Kenya African National Union party. Government jobs would be filled exclusively from its ranks.

The consolidation of a new ruling class drawing its power and wealth through the state itself was an idea that Marxists had never fully expected, though that pattern was common in antiquity and in precolonial Third World empires. As George Orwell wrote, socialists had "assumed that what is not hereditary cannot be permanent." The essence of continuous power, however, was not father-to-son inheritance of wealth. Hereditary aristocracies are always short-lived compared to co-optive institutions like the Catholic Church. Orwell concluded, "A ruling group is a ruling group so long as it can nominate its successors. The Party is not concerned with perpetuating its blood but with perpetuating itself." The structure is more important than the specific individuals wielding power.

Continuity for the modern dictatorship is easier because it controls the state, judiciary, ideology, and economy. Wealth and power are the collective property of the ruling elite rather than, as in the traditional dictatorship, of a few families and cronies. But this also means that economic efficiency takes a backseat to the interests of a politically directed group rather than being the prime concern of a commercially oriented one. Consequently, if pure capitalism's drawback is that a greedy minority enjoys an oversize portion of the cake, nondemocratic socialism limits the size of the cake as a whole, even when it is somewhat more fairly distributed.

The new elite is consolidated around the dictator in several ways. Long personal comradeship during years of struggle for independence or against a traditional dictatorship builds powerful bonds of loyalty. Many of their countries' key leaders today are men or sometimes women who fought with Castro in the Sierra Madre or with Samora Machel in the Mozambican bush; conspired in tiny, secret meetings with Saddam Hussein, Assad, or Qaddafi; stood entranced in rallies listening to the speeches of a Julius Nyerere or Jomo Kenyatta. These people freely accepted their leaders, dedicated lives to the cause under their command, followed their orders, marveled at their skill, and saw their popularity among the common people. These are not experiences easily forgotten or loyalties lightly discarded. And in each of these cases the leader of the movement did precisely as he claimed, becoming leader of the nation. The very fulfillment of this promise underlines the worth of his judgment and charisma.

A country built on struggle reverses the proprieties of a long-established stable society. Moderate forces tend to be at a disadvantage since they were—or are thought to have been—more willing to compromise with the old system of traditional dictatorship or colonialism. Similarly, lack of acceptance by the West is a badge of honor, and the opposite can cause shame and suspicion. Politicians find peasant origins an advantage; time in prison is a source of pride. What is deemed moral and proper by the West is often seen as part of an exploitative system, and terrorism can be rationalized by various arguments.

The existence of so many grievances, justified or otherwise, creates a symbiotic relationship between the general population and a leader who promises to free and discipline its power to resolve these problems. Continued hatred of the old regime and fear that it might return is a powerful force guaranteeing a certain amount of popularity for the new system. "At one point we intended to kill Somoza," recalled Sandinista leader Henry Ruiz shortly after the revolution in Nicaragua, "but this was where [Sandinista chief] Carlos Fonseca's great foresight came in. Carlos maintained that Somoza was an invaluable asset who personified all our country's contradictions. . . . In short, dictatorship and class oppression were clearly identified in the person of Somoza."

The dictator probably stands above colleagues in ability, and his superiority must be augmented by their deference to him. Where the dictator's superiority is questionable, he must be all the more careful to buy or frighten his colleagues into backing him. As always, Idi Amin operated on the most direct and basic level to counter this possibility. Every Tuesday a Boeing 707 cargo plane took off from London with a load of fine clothes, whiskey, cigarettes, gourmet foods, watches, and sunglasses for delivery to his officers' rent-free suburban houses, where they parked their Peugeots and Fiats, taken at gunpoint from civilians. But loot alone is not enough; mercenaries are reliable only as long as they are regularly paid.

Yet this small "band of brothers," in Shakespeare's phrase, can, and often does, turn to fratricide. So more reliable, additional methods must be found to hold the elite together in battles against rival power seekers, groups and classes deemed enemies, and real or imagined foreign conspiracies. Ethnic, regional, or tribal ties can be important in the supplementing of the ruling group's unity—among Syria's Alawis, Iraq's Sunnis, Kenya's Kikuyu, Ethiopia's Amhara—but must be transcended by the bringing in of new recruits if the regime is to succeed. Identity is also reinforced through institutional ties, particularly a party, and the urge to protect collective benefits.

The relationship between leader and lieutenants can be glimpsed by watching Mozambique's President Samora Machel and his ministers. Machel is playful, teasing men who clearly do not quite know how they stand or whether a steel edge lies behind the jokes at their expense. The dictator is the only one allowed such a public sense of humor and the nation's only truly free man. No wonder he seems so animated with energy, so colorful, because he is surrounded by men whose grayness is a form of self-protection. He would not necessarily mind being considered, as a dictator of Bangladesh was called, a "hero among zeros." In Zaire only dictator Mobutu's picture can be publicly displayed. In Egypt Anwar al-Sadat was ridiculed as "Mr. Yes" during the long years that he understudied

Nasser. In some places, of course, subordinate leaders have their own power bases in military or party units. The leader must consult them on key decisions, and they have a margin of real independent decision-making authority.

Just as the dictator's personality must bind together the leadership cadre, it must also tie the ruling group to at least a large section of the people. One of the most impressive records at forging the relationships between the leader and ruling elite and between the leader and the masses has been compiled by Fidel Castro.

Castro's career is a demonstration of a modern dictator's instrumental use of ideology. He did not become a dictator because he was a Communist but rather became a Communist because he saw it as the only way to ensure his continued personal power, regime's survival, and the achievement of his goals. To reach his objectives, Castro concluded that a permanent government with sweeping powers was required. Marxism-Leninism offered the best means to construct such a structure of power.

When Castro marched into Havana in 1959 at the head of a guerrilla army, no one including Castro himself knew how he would govern. In his first public speech after victory he proclaimed, "We are going to make the revolution. The revolution that never came about in 1898 or 1933. This time we're going to make it come true." His entrance into Havana was like an apotheosis. From the presidential palace's balcony Castro asked the multitudes to open a path for him, proclaiming, "The people are my bodyguard." And, wrote Carlos Franqui, a fellow fighter whom Castro asked to be the revolution's historian, "Like Moses parting the waters, he crossed the sea of people that ran from Misiones Avenue to the bay, a hero out of Greek mythology and a collective orgasm." The crowd was delirious, chanting over and over again, "FIDELFIDELFI-DELFIDEL."

Castro had been a stalwart of the traditional liberal reform party, and the Communists had given no help to his own July 26 Movement. Once in power, however, he realized that a turn toward communism would provide him not only with Soviet help against a United States whose historic relations with Cuba made it irredeemably imperialistic in his eyes but also with a ready-made blueprint for a vanguard party, ideology, and development program that would ensure his total, lifetime rule. Above all, he wanted an irreversible revolution after all the failed or "betrayed" ones he had seen in Cuba—the defeated revolutions in 1898 and 1933—and elsewhere. Castro would not allow this to happen to him. To ensure success, he concluded that one must be ruthless and willing to sacrifice democracy for strength. His claim to have always implicitly been a Marxist was a reference to his belief that as a sincere seeker of national liberation and modernization, he could follow no other path.

Castro told Franqui that when he was a child, "Everyone lavished attention on me, flattered, and treated me differently from the other boys we played with. . . . This tends to make boys grow used to a privileged situation and take on the attitude that whatever they receive is rightfully theirs." Like Nasser and many other future dictators, Castro grew up in a world of political instability and student demonstrations and developed contempt for the "unbelievably frustrating and disorganized" reformers who were always defeated or overthrown by traditional dictators and juntas. In his travels abroad he came into contact with Peronists, followers of other populist leaders, and Marxists who had a different plan for exercising power.

So he added not only the entire prefabricated apparatus of Marxist-Leninist rule but also the populist personalism of Perón and Nasser. Castro was always ready to improvise and never willing to share power. The revolution—as in Nicaragua, Iran, and most of Africa—was made by the great majority, yet, commented Franqui, "The people, the true protagonists of the victory, are obliged to thank the heroes because they are now free." Even while promising elections in 1959, Castro warned they might mean the return "of oligarchy and tyranny." In May 1960 he gave a speech entitled "Elections—What For?"

Such, however, is the prerogative of leadership. The new

style of democracy—"direct democracy" Castro later called it—was shown when he asked a mass meeting at the national palace whether the "people" agreed that the murderers and torturers in the fallen Batista regime should be shot. "Put 'em up against the wall!" some shouted. Then a massive shout of "Yes!" answered his question. The execution of these genuine criminals set a precedent, giving the government and security forces the power of life and death over other citizens. But it was also a popular act, as with the execution of the Shah's minions after Iran's revolution. In both cases U.S. criticism only discredited its later complaints over human rights. "Of course," added Franqui, with a cynicism felt elsewhere in the Third World, "they said nothing about Trujillo, Somoza, [Venezuelan President Marcos] Pérez Jimenez, [Carlos] Castillo Armas" and other dictators friendly to the United States.

Castro then moved to destroy all institutions that posed alternatives to his power. The old regime was quite dead, and the new threat came from other revolutionary leaders, the middle class, unions, newspapers, or peasant associations. What traditional caudillos had merely taken over and tried to manipulate, Castro reorganized from top to bottom. He took over the university student group, a step Batista never would have dared take. Its head, a member of the July 26 Movement, later died in prison.

The old Communist party furnished an infrastructure to replace Castro's more independent-minded comrades just as the USSR provided a ready alternative to the United States. Ironically, the Communists had collaborated with the Batista dictatorship in exchange for legality and control of the labor movement. Many men promoted under Castro had worse records than those who were purged, but as always, those with the most to hide are often the most eager and uncomplaining in collaborating with the new regime. Their very vulnerability makes them hate and fear idealistic revolutionaries. Those who become dissidents will find themselves written out of history as photos are airbrushed. Becoming a hero is often a matter of dying at the right time.

Castro, like other dictators, made the definition of resist-

301

ance his own personal property. To get rid of the moderate first postrevolutionary president, he threatened to resign, a tactic also used by Perón and Nasser. To eliminate a colleague who had criticized his arbitrary style, Castro announced, "Either Huber Mateos is a traitor or I'm a liar." With such epithets hurled at proved revolutionaries, the margin of acceptable dissidence became increasingly narrower. Torture began early. Castro justified it by claiming that some people charged with counterrevolutionary activity were released because there was no proof and had to be recaptured after committing sabotage. Torture and the abandonment of legal due process could save the lives of revolutionaries, even the revolution itself. And if hundreds of thousands of people fled, their departure only strengthened the regime by removing opponents.

Franqui quoted Castro as writing him, "All criticism is opposition. All opposition is counterrevolutionary." This is true in the sense that a regime threatened at home and abroad may be easier to overthrow if it permits dissent. But Castro's formula also bars any possibility of peaceful change, rejects the best mechanism for self-improvement, and helps incompetents and opportunists stay in office. The revolution is saved in form by a method that guarantees it destroys itself in content. It devours not its children but its most devoted parents. Thus, while the Cuban Revolution and other modern dictatorships brought benefits particularly by redistribution of wealth, they also involve incredible waste and mismanagement that threaten development. Centralized planning permits a greater concentration of efforts but also is victimized by endemic problems of underdevelopment—insufficient information, experience, skills, and resources. The limits of Castro's style and system were shown by his ridicule of peasants who rightly questioned one of his plans, "Your problem is that you're all a bunch of conservatives. . . . I'm going to prove it to you here the way I did . . . when they told me no one could start a revolution here."

There were, no doubt, also material reasons for the strong bond between Castro and his subjects. For many of those who stayed in Cuba, however, there were direct benefits: an end to the plantation system, a successful literacy campaign, new schools, improved housing, better medical care, and reduced unemployment. The regime democratized access to leisure activities, consumer goods, and the existing national wealth. Living standards were improved for the poorest, and many people from that class were educated and promoted into higher-status, prestigious positions opened by development (the need for more teachers, for example) and by the departure of much of the middle and professional classes.

Many people supported the regime not only because of discontent with the old order but also because of nationalist fervor. The takeover of foreign oil companies in 1960 was made into an anti-imperialist festival, as Nasser had done when he seized the Suez Canal company four years earlier. In Cerro Stadium the crowd formed a rumba line, singing, "Hey, Fidel, go ahead, hit the Yankees on the head!" The CIA generally preferred to back the most subservient, reactionary elements in the opposition, which generally discredited the anti-Castro forces and seemed to demonstrate that the United States simply wanted to reimpose the hated old regime.

The new system abolished many characteristics of pre-revolutionary society: landlords, the independent middle class, laws discriminating against the poor, the political competition of parties, and the economic competition of the market system. "But," noted Franqui, "it never abolished the Communist party, the state, the police, the army, money, and salaries." The party ruled the state or the state was grafted onto the party. "Where before there were thousands of private properties, large or small, now there was only one, which belonged to the state. Where before there was anarchy in production, which led to inequalities and injustice, now there was a tyranny in production that paralyzed the economy and life itself." Elite privileges replaced class privileges.

Yet from a strictly power politics standpoint, this analysis is misleading. A considerable constituency still recognizes the ruling group's qualifications. The new elite may be, as a Third World politician phrases it, a "dictatorship of the enlightened" whose "self-proclaimed tutorship" is designed to make the masses over into its own image. Yet these are the people whose skill and educational advancement the majority seeks to imitate and into whose ranks it wishes to send its children.

Popular support for the modern dictatorship's system is also strengthened by the anticapitalist sentiment that pervades so much of the Third World. These societies never experienced the socially responsible welfare state capitalism of the New Deal or Western Europe's Social Democratic reforms with strong trade unions, mass culture, and an internal market based on workers' ability to buy consumer goods. Instead, its point of reference is a capitalism in which extremes of wealth and power are concentrated in a small group and workers and peasants have few rights and no protection. The government protects but never restrains the wealthy, who, for their part, lack any sense of social responsibility. It is more akin to the nineteenth-century early industrial capitalism of sweatshops, Dickensian cities, dark satanic mills, twelve-hour days, and robber barons. Here is one reason for the contradiction between admiring American progress and rejecting America as a model: the U.S. (and European) experience does not seem to be easily transferrable to Third World observers.

The democratic small-scale capitalism of merchants, craftspeople, and independent farmers or self-sufficient peasants survives in many modern dictatorships. But the most advanced type of capitalist enterprise—modern, technically advanced, mass-producing heavy industry—seems out of reach for much of the Third World's entrepreneurs operating on private capital. Unable to create their own IBM, General Motors, U.S. Steel, or General Foods, Third World states have to allow subsidiaries of such companies on their soil or as customers for their raw materials. Yet nationalism rejects allowing such power for foreign companies or so much dependency on decisions of alien entities that will always put their own interests ahead of the country's well-being. The state is the only conceivable partner or competitor to this frightening economic force, just as it also claims a monopoly on politics to unite the nation in the face of foreign great powers. Since these seem the only alternatives, the domination of a governmental elite is accepted as pragmatically and patriotically preferable to that of a foreign elite.

These conditions of national, economic, and political insecurity allow a modern dictatorship to reinterpret politics. Socialism claims to promote development under central control, warning that progress is possible only with limits on private accumulation of wealth and the transfer of resources into foreign hands. Trade unions, the media, and other institutions must be mobilized and disciplined for the development struggle; divisive electoral and pluralistic democracy is inferior to the unity of mass-line, populist democracy. "I have no opponents," says Ivory Coast President Houphouët-Boigny during a five-and-a-half-hour speech to the 1985 national congress of his African Democratic party. "My opponent is poverty."

Repression against those violating this desperately needed and universally beneficial civic unity is something to be recounted with pride. Thus, when those exiled as unreliable intellectuals during the Cultural Revolution demonstrated, asking to return home to the cities, Peking's deputy mayor complained, "Their individualistic actions jeopardize the interests of the state." Nicaragua's Minister of the Interior Tomás Borge tells his people, "You must have no shame to say that in Nicaragua there is a state of siege and martial law." When *turbas*, mobs organized through the neighborhood Sandinista Defense Committees, intimidated the opposition, Borge called them "divine" *turbas*, and his colleague Daniel Ortega commented, "We are not ashamed to be *turbas* because to be part of the *turbas* is to be part of the people." After Iran's urban middle class had complained about the Revolutionary Guards' harassment, Iranian leaders traveled to the force's camp to proclaim, "We are all Revolutionary Guards."

Such attitudes led a Turkish scholar to point out that the real class distinction in the Third World struggle is not between economic groups but between the rulers and the ruled. The former come from many different places and backgrounds, but "Once they are entangled in the wheels of the organization called State," they adopt a peremptory manner. "Instead of marching with the masses [whom] they are supposed to guide," they act like a man riding a horse, cracking the whip and pulling the reins when necessary. "It is the disease of the so-called intelligentsia," he concluded, "who think . . . they have been created to rule the nation."

This superior attitude meshes perfectly with Leninist notions of a scientifically guided, disciplined vanguard directing the fallible masses. We are modern and educated, say the leaders, and must rouse this mass of passive peasants and declassed urban poor. We know what needs to be done; they are sunk in backwardness and need to be told what to do. What point is there in consulting them in a formal manner when they may only be tricked—as they have been before—by the old dominant groups or foreign agents? Third World states are not so tame as more stable, democratic ones. He who would bust a bronco needs to keep a tighter hold. Traditional dictators, too, have made this point. The Shah was fond of saying that he would rule Iran like Switzerland when the Iranians began to behave like Swiss.

Like traditional dictators, then, modern dictators purport to provide their people with peace and unity. In addition, they claim other benefits: the destruction of an old, oppressive order; the discipline, pride, and puritanism required by primitive accumulation; the induction of new blood into the elite; the revival of the nation in the face of its enemies. Thoroughgoing change, the government argues, requires unrestricted controls.

The centralization of power and resources allows for all sorts of campaigns, depending on the country's resources and requirements. New service personnel—nurses, midwives, paramedics, doctors, agronomists, and teachers—are trained. There are literacy campaigns, insect and disease eradication programs, cooperatives and mutual help teams, state-built dams and roads. The traditional state took its cut and gave back little except alleged protection, and often people needed protection from the state. The new regime demands more but gives more in return.

Ideological and psychological indoctrination and encouragement are a major part of this process. It is hard to mobilize a people made passive by long years of familiarity with the limits of possibility and by fear of repression and change. Peasant conservatism is based not on ignorance but on the experience that change is more often for the worse than for the better, that instability breeds famine, and that if the peasants produce more, it will be appropriated by the state. All these attitudes must be changed if modernization and development are to succeed. Sometimes the behavior of the modern dictatorship, despite its slogans, only reinforces these expectations.

There is an additional problem. Even the new order can at best offer only limited and gradual material benefits while demanding real and immediate sacrifices. In exchange, it can promise only a distant, still nonexistent better world. The dictator must convince his people that present work will produce future benefits by building a relationship of popular support and trust. After returning from studies in Britain and the USSR in 1946, Kenya's Jomo Kenyatta addressed mass proindependence meetings of up to 30,000 people. When some Kenyans turned to violence, the British imprisoned Kenyatta. He was released to become the country's first president and beloved founding father, the only national leader it had ever known.

Kenyatta played well the dual role of sophisticated chief executive and tribal superchief. He could write scholarly anthropological analyses of tribal culture or twirl across the stage at meetings with tribal dancers. As writer Sanford Ungar observed, "His picture is still on the wall of many homes in Kenya, however humble; his thoughts and actions—his aphorisms for daily life—for a time enjoyed a status roughly equivalent to those of Mao Zedong in China." Kenyatta spoke to the people in terms they could understand. At rallies he often gave three separate speeches, noted Ungar. The English text, addressed to an international audience and British settlers, stressed economic stability and the Africans' willingness to forgive the past. In Swahili, the cross-tribal trading language, he emphasized national unity and Africanizing the economy. The version in Kikuyu, the language of his own tribesmen, assured them of their dominant position.

Kenyatta put forward the motto of *Harambee*, Swahili for "Let's all pull together," trying to build on traditional village communities. His regime promoted self-help projects. It built schools, cattle dips, and community centers, giving the country something that the West takes for granted: a government that serves people's needs rather than one that only collects tribute. Leaders must be able to mix modern technology and traditional images, a tactic also common in Western politics. Sally Mugabe, wife of Zimbabwe's Prime Minister Robert Mugabe, appealed over radio for higher moral standards by saying, "The gods and spirits are watching us. They are not pleased with us."

Using appeals, incentives, and coercion, the revolutionaries try to move the population through three stages of activity. They start from the lowest possible gear of participation—passive acceptance of tradition or foreign rule, pessimism, localism, family loyalty, ethnicism, lack of self-confidence, etc. By agitation and organization, they advance into the high gear of political campaigns or revolutionary struggle—self-sacrifice, unity, confidence, belief in future, mutual help, strikes and violence. After victory they shift into the middle-gear modern dictatorship stage of mobilization—institutionalization, respect for the leadership, hard work, hope for the future without excessive demands on the present, discipline, unity behind the government, and patriotism as defined by the dictator. This program combines what is self-serving for the regime with a crash course on some of the characteristics required by a modern nation-state.

In this context participation is no mere political gimmick but a way to persuade the population to implement policies and take on behavior patterns it might otherwise resist. Mistrustful peasants will, in times of instability or poor prices, shift from cash to subsistence crops. Urban workers must be pressed to work harder in the belief that greater effort will bring them some advantage.

308

In 1979 Flight Lieutenant Jerry Rawlings staged a coup in Ghana. A few months later, following what the West would praise as the proper pattern, he returned power to an elected government. But the civilian regime failed to cope with the country's monumental economic problems and harassed Rawlings and his ex-junta fellows. So, in 1982, Rawlings staged coup number two. This time he dug in for a longer term, establishing a Provisional National Defense Council (PNDC) as the ruling body and naming a cabinet that included civilians. Enhancing his populist reputation, he promised to redistribute wealth and reduce foreign influence and bureaucracy. Rawlings also pledged to crack down on hoarding, overpricing, smuggling, and corruption, all of which were rampant.

Obviously the government did not have the facilities for doing all these things. By appealing for mass participation, Rawlings could marshal support for his government and begin to reverse the cynicism and demoralization that had set in from the failure of previous regimes, going all the way back to Ghana's first president, Nkrumah. Thus, he set up People's Tribunals (no appeals permitted) to expedite trials, decreed reductions in rents and transport costs, established People's Shops, and improved the efficiency of tax collection. Students and soldiers were put to work, bringing cocoa from rural areas to port. This helped reduce smuggling, which had reached 20 percent of the crop, because farmers received only 17 percent of the black-market price. The students and other supporters also provided a volunteer force to combat hoarding and rising prices, trying to control the country's chronic inflation. He toyed with an alliance with Libya and with claiming that the United States, Britain, and France planned to invade Ghana. But Qaddafi was not likely to give much aid, and Rawlings soon moderated his foreign policy rhetoric. Rawlings's favorite slogan was that Ghanaians must directly "take over the destiny of this country, your own destiny" through involvement.

The story has no clear happy ending. Ghana's huge external debt did not disappear, although there were some improvements. Where once Ghanaians referred to the protruding bones of the undernourished a "Rawlings collar" they now called added weight a "Rawlings overcoat." Considering the size and stubbornness of the nation's problems, the political solution was about as good as could be expected.

Rawlings told an interviewer from *Jeune Afrique*, "The greatest problem with governing countries of the Third World is the apathy and ignorance of a greater part of the people. Some of them see the government as an unpleasant machine, when taxes are increased, for instance, but interesting when a new hospital is built. They must be taught to participate in the life of the state."

And even in tiny Burkina Faso, where the Sankara regime's theatricality sometimes verges on farce, the play is at least adapted to its audience. A national administration modeled on French practice and a provincial government based on the chiefs give way to Committees for the Defense of the Revolution. Street children are organized, given places to sleep, and sometimes training in making handicrafts that can be sold. Vaccination campaigns are organized, and officials drive Renaults instead of the Mercedes-Benz limousines previously used.

Leaders do not abandon their lust for power but also see the preservation of their rule as integrally related to maintaining a popular base. Few Third World modern dictators come to the point of believing the nation sufficiently stable or their ambitions suitably met to allow for retirement. Léopold Senghor, Senegal's founding leader, voluntarily left office in 1980 at age seventy-four; Ahmadou Ahidjo of Cameroon retired to France soon afterward following twenty-two years in power. But even Ahidjo was soon complaining that his handpicked successors were blaming problems on him. If so few of the founding fathers, chosen by acclaim, are willing to step down, even less hope can be pinned on their heirs or of coup makers and revolutionaries. Asked to explain his revolution's principal achievement, Sandinista leader Bayardo Arce—before going on to list better housing, land reform, greater literacy, and political activization of the people—replied, "The principal achievement is that I am here in this office in Managua giving you this interview."

Even many modern dictatorships recognize the friction

between the urge toward power and the goal of transformation. As the guidelines of Tanzania's ruling TANU party point out, "The truth is that we have not only inherited a colonial governmental structure but have also adopted colonial working habits and leadership methods . . . in which one man gives the orders and the rest simply obey them." If people are not truly involved and given some say in decision making, they will feel that the institutions do not belong to them and the government does not represent them. They then become cynical and "adopt the habits of hired employees." To be successful, modernization must stress the "development of people and not things." It is far easier to gain access to the latest technology or consumer goods than it is to build a society capable of producing, widely distributing, and using them. Hence the idea common in the Third World that the government must foster the creation of a "new man" is a goal both utopian (people must be unselfish, honorable, self-sacrificing) and necessary for development (people must be reliable, skilled, patriotic, civic-minded, willing to take responsibility).

Modern dictatorships, however, find it hard enough to create such "new men" among their own leaders, whose unconstrained power undermines ethical values. Party and government officials, warns TANU, must not become arrogant, extravagant, contemptuous, and oppressive. They should be, in short, not tyrants to the people but champions of the people. The party should serve as watchdog and combat misbehavior by its cadre. In view of the nature of the system, these rules are everywhere breached more than they are observed.

It is equally easy to declare tribalism, religion, or factionalism obsolete but quite another thing to change the thinking of those familiar with no other arrangement. Guinea-Bissau's Amilcar Cabral, the architect of his country's liberation struggle, was murdered in 1973 by members of his own party to whom the Portuguese colonialists had promised independence if they first eliminated the lighter-skinned Cape Verde islanders in general and Cabral in particular. The tribal-based factionalism behind the "ideological" struggles of South Yemen's "Marxist-Leninists" have led to one bloody coup after another.

311

Afghanistan provides a good example of how the passion to modernize people regardless of their own wishes can turn into tyranny, with the enlightened "vanguard" becoming its countrymen's worst enemy. The two tiny Communist parties recruited from relatively Westernized sectors of the urban middle class. After taking power in a 1977 coup, they immediately began to impose their vision on the country without considering its real conditions. The flag, modeled on Islam's green banner, was replaced with a copy of the USSR's red one. Elimination of the bride price, a step intended to improve women's status, was ordered overnight in a way that disrupted the society. Revising lending practices made credit unavailable; an ill-considered land reform challenged clan and family ties. All these steps, widely perceived as anti-Islamic, alienated the people they were supposed to benefit. The country rose in rebellion. The Soviet invasion of December 1979, intended to preserve some form of Marxist regime, only demonstrated its unpatriotic nature. New gestures intended to redress popular complaints were too late. As with Pol Pot in Cambodia, the Afghan dictators decided it was necessary to destroy their own country and people in order to "save" them. And all along, in both Afghanistan and Cambodia, the Communists fought viciously among themselves as well.

The single party may be a modern dictatorship's dominant factor, the arena for the conduct of politics, or an empty symbol. This last definition was the case for Ethiopia's military junta, which postponed introducing a party for five years because officers feared it might become the instrument of civilian Marxist politicians. At last, in late 1984, the Workers' Party was organized with officers filling seven of eleven Politburo seats and more than two-thirds of the central committee. The idea of a military dictatorship presenting itself as a Marxist-Leninist proletarian party would be farcical if the same format had not already been used to rationalize so many other kinds of rule by a small elite. Nevertheless, the Ethiopian military was aware of the fact that formation of a single ruling party, as Africa specialist Ruth Collier wrote, provides a way to draw in civilians: by "patronage, jobs, and the dispensing of governmental favors." In other places the party plays a more definitive role. In Nicaragua it has become increasingly entwined with the state. Instead of the Nicaraguan Television Network or Nicaraguan Army, there is the Sandinista Television and the Sandinista Army. Since a legal opposition still exists, the domination of the Sandinista party must be broadcast and inculcated at every opportunity. By way of contrast, in Kenya the KANU party serves as the overarching national political institution, and real politics takes place within its domain. As many as eight or ten candidates compete for each parliamentary seat. Under this umbrella approach some Kenyans say they have a "no-party system," but this came about only because other parties were eliminated and a national consensus was created to accept KANU's status as the permanent government.

Elections play a subordinate but not altogether useless role. Academic studies of one-party competitive elections in Africa, concluded Collier, show they do "build support and legitimacy for the government" by convincing people they have some say in choosing leaders and making them responsive. Many common people would agree with the dictators' idea that multiparty elections are an inferior way of choosing leaders. As Rawlings put it after allowing that system another chance, political parties have failed. "To give the people a choice between candidates . . . designated by others is no democracy; especially when [in seeking] votes, these candidates try to outdo one another in promises that cannot be fulfilled. Of course," Rawlings acknowledged, such arguments can be used to justify a dictatorship like Idi Amin's. "It is, finally, the people's confidence that counts" in defining a proper regime.

The modern dictatorship is caught in a vicious circle since in order to maintain that it enjoys the people's confidence, the regime is unlikely to risk any test of a free election or an unfettered opposition. Speaking of a rigged 1985 election won by dictator Samuel Doe in Liberia, U.S. Assistant Secretary of State Chester Crocker pointed out, "In claiming only 51 percent of the vote, Doe publicly acknowledged that a large segment of society—49 percent of the voters—supported other points of view and leadership than his own." The result fulfilled a modern dictator's worst nightmare. Angered at the stolen election, the opposition united and protested. A small group, including one of Doe's most trusted fellow officers, launched a coup. Although the radio station briefly fell to the insurgents, Doe called in the loyal 1st Infantry Battalion to suppress the revolt. Doe is unlikely to call elections again; other African officers will even more closely associate ballots with instability.

Dictatorships obviously prefer to have a framework of permanent local authority to fall back on so as to avoid having to call pluralistic elections. During Guinea-Bissau's independence war the PAIGC liberation party organized elections of village committees of five (at least two women), with a leader as the principal political officer, a deputy responsible for the militia, and other members charged with administration, social issues, supply, and production. Above these were zone, regional, and national committees.

In Nicaragua, as in Cuba, Iran, Ethiopia, and other places, neighborhood committees form a reliable cornerstone for the regime. The government claims these are the revolution's eyes and ears, allowing it better to serve popular needs and hear grievances. The opposition says the purpose is to monitor and ensure the obedience of the people. Both sides are right. Such institutions allow the more efficient distribution of food ration cards, housing, and other benefits. They also help direct repression. Possessing both aspects, they are ideal instruments for a modern dictatorship.

Since the government controls the law rather than vice versa, since all other public institutions are subordinate to the regime, and since elections have only limited influence, the kind of arbitrary behavior which TANU's rules try to control is inevitable. Student groups are intended to criticize bad teachers; labor unions are expected to protect members from dangerous conditions; and women's groups are supposed to free their members from traditional roles, provide new choices and opportunities, and improve treatment in the family. They may be able to achieve some of these objectives but only if the goals or specific targets for complaint correspond with the regime's objectives.

"Our best guarantee against all forms of despotism, against all forms of injustice," says a veteran Cuban revolutionary, "is Fidel himself. He does not tolerate abuses of power." But no matter how popular the dictator—indeed, in direct proportion to the dictator's popularity—no one is protected against his protection. After all the theoretical elaborations, the final, and far from satisfactory, rationalization is that of Khomeini: A just and rightly guided man in power will govern justly. Still, this lack of structural restraint on government does not indicate that everyone is dissatisfied or victimized by it. Elimination of the old order, reforms that benefit a large portion or majority, new opportunities, ideas that persuade, identification with the dictator, ethnic or other links with the ruling elite, and institutions that allow for at least some participation and distribution of power can build a wide base of support.

The appeal to nationalism is the icing on the cake. Writing in a prenationalist age, Machiavelli commented, "When a powerful foreigner enters a province, all the less powerful inhabitants become his adherents." Yet the rise of patriotic sentiments reversed this rule. When a regime has any large degree of popular support and legitimacy, a foreign state's force, pressure, and propaganda directed against the country may only cause the people to rally around their government.

This principle is reinforced by Third World feelings that advanced industrial states, particularly Western ones, mistreat, oppress, and act hypocritically toward them. Some regimes project their authenticity largely as a function of their anti-Western rhetoric or actions. "The secret of the success of the revolution," said Iranian Member of Parliament (and former Deputy Foreign Minister) Ahmed Azizi in May 1985, "lies in its belligerence, in both words and deeds." Modern dictatorships try to demonstrate that they have transformed their country from the subordinate subject of history and manipulation into a powerful force in the world. Iranian Prime Minister Mir-Hussein Musavi boasted that "on account of its sensitive geographical location and vast natural resources, Iran has al-

315

ways been a target of the ominous plots of East and West."
Parliament Speaker Ali Akhbar Rafsanjani proclaimed, "The
U.S. president nightly scrutinizes the satellite photos of the
[Iran-Iraq War]. . . . This is a sign of the greatness of the
revolution."

There is a duality here between inferiority and egomania,
between feelings of power and fear of powerlessness that characterizes contemporary Third World nationalism. The violence and extremism of their rhetoric are partly a reflection
of material weakness. Expressions of hatred for the West are
mixed with an obvious desire for Western respect (even in the
form of fear) or approval.

As in other areas, the gap between rhetoric and reality
can produce farcical situations. Libya's Qaddafi is fond of making sweeping promises of aid to various revolutionary causes
and states, but the money pledged usually never appears. A
Burkina Faso official commented, "We never plan on the basis
of these promises, and would be happy to receive the cement
and other aid [Qaddafi] has promised in the past." Money
pledged by Arab states to each other or to the PLO often does
not appear. A State Department officer stationed in a Persian
Gulf emirate once asked a high local official whatever happened to the funds he had promised the PLO at the last Arab
summit. In response the government quickly issued a statement bragging about the donation, which was apparently never
made. By October 1985 thirty-six of forty-six Organization of
African Unity member states had not paid their pledges to its
Liberation Fund. While issuing thundering denunciations of
apartheid and demanding Western boycotts, many African
states continue extensive secret trading with South Africa.

Thus, the West should always remember that the rhetoric
of modern dictators is of limited use in understanding their
actual practices. Their threats are mitigated by a need to exercise caution in order to survive in power, and their demands
are constrained by the demands of reality. Not for one moment
should the differentiation be forgotten between dictators and
the people in whose name they claim to speak. Hypocrisy is
the medium of exchange of those who plead on behalf of the

rights, lives, and livelihoods of those whom they themselves are trampling on. The sweeping talk of nationalism, Pan-Africanism, Arab unity, and so on are often an integral part of domestic demagoguery; demands for Western concessions to the poor and powerless are made by those themselves rich and powerful who do little for these causes and who take a large percentage of any aid provided.

Although nationalistic statements made by Third World governments often should not be taken seriously as indicating intentions, they can still be important as illustrating perceptions. To develop one's own identity is to define a self apart from others. The appeal of a Western culture so effectively communicated around the world makes it more frightening. Thus, Tanzania has tried to bar tight or bell-bottom pants for men, shorts or short skirts for women. State-run radio stations limit the playing of foreign music. Economic protectionism, saving foreign exchange for higher-priority items, goes hand in hand with cultural protectionism.

Political scientist Fouad Ajami has written cogently on this point: "Some of the 'things' of the West—its weaponry, its fashions, its machines—are coveted and stockpiled by states that can afford them, by individuals who can afford quick trips to London, Paris and New York. But the Western 'way' is another matter. The susceptibility to Western judgment is no longer there." In that sense Fanon's views have triumphed.

While the West's failure to understand Third World attitudes has been the source of many foreign policy errors, the Third World has had an equal or even greater problem in understanding Western society. As one Arab newspaper in Bahrain put it, "The United States is a strange country full of secrets and motives, and no rule applies to it." The statement was made in an article suggesting that a 1981 assassination attempt against President Ronald Reagan was actually a coup attempt by Secretary of State Alexander Haig. An Egyptian newspaper claimed that the most important factor behind U.S. foreign policy was "religious fanaticism." Many similar examples can be cited. Soviet disinformation is sometimes responsible for anti-American or anti-Western articles in the

Third World media, but the real story is about why criticism or slander is so willingly received and readily believed. Soviet culture is too unattractive to be threatening, and the USSR's political behavior is more easily understandable among fellow modern dictatorships.

On a more immediately political level are allegations about Western companies that buy, control, or "rob" national resources and of great powers that manipulate or replace Third World governments not to their liking. Western guilt for past or present misdeeds must be carefully evaluated since it is sometimes real and sometimes the product of exaggeration or of modern dictatorships' ingenuous blaming of problems on foreigners.

The fact that such attitudes are historically comprehensible does not necessarily make them ethically superior. To say that one man's terrorist is another man's freedom fighter is no more impressive than to argue that one man's Gestapo agent or KGB informer is another man's defender of Nazi Germany's fatherland or Soviet Communist security. And it is often forgotten that throughout the 1920s and most of the 1930s Germany and the USSR were viewed as oppressed nations rightfully seeking their places in the sun against a background of past mistreatment and present insecurity. Individual actions and cases must be judged on their merits.

Nonalignment was a partial answer in the drive for Third World identity. To fall into either bloc would be a dependence inadmissible to those whose pride is so delicate. The structural similarities between modern dictatorships and Moscow and the effort of some Third World Communist states, particularly Cuba, to push for a nonaligned-Soviet alliance give the USSR some advantage. But the 1981 conference of nonaligned nations rejected this path, and the West holds too many cultural, economic, and strategic cards to be so easily discarded.

More often nonalignment has become a matter of a modern dictator's trying to limit the influence of both "superpowers" in his own country or neighborhood while seeking to play them off for his own best advantage. "To define my regime in pro-Soviet or pro-American . . . terms is Manichaean," says

Madagascar dictator and President Didier Ratsiraka. "We cooperate with all countries which respect our sovereignty and
our independence." Nonalignment is part of his regime's doctrine, as announced in the Charter of the Revolution (the Red
Book). He is happy to take aid from France, the USSR, or any
other state.

Despite all the talk about nation building, the disintegration of nations is an equally important—and more often seen—
issue today. Just as laissez-faire politics has been replaced by
an increasing role for the state in both democracies and dictatorships, international affairs have evolved toward a greater
demand for order. A world of states views with disapproval
the invasion, takeover, or disappearance of other states. This
new attitude—which imposes constraints on at least Western
behavior—is a life insurance policy for nations. It makes possible the continued existence of unstable or weak Third World
states which would have fallen victim to Darwinian laws in the
nineteenth century's imperial era. Similarly, no matter how
big a country's debts or economic problems, the safety net of
the International Monetary Fund, World Bank, big bank loans,
and foreign aid protects it from bankruptcy. This is an important new state of affairs that has altered the nature of
international politics.

During the 1960s and 1970s the Third World's emergence
first posed new problems and then provided new arenas for
the U.S.-Soviet conflict. By the 1980s it was clear that nonalignment had failed to provide immunity from entanglement
in great power competition. Internal and local conflicts motivated individual leaders and factions to seek outside support.
Economic contingencies, the search for sources of arms, and
ideological borrowings undid regional blocs. Throughout this
epoch, global responsibilities and the new, disorderly international order posed major problems for U.S. foreign policy.
These will be considered in the final chapter.

But first it is necessary to say some additional words on
the modern dictatorship itself. The final question is, If there
is so often a lack of alternative to modern dictatorship, is it a
justified, if not justifiable, system? Judgment must be based

on whether it is capable of laying a foundation for something better to supersede it, a system offering more democracy (real, if not formal), real development (benefiting the largest possible number), economic and political human rights, and cultural pluralism.

Ironically, the exaggerated complaints about Western imperialism occur at a time when these powers show more respect for third world sovereignty than at any previous time in history. Scapegoating the West, useful as it is for modern dictators in domestic politics, also prevents examination of their own misrule and of the main internal causes of oppression and underdevelopment.

It is necessary to understand the roots, even the inevitability, of modern dictatorship in many countries but this does not mean to sympathize with the phenomena or to apologize for its crimes. Traditional societies produce traditional dictatorships, changing societies modern dictatorships or, as frequently seen in Latin America and Asia, modernizing juntas. Modernizing juntas often give way, at least temporarily, to civilian rule. But what will modern dictatorships produce?

History is full of ironies in this regard. A traditional imperial system in Japan, modernized by a ruthless clique of officers, led the country to a terrible disaster in World War II. A U.S. military occupation imposed democracy and opened the way to a new era of peaceful, fantastically successful growth in which Japan retained and developed its traditional values. And after all, Hitler was a German, Mussolini an Italian, Napoleon a Frenchmen. Either modern dictatorship is a transitional era or its modern techniques and technology will allow it to leave a permanent mark on Third World societies. Hoping for the former outcome but fearing the latter result, Julius Nyerere put it best: "A man who tries to control the life of another does not destroy the other any the less because he does it, as he thinks, for the other's benefit. It is the principle which is wrong . . . of one man governing another without his consent."

If democracy is usually the product of modernization, the

Third World might eventually follow the same pattern. Nevertheless, Communist regimes show no sign that economic development cannot coexist with dictatorship. Possibly, modern dictatorship is a passing stage in the lives of the Third World nations but today this does not seem very likely.

The survival instinct, however, may push modern dictatorships toward a type of radical pragmatism rather than rigid fanaticism in foreign policy. Sadat rebuilt relations with the United States and later made peace with Israel. Qaddafi reduced his backing for terrorism because of U.S. military pressure. Facing an unwinnable war with Iraq and a difficult economic situation, some of Khomeini's top lieutenants held secret talks with the United States in 1986.

In dealing with Washington, Iranian politicians had to strike a balance between their practical needs (arms, money, and breaking out of isolation) and radical constraints (Khomeini's wish to continue fighting the war and reviling America, rivals' exploitation of any treasonous "moderation," and difficulty in justifying actions to their own supporters).

U.S. policymakers only dimly understood Iran's situation, which they judged by outmoded expectations of national-interest pragmatism and inevitable moderation. The Reagan White House sold Iran arms, seeking a quick diplomatic success and release of Americans held hostage in Lebanon. The result was a debacle, but the experience underlines America's need to learn how to cope with modern dictatorships.

CHAPTER TWELVE

America and the Dictators

Dealing with Third World dictatorships has tested both the power and values of the United States. The rise, fall, wars, and courting, or criticizing, of Third World dictators has been the central issue shaping its foreign involvement, particularly since the U.S.-Soviet nuclear stalemate makes the Third World the arena of superpower competition. The behavior and troubles of Third World dictators have allowed each side to measure its strength as well as bred regional conflicts and set afire crises.

Each era of U.S. foreign policy is marked by its view of these problems and ability to handle them. Liberals and conservatives chose distinctive approaches to the collapse of allied dictators and to friction with their replacements in China, Cuba, Vietnam, Ethiopia, Iran, and Nicaragua. The puzzle of how to deal with terrorism from Syria and Libya, idiosyncratic dictators in Africa, modernizing juntas in Latin America or South Korea, and struggles for democracy in the Philippines and Nicaragua preoccupied U.S. leaders while challenging Americans' ideas about the rest of the globe, setting off passionate, fundamental debates at home.

Americans are unusual among nations in demanding that

their foreign policy stand for something rather than merely provide a tool for security and survival. Debates over how best to define this purpose have followed a curious cycle, as different lessons have been drawn from apparently contradictory historical experiences. Entanglements abroad or the fall of pro-U.S. traditional dictators encourage liberal critiques; Soviet aggression or the birth of anti-American modern dictatorships reinforce conservative arguments.

The American thought that foreign policy should improve the world made another country's style of government a factor relevant to the conduct of diplomatic relations. The popularity of this idea is shown by its centrality in the thinking of two such different Presidents as Jimmy Carter and Ronald Reagan. Carter's human rights policy aimed to encourage better treatment of citizens by all kinds of Third World dictatorships and suggested that the United States align itself with seemingly inevitable tides of change. Reagan's doctrine equated communism with tyranny and advocated U.S. assistance to guerrillas battling Third World leftist modern dictators.

The idea that America might escape the world or reshape the globe in its own image is a legacy of geography and history. Protected by Atlantic and Pacific moats, the nineteenth-century United States was secure in its distance from other great powers. Preoccupied with its own expansion and development, U.S. political culture came to view international activism as unwelcome and dangerous. Presidents starting with Woodrow Wilson tried to justify an energetic foreign policy by portraying it as a struggle for freedom which would "make the world safe for democracy." With an unbroken tradition of representative government and progress at home, Americans could see dictatorship and international conflicts mainly as aberrations that could be eliminated by better international understanding and greater diplomatic effort.

"Nowhere," historian Walter Laqueur wrote, "has there been so little understanding of how a dictatorship works or so little appreciation of the importance of ideology (or religion or nationalism) in politics. In no other country has there been so much good will—which is to say willingness to ignore or at

323

least belittle the existence of genuine conflicts among nations, ideologies, and political systems." Consequently, Americans are more inclined than other nations to want to convert foreign dictatorships into democracies but are less equipped to understand how such systems work and why they survive or fail.

The prevailing American understanding of and attitude toward dictatorship, then, have both admirable and naïve elements. Reality often makes the United States modify its reformist impulse. Responsibilities and self-defense force it to deal with or even support many governments—to avoid or defuse conflict if for no other reason—whose political systems are not to Americans' liking. In a tough, dangerous world, practicality must often take priority over preference or purity.

Those arguing that the United States should take a more thoroughly realpolitik approach delight in quoting the early statesman and President John Quincy Adams that America "goes not abroad, in search of monsters to destroy. She is the well-wisher to the freedom of all. She is the champion and vindicator only of her own." But even Adams shared the American obsession with foreign policy as a struggle for justice and progress: "The Royalists everywhere detest and despise us," whose political principles "make the throne of every European monarch rock under him." Democracy was "destined to cover the . . . globe." He cautioned against intervention only because he considered the young nation too fragile to risk it, the international struggles too imperialistic to make involvement worthwhile, and the favorable outcome for the forces of freedom so inevitable as to make it unnecessary.

Adams was correct in explaining that idealism can be practiced only when firmly rooted in a realistic assessment of the world. Yet American idealism also has something practical to teach realism: Morality and self-interest often converge. The United States has a successful political and economic system which makes it a more attractive ally and model than the USSR. American objectives like peace, stability, and development can be more effectively realized through a proliferation of democracy. Democratic states make stronger allies—less subject to revolutions that produce anti-Americanism and dictator-ships—and benefit both U.S. interests and their own citizens.

This strategy can work, of course, only in countries like Argentina or the Philippines, where there already are strong moderate, democratic traditions and political forces. And this predominantly liberal thesis fell into disfavor after revolutions in Iran and Nicaragua had replaced traditional, pro-U.S. dic-tatorships with modern, anti-American ones. Conservatives argued that the United States would have been better off to have supported the old regimes. Liberals equate pro-Ameri-canism with democracy; conservatives equate democracy with anticommunism.

Of course, the liberals' prodemocratic strategy also criti-cizes the Soviet bloc's human rights record while conservatives sometimes pressure rightist, pro-U.S. dictatorships. The point here is the two versions' common themes: U.S. foreign policy should side with democracies against dictatorships and try to convert dictatorships into democracies. Both sides argue that such a strategy strengthens U.S. interests, combats Soviet ex-pansion, contributes to regional security, and promotes the welfare of Third World people.

Routine diplomacy requires the United States to work with incumbent rulers to obtain base rights, economic benefits, re-gional and global cooperation, and denial of all these things to the Soviets. Corporate interests, demanding protection of their holdings, may influence accommodation or antagonism toward individual dictators. These factors make human rights and democracy seem troublesome, irrelevant considerations. Ironically, even the most humanitarian policy presupposes U.S. interaction with dictators because its influence, including le-verage in promoting change, presupposes trade, aid, or dip-lomatic relations. Policymakers need a long-term perspective, remembering that a country and people will exist long after a specific ruler or regime has passed from the scene.

The principal issue setting U.S. policy toward other gov-ernments is usually their behavior toward the United States and USSR. Distinctions must also be drawn between greater and lesser evils. The USSR's aggressive behavior and efforts to destroy U.S. influence encourages the United States to block the emergence of Soviet client or puppet regimes. What can or should be justified in the name of the U.S.-USSR conflict has always been a matter of great priority as well as one of tremendous controversy. The phrase "Free World," once proudly used to describe the U.S.-led alliance, became a mockery because the United States so frequently aligned itself with dictatorships or helped overthrow democratic regimes.

Yet the Cold War and the issue of dictatorship versus democracy—of which, after all, the U.S.-Soviet struggle is a case in point—cannot be fully separated. The conflict is not merely a competition between two great powers, as the realists would have it, or of two essentially identical superpowers, as much of the Third World claims, but between a free society and a dictatorship. American conservatives have rightly pointed out that the idea of "moral equivalency" between the United States and the Soviet Union is very much at variance with the facts. But liberals are correct in bringing out the sad reality that U.S. support for traditional dictatorships has helped bring death and misery to people around the world, who experience the United States' raw power as often as they do its good intentions. Such actions, even when unintentional, discredited the United States and encouraged the view that Washington and Moscow were, in fact, interchangeable. Discarding the U.S. qualitative superiority over the USSR is to lose one of America's greatest advantages in the struggle.

The Cold War context affected domestic U.S. debates about dictatorships in another way as well. Conservatives often argued that traditional dictatorships should be defended against all comers because they were anti-Communist, sometimes implying that they were more consistently, effectively so than alternative civilian democratic governments. A corollary was to assume that radical nationalist modern dictatorships and most opposition movements were necessarily pro-Soviet. Liberals, in contrast, often idealized forces fighting against traditional dictators while accepting at face value modern dictatorships' claims of success and rationalization for repression. The accuracy of these varying views of dictators depended on the specific country in question. Neither set of assumptions was always right or always wrong.

While the American world view, Cold War conflict, and diplomatic expediency all shaped U.S. policy toward Third World dictators and revolutions, ignorance of local conditions was also an important factor. Policymakers often misread the survivability of the incumbent regime, understated the likelihood of political upheaval, and confused nationalist or neutralist forces with irrevocably pro-Soviet ones. As has been already pointed out, most modern dictatorships—even those with radical or Marxist views—are not Soviet satellites. But, of course, these modern dictators are also not democratic.

A lack of knowledge about Third World societies has repeatedly caused problems for the United States. An illustrative tale about the ignorance factor is reporter Bernard Diederich's description of an incident during then Vice President Richard Nixon's visit to Haiti in the 1950s. Nixon stopped a young peasant woman riding a donkey. "Tell this cocoye to let me go on my way," she said in Creole, using an unflattering Haitian expression. Nixon's interpreter translated this as "She says she is happy to meet the Vice President." Nixon asked about her family. The woman answered she had no husband and three children. The translator rendered this as "She is engaged." Nixon then placed a hand on the donkey's rump and asked, "What is the donkey's name?" Her reply was "He is crazy. It is called a donkey." The interpreter said, "She says it hasn't got a name, and asks to be excused because it is getting late." It is often hard to translate between differing cultures and types of politics. Such misleading dialogues, tragic or comic, have been common in the history of U.S. foreign policy.

Americans have additional perceptual shortcomings in coping with Third World dictators. A false analogy between domestic politics—where the U.S. government has far greater control—and foreign policy means that Americans overestimate U.S. responsibility and power for shaping international events. And foreign rulers do not necessarily look at the world or define proper behavior in the same way as do Americans.

Their actions may be judged by American values, but they must first be understood in their own contexts of history, psychology, and beliefs.

Thus, Third World dictators often take extreme positions or seemingly suicidal actions that appear irrational to Americans but are the reflection of the dictatorship's ideology and requirements for staying in power. This factor explains Iran's handling of the hostage crisis and Khomeini's continuation of a bloody war with Iraq, the domestic and regional political advantages for Arab leaders refusing to make peace with Israel, Mexico's friendly stance toward Cuba and Nicaragua, the Argentine junta's attack on the Falklands, Tanzania's stubbornly disastrous agricultural policy, and Soviet behavior as well. All these dictatorships operate on different criteria from those of democracies, not only because their nations' histories and regional situations are different but also because their internal politics are different. They are not held accountable by elections or by an independent press or judiciary. Dictators generally do not cut military spending to protect living standards, for example, because they have to worry about the army's loyalty, not about parliamentary votes or demonstrations.

Equally, the idea that international conflicts result mainly from misunderstandings disregards the fact that there often are real clashes between nations' interests and goals. While diplomacy can be an important and productive means of limiting or resolving problems, leaders—figuratively as well as actually—speak different languages. Nor is the solution merely a matter of persuading Qaddafi, Castro, or Khomeini that the United States has good intentions. Even aside from the fact that these leaders' world views and interpretations of history are inherently hostile, the use of anti-Americanism as a tool for domestic control and mobilization may preclude policies that would make possible good relations with the United States.

International terrorism, for example, is less and less the work of crazies—or those driven to distraction by philosophical angst or unbearable grievances—and more and more the product of careful political calculation. Most terrorism in the Middle East functions as an adjunct of Libyan, Syrian, or Iranian foreign policy and is designed to achieve very specific aims. These include such major objectives as: Libyan efforts to dominate the Arab world and to overthrow all moderate regimes; Syrian attempts to dominate Lebanon and prevent Jordan from making peace with Israel; Iranian goals of sparking Islamic fundamentalist revolutions and gaining hegemony over the Persian Gulf; PLO objectives of destroying Israel, mobilizing support for its intransigent policy, and wiping out any independent-minded Palestinians. All these forces want to eliminate U.S. influence in the region; Syria, Libya, and PLO are closely allied with Soviet regional interests. Similarly, since Khomeini, Qaddafi, and Assad each seek to dominate the Middle East, U.S. support for the countries they would have as their victims—not only Israel but even more immediately such states as Egypt, Tunisia, and Saudi Arabia—raises the dictator's wrath and leads to terrorist attacks against Americans. The regime itself often sets off a confrontation by its own behavior, making America a more determined enemy by treating it as one. Obviously, it is very difficult for the West to compromise with these motivations. A belief that the central problem is one of a lack of communication fails to comprehend the ruthless and aggressive nature of these regimes.

The American belief in the illegitimacy of dictatorship as a form of government may also lead to underestimating its staying power. Dictators are seen as innately unpopular, repression as intrinsically unsuccessful, and misgovernment as creating an inevitably successful democratic opposition. Such a view emerges from the history of nineteenth-century democratic revolutions but does not take into account contemporary dictators' more sophisticated techniques for control and generating support. In politics, after all, victory often does go to the most ruthless.

Many of the West's romantic illusions about the Third World have been dispelled. Regimes there proved as aggressive, bigoted, and brutal as any imperialists toward their own people and neighbors. There is much truth in a comment by Martin Herz, a career Foreign Service officer, that only after observing how an opposition behaves after coming to power can one appreciate how easy it is for those outside government to condemn dishonesty and corruption while claiming to have "the purest motives, to be selfless in their devotion to the public weal, incorruptible, and [to possess] policies that promise instant solutions to the country's problems."

Nor is the miscomprehension all on one side. On the one hand, Third World governments alternately fear the U.S.-Soviet rivalry as a threat to their sovereignty or seek to exploit it for their own advantage. President Nyerere once warned that U.S.-Soviet competition might set off a new "scramble for Africa." On the other hand, the motives and objectives of the United States are often caricatured.

These myths about the United States overestimate its omnipotence, omnipresence, and belligerency. Modern dictators both believe and propagandize that previous traditional dictators were dependent on the United States; traditional dictators often try to cow their own people by claiming a U.S. mandate to rule. These assertions may have a historical basis—as with the U.S. role as patron in Latin America—or can be a hysterical overreaction or cynical organizing tactic. "To be anti-American nowadays is to shout with the mob," wrote British writer and socialist George Orwell in 1948. Today such sentiments can activate powerful nationalist emotions and very large crowds.

Such patterns can be seen even in a rightist traditional dictatorship like Chile. In 1985 the U.S. National Aeronautics and Space Administration sought to extend by 500 yards an airstrip on Easter Island—a Chilean-ruled dot of land in the Pacific Ocean—as an emergency landing site for the space shuttle. Wild rumors spread through Chile that the United States was building a missile base. Christian Democratic leader Radomiro Tomic charged, "The security and sovereignty of . . . the entire country could be affected"; the left claimed Chile would become a target for Soviet missiles. Student demonstrators protested that the United States was backing the Pinochet dictatorship in exchange for a base. The opposition branded the government as a traitor and U.S. puppet. But actually General Pinochet wanted this controversy publicized to give the impression that he enjoyed full U.S. support, and he accordingly waived the usual heavy press censorship. As Latin America expert Mark Falcoff explained, the regime "desires these relations desperately—as if in fact its survival did depend upon it." The Shah and Marcos also tried to convince their people that the United States uncritically backed them, a strategy which heightened anti-Americanism among those opposing the dictators.

Modern dictatorships often use purported U.S. enmity for the same reason. Anti-Americanism can be both a sincere belief partly justified by history and a useful strategy for ruling at home and advancing ambitions abroad. Fidel Castro portrays his revolution as liberating Cuba from U.S. domination. True independence, he argues, necessitates a radical break with this past, when reformers were too moderate and compromising to succeed. Castro has manipulated anti-American nationalism to label certain groups (the middle class) and institutions (free speech) as partners of foreign imperialism. And this tactic rationalizes the controls the dictator needs to maintain power permanently. Restraints on freedom have been justified as guarding against Yankee intervention or a return to the hated old U.S.-sponsored order. Finally, anti-American ideology reinforces Castro's regional strategy. Those opposing the dictator's aggression or subversion are deemed betrayers of their nation's and region's interests and identity. U.S. countermeasures against the expansion of Cuban influence in Latin America "prove" hostile U.S. intentions and reinforce the regime's claims.

Sometimes, of course, suspicion of the United States is quite rational. Opponents who come to power are bitter about U.S. support for the old regime: Radicals are angry about past American backing for conservatives; civilians complain about U.S. involvement in military coups. A whole generation may have to pass—the modern dictatorship entrenched, memories faded, ambitions moderated—before antagonisms are soothed. The evolution of Egypt from Nasser to Sadat and of China from Mao to Deng Xiaoping are two examples of this pattern.

Anti-Americanism may also be a reaction to Western cultural influence. America's power and success breed both jealousy and fear. The incredible spread of U.S. films, products, music, and literature overruns markets and threatens to drive local artists and artisans out of business. In adapting so fully to these goods and ideas, elites in traditional dictatorships may be alienated from their own people—a problem symbolized by the Shah's skiing trips to his Swiss chalet and Somoza's West Point training—making it easy for opponents to question their nationalism. A loss of cultural distinctiveness is often thought to presage the destruction of independence.

Similarly, U.S. economic power—multinationals that export their profits and compete with local enterprises, banks to which the country is indebted—stir resentment that the modern dictator shares and exploits, claiming Western companies underpay for crops and resources, mistreat workers, remove potential development capital, and meddle in local politics. Third World leaders attribute the lack of past progress to Western exploitation. Nationalizing foreign-owned land or companies provides a simple, popular way of raising cash and concentrating wealth in the regime's hands. Profits can be plowed into domestic projects; landholdings can be redistributed to peasants, who become government supporters.

While historical, cultural, and economic issues create friction between modern dictatorships and the United States, there are also countervailing forces. Third World regimes, particularly in Africa, desperately need American aid and avidly seek U.S. investment, technology, and loans. But compromise is often accompanied by an increase in radical rhetoric and political control in order to prove the regime has neither sold out nor gone soft. Dictators are determined to ensure that an opening to the West does not imply any import of U.S. influence, political structures, or capitalism.

Often the United States is popular among the common people as a symbol of high living standards, more rights, and a source of movies, music, and mass-produced goods. Traditional dictators also have an incentive to like the United States as a sugar daddy for aid, weapons, and support against internal opposition or radical neighbors. A modern dictator's interests can be quite different. He has often overthrown a pro-U.S. regime, struck against U.S. business, and received arms from the USSR. He is tempted to alter Franklin Roosevelt's dictum and conclude that the Soviets may be SOBs, but they are his SOBs. The dictator must consider whether better relations with the United States will reinforce or threaten his rule. The more popular America or things American are among his own people, the harder the modern dictator must work to defuse and discredit its appeal.

All these themes can be clearly seen in the history of U.S. relations with Third World dictators. If they do not recall and understand these experiences, Americans are doomed to be shocked, confused, and disappointed by future developments. The evolution of U.S. policy toward Third World dictatorships can be traced through several overlapping periods whose premises and lessons have become part of contemporary thinking on the issue: the Cold War period, the 1960s, and the period of the Vietnam War.

Clearly, the Cold War competition with the USSR, the single most important issue for U.S. foreign policy since 1945, had a major effect on American policies and attitudes toward dictatorship. Experience with Soviet deceit and aggression led to a vision of a Manichaean world in which all states must be either pro-U.S. or pro-Soviet. Thus, dictatorships friendly with the United States were judged much less critically than those evincing Marxist or pro-Soviet sympathies. Indeed, American conservatives often saw Latin American juntas as more secure and stable rulers than reformist or left-leaning civilian regimes, allowing Third World rightists to justify coups and repression by claiming that they were only countering Communist threats.

U.S. experience in the 1940s and 1950s was taken as confirming the two-camp theory and the danger of new-style modern dictatorships aligning with the Soviets. The overthrow of Chinese dictator Chiang Kai-shek and the Communist victory in 1949 began a pattern of foreign revolution and domestic controversy that was to be repeated over Cuba, Vietnam, Iran, Nicaragua, and elsewhere. Chiang's regime had been accurately criticized by China experts as too corrupt, unpopular, and badly organized to defeat Mao's Communist forces. In addition to doubts over whether Chiang could be saved, Presidents Roosevelt and Truman rejected intervention in China as too huge a task for the United States. State Department specialists knew Mao was a dedicated Communist but believed that Chinese nationalism would ultimately prevail over Soviet domination.

Although these perceptions proved accurate in the long run, the People's Republic of China first became a firm ally of the USSR as well as a doctrinaire Communist state. American conservatives attacked the White House and State Department for "allowing" China to become Communist. Senator Joe McCarthy and the Republican party even branded U.S. China policy as treason. The controversy over China had a lasting effect. Although Americans remained uncomfortable about traditional dictatorships, the danger of Communist takeovers and the fear of domestic political uproars discouraged later U.S. Presidents from pressuring such allies to change. Movements that appeared nationalist or radical were viewed with suspicion as pro-Soviet Communists in disguise.

This lesson was applied elsewhere. President Dwight Eisenhower wrote of Egypt's Nasser in his memoirs, "If [he] was not a communist, he certainly succeeded in making us very suspicious of him." Fear that Iran's nationalist Mossadegh government was or would become a Communist-dominated regime was a major incentive for launching the U.S.-backed pro-Shah coup there in 1953. Similarly, the U.S. ambassador to a Guatemalan reformist regime, overthrown by a U.S.-organized coup in 1954, commented, "The Arbenz government, beyond any question, was controlled and dominated by Communists." When early modern dictators like Nkrumah in Ghana, Lumumba in the Congo, and Sukarno in Indonesia came to power, they were also viewed with extreme mistrust. After the Cuban Revolution left-of-center politicians in Latin America were often seen as potential Communists or men who would pave the way for Castroite rule. Many of these leaders were overthrown by coups welcomed or even assisted by the United States.

The early Cold War thus shaped U.S. policy toward Third World dictatorships in three ways: First, by increasing its international involvement, including foreign aid and the establishment of military bases abroad, the United States developed closer relations with many dictatorships. Second, seeking allies against the USSR and keeping China's fate in mind, the United States was soft on traditional dictators, lest pressuring or weakening them enabled pro-Soviet movements to seize power. Finally, emerging nationalist modern dictators and even some reformist democratic politicians were seen as politically dangerous.

Despite these premises, however, the need to face dramatic changes in the Third World required readjustments in the 1960s, the second period in the development of U.S. policy toward dictatorships. Liberals pointed out the costs of complacency: The United States was losing ground. Shame over past U.S. policies, rising anti-Americanism, and clashes with Third World populist regimes showed that the original Cold War paradigm did not fit the new circumstances. Liberals blamed U.S. policy for fostering immoral and unstable traditional dictators and driving Third World states toward the USSR.

Decolonization was politically reshaping the world. Emerging states and changing consciousness created heightened expectations of economic development and demands for independence or national equality. Experience with the new African states showed that nationalist modern dictators were not Communists. With dozens of independent countries pursuing their own interests, neutrality in the East-West struggle became common.

Acknowledging this new complexity in a 1964 essay, Henry Kissinger wrote, "In contemporary international affairs a country suffers fewer disadvantages from being neutral and may gain some international stature through the competition of the major powers for its allegiance. . . . Neutrality then becomes an invitation to be wooed." Yet this adds "a new element of volatility" because these nations "feel free to practice vis-à-vis their own neighbors the kind of power politics which they urge the great powers to abjure." Alongside and entwined with the East-West conflict were Third World leaders' own ambitions. Such dictatorships had to be dealt with as independent factors, not as mere surrogates of Washington or Moscow.

The first U.S. experiment with these issues—conducted, ironically, by an Eisenhower administration known for its rigid Cold War classification of dictators—turned out badly. The United States refused to support Fulgencio Batista's traditional dictatorship in Cuba against Fidel Castro's guerrillas, who finally marched victoriously into Havana in January 1959. Events in Cuba seemed to follow a pattern similar to the Chinese Revolution. A traditional dictator had again fallen only to be replaced by an anti-American, pro-Soviet modern dictatorship.

President John Kennedy interpreted Castro's Marxist course as more proof of the need for a new kind of strategy toward the non-Communist Third World: help in nation building to promote stability, democracy, and non-Marxist roads to development; the favoring of democratic "third" forces that were neither Communist nor traditional dictators; and to court modern dictators who might moderate their foreign policy.

Before taking office, Kennedy had warned about the danger of thinking "that all Latin American agitation is Communist-inspired—that every anti-American voice is the voice of Moscow—and that most citizens of Latin America share our dedication to an anticommunist crusade to save what we call free enterprise." He advocated competing with Moscow and Havana for the support of reformist and nationalist forces. "Can any American looking at the situation in Latin America feel contented with what's happening today," he said soon after taking office in 1961, "when a candidate for the presidency in Brazil [Janio Quadros] feels it necessary to call not on Washington during the campaign, but on Castro in Havana" to muster support at home? "The big struggle will be to prevent the influence of Castro spreading to other countries." But while Castro supported and armed guerrillas, traditional dictators and juntas that antagonized their own people were the true recruiting agents for revolution and communism.

In very different ways the Peace Corps and Green Berets symbolized U.S. policy's attempt to adapt to changes animating the Third World. They were designed to teach Third World regimes how to build nations, encourage citizen participation, create stability, and provide a non-Communist model for development while discouraging and defeating insurgencies. To compete with traditional dictators' use of repression and entrenched custom as well as modern dictators' combination of repression, change, and rewards, moderate politicians must organize popular support for reforms, mobilizing and organizing the masses to carry out and preserve democratic revolutions that provide real progress and benefits. Such later political figures as José Napoleón Duarte in El Salvador or Corazon Aquino in the Philippines demonstrated the possibility of this kind of politics.

Despite these tactics, however, the United States was again backing military coups in Latin America by the second half of the 1960s. The United States hoped, along with many middle-class Latin American civilians, that junta rule would better maintain stability and more effectively defeat Marxist guerrilla movements. Within a year of Kennedy's assassination Washington guaranteed Brazil's link with U.S. influence by supporting a coup. In short, when faced with a threat from a real or apparent pro-Soviet group, liberals retreated to the original Cold War preference for traditional dictators rather than risk the possibility of a radical alternative. Nevertheless, liberals still maintained that weak, unpopular, and economically incompetent traditional dictators were at the root of conditions that gave rise to revolutions producing anti-American modern dictatorships.

Conservatives favored action to protect traditional dictatorships against communist or alleged Communist takeovers; liberals sought to inoculate against these threats by helping form new regimes immune to them. Liberal advocacy of pressing traditional dictators to democratize while trying to improve

337

relations with non-Communist modern dictatorships was the exact reverse of the conservative version of Cold War thinking.

The Vietnam War, by testing the liberal and conservative perspectives on dictatorship, frustrated and reinforced them both. In contrast with its relative inaction over China and Cuba, the United States made an all-out effort in Indochina first to transform—as the liberals had suggested—and later to save—as the conservatives demanded—a traditional dictatorship from a Communist-led revolution.

There were bitter paradoxes for both sides. Critics of the war correctly understood the psychological, organizational, and nationalist assets enjoyed by Hanoi and the National Liberation Front, but many of them were fooled into thinking that the anti-Saigon forces were independent and non-Communist. They also correctly analyzed the corrupt, unpopular nature of the South Vietnamese and Cambodian governments but went on to conclude that these shortcomings meant such regimes—and inevitably their subjects as well—deserved to fall to Communist rule.

Supporters of the war also faced dilemmas. They argued, on practical grounds, that a U.S. defeat and a takeover of Indochina by pro-Soviet Communists would damage American prestige and power around the world. But the cost of the war was so tremendous as to have the equivalent, counterproductive effect. Supporters claimed, on moral grounds, to be preserving a future democratic option for the Vietnamese people. But this was a difficult position to sustain when tens of thousands were being killed and the country destroyed in order to save them. And through it all there was no strategy capable of obtaining victory because the enemy would not give up, and ultimately, the South Vietnamese government could not sustain itself.

During the war's first phase the United States tried Kennedy's strategy of trying to help, cajole, or force the Ngo Dinh Diem dictatorship to become stronger, more efficient, and more popular. When it proved incapable of doing so, the administration backed a military coup. The resulting juntas, however, were even more unstable and less politically astute than Diem had been.

Despite all the aid and civic action programs, the war came to be fought as a strictly military engagement, costing the United States a decade of effort, tens of thousands of lives, a serious loss of prestige, and billions of dollars. North Vietnam, a streamlined modern dictatorship, was able to combine Sino-Soviet aid, disciplined organization, nationalism, Ho Chi Minh's charisma, and repression to win victory over an uncertain, rickety traditional dictatorship. U.S. intervention shored up the Saigon regimes but also provided North Vietnam with a nationalist rallying cry. "The Communists won the war by their resort to systematic brutality," commented an April 1985 *New Republic* editorial, "the anti-Communists lost it by their resort to capricious brutality." Brutality alone would have been insufficient, but the contrast between a well-organized, disciplined Hanoi and a dispirited, drifting Saigon was quite real. North Vietnam and its southern allies could—while South Vietnam could not—inspire, command, or intimidate people into enthusiastic support.

The Vietnam War created syndromes that pushed both conservatives and liberals toward more extreme versions of their earlier views. The former were all the more certain of the need to defend traditional dictatorships and the centrality of the Communist threat and Soviet aggression. Former President Nixon wrote, in a book significantly entitled *No More Vietnams*, that the U.S. mistake in Indochina was not to back the French colonial authorities in the 1950s. "Obsessive fear of association with European colonial powers blinded successive administrations [to the] very simple fact: communism, not colonialism, was the principal cause of the war in Indochina." In short, it was neither popular complaints (social injustice, nationalism) nor identification of the United States with unpopular causes (colonialism, traditional dictators) that created revolutions and modern dictatorships but rather Soviet-hatched conspiracies. The Vietnam defeat was due to a lack of resolve, not to a mistaken policy.

Nixon was wrong because although communism was the central factor in Hanoi's system, its major asset was the kind of nationalist, expansionist ambition that marked other Third World modern dictatorships. Further, it was not communism that gave credibility to nationalism but vice versa. If anticolonial and anti-American sentiments had not existed, alongside opposition to the Saigon dictatorship, hard-core Communists might have had the same beliefs but would have been unable to mobilize so many other people. Conversely, traditional dictatorships did not fall because they were more evil than modern dictatorships so much as because they were more vulnerable.

Many liberals drew their own lessons from Vietnam. They attributed the defeat to the undemocratic nature and lack of nationalist appeal by Saigon's rulers—to the inherent weakness of traditional dictators. Moreover, the Sino-Soviet split and other events demonstrated that radical, even independent Marxist states were not necessarily a threat to U.S. interests. The loss of prestige over Vietnam and other past policies required a special effort to prove American willingness to support the forces of democracy, development, and national sovereignty in the Third World which otherwise might turn toward the Soviet Union. If U.S. toughness had produced the crisis, U.S. flexibility, even compassion, was needed to escape it.

This approach had some weaknesses. It tended to underestimate the USSR's subversive role and the intrinsic conflicts of interest that made it impossible or dangerous to woo some modern dictators. Reacting against traditional dictators' sins, it could be naïve about their opponents' objectives. Disillusioned with interventionism's high cost and inability to save traditional dictators, these liberals were also reluctant to act decisively in crises to press their own strategy for democratic transformation. To take such a strong stand, after all, would also require a form of intervention.

The Carter administration's human rights policy was popular in theory—building on a peculiarly American discomfort of being allied with dictators—but controversial in practice. Believers in realpolitik asked whether it advanced U.S. interests to interfere with other states' internal affairs. Conservatives felt that too much pressure was focused on traditional dictatorships friendly to the West rather than on leftist modern dictatorships favorable to the USSR.

Carter also criticized the predominance of U.S.-USSR competition in shaping Washington's Third World policy. By questioning an "inordinate fear of communism" or denying the Soviets were "ten feet tall," Carter was urging that the United States not let an overestimate of Soviet power and craftiness make it obsessively support traditional dictatorships, assume that modern dictators would inevitably side with Moscow, or be convinced that Communists were always better placed to succeed against traditional dictators. His handling of revolutions that replaced traditional dictatorships with modern dictatorships in Iran and Nicaragua made Carter subject to much criticism and threw his premises into question.

Ironically, the defeat of democratic anti-Somoza forces in Nicaragua was due not only to the Carter administration's reluctance to intervene decisively in the transition but also to past conservative policies identifying the United States with the old dictatorship. In Iran the United States had far less leverage, and there was no real democratic force or even a mass constituency for one. Some form of modern dictatorship was inevitable. These upheavals and resulting problems grew out of a long-term U.S. backing for unpopular dictators, liberals argued, while conservatives responded that instability was largely caused by U.S. meddling and Soviet subversion.

Reacting to these same crises, conservatives produced ideas extending their own past theses. First, respect for U.S. power, rather than an attempt to make America more popular, was the main priority. Iran dared to hold U.S. hostages only because its Islamic rulers felt that America, to use an earlier Nixon phrase, was a "pitiful, helpless giant."

Second, apparent successes for Moscow in the Third World and the Soviet invasion of Afghanistan reinforced the appeal of a Cold War dichotomy in evaluating dictatorships. Moscow was again seen as the central force undermining traditional dictatorships and creating new ones. "The Soviet Union and

341

its proxies," wrote Nixon, " . . . licked their chops and gobbled up South Yemen, Angola, Mozambique, Afghanistan and Nicaragua. . . ."

Third, these years also brought deep disillusionment with the promises and inflated claims of revolutionary transformation, a cynicism well expressed by W. B. Yeats's poem "The Great Day," reflecting a similar experience in Ireland's turbulent history:

> Hurrah for revolution and more cannon-shot!
> A beggar upon horseback lashes a beggar on foot.
> Hurrah for revolution and cannon come again!
> The beggars have changed places, but the lash goes on.

In considering the era just past, the dominant voices in the public debate blended these factors together. "The Soviets concluded that the global 'correlation of forces' was shifting in their favor," said Secretary of State George Shultz in an April 1985 speech. "American weakness turned out to be the most destabilizing factor in the global scene." During the Vietnam War U.S. force had seemed the principal villain behind the suffering. Columnist Anthony Lewis wrote at the time that nothing "could be more terrible than the reality of what is happening in Cambodia now." The massacres following the Communist takeover belied that statement: History showed that things could be far worse than they had been under a traditional dictator. As Shultz commented, "The communist subjection of Indochina has fulfilled the worst predictions of the time."

Shultz was also essentially correct in adding that while South Vietnam was "not a Jeffersonian democracy with full civil liberties by American standards . . . there was a vigorous, pluralist political process, and the government intruded little into the private lives of the people." Yet the pluralism was disruptive and against the Saigon dictatorship's will; unable either to stifle or to be transformed by dissent, the regime was only weakened by it. The lack of intrusion was not benevolence but the government's inability to mobilize fully for war or even to exercise control over its own territory. The dictatorship's limited "virtues" helped cause its defeat.

By accepting the idea that change and revolution were inevitable, said the aforementioned *New Republic* editorial, U.S. policy had shown antidemocratic adversaries "that if they are fanatical enough and seem unyielding enough there will be plenty of Americans who will argue that they are not to be resisted at all. Thus the victory of the implacable becomes irresistible: zeal becomes its own reward, and perversely even an index of justice." Shultz rejected the criticism "that we, and our friends, are the representatives of evil." In a world where Pol Pot massacred fellow Cambodians, Qaddafi ordered terrorism, and the Soviets seized Afghanistan, the focus of approbation must be turned elsewhere.

But there were two ways of acting on the conclusion that revolution against a traditional dictator could produce something worse. The liberal interpretation favored even greater urgency for pressing regimes toward reforms that could avoid an explosion; the conservative alternative argued that liberal tinkering was destabilizing, making a blowup more likely, and urged instead even more steadfast support of friendly dictators.

In the latter category was Kissinger's warning in a September 1979 interview: "Trying to bludgeon societies into behavior analogous to our own [will] either lead to a deadlock and American irrelevance, or it will lead to the collapse of existing authority without a substitute compatible with our values and, therefore, the emergence of a radical outcome, as in Iran and Nicaragua. . . . If there is no moderate alternative and our choice is between the status quo and the radicals, it is a serious question whether the radicals are more in our long-term interest than the status quo."

In reality, the Nicaragua and Iran crises presented the United States with situations in which the status quo was no longer a viable option. U.S. policy was not one of gratuitously bludgeoning Somoza into reforms but faced a situation in which Washington's backing for Somoza would have driven Nicaraguans to despair, radicalism, and revolution, ensuring the worst-case outcome that the United States was trying to avoid. By the time Khomeini's radical leadership came to dominate the opposition, Iranians had already concluded that the Shah's regime could neither survive nor offer any major reforms. The unpalatable choices emerging at the last minute in both countries—dogged support of a failing traditional dictator or acceptance of an anti-American modern dictatorship—were due to months of failure by U.S. policymakers to realize the depth of the crisis and to take decisive action supporting a different result.

The view of Kissinger does not flinch from recognizing a leader's duty to choose among unattractive alternatives yet also presumes foreign revolutions take place only at the behest of the United States. Kissinger sounded similar themes in a February 1979 interview on the Iranian Revolution, claiming that the Shah did not fight back more forcefully "because he must have had doubts about our real intentions." An ongoing revolution cannot be moderated by concessions, Kissinger added, and these should come only after order has been restored. This argument fails to understand that revolutions are produced by a heterogeneous alignment of forces, united mainly by their opposition to the existing order, which can be separated out, particularly in the earlier stages, by reforms or moderate alternatives.

Kissinger's analysis also neglects the foreign country's internal politics and problems that shape the crisis. In Iran these included the Shah's personal weakness, the opposition's breadth, the army's ineffectiveness, Khomeini's charismatic appeal, and a range of economic problems and sociological changes that stirred passionate grievances. Ultimately Kissinger's conception is analogous to explaining the American Revolution as the result of French meddling and King George III's lack of firmness.

The most comprehensive, sophisticated argument for the conservative analysis of dictatorship was made by Jeane Kirkpatrick. In *Dictatorships and Double Standards* she argues that traditional dictators were less burdensome for their subjects than are their replacements. The Shah and Somoza, for example, through their long tenures, brought relative domestic tranquillity, allowed their people to maintain their customary life-styles, increased national wealth, and were friendly to the West. After decades of cooperation, however, the United States dropped them when they were being attacked and helped into power "new regimes in which ordinary people enjoy fewer freedoms and less personal security than under the previous autocracy—regimes, moreover, hostile to American interests and policies." U.S. support "for 'change' in the abstract ends up by aligning us tacitly with Soviet clients and irresponsible extremists. . . ." Again, her analysis assumes that keeping Somoza and the Shah in power was a viable option and one within U.S. capabilities.

Kirkpatrick also misjudges who is a Soviet client; she was wrong about the successful turnover of the Panama Canal and in labeling Panamanian dictator Omar Torrijos a "Castroite." Her liberal critics have sometimes been naïve about the pro-Soviet and dictatorial leanings of revolutionaries and liberation movements. But like Kissinger, Kirkpatrick overstates the Soviet role in creating the discontent and revolts that emerge in traditional dictatorships. "The deep historical forces at work in such diverse places as Iran, the Horn of Africa, Southeast Asia, Central America, and the United Nations look a lot like Russians or Cubans," wrote Kirkpatrick. Yet revolutions do not gain impetus if there is no strong basis for them; otherwise, the Soviets and Cubans could create upheavals and turn regimes into puppets much more easily than has actually been the case. Merely sending in guerrillas or arms, as Che Guevara discovered in Bolivia, does not ensure success. Kirkpatrick is right, however, in noting that Soviet and Cuban support may offer victory in appropriate circumstances to one of several contending opposition factions and ideologies or may help a client regime stay in power.

One of Kirkpatrick's most interesting insights is to explain why modern dictators may be more appealing to Americans than their traditional counterparts. The latter's open distribution of power through kinship and cronyism "rather than on the basis of objective 'rational' standards violates our con-

345

ception of justice and efficiency." Americans dislike regimes that prefer stability over the change that has been our historic choice. Extremes of greed and conspicuous wealth next to grinding poverty are interpreted as deliberate cruelty rather than inherited reality. Their replacements, in contrast, usually glorify "modernity, . . . reason, science, education and progress. . . . They speak our language [promising] a hopeful future, . . . egalitarianism rather than hierarchy and privilege, liberty rather than order, activity rather than passivity."

In Kirkpatrick's writings, however, a revolution seems to be more the product of a conspiracy rather than a reflection of wide discontent. "The Somoza regime had never rested on popular will (but instead on manipulation, force, and habit)," she writes, and fell not because of the masses' sentiments but because of the Sandinistas' arsenal. This is technically true. As modern dictatorships show, regimes are not overthrown merely because they are oppressive as long as the opposition lacks guns and organization. Nonetheless, the Sandinistas were a tiny, isolated group until the regime's behavior sparked a mass uprising and general strike supported by the vast majority of Nicaraguans. Non-Communist states like Colombia, Venezuela, Costa Rica, and Mexico also acted against Somoza. These forces all would have preferred a democratic alternative— particularly if the United States had backed one—but were willing to support almost anyone against Somoza, a judgment that can only be taken as a popular and regional rejection of the regime.

A central point in Kirkpatrick's argument is "that traditional authoritarian governments are less repressive than revolutionary autocracies, . . . more susceptible of liberalization, and . . . more compatible with U.S. interests." This statement contains much truth and some misleading conclusions about repression, liberalization, and U.S. interests.

Certainly, traditional dictatorships are generally less pervasive in their efforts to shape society, but less activist government is not necessarily better or more popular. Maintaining customary patterns—inequitable landlord-tenant relationships, for example—may be more oppressive than altering them. Further, the new regime may change the focus of repression from being a weapon of social control against workers and peasants into being a tool of vengeance and political control against the wealthy, the old middle class, or opposition activists. Those who are no longer being punished or who benefit from economic change—land reform, nationalizations, enlargement of the elite—are unlikely to see the new system as more repressive and are much more likely to find it psychologically appealing. The fact that traditional dictators did not alter the distribution of goods, status, and power was not so much an act of kindness as a failure to meet the dramatic changes and demands for development already shaking their countries.

As for liberalization, Kirkpatrick accurately notes, "Although there is no instance of a revolutionary 'socialist' or Communist society being democratized, right-wing autocracies do sometimes evolve into democracies." Third World traditional dictatorships are more likely to become democratic than are modern dictatorships, but by the same token, they are also just as likely, particularly outside of Latin America, to become new modern dictatorships. Kirkpatrick's academic research had been on Latin America, where traditional dictatorships have generally alternated with civilian rule. In other regions, however, there are few traditional dictators left. The point is that, as political systems, traditional dictatorships in our time are more systemically unstable than modern dictatorships. Consequently, U.S. interests are not best served by a laissez-faire policy toward traditional dictatorships; it is all the more important to act decisively at critical turning points in order to avoid their replacement by more entrenched dictatorial regimes.

Actually the Carter administration was never eager to "overthrow" the Shah and Somoza, and human rights considerations had little practical effect on U.S. policy toward them. When revolts did begin, the first phase of U.S reaction was a denial that any problem existed. Having justified bilateral relations so long on the basis of realpolitik and having seen previous challenges fail, Washington doubted the dictators were in real trouble.

Only after months when the regime's incapacity had been demonstrated did the Carter administration begin to act. Even then it was paralyzed by heated debates over whether the United States should press the ruler for concessions and by fear of a conservative backlash at home. Washington did not push the Shah or Somoza far or fast enough to yield to the moderate democratic opposition. Demands grew greater as the regimes showed both weakness and inflexibility. When moderates saw no alternative, they began to throw their support behind the radicals—Islamic fundamentalists and Sandinistas respectively. The chain of events was quite different from what Kirkpatrick portrayed.

Again, it is true that U.S. relations with prerevolutionary Cuba, South Vietnam, Iran, Syria, Egypt, Iraq, and Nicaragua were better than with the successor regimes. Some anti-Americanism can be traced to specific U.S. policies; a great deal of the antagonism was adopted for ideological and domestic reasons. Those dependent on Moscow or who seek to lead regional or global revolutions are not going to be swayed by U.S. arguments or demonstrations of goodwill. Kirkpatrick makes a persuasive case against romanticizing modern dictators or naïvely expecting that nothing can be worse than existing traditional ones.

Yet her analysis has also been criticized as an apology for traditional dictatorships, a rationale for a U.S. policy of shoring up an existing dictatorship rather than pressing the dictator for change or a peaceful yielding to democratic rule. In two specific cases, El Salvador and the Philippines, this is precisely how Kirkpatrick herself argued.

"To many Salvadorans," Kirkpatrick wrote, past violent repression "seems less important than the fact of restored order and the . . . years of civil peace that ensued." Obviously this is more likely to be true of the Salvadoran landowning and army elite than of the lower-class majority and much of the urban middle class as well. Moreover, if this view of public

opinion is accurate, it applies even more to modern dictatorships, which are generally better able to maintain order through
propaganda and repression, than to traditional ones. But an
obsession with order can also block progress, evolving into a
system unacceptable to increasingly larger sectors of the populace. The real question is how much of the public is willing
to accept and pay the personal and social costs for the kind
of order provided.

If a liberal error was to see any change as improvement,
the conservative mistake was to think that mere willpower
could prevent change. Thus, in El Salvador during the 1980s
a stubborn determination to maintain the existing order would
have been suicidal. The Reagan administration rightly strove
to avoid the emergence of an anti-American, pro-Soviet modern dictatorship in El Salvador by providing aid and military
training to the government. But it also believed the surest way
to "save" El Salvador was by backing the military-landlord elite.
The administration saw issues of democracy, human rights,
and land reform as a disruptive distraction from successful
waging of the war. Fortunately pressure from Congress and
public opinion forced the administration to condition aid on
the holding of elections and other reforms which, while still
inadequate, undercut the appeal of Marxist revolution. If not
for President Duarte and a heroic group of Christian Democrats, the army's brutality and the oligarchy's reactionary policies would have alienated tens of thousands of professionals,
workers, and peasants into joining forces with the guerrillas.

Similarly, Kirkpatrick failed to understand the Philippines
crisis of 1985–86. Aside from the Communists waging guerrilla warfare, there was a much larger moderate opposition to
President Ferdinand Marcos. Kirkpatrick saw only two alternatives: preserving Marcos or allowing the Communists to take
over. In fact, trying to do the former was the best way to
guarantee the latter result. Marcos's failures were not extraordinary, she wrote in a December 1985 column, "Of 159 member states of the United Nations, at least 100 are probably
governed more poorly than the Philippines." Once again, the
United States was showing "obsessive intolerance [toward] a

government in a nation of great strategic importance. . . . Remember Batista, Ngo Dinh Diem of Vietnam, Lon Nol of Cambodia, the Shah of Iran, Anastasio Somoza?" Each's shortcomings were manipulated to fool Americans and replace them with "repressive, aggressive dictatorships." She cautioned against pressuring Marcos, concluding that political change in the Philippines was ultimately not the business of the United States. It was a formula characterized by *Washington Post* reporter Sidney Blumenthal as "Stand by your strongman."

Yet if the United States had not supported the opposition after Marcos stole the February 1986 election or had not pressured Marcos to institute reforms and ultimately to step aside, the situation would have become far worse. The crisis was real: The economy was in ruins, government forces were murdering peasants, the army could not contain the guerrillas, and the Catholic Church had joined the opposition. Increasingly desperate opponents were reaching the point where they would prefer and work for a Communist victory rather than continue to live under Marcos's rule. What to Kirkpatrick was "meddling" and "interference in Philippine politics" was a desperate effort to avoid full-scale civil war. If American policymakers had followed her advice to "cease" their "interference," the Philippines would ultimately have gone the way of Vietnam or Cambodia.

Fortunately, knowledgeable officials in the State and Defense departments, aided by Congress, forced the White House to face reality and support Corazon Aquino, the true winner of the presidential election. The key factor, however, was the determination, democratic traditions, and courage of the Filipinos themselves.

While the Philippines crisis provided the administration with some education about traditional dictators, there were fewer pro-U.S., rightist or traditional dictatorships left, with South Korea and Chile being the most controversial. The White House had already developed a new policy toward some modern dictators, inspired by the emergence of guerrilla warfare against modern dictatorships in Angola, Afghanistan, Cambodia, and Nicaragua. Since domestic reluctance and changes in the international environment make it harder for the United States to arrange covert operations or coups to overthrow hostile Third World governments, support for opposition guerrillas seems a promising way to reach the same goal.

Conditions in these four countries varied considerably. The Afghan guerrillas, fighting a Soviet invasion and a puppet government, were themselves Islamic fundamentalists. The administration never used its considerable leverage over the Nicaraguan Contras to make them more observant of human rights or to strengthen the moderates among them. In Angola Jonas Savimbi may have had as good a claim to governing as did the ruling party, but he primarily represented a tribal constituency. And most of the Cambodian guerrillas were led by the very Communists who had murdered so many of their own people when in power. Thus, while all these movements were anti-Soviet and pro-United States, none of them was particularly democratic-minded. Some of them were unable to build broad bases of support, unity, and nationalist legitimacy. Their U.S. supporters found it difficult to see how these were prerequisites for success.

If conservatives tended to be complacent about traditional dictatorships as long as they were anti-Communist, many liberals have been too lenient on Third World modern dictatorships and the claims of movements fighting traditional dictators. The left still tends to think that nothing could be worse than the old order, believing that only an opportunist or worse could support the wretchedness of today compared with the beautiful vision of tomorrow purveyed by the modern dictators. To criticize such heroes of equity and social justice is equivalent to intellectual treason.

Past Western and U.S. bullying, racism, and colonialism erode the confidence of the West or at least portions of its intelligentsia. It is important to remember, however, that there are different stages of wisdom about international affairs. One level is to understand that other people also believe their country and leaders correct, that we are not always right, and that another country's behavior cannot be comprehended without considering its society, history, and national viewpoint. Nonetheless, a still higher level of comprehension is to learn that cultural relativism does not necessarily mean that the other side is right, that belief in human equality does not mean being fooled into thinking humanity is homogeneous, and that to understand another nation is not necessarily to agree with it. The Iranian regime and many of its citizens may believe that the United States is the Great Satan, Libya may think that it has a perfect right to support international terrorism, other nations may conclude that economic development requires the persecution or torture of "class enemies" or dissidents; but sincerity is not what is at issue here. Political analysis also requires a differentiation between subjective beliefs and objective reality.

Much of the Western left and some liberals have become apologists for modern dictators, accepting their claims and statistics at face value, something they would never do with their own governments. In the case of Nicaragua, for example, they have denied the Sandinistas' Marxist-Leninist objectives and harshly criticized those documenting inequities as giving aid and comfort to the right. Naïve and sympathetic American visitors have traveled to various modern dictatorships and returned with reflexive, unqualified praise.

This deeply emotional defensiveness is based on hatred of the oppressive traditional regimes and equation of the new ones with progress. Once "liberated," the country becomes a cause to be protected rather than a society to be evaluated. Being willfully naïve about how power is actually exercised, the left sees the unexamined new order as a festival of rule by the "people." This kind of debate has been going on since the French Revolution. One could admire the motto of Liberty, Equality, and Fraternity or point to the liberal use of the guillotine. Those doing the latter could be accused of indifference to the old monarchy's daily oppression. Today those who point out the shortcomings of African governments can be unfairly accused of a preference for colonialism, or, in Nicaragua's case, for Somoza.

Confusion also arises from the idea that poverty, malnutrition, and disease are the direct causes of revolution. If this is true, then the rebellion can be seen as an inherently virtuous protest against dreadful conditions. But if it is understood that the strain of change and development is the real cause of political upheaval, then the new regimes must be judged by what they produce rather than by what they negate.

The modern dictators and their apologists convinced the Western left and some liberals that the Third World's ruling classes are not responsible for their own misrule, that it is bad form to expose their corruption or to reveal their repression. Such criticisms were to be dealt with as the intellectual equivalent of pornography. Its authors could be told, as translator Robert Hass lectured one critic, "No American writer is in a position to lecture a Nicaraguan writer on the forgiveness of sins." After all, he who carps is "exposed to no danger, require[d] to perform no action," nor does he mitigate anyone's suffering. "It would take a good deal of self-intoxication to lecture [Minister of Culture] Father [Ernesto] Cardinal, or anyone else, from that particular platform." But all this omits the fact that regardless of the past, the Cardinals are now in power and doing the persecuting of democratic-minded opponents. The dictators themselves are also "exposed to no danger."

A combination of guilt, dissatisfaction with their own society, yearning for utopian solutions, and romanticism can become a brew that turns the liberals' original humanitarian goals and beliefs on their head. Sartre rationalized Third World violence in his preface to Frantz Fanon's *Wretched of the Earth*: "By this mad fury, by this bitterness and spleen, by their ever-present desire to kill us, by the permanent tensing of powerful muscles which are afraid to relax, they have become men. . . . Hatred, blind hatred . . . is their only wealth." Such a simultaneously masochistic and patronizing view—they once lived just to serve us; now they exist only to punish us—quickly turns into an apologia for massacres, torture, terrorism, anti-Semitism, and endless lies.

The problems posed for U.S. policy by Libya and Sandinista Nicaragua provide some guidance on how to formulate a strategy toward such hostile regimes. In both cases most

Americans would like to see the current rulers removed or forced to change their policies.

A century ago Qaddafi's involvement in subverting his neighbors and terrorism would have brought on a Western invasion; a few decades ago it would have brought a U.S.-sponsored coup. Today, however, American conscience and debate, regional nationalism, Soviet intervention and the structure of modern dictatorship effectively rule out these options.

To stage a coup, a dissident Libyan colonel would have to organize colleagues and be sure that subordinate officers and troops would follow his order to rebel. This is a far more difficult task than it was for Qaddafi himself under the monarchy. Loyalty is highly institutionalized; security measures are stronger. Qaddafi's five separate intelligence agencies, some led by relatives, watch one another and the armed forces. Soviet bloc advisers who help protect Qaddafi will neither sympathize with nor be bought off by opponents. Better means of expanding the ruling elite, ideology, surveillance, and repression have reduced the number of coups in the Arab world. The last successful military takeovers in major Arab states were in Syria (1970) and Qaddafi's own coup in Libya (1969).

Qaddafi not only used repression but also provided a variety of material benefits, patriotism, and his own charisma. He came to power at the moment when oil money began to pour into Libya. Despite his massive arms spending, there were billions of dollars left for raising living standards. Qaddafi also transformed Libya from a backwater into an important country, suffused with pride and extreme nationalism. In addition, he skillfully manipulated symbols and the media to portray himself as the nation's embodiment, a man who serves the people's interests and someone with whom all good Libyans should identify.

But Qaddafi's modern dictatorship also has some significant weaknesses. His wasteful ways, shoddy planning, and economic errors, combined with an oil glut that drastically reduced revenues, forced major cutbacks in politically beneficial spending. Qaddafi's anarchic tendencies prevented him from building as strong a network of loyal groups as could be found in Egypt, Syria, Iraq, or Iran. More than the others, Qaddafi led a "one-bullet" regime vulnerable to his assassination. On the regional level his personal instability and aggressiveness made him unpopular among fellow Arabs. Internationally Qaddafi could not rely on Soviet help; he had to fear, while simultaneously ridiculing, retribution from the United States.

The fact that Qaddafi is not crazy and wishes to remain in power gives the United States a great amount of potential leverage against him. The Libyan dictator used terrorism, demagoguery, bribery, and other such techniques not as ends in themselves but as instruments in furthering his ambition. This very goal-oriented quality makes him more vulnerable to deterrence and discouragement. Consequently, the application of a judicious amount of force, as in the U.S. air attacks of 1986, can have a positive effect. The pressure should be enough to weaken Qaddafi and demonstrate to him the costs of his anti-American and subversive activities but not so much as to make him feel so cornered as to escalate his efforts at regional destabilization and international terrorism. U.S. actions will not reduce terrorism or Qaddafi's trouble-making to zero but it can restrain Libya, cutting down the number of incidents, saving lives, making it harder for terrorists to act or escape, and discouraging others from imitating Qaddafi.

In themselves, highly publicized confrontations with the United States allowed Qaddafi to posture both as a Libyan and an Arab nationalist. But such activities do him little good in the region. Anyone who has long observed the Middle East has seen that Arab solidarity can be a greatly overestimated factor. All the Arab governments had to make ritual, rhetorical criticism of anti-Qaddafi actions but none of them did anything to help Libya and many are not displeased by a weakening of Qaddafi. The Libyan leader himself well understood his own isolation and the dangerous situation he was facing.

Since Qaddafi wanted to stay in power, he had to take into account both the lack of Arab support and the military and economic pressures that threaten to force him into choosing between changing his behavior or seeing his rule undermined. Qaddafi will choose to stay in power but this very decision will also force him to be more restrained in his actions. Even if many Libyans rally to him out of patriotism, it does not change this essential fact.

Economic pressure from the United States and Western Europe, including embargoes and bars on citizens working in Libya, would cause further declines in living standards and challenge Qaddafi's popularity. Since Qaddafi overestimates U.S. power, quiet and open operations against him—particularly those with minimal publicity—will feed a sense of panic within the regime. These measures can have an effect, however, only if coupled with diplomacy that allows Qaddafi a face-saving retreat. While Qaddafi's ambitions and ideology pose the real problem—he is an adventurist even by modern dictators' standards—U.S. policy could limit and help control his destabilizing activities.

Similar points can be made about Nicaragua. As in the case of Libya, the Sandinistas gained support by their leading role in destroying the old order, providing benefits for many, seizing a monopoly on patriotism, and indoctrinating the young. They were better organized than Libya and not so dependent on one leader. But on the negative side their economy was more precarious, the regional balance more unfavorable, U.S. power closer at hand, and the opposition more deeply rooted.

Nicaragua's rulers moved hesitantly down the road to modern dictatorship not out of any compunction but because of three political factors: They were afraid that the United States would increase aid to the Contras or even stage an invasion; the Soviets and Cubans, overextended and wanting to avoid confrontation with Washington, gave Managua only limited help; and domestic opponents—including the church, independent labor unions, and the remaining private sector—were still strong enough to checkmate a regime that could harass but not destroy them. The best strategy for the United States was to make use of these constraints.

Washington's main objectives vis-à-vis Nicaragua were to prevent the establishment of Soviet bloc bases, limit the further entrenchment of Soviet-Cuban influence, and stop the Sandinistas from continuing to subvert their neighbors. Support for democratic opposition forces in Nicaragua was valuable not only on its own terms but also because some degree of pluralism was the best guarantee of moderating the regime's foreign policy and stopping the advance to full modern dictatorship.

The Contras, in and of themselves, could not obtain these results. Militarily they were unable to defeat the Sandinistas; politically they were ineptly organized. Their obvious dependence on U.S. support eroded their patriotic appeal, ceding the powerful weapon of nationalism to the regime. The ex-Somoza officers who led Contra military forces were not impressive fighters. Other than bullying the peasantry, their sole experience with war was being defeated by the Sandinistas. The Contras' tactic of terrorizing the populace was not just an ethical problem but also showed they had no idea of how to build a base of support or create liberated zones. The Reagan administration made no serious effort to democratize the Contras themselves or purge Somocista elements. Yet without such steps Congress would give only limited support to a movement that seemed likely to return Nicaragua to traditional dictatorship or even to drag the United States into war.

Again, U.S. strategy needed to combine military-economic pressure with diplomatic activism. Even those who opposed funding the Contras or criticized the economic boycott against Nicaragua could still agree with the use of such already existing leverage as a point of departure. The Sandinistas, in short, must be pushed to the point where they have to make a choice between changing their policies or risking the loss of power altogether. But, to be effective, this U.S. policy must present the dictatorship with a way out. Otherwise, the modern dictatorship can toughen its policy and fight to the end. With no incentive to limit domestic repression, links to the Soviet bloc, and foreign subversion, the regime will pose a much greater danger to the United States than it did before the onset of the confrontation. Given the continued constraints on the United States, particularly against a direct invasion, and the tools that a modern dictatorship can bring to bear, the Sandinistas might well win out in the end. They would then be far more entrenched as well as virtually impervious to U.S. influence. After all, this is precisely what happened with Castro's regime in Cuba.

The best negotiating option is represented by the Contadora accords, promoted by most Latin American governments, which sought to ensure the removal of foreign bases, military buildups, and cross-border subversion from Central America. These were all high-priority aims of the United States but no diplomatic solution was possible without active U.S. involvement. Instead of allowing itself to be seen as the main factor blocking negotiations, the United States should have been demanding that Nicaragua negotiate, both bilaterally and multilaterally. In such circumstances, U.S. leverage and the support of the region's nations could have been effectively brought into play to reach a solution satisfying American interests.

As in the case of Libya, the Reagan administration failed to appreciate the powers and advantages that a modern dictatorship could bring into play. It underestimated the ease of overthrowing such a regime, thereby weakening its ability to influence such a government even against the dictatorship's will.

By a combination of carrots and sticks, conditioned on Nicaragua's behavior, tough negotiations, and support for the internal democratic opposition, the United States could gain the upper hand. Whether or not Nicaragua became democratic, much of its threat to the area would have been defused and domestic repression reduced. If Nicaragua violated the treaties, the United States would have the power—and much wider domestic and regional support—for decisive action to force them back into line. Ultimately, a successful policy must be both tough and flexible. Many liberals have underestimated the Sandinistas dictatorial ambitions and Marxist-Leninist politics. Yet conservatives have not accurately assessed how best to challenge these factors and have not appreciated the resources such a regime can use to stay in power even against—

one might say, particularly against—a foreign-backed guerrilla war. The fact that the Sandinistas can credibly portray the Contras as flunkies of the United States goes a long way toward rationalizing Managua's own policy toward Havana and Moscow. A situation in which the Sandinistas can credibly claim that the Contras want to return to an oppressive traditional dictatorship helps immeasurably to secure passivity or even support for their own repressive measures.

In dealing with modern dictatorships, there are no total solutions. Since the United States was unwilling or unable to overthrow the Tripoli and Managua regimes, the goal of U.S. policy should be to achieve some coexistence under the best possible terms for the United States by making the maximum use of their insecurities to place the greatest limits on their foreign and domestic abuses. In general, modern dictators require their citizens to accept limits on rights and living standards which are unpalatable even when nationalism, necessity, and ideology are offered as rationales. The governments themselves can neither trust the USSR for aid and protection nor solve their own development problems. These shortcomings offer opportunities for U.S. strategic and military leverage, human rights and material advantages, and our technological and economic edge over the USSR.

Economically backward and strategically overextended, Moscow has limited resources and even more limited generosity. In sub-Saharan Africa, for example, the USSR supplies less than 1 percent of economic assistance. But it also provides an estimated 48 percent of military aid and, in some cases, Cuban soldiers. These are impressive assets in some situations. S. 'l, most modern dictators are eager to improve relations with the West to obtain aid, goods, and technology that the Soviet bloc cannot or will not provide. The U.S. role in mediating regional conflicts provides an enormous advantage. Time after time the Soviets have been disappointed in their attempts to court or control rulers.

While the United States has suffered from the conversion of traditional dictatorships to modern dictatorships, the Soviets and their allies have learned the fickleness of the latter.

Like the United States, they have discovered that the structures and rhetoric of modern dictators do not mean that they are Communists. As a Polish writer, Ignacy Sachs, put it in 1966, "In practice, we sometimes invert the correct assertion that foreign policy is an extension of domestic policy, and whenever, on the international scene, a country practices neutralism or seeks cooperation from us, we endeavor to find leftist trends in its domestic policy." Moscow's concern, of course, is to create situations where ideological affinity, factional manipulation, security and economic dependence, or even outright occupation would cement the regime's allegiance as puppet or client.

Again like the United States, the Soviets find it difficult to decide in many cases whether to support opposition movements or the government in power. Sometimes they have bet on the revolution and ruined their relations with the rulers. In other cases Moscow has outlived its usefulness when its influence came to threaten the dictator's most precious possession: his own power. Motivated by ego, nationalism, or greed, the dictator has reined in or expelled the Soviets. Thus, Moscow has been forced out of one country after another: Egypt, Sudan, and Iraq in the Middle East; Somalia, Guinea, and Ghana in Africa. After three decades of independence for Africa, after three decades of Soviet priority on the Arab world, and three decades after the Cuban revolution in Latin America, Moscow's gains are not really impressive.

From the standpoint of the East-West conflict and of U.S. interests generally, four types of Third World dictatorships can be distinguished. First, there are regimes aligned with the USSR, supporting Soviet strategic aims, allowing Soviet use of their soil for bases and other facilities, and engaged in close security and intelligence cooperation. In short, the identity and survival of the regime seem tightly linked with the Soviet bloc. These criteria apply to such close allies as Cuba, Vietnam, and Afghanistan. To a lesser but still impressive degree these conditions can be found in clients like Syria and Nicaragua, Angola and Ethiopia, though none of them is a Soviet satellite.

Second, there are countries engaged for their own reasons in the systematic subversion of neighbors, antagonism to U.S.

interests, attacks on U.S. friends, and support for international terrorism. These states include Libya and Iran, and both Nicaragua and Syria could also be placed here.

Most modern dictators, however, want good relations with the United States and regional stability. They (like Egypt and Tunisia) are interested in U.S. support or (like most African regimes) view U.S.-Soviet competition as a chance to play off both sides for their own benefit and maximum independence.

Finally, there are the remaining traditional dictators friendly with the United States. Some of them, like the Arab monarchies, still enjoy a large amount of traditional legitimacy, but this can be expected to decay over the coming decades. In Asia and Latin America a return to civilian democratic rule may prove a safety valve. But if these dictators mistreat their people, fail to provide benefits, and face confident, organized oppositions, serious instability can result. Traditional dictators, then, threaten U.S. interests not by themselves becoming pro-Soviet or anti-American but by providing fertile ground for such regimes to arise.

Consequently, the U.S. rationale for such "abnormal" diplomatic steps as support for human rights, democratization, and opposition movements is justified by different considerations for friendly and hostile states. In the former case such actions can stem the deterioration that might bring antagonistic dictatorial forces to power. Where regimes are already hostile, these measures can be constraints, challenging the narrow monopoly on power that allows a regime to benefit from concentrating power, stifling dissent, using Soviet repressive aid, and destabilizing its region.

All these circumstances and problems are quite different from past expectations. America's founders of the late eighteenth century and most nineteenth-century Western political thinkers believed the world would follow a straight line of progress from monarchies to representative democracies. In our century, however, a new kind of dictatorship arose from the collapse of countries in the catastrophes of war and revolution, the strains of socioeconomic change, and the manipulation of new organizational, ideological, and technological tools. The praxis of unscrupulous or well-intentioned ideologues as well as the acts of desperate people has severely shaken the dream of progress.

Nevertheless, all the facts are still not registered. The preliminary results have thrown into doubt the deterministic optimism of the past. It has yet to be seen whether more industry, urbanization, and the fruits of modern communication, education, and ideas will, in turn, produce a popular demand for more rights. Nor can it yet be determined whether the need to create an internal market will create a large, democratic-minded middle class. Even the practical failures of modern dictatorships do not mean that they will crumble. After all, the most economically and technologically advanced such regime is the Soviet Union, a state that hardly seems to be following a trend toward democracy. Furthermore, the new middle class in Africa and the Middle East—dependent on government employment or intellectually committed to radical nationalist ideology—has been, despite many exceptions, more of a pillar of than a challenger to the system of modern dictatorship.

Modern dictatorship, then, seems a type of government that has great staying power in the future Third World. Traditional dictatorship seems the structure most threatened by change and development. While the influx of much oil wealth has postponed the showdown, Saudi Arabia and other Arab monarchies may be expected to face serious problems in the coming decade. Unless those in power in Latin America's current springtime of democracy are capable of making major innovations, the cycle of military rule can be expected to return. In Asia, the Third World region most successful at making economic progress, the traditional dictatorships and modernizing juntas in South Korea and elsewhere may be expected to reach a crossroads, with one path leading to modern dictatorship and the other to a more democratic society.

An additional question is the underlying insecurity of the industrialized democratic states—the United States, Canada, West Europe, Israel, and Japan among them—that they are less qualified for survival than the modern dictatorships. The idea, which the dictatorships themselves spread, is that the disunity, lack of discipline, openness, and lack of brutality of democratic states make them weaker and less able to compete.

History has shown, however, that these fears are not well grounded. Modern dictators put society under a discipline and coordination of energy that protect their own rule and may mobilize resources and manpower more effectively than might otherwise happen. But these very same techniques also sabotage the system by removing the pluralism and personal initiative that are the best safeguard against waste and inefficiency. Objectively, free people are more productive, at least after a certain level of development. This factor can be very important in competition among countries, but it does not necessarily apply to the political struggle within specific countries, where the forces of dictatorship may enjoy the significant advantages enumerated above.

Individual governments and types of rule should be judged on how much they actually do for their citizens, including their ability to provide justice, progress, material well-being, and freedom. U.S. relations with other governments will be based in the first place, but not exclusively, on their foreign policies. Yet history has shown that a nation's internal conduct often plays a central role in determining its external behavior. One hopes for a day when there are no more dictatorships of any kind on the earth, but dictatorships—like democracies—have survived because of an ability to evolve and to take on new forms.

Selective
Bibliography

FBIS = Federal Broadcast Information Service
MEA = Middle East and Africa
LA = Latin America
JPRS = Joint Publications Research Service

BOOKS

Adamolekun, Ladipo. *Sékou Touré's Guinea*. London: 1976.

Ahmad, Jalal Al-I. *Occidentosis: A Plague from the West*. Berkeley, Calif.: 1984.

Ajami, Fouad. *The Arab Predicament*. Cambridge, England: 1981.

Akhavi, Fuad Ajami Shahrough. *Religion and Politics in Contemporary Iran*. Albany, N.Y.: 1980.

Alexander, Robert. *Juan Domingo Perón*. New York: 1979.

Amnesty International. *Report 1980*. London: 1980.

———. *Report 1985*. London: 1985.

Arnold, Anthony. *Afghanistan's Two-Party Communism*. Stanford, Calif.: 1983.

Atatürk, Mustafa Kemal. *Quotations*. Ankara: 1982.

Selective Bibliography

Baker, Raymond. *Egypt's Uncertain Revolution Under Nasser and Sadat.* Cambridge, Mass.: 1978.

Baloyra, Enrique. *El Salvador in Transition.* Chapel Hill, N.C.: 1982.

Berger, Peter. *Pyramids of Sacrifice.* New York: 1975.

Bienen, Henry. *Political Participation Under Military Regimes.* Beverly Hills, Calif.: 1976.

———. *Tanzania.* Princeton, N.J.: 1970.

Braunthal, Julius. *History of the International,* vol. 2. New York: 1967.

Browning, David. *El Salvador.* Oxford, England: 1971.

Cabral, Amilcar. *Revolution in Guinea.* New York: 1970.

———. *Unity and Struggle.* New York: 1979.

Calvocoressi, Peter. *Africa and the World.* New York: 1985.

Canetti, Elias. *Crowds and Power.* New York: 1962.

Carter, Gwendolen, and Patrick O'Meara. *African Independence: The First Twenty-Five Years.* Bloomington, Ind.: 1985.

Cartey, Wilfred, and Martin Kilson. *The Africa Reader.* New York: 1970. 2 vols.

Castro, Fidel. *Fidel Castro Speaks.* New York: 1969.

———. *History Will Absolve Me.* New York: 1961.

Chaliand, Gerard. *Revolution in the Third World.* New York: 1977.

Cohen, Stephen P. *The Pakistan Army.* Berkeley, Calif.: 1984.

Collier, David. *The New Authoritarianism in Latin America.* Princeton, N.J.: 1979.

Collier, Ruth. *Regimes in Tropical Africa.* Berkeley, Calif.: 1982.

Crassweller, Robert. *Trujillo.* New York: 1966.

Crawley, Eduardo. *Dictators Never Die.* New York: 1979.

Davidson, Basil. *Black Star.* New York: 1974.

Devlin, John. *A History of the Baath Party.* Stanford, Calif.: 1976.

———. *Syria.* Boulder, Colo.: 1983.

Diederich, Bernard. *Papa Doc—Haiti and Its Dictator.* Hammondsworth, England: 1972.

———. *Trujillo.* Boston: 1978.

Djilas, Milovan. *The New Class.* New York: 1957.

Dostoevsky, Fedor. *The Brothers Karamazov.* New York: 1976.

El Fathaly, Omar, and Monte Palmer. *Political Development and Social Change in Libya*. Lexington, Mass.: 1980.

Entelis, John. *Algeria: The Revolution Institutionalized*. Boulder, Colo.: 1985.

Fanon, Frantz. *The Damned*. Paris: 1963.

Feinberg, Richard. *The Intemperate Zone*. New York: 1983.

Fiechter, George. *Brazil Since 1964--Modernisation Under a Military Regime*. New York: 1975.

First, Ruth. *Power in Africa*. New York: 1970.

Fischer, Michael. *Iran: From Religious Dispute to Revolution*. Cambridge, Mass.: 1980.

Franklin, H. Bruce. *The Essential Stalin*. Garden City, N.Y.: 1972.

Franqui, Carlos. *Diary of the Cuban Revolution*. New York: 1980.

———. *Family Portrait with Fidel*. New York: 1984.

Gran, Guy. *Zaire*. New York: 1979.

Halliday, Fred, and Maxine Molyneux. *The Ethiopian Revolution*. London: 1981.

Halperin, S. William. *Mussolini and Italian Fascism*. Princeton, N.J.: 1964.

Harik, Ilya. *The Political Mobilization of Peasants*. Bloomington, Ind.: 1974.

Harris, Lillian. *Libya*. Boulder, Colo.: 1986.

Harrison, Paul. *Inside the Third World*. New York: 1982.

Heikal, Mohamed. *The Road to Ramadan*. New York: 1975.

Herskovits, Jean. *Nigeria*. New York: 1982.

Hitler, Adolf. *Mein Kampf*. Boston: 1943.

Hollander, Paul. *Political Pilgrims*. New York: 1981.

Horowitz, Irving Louis. *Cuban Communism*. New York: 1981.

Hourani, Albert. *Arabic Thought in the Liberal Age, 1798–1939*. New York, 1970.

Jackh, Ernest. *The Rising Crescent*. New York: 1944.

Jorge, Paulo. *MPLA ANGOLA*. Richmond, B.C., Canada: 1973.

Kapuscínski, Ryszard. *The Emperor*. New York: 1983.

———. *Shah of Shahs*. New York: 1985.

Karpat, Kamal. *Social Change and Politics in Turkey*. Leiden, Netherlands: 1973.

Kelly, Sean. *Access Denied: The Politics of Press Censorship*. Beverly Hills, Calif.: 1978.

Kinross, Lord. *Ataturk: The Rebirth of a Nation.* London: 1964.

Kirkpatrick, Jeane. *Dictators and Double Standards.* New York: 1982.

Kitchen, Helen. *Africa from Mystery to Maze.* Lexington, Mass.: 1976.

Lamb, David. *The Africans.* New York: 1984.

Laqueur, Walter. *A World of Secrets.* New York: 1985.

————, and Barry Rubin. *The Human Rights Reader.* New York: 1979.

Lenin, V. I. *What Is to Be Done?* New York: 1969.

Lewis, Bernard. *The Emergence of Modern Turkey.* New York: 1969.

Liehm, Antonin. *The Politics of Culture.* New York: 1968.

Lowenthal, Abraham. *The Peruvian Experiment: Continuity and Change Under Military Rule.* Princeton, N.J.: 1975.

Luttwak, Edward. *Coup d'Etat: A Practical Handbook.* Cambridge, Mass.: 1979.

Machiavelli, Niccolo. *The Prince.* New York: 1977.

Meredith, Martin. *The First Dance of Freedom.* New York: 1985.

Millett, Richard. *Guardians of the Dynasty.* Maryknoll, N.Y.: 1977.

Mussolini, Benito. *The Corporate State.* New York: 1975.

————. *Fascism: Doctrine and Institutions.* New York: 1968.

Nasser, Gamal Abdel. *Philosophy of the Revolution.* New York: 1960.

Neto, Agostinho. *Message to Companions in the Struggle.* Richmond, B.C., Canada: 1972.

Noland, David. *The Ideology of the Sandinistas.* Miami, Fla.: 1984.

Nutting, Anthony. *Nasser.* New York: 1972.

Nyerere, Julius. *Quotations from President Julius Nyerere.* Morogoro, Tanzania: 1970.

————. *Uhuru na Ujamaa: Freedom and Socialism.* London: 1968.

Olorunsola, Victor. *The Politics of Cultural Sub-Nationalism in Africa.* New York: 1972.

Page, Joseph. *Peron, a Biography.* New York: 1983.

Pálóczi Hórvath, George. *The Undefeated.* London: 1959.

Parker, Phyllis. *Brazil and the Quiet Intervention, 1964.* Austin, Texas: 1979.

Potash, Robert. *The Army and Politics in Argentina.* Stanford, Calif.: 1980.

Quandt, William. *Revolution and Political Leadership: Algeria, 1954–1968.* Boston: 1969.

Rabinovich, Itamar. *Syria Under the Ba'th 1963–66.* Jerusalem: 1972.

Riding, Alan. *Distant Neighbors*. New York: 1985.

Robbins, Carla Anne. *The Cuban Threat*. New York: 1983.

Rosberg, Carl, and Thomas Callaghy. *Socialism in Sub-Saharan Africa*. Berkeley, Calif.: 1979.

Rubin, Barry. *The Arab States and the Palestine Conflict*. Syracuse, N.Y.: 1981.

————. *Paved with Good Intentions: The American Experience and Iran*. New York: 1980.

————. *Secrets of State: The State Department and the Struggle over U.S. Foreign Policy*. New York: 1985.

Sachs, Ignacy. *The Discovery of the Third World*. Cambridge, Mass.: 1976.

el-Sadat, Anwar. *In Search of Identity*. New York: 1978.

Saul, John. *The State and Revolution in East Africa*. New York: 1979.

al-Sayyid-Marsot, Afaf Lutfi. *Egypt's Liberal Experiment: 1922–1936*. Berkeley, Calif.: 1977.

Segal, Ronald. *African Profiles*. Baltimore, Md.: 1962.

Smith, Peter. *Argentina and the Failure of Democracy*. Madison, Wis.: 1984.

Somoza, Anastasio. *Nicaragua Betrayed*. Boston: 1980.

Stalin, Joseph. *Foundations of Leninism*. Westport, Conn.: 1975.

Stepan, Alfred. *The State and Society: Peru in Comparative Perspective*. Princeton, N.J.: 1978.

Stephens, Robert. *Nasser*. New York: 1970.

Tanganyika African National Union. *Tanzania: Party Guidelines*. Richmond, B.C., Canada: 1973.

Tannenbaum, Edward. *The Fascist Experience*. New York: 1972.

Tordoff, William. *Government and Politics in Africa*. Bloomington, Ind.: 1985.

Turner, Henry. *Reappraisals of Fascism*. New York: 1975.

Ungar, Sanford. *Africa*. New York: 1985.

U.S. State Department. *Report on Human Rights in Countries Receiving U.S. Aid*. Washington, D.C.: 1979.

Vatikiotis, P. J. *Nasser and His Generation*. New York: 1978.

Waterbury, John. *Commander of the Faithful*. London: 1970.

————. *The Egypt of Nasser and Sadat*. Princeton, N.J.: 1983.

Wesson, Robert. *Democracy in Latin America*. New York: 1982.

Wiarda, Howard. *Dictators and Development*. Gainsville, Fla.: 1968.

Wiles, Peter. *The New Communist Third World*. New York: 1982.

World Bank. *Toward Sustained Development in Sub-Saharan Africa*. Washington, D.C.: 1984.

———. *World Development Report*. Washington, D.C.: 1985.

Wynn, Wilton. *Nasser of Egypt*. Cambridge, Mass.: 1959.

Yeager, Rodger. *Tanzania: An African Experiment*. Boulder, Colo.: 1982.

Zabih, Sepehr. *Iran Since the Revolution*. Baltimore, Md.: 1982.

ARTICLES AND SPEECHES

Adeniran, Tunde. "Olusegun Obasanjo." *Africa Record* (May–June 1976).

Ajami, Fouad. "The Fate of Nonalignment." *Foreign Affairs* (Winter 1980–81).

Alfonsín, Rául. Speech at Armed Forces banquet, July 6, 1985. FBIS/LA, July 8, 1985, pp. B1–8.

Anderson, Lisa. "Qadhdhafi and the Kremlin." *Problems of Communism* (September–October 1985).

Arce, Bayardo. Interview with Nicaraguan News Agency, July 17, 1985, in JPRS-LAM-85-017-L, August 22, 1985.

Associated Press. "Winners Harass Losers: Opposition Backers Beaten in Zimbabwe." *Washington Post*, July 9, 1985.

Babangida, Ibrahim Gbadamasi. Discusses coup in Nigeria, Lagos Radio, August 27, 1985. FBIS/MEA, August 28, 1985, pp. T2–4.

Baird, Jane. "Latin America's Free-Market Failure." *Institutional Investor* (July 1982).

Bell, Peter. "Democracy and Double Standards: The View from Chile." *World Policy Journal* (Fall 1985).

Bienen, Henry. "African Militaries as Foreign Policy Actors." *International Security* (Fall 1980).

———. "Military Rule and Military Order in Africa." *Orbis* (Winter 1982).

Blumenthal, Sidney. "An Ideology That Didn't Match Reality." *Washington Post*, March 2, 1986.

Borge, Tomás. May Day speech, May 1, 1982. FBIS/LA, May 3, 1982, pp. 12–19.

———. Speech on Fourth Anniversary of Sandinist Defense Committees, April 27, 1985. FBIS/LA, May 3, 1985, pp. 13–18.

Calderón, Manuel. "Government Control of Mass Media Analyzed." *Le Monde Diplomatique* (Mexico City; June 1985).

Chalmers, Douglas, and Craig Robinson. "Choose Liberalization: Perspectives from South America." *International Studies Quarterly* (March 1982).

Clement, Peter. "Moscow and Southern Africa." *Problems of Communism* (March–April 1985).

Cox, Robert. "The Souring of the Argentine Dream." *Harper's* (May 1985).

Craig, Alexander. "Military Regimes Face Problems of Political Participation." *International Perspectives* (January–February 1976).

Crocker, Chester. "Recent Developments in Liberia." U.S. State Department Current Policy No. 773 (December 1985).

Cuadra, Pablo Antonio. "Notes on Culture in the New Nicaragua." *Vuelta* (Mexico City: August 1985). Translation by Mark Falcoff.

David, Steven. "The Role of Foreign Assistance in Protecting Third World Regimes from Coups d'Etat." Unpublished paper.

Dawisha, Adeed. "Arab Regimes, Legitimacy and Foreign Policy." Paper presented to the American Political Science Association, November 1984.

Dessouki, Ali Hilal. Quoted in *Washington Post*, July 31, 1985.

Diamond, Larry. "Nigeria: The Coup and the Future." *Africa Report* (March–April 1984).

———. "Nigeria in Search of Democracy." *Foreign Affairs* (Spring 1984).

Doe, Samuel. National Day speech. Monrovia Radio, July 26, 1985. FBIS/MEA, July 30, 1985, pp. T1–2.

Falcoff, Mark. "The United States and Chile." American Enterprise Institute paper (Washington, D.C.: 1985).

Frankel, Glenn. "Mugabe Struggles in Vain to Curb Officials' Get-Rich-Quick Attitude." *Washington Post*, December 23, 1984.

———. "Zaire's Mobutu: Self-Made Ruler." *Washington Post*, May 23, 1985.

French, Howard. "Letter from Burkina Faso." *Washington Post*, December 17, 1985.

Funk, Gerald. "Can Ethiopia Survive Both Communism and the Drought?" *Africa Notes* (March 15, 1985).

Gertzel, Cherry. "Uganda After Amin: The Continuing Search for Leadership and Control." *African Affairs* (1980).

Gott, Richard. "Booming Brazil Is Now Dangerously Vulnerable." *The Guardian* (London: December 22, 1973).

Gunn, Gillian. "Post-Nkomati Mozambique." *Africa Notes* (January 8, 1985).

Hamilton, David. "Ethiopia's Embattled Revolutionaries." *Conflict Studies* (April 1977).

Handler, Bruce. "Flying High in Rio." *New York Times Magazine* (June 8, 1975).

Hansen, Emmanuel. "The Army, the State, and the Rawlings Revolution in Ghana." *African Affairs* (January 1980).

Harden, Blaine. "Despite Vast U.S. Aid, Ethiopia Stays Hostile." *Washington Post*, April 14, 1985.

Harman, Nicholas. "A Survey of Nigeria." *The Economist* (January 23, 1982).

Hass, Robert. "Cardenal and Nicaragua." *Washington Post Book World*, July 21, 1985.

Henderson, George. "Libya: Redefining the Revolution." *Africa Report* (November–December 1984).

Hills, Denis. "Horror in Uganda." *New York Review of Books* (September 16, 1976).

Horowitz, Irving Louis. "From Dependency to Determinism: The New Structure of Latin American Militarism." *Journal of Political and Military Sociology* (Fall 1977).

———. "Military Origins of Third World Dictatorship and Democracy." *Third World Quarterly* (January 1981).

———. "State Power and Military Nationalism in Latin America." *Comparative Politics* (January 1976).

Houphouët-Boigny, Félix. Interview in *Jeune Afrique* (August 14–21, 1985).

Hughes, Arnold. "The Army as 'Social Engineers' in Nigeria." *Contemporary Review* (December 1977).

Johnson, Nels, and Marina Ottaway. "Marxism-Leninism and Islamic Fundamentalism: The Convergence of Third World Radical Ideologies." Unpublished paper, June 1984.

Jordan, David. "Argentina's Military Commonwealth." *Current History* (February 1979).

Joseph, Richard. "The Overthrow of Nigeria's Second Republic." *Current History* (1984).

Kaufman, Michael. "A Reign of War in the Land of Sheba." *New York Times Magazine* (January 8, 1978).

Kirkpatrick, Jeane. "Marcos and the Purists." *Washington Post*, December 16, 1985.

Kissinger, Henry. Interview in *Time* magazine (September 24, 1979).

———. "Power and Diplomacy." *The Dimensions of Diplomacy*, E. A. J. Johnson, ed. Baltimore, Md.: 1964.

Kraft, Joseph. "Letter from Addis Ababa." *New Yorker* (July 31, 1978).

Kraus, Jon. "The Decline of Ghana's Military Government." *Current History* (December 1977).

———. "Rawlings's Second Coming." *Africa Report* (March–April 1982).

Laqueur, Walter. "Is There Now, or Has There Ever Been, Such a Thing as Totalitarianism?" *Commentary* (October 1985).

―――. "Third World Fantasies." *Commentary* (February 1977).

Lee, William. "Ethiopia: A Review of the Dergue." *Africa Report* (March–April 1977).

Leiken, Robert. "The Nicaraguan Tangle." *New York Review of Books* (December 5, 1985).

―――. "Nicaragua's Untold Stories." *New Republic* (October 8, 1984).

Lowenthal, Abraham. "Dateline Peru: A Sagging Revolution." *Foreign Policy* (Spring 1980).

Malwal, Bona. "The Sudan: The Unsettling Political Future." *Middle East Insight* (October–November 1985).

Meister, Ulrich. "Liberia After the Coup." *Swiss Review of World Affairs* (October 1980).

Miremont, Auguste. "The Elephant Continues Its Progress." Abidjan: *Fraternité Matin*, July 19, 1985.

Momoh, General. Speech at City Hall. Freetown Radio, August 28, 1985. FBIS/MEA, August 30, 1985, pp. T2–3.

Mugabe, Robert. Speech Radio Maputo, July 15, 1985. FBIS/MEA, July 16, 1985, pp. U7–8.

Musavi, Hussein. Interview in *Kayhan International* (Tehran: December 22, 1985).

"The Myths of Revolution." *New Republic* (April 29, 1985).

Neff, Richard. "Peru: An End to the Ruling Class." *Contemporary Review* (July 1978).

Niedergang, Marcel. "From Coffee to Petrochemicals." *The Guardian* (London: September 30, 1972).

Nyerere, Julius. Recommends Ali Hassan Mwinyi Succeed Him. Dar es Salaam Radio, August 15, 1985. FBIS/MEA, August 19, 1985, R2.

O'Connell, James. "Power and Succession in a Military Regime: The Case of Nigeria." *Contemporary Review* (May 1976).

Ottoway, Marina. "Social Classes and Corporate Interests in the Ethiopian Revolution." *Journal of Modern African Studies*, vol. 14, no. 3 (1976).

Perlmutter, Amos. "The Comparative Analysis of Military Regimes." *World Politics* (October 1980).

Philip, George. "Military Authoritarianism in South America, Brazil, Chile, Uruguay and Argentina." *Political Studies* (March 1984).

"Press Law Allows Offended to Have Right of Reply." *Iran Times*, November 15, 1985.

Preston, Julia. "What Duarte Won." *New York Review of Books* (August 15, 1985).

Randal, Jonathan. "Ghana Moderates Its Policies." *Washington Post*, May 24, 1985.

Richter, William. "Persistent Praetorianism: Pakistan's Third Military Regime." *Pacific Affairs* (Fall 1978).

Rothchild, Donald. "Military Regime Performance: An Appraisal of the Ghana Experience, 1972–78," *Comparative Politics* (July 1980).

———. "The Rawlings Revolution in Ghana: Pragmatism with Populist Rhetoric." *Africa Notes* (May 2, 1985).

Ruiz, Henry. Interview. *Nicarauac* (May–June 1980).

Sankara, Thomas. Speech on Second Anniversary of Revolution. Ouagadougou Radio, August 4, 1985. FBIS/MEA, August 6, 1985, pp. T1–4.

Sarney, Jose. Quoted in "Sarney: Politician, Writer, President." *O Estado de Saõ Paulo*, April 22, 1985, JPRS 850057, July 3, 1985.

Sartre, Jean-Paul. "The Society That Came In from the Cold." *Evergreen* (November 1970).

Schoenhals, Michael. "Elite Information in China." *Problems of Communism* (September–October 1985).

Shaw, Terri. "Block Clubs Oversee Cuba's Daily Life," *Washington Post*, December 30, 1974.

Shultz, George. "The Meaning of Vietnam." Speech of April 25, 1985, text from Department of State.

Szulc, Tad. "Letter from Brasilia." *New Yorker* (March 10, 1975).

Tannahill, Neal. "The Performance of Military and Civilian Governments in South America." *Journal of Political and Military Sociology* (Fall 1976).

Vargas Llosa, Mario. "Intellectuals, the 'Cuban Solution' and Double Standards." *Atlantic Monthly*.

Videla, Jorge. Quoted in *Washington Post*, September 11, 1976.

Viorst, Milton. "Peru: The Mismanaged Revolution." *Atlantic Monthly* (February 1978).

Wai, Dunstan. "Revolution, Rhetoric, and Reality in the Sudan." *Journal of Modern African Studies*, vol. 17, no. 1 (1979).

———. "The Sudan: Domestic Politics and Foreign Relations Under Nimiery." *African Affairs* (July 1979).

Walzer, Michael. "On Failed Totalitarianism." *1984 Revisited*, Irving Howe, ed. (New York: 1984).

———. "Totalitarianism vs. Authoritarianism." *New Republic* (July 4 and 11, 1981).

Werlich, David. "The Peruvian Revolution in Crisis." *Current History* (February 1977).

Wolpin, Miles. "Military Radicalism in Latin America." *Journal of Interamerican Studies and World Affairs* (November 1981).

Zaid, Gabriel. "The Sandinista Path." *New Republic* (May 20, 1985).

Zalaquett, José. "Guinea's Worth." *New Republic* (August 12 and 19, 1985).

Index

375